N · DON CORYELL · DICK SPRAGUE · MILT BOHART · WENDELL N

OREDT · GEORGE FLEMING · DON _____ AVIDSON · CH

· RICK REDMAN · BILL DOUGLAS · _____ LL · DAVE WIL

NNIS FITZPATRICK · RAY PINNEY · MIKE BALDASSIN · MIKE ROHF

· JEFF LEELAND · ROBERT "SPIDER" GAINES · TOM TURNURE · RC

MIKE LANSFORD · MARK STEWART · RAY HORTON · CHUCK NEL

A JR. · MARK PATTISON · JACQUE ROBINSON · TIM MEAMBER ·

· DANA HALL · MARIO BAILEY · STEVE EMTMAN · MARK BRUNELI

T · BENO BRYANT · NAPOLEON KAUFMAN · MARK BRUENER · D.

ONY PARRISH · BENJI OLSON · JEROME PATHON · BROCK HUARI

OHN ANDERSON · CODY PICKETT · RICH ALEXIS · ZACH TUIASO

· BUD ERICKSEN · WALTER HARRISON · DON CORYELL · DICK SP

R CARR · CHUCK ALLEN · BOB SCHLOREDT · GEORGE FLEMING

ICKS · JIM LAMBRIGHT · DAVE KOPAY · RICK REDMAN · BILL DO

SONNY SIXKILLER · BILL CAHILL · DENNIS FITZPATRICK · RAY PIN

CHAEL JACKSON · NESBY GLASGOW · JEFF LEELAND · ROBERT "S

MARTIN · JOE STEELE · TOM FLICK · MIKE LANSFORD · MARK STEV

Y ALLEN · STEVE PELLUER · JIM MORA JR. · MARK PATTISON · JA

· DONALD JONES · ED CUNNINGHAM · DANA HALL · MARIO BA

WHAT IT MEANS TO BE A HUSKY

DON JAMES
AND WASHINGTON'S GREATEST PLAYERS

GREG BROWN

TRIUMPH
BOOKS
CHICAGO

Library of Congress Cataloging-in-Publication Data

What it means to be a Husky : Don James and Washington's greatest players / edited by Greg Brown.
    p. cm.
ISBN-13: 978-1-57243-806-4 (alk. paper)
ISBN-10: 1-57243-806-1 (alk. paper)
    1. University of Washington—Football—History. 2. Washington Huskies (Football team)—History. I. Brown, Greg, 1957–
GV958.U5865W53 2007
796.332'6309797772—dc22

    2007012969

This book is available in quantity at special discounts for your group or organization. For further information, contact:

Triumph Books
542 South Dearborn Street
Suite 750
Chicago, Illinois 60605
(312) 939-3330
Fax (312) 663-3557

Printed in U.S.A.
ISBN: 978-1-57243-806-4
Design by Nick Panos
Editorial production and layout by Prologue Publishing Services, LLC
All photos courtesy of the University of Washington and Collegiate Images unless otherwise indicated

CONTENTS

FOREWORD

What It Means to Be a Husky

BEING A HUSKY IS A WONDERFUL opportunity and carries great responsibility. We talked about it all the time during my 18 years as the head football coach at the University of Washington.

We told our coaches and players to remember the guys from the past—the Redmans, the McKetas, the Heinrichs, and the McElhennys. The UW is steeped in the tradition of talented athletes.

A rich football tradition marks time and touches all generations.

I'm proud of the accomplishments of the coaches and players who added to Husky football history during my time at the UW from 1975 to 1992. We won the school's first national football championship, went to six Rose Bowls, 14 bowls in total, and compiled a 153–57–2 record, winning almost three out of every four games overall.

Whatever legacy those teams left behind, the immeasurable accomplishment is how being a Husky turned boys into men and, hopefully, gave those who endured the skills to be successful long after their last game at Washington.

When we recruited players to become part of Washington history, we told them the UW could offer them three things: 1) we told recruits the University of Washington offered a great education; 2) we said the program would give them a chance to win; and 3) we believed the program could take them as far in football as they could go.

All head coaches bring to a program the sum of their experiences. My ideas were shaped by many programs and coaches. It all started at Washington. Washington High School, that is, in Massillon, Ohio.

I made my mind up while playing high school football that I wanted to be a football coach. All the guys I idolized the most were my coaches. Legendary Paul Brown started his coaching career at my high school. We had a tradition of winning legendary state and national titles long before I played quarterback there in the late 1940s. My high school head coach, Chuck Mather, had six years with only two losses. We won two state titles while I was there. I was an average quarterback. We had three great running backs. I didn't throw too much, but showed enough talent to receive a football scholarship to the University of Miami.

The Hurricanes were really good my first two years, and we went to the Orange and Gator bowls. My junior and senior seasons we lost some players. Throwing in those days was nothing like now. We'd throw in a season what they do in two or three games now. Still, I threw some good passes and set five UM passing records.

After my last pass, and with an education degree in hand, I got married to Carol and spent two years in the army.

I got my master's degree in education at the University of Kansas and was a graduate football assistant. I couldn't find a college coaching job, so I was a high school assistant coach at Miami Southwest High. I stayed in contact with my former Miami coaches, and they helped me land an assistant job at Florida State for seven seasons. I then joined the Michigan staff for two years and Colorado for three.

I befriended Colorado State head coach Mike Lude while at Colorado. So when he landed the athletics director job at Kent State, he gave me an interview for the head coaching job.

I believed I was ready. I had seen the program philosophy at Florida State and how it's done in the Big Ten with a lot of the Bud Wilkinson–Oklahoma philosophy under Eddie Crowder. I paid attention to all the coaches I met.

I wanted to be disciplined and organized. I didn't like wasting time. I remembered sitting in meetings and spending two hours deciding what color ties we were going to wear. That kind of wasted time just killed me.

In my second season, we won Kent State's first and only Mid-America championship.

Meantime, Jim Owens announced he was going to retire at Washington. Athletics director Joe Kearny started a true nationwide search. He and Don Smith went around the country and interviewed prospects. They interviewed me. It came down to five coaches, then three dropped out. It came down to Darryl Rodgers and myself.

I had never been in Seattle, but I knew Washington had a great tradition and the team just happened to be down at the time.

When I was hired, Jim Owens spent a lot of time with me going over players and coaches. I brought four coaches from my staff and hired Jim Mora Sr. from UCLA. I kept three UW coaches, including Jim Lambright. Recruiting was the first priority. My second day on the job, I flew around the state. That day we landed Michael Jackson (the UW all-time leading tackler) and tight end Scott Greenwood. Starting lineman Joe Sanford and Roger Westlund were important early signings. We knew we had to get the best in-state players.

It was also important to me to set up academic counseling, which was well underway with Gertrude Peoples, year-round strength training, and a recruiting philosophy.

That spring we got a little lucky. We had wrapped up recruiting. Assistant coach Chick Harris came in one day and said there was a quarterback at West Los Angeles Junior College that he wanted to bring in. We were not in the recruiting mode. His name was Harold and was only a freshman. I said, "Wait a minute." All my coaching life I was told you don't get a junior-college player that has eligibility. You won't ever be able to go back to that school for stealing their player, and they are going to kill you throughout the whole state of California.

Harris said, "No," this quarterback named Harold Warren Moon had an agreement with his coach, saying if he could go to a four-year college after his first J-C year, he would permit it. We called the coach to verify that. So we went down, recruited him, and signed him. We got lucky.

There were two traditions I wanted to change once I got to Washington—one I did, one I didn't.

Owens had the idea to reward top players with purple helmets, while the rest of the team wore gold. And I didn't like the idea of guys playing with two different helmets. So I came in with a uniform scheme sort of like the 49ers, and we got everyone dressed alike. Then I wanted to have our team on the south side when we played at Husky Stadium so we would be in the shade on sunny days. And that would've been a break in tradition. But the Pac-10 had a rule that the home team always had to sit with the student body section. That's because of problems with 'SC and Stanford.

One team tradition I brought from another program was the "final hit" for seniors. I thought it was a good idea to recognize the seniors, whether they were star players or not. At the last home game, we'd bring them out one at a time. In the last practice, we'd make two lines and put out a dummy. We usually would have an opposing jersey on the dummy. The seniors would give it a forearm shiver or something. The guys would have some fun with it and clown around.

My most important speeches to the team were on Thursdays. This came from the philosophy of Paul Dietsel, Bear Bryant, and Sid Gilman, who contended that pregame speeches were too late. If a player is not ready on game day, a fiery talk wouldn't make a difference. On Thursdays, before practice, was the time to cut out all the bull. There wasn't any joking around. I wanted 100 percent focus on practice and things done right. We normally rested on Fridays and on the road walked through some situations without pads to give them an opportunity to get into their game-day cleats.

In 1975, my first year, we came within a field goal of going to the Rose Bowl. We did beat both USC and UCLA for the first time since 1964. We went for touchdowns instead of field goals against Stanford and California and failed. In retrospect, a field goal in either could have sent us to Pasadena.

We had a miracle comeback in our final game against Washington State. They got a little greedy and tried to throw a play-action pass, and Al Burleson picked it off for a touchdown. That was a game we didn't deserve. A 6–5 record was a solid start.

We lost about 40 seniors after that first season. We played a lot of young kids that second year and were 5–6.

That critical third year started with close losses to Syracuse and Minnesota. We were 1–3 going into Oregon. That's when we turned it around and had a really exciting year with a Rose Bowl berth. The players had to get caught up in what we were doing. We had enough talent and got some breaks. We were decided underdogs to Michigan. I don't think anyone thought we were as good as they were. Then we pulled that thing off.

I had the impression that after we got all the film from Michigan that there was a feeling we might not have a chance against these guys. Not many may remember, but I just went in and told the coaches and players that we were going to change our goals. I told them I didn't want to get caught up in the idea that this was a must-win game or that life was going to come to an end.

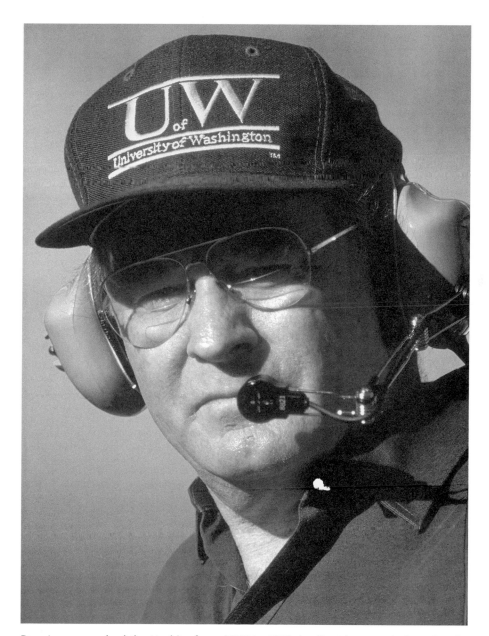

Don James coached the Huskies from 1975 to 1992, leading them to six Rose Bowls, an Orange Bowl, and the 1991 national championship. In 18 seasons, James's teams went to 14 bowl games (10 wins, four losses) and compiled a 153–57–2 record.
Photo courtesy of AP/Wide World Photos

We were going to do a couple things. We were going to go down two weeks early. We were going to have fun, go to Knott's Berry Farm, Disneyland, and Universal Studios. During the game we had two goals: 1) gain the respect of Michigan players (because I didn't think they respected us at all); and 2) gain respect of the people who reported the game—the writers and the radio guys. I wanted them to say, regardless of the score, that it appeared as though the Huskies wanted to win the most. It took the pressure off of the must-win attitude. "We are going to go down and have fun," I told them. "We are going to do the best we can to prepare hard and try to gain respect." I thought it took some pressure off.

We prepared for all our bowl appearances the same way. If the game was on a Monday, we made that a Saturday from our regular week's schedule and backtracked. We tried to get them on a schedule that we had in season.

The thing I learned is that players, when you travel with them to bowl games, need to see and do everything. They need to get out and have fun.

The goal was to get them to practices. Let them do their social thing, then get serious the last four or five days, and the last two nights let the team captains do the bed checks.

The bowls were fun for me, too. It was like the same enjoyment a father gets taking his kids to Disneyland. That's how I felt about going to bowls, especially the Rose Bowl. To give these guys the experiences. It was fun to see the team experience those trips.

I felt like there were three stages of football, and it would be hard to win all three stages—offense, defense, and kicking. The kicking game was key to us turning around the program. There's nobody we played who worked harder than we did at our kicking game. We had ways of figuring out yards versus points. We'd consistently end up winning the kicking game. It was the big part of our early success before we could catch up with physical talent.

We always set high goals at the beginning of every season. Winning a national championship was always a goal. As all Huskies fans know, our 1991 team went undefeated and shared the national championship with Miami.

To get there, we made some changes in how we recruited.

After our Orange Bowl win over Oklahoma, when we finished No. 2 in the nation, I think we kind of slacked off. I think either I, or my staff, got a little lazy and started making some recruiting mistakes on speed positions. We became big and slow.

We played Penn State in the Aloha Bowl, and it opened our eyes. Their guys were a couple inches shorter but quicker than our guys. I told our staff I was sick and tired of making recruiting mistakes.

The high school coaches knew what to tell you. We'd have coaches tell us a guy could run a 4.6, and we'd get him, and he'd run a 4.9. We needed a way to confirm speed. We started to get data on the vertical jump. The high school coaches didn't have the same data. The NFL had it, and we had it. You just reach up and measure your reach and just jump. We knew if you couldn't jump, you couldn't run. If you're vertical jump is 8 to 12 inches, that's not good enough, unless you weigh 300 pounds.

We tried to get recruits into our football camps, or if they ran track, we'd get their legitimate times. But the guys who were question marks because we couldn't confirm their times, we had them do a vertical jump. It was a quick test we could do and wasn't considered a workout. We knew speed guys needed to jump at least 30 inches high.

As a result, we got faster. We changed our defense to an attacking style and opened up our passing offense. We got some breaks, too. Not a lot of people knew about a lineman in Cheney named Steve Emtman, who became the most dominant nose guard in our history. Two of four captains from that 1991 team came from Virginia—Donald Jones and Ed Cunningham. That's a break.

The biggest thing about that season was that Billy Joe Hobert was able to step in for Mark Brunell, who got injured in the spring, and win our first two games on the road—against Stanford in the opener and then at Nebraska.

We had youth, experience, size, and speed, plus a lot of talent. I could have coached another 10 to 15 years and not have had that combination again.

My biggest disappointments were when players stayed with us four and five years and didn't get their degrees. Every player who finished the program was offered a full scholarship to come back and finish his education. They could come back after 10 years and we'd pay for it.

Every player, top to bottom, was important to the program. Every year we had walk-ons. They were very important in our game preparation as members of the scout team and some became starters. We lettered every walk-on who stayed through his senior year.

When we went to a bowl, we took the walk-ons with the team or had them fly down for the game when we were limited by rules of the bowl. And everyone, including the walk-ons, got bowl rings and the other bowl gifts players received under NCAA rules. I can name several walk-ons who played in the NFL. We constantly tried to recognize their contributions.

There were a lot of players who I wished had a chance to play but didn't because of the numbers. They were really great young guys, many who went on to be very successful off the field. They were all part of Huskies football.

What I hoped young men learned was teamwork, discipline, and organization. I truly believe that the lessons you learn on a competitive team you can take into the business world—work hard, be a team player, be a leader. Those are the types of people who are successful. I've had a lot of players come back and say the things they learned in Huskies football helped them in their jobs.

Being a Huskies football player is a great opportunity to be part of a long tradition—to play Division 1-A college football, to play in a venue like Husky Stadium, with the hugely supportive fans, and to play in the Pac-10. It's a special responsibility to live up to the past. There are a lot of guys who treaded down that tunnel who were tired, beat up, and sore, and still sucked it up and went through it and got better. As this book tells, every player who ran through that tunnel has a story to tell…

—Don James

EDITOR'S ACKNOWLEDGMENTS

FIRST I'D LIKE TO THANK University of Washington Director of Athletics Todd Turner and Executive Associate Athletics Director Jeff Compher for the access to Athletic Office information and photographs.

I'm very grateful to Don James for giving of his time and sharing his thoughts in writing of the foreword.

A special thanks is in order to Greg Lewis, executive director of the Big W Club, for helping me track down players, and Brian Tom, assistant director of communications, and his assistants, for researching player files for the photos in this book.

The volume of audiotapes required help to accurately transcribe more than 100 hours of player memories. This book could not have been completed without the diligent transcription support from Benji Brown, Lauren Brown, and Becky Wheless. Thank you all so much!

This book also would not have been created without the support of my wife, Stacy. The time needed to compile these stories was subtracted from nights and weekends that put much of our lives on hold for 20 months.

Finally, on behalf of myself and all Huskies fans who will appreciate reading these stories, I thank all the Huskies players who gave their time and memories.

INTRODUCTION

The highest team honor bestowed on a Huskies football player is to receive the Guy Flaherty Award, awarded each year to the player voted by teammates as the "most inspirational."

Flaherty played every minute of football at Washington during the 1906 and 1907 seasons. He only played in the first and last games of the 1908 season because of a severe case of boils on his arm. Still, Flaherty attended every practice and game, and performed manager and assistant manager duties.

Flaherty's teammates were inspired by his unselfish devotion to Washington football. The senior class established the award in Flaherty's honor. The Guy Flaherty Award is believed to be the first intercollegiate inspirational award.

It's too bad the award is only given to one Husky a year. Each football season produces dozens of unbelievable stories of players whose perseverance and courage overcame the challenges of playing big-time college football. Some were demonstrated on the field with unforgettable plays on the field. Others were small acts only known to their teammates or themselves.

I had an inside view of Huskies football while attending the UW from 1975 to 1979 and playing on the baseball team. I got to know some football players in the classroom, in the weight room, or crossed paths in the training room. To see Warren Moon, and many others, barely able to walk into the training room for treatment midweek and then perform gracefully on Saturday put my aches in perspective.

I also had the opportunity to cover the Huskies periodically as a sportswriter. I always looked for the uplifting story lines. I didn't have to look far.

I've always believed sports teaches life lessons. Before this book, I had writ-ten 28 autobiographies with America's most famous athletes. This book is really 92 autobiographies. You'd think two years would be enough time to track down former players, interview them, transcribe and edit their words, and allow them to review their words before publication. But it really wasn't enough time and there was not enough space. Hundreds more stories deserved to be told in this collection.

While interviewing Huskies who played from the 1930s to the 2000s, I was struck by how their experiences were so similar. With a few rare exceptions, almost to a man, players admitted they were scared to death during the first weeks of practices, had self-doubt along the way, and contemplated quitting at some point. Running out of the Huskies tunnel onto the field was an out-of-body experience for every player who wore the uniform. Each era had its superstars and its scandals. All those who went on to play professional foot-ball, in retrospect, said playing football at Washington produced the greatest bonds and their most cherished memories.

Their stories show glimpses of the times and attitudes in which they played. More than anything, they tell how winning isn't necessarily just about the scoreboard but about tackling your personal challenges and being part of something bigger than yourself.

Many players were brutally honest. What Michael Jackson, Washington's all-time leading tackler, says about the toll football took on his body is sober-ing. George Fleming tells about the unconscionable excuses white coaches gave in the 1960s as to why African American players couldn't play certain positions. Joe Steele talked candidly about his season-ending knee injury and how one play changed his life. What happened to Tim Cowan that made him bawl for three hours was heartless.

And there were the many personal triumphs, such as the walk-on stories of Hugh Millen and Jeff Leeland. Ink Aleaga shares how he didn't have the grades to attend the UW, sat out a year to improve his grades, then excelled on the field and in the classroom and now has a job with the UW. The sto-ries about the Rose Bowl scene with Curtis Williams, paralyzed by a tackle that later took his life due to complications, are touching. Isaiah Stanback talks about how he was never ashamed to be a Husky, despite going through one- and two-win seasons.

There were some interesting twists of fate as well. You couldn't make up Jacque Robinson's story about how he got onto the Rose Bowl field to become the MVP of the game as a freshman. Anthony Allen tells how after the 1982 Aloha Bowl game he was left behind at the stadium, in game uniform, with no way back to the hotel. Don "Air" Coryell, the father of the modern passing attack, played mostly defense while at Washington in the 1940s. Teammates convinced Sonny Sixkiller and Greg Lewis not to quit the program.

In all, these players' stories show the depth of Washington's long football tradition and insight into what it really meant for the players to be Huskies.

The THIRTIES

JAMES M. "JIMMIE" CAIN
RUNNING BACK
1932–1936

WHEN I CLOSE MY EYES AND MEMORIES SWIRL, next to my family, I remember my days at the University of Washington. Playing UW football ranks as one of the great experiences in my life accomplishments.

Of course, at my age, just making it to the next day is an accomplishment. I turned 94 on September 5, 2006. I live in Rancho Mirage, California, and get around with the help of a wheelchair and a walker. My wife of 55 years, Grace, passed 10 years ago. My two daughters and two grandchildren have given me a lifetime of joy, and I'm proud of all of them.

Thanks in part to my popularity as a Huskies football player, I built an insurance agency in Seattle, knew many people, and counted most of them friends. I sold them lots of insurance. I loved this community. I belonged to many organizations, such as Shrine Masons, Rotary, Lions, and Navy League, and was president of the Washington Athletic Club and UW Alumni Association. I refereed Pac-8 and Pac-10 football games for 25 years. I am the only person to be both a player and a referee in the Rose Bowl. I refereed the East-West Shrine Game while I was potentate of Nile Temple. I was involved in fund-raising for the Red Cross and March of Dimes, and helped pass school levies. I enjoyed all sports and played tennis well into my eighties. I had a wonderful life there in Seattle and wanted to give back as much as it gave me.

Football literally pulled me out of the gray Oklahoma dust bowl and gave me a colorful future. My father died when I was 10. My mother and I struggled to make ends meet. I always had a job. We were living in a half-burnt-down house, almost starving, in Wetumka, Oklahoma. Tom Phillips, owner of the Holdenville *Daily News*, came and took me to Holdenville, 20 miles away. My mom moved to Muskogee. A high school football coach named D.M. "Doc" Wadley changed my life. He "recruited" me to play at Holdenville High School. He promised to take care of me if I played for his team. We both kept our promises.

The Great Depression started with the U.S. stock market crash during the 1929 football season of my sophomore year in high school. Not the best of times to come of age. I poured myself into my studies and sports. Even though I was just 5'8", I stood out. I was fast. I played basketball, baseball, and ran track, but football was my ticket. I was all-state my senior year with a bunch of touchdowns, including four in my final high school game, all on runs of 50-plus yards.

Being a straight-A student, I had many colleges after me. I picked the University of Washington because the coaches offered to pay for my education with a four-year scholarship.

I arrived by bus with $15 in my pocket and thought the UW campus was the most wonderful place I'd ever seen. The evergreens, water, and mountains were spectacular sights for an Okie flatlander.

There was a national movement by reformers to de-emphasize college football about the time I arrived at Washington. During my senior year in high school, a Yale football player had died, and the death rate from head injuries of college football players tripled from the previous year. A Carnegie Foundation report called for fewer college football games. The report said alumni dollars and massive press coverage were corrupting the sport, making it quasi-professional. The general public dismissed such thoughts, especially at Washington. Washington had the most adoring and loudest crowds in the nation at the time. The greatest thing about playing football at Washington was the crowds. They were very supportive. We had the best spirit and the highest attendance of any school.

During my first Huskies football practice, I thought I'd never hear the crowd's roar from the field. My first thought at practice: "I'm not going to make this team."

3

Such thoughts were out of character for me, being a normally positive person. I didn't let anyone know what I thought. In fact, to counteract my fear, I boldly told UW head coach Jim Phelan: "I *am* going to make it."

I had made predictions before. I told friends in Oklahoma before I went to the UW that I was going to be an All-American and that I was going to play in the Rose Bowl.

Being small was my biggest challenge. I had to show them I could play.

In those days, freshmen were not allowed to play varsity. We had an A team and a B team in practices. Freshmen were always on the B team. I never considered quitting and I was never homesick. During the summer, Coach Phelan lined up cannery jobs in Alaska for players who needed money. It was tough work, but it paid well. I also held jobs at a men's store and rode my bike around campus, advertising and handing out samples of Beech-Nut chewing gum.

I was blessed with an athletic body—broad shoulders and rippling muscles. But I needed to gain weight. I did it with milk. I drank about five glasses of milk at every meal. I loved hot dogs and ice cream, too, but didn't care much for vegetables. I gained a solid 10 pounds and played at 175 pounds in college.

My sophomore year I played in our first game and was a starter the rest of my UW career, on both offense and defense.

It was thrilling to play. I was determined I wouldn't fail the team. Each one of my professors started coming to see me. I guess they couldn't believe I could play football at 5'8".

The press always loves a good story, and I became a good story. My senior year I played every position in the backfield as I filled in for injured teammates. Our senior backfield was made up of Ed Nowogroski, fullback, Elmer Logg, quarterback, and Byron Haines and me as halfbacks.

The Seattle newspapers covered our team from every angle. I was dubbed "Hurry-Cain," "Sugar-Cain," and "Raisin' Cain." They called me the team's "little chunk of dynamite."

Looking through scrapbooks of newspaper clippings might surprise some with the outlandish pandering photo opportunities. Washington was *the* only sport in town. One showed a teammate and I in glorified women's ballet outfits at a ballet bar. We were listening intently to two women giving us dance lessons for the upcoming Meany Hall fund-raiser in which we performed in the "Moose Ballet." We had fun with it.

Jimmie Cain electrified Huskies fans as a 5'8" running back and earned All-America honors in 1936.

Playing football, as always, was a serious, dangerous matter. We didn't have the protective gear of today. Our helmets were heavy padded leather without face masks. I only broke my nose once (in high school). Interestingly, we wore the *W* logo on the back of our helmets, instead of on the side as they do now.

At Washington I had only two injuries, a dislocated hip and a broken rib. I broke a rib my senior year in mid-season against Cal. I played two weeks later against the Oregon Ducks, thanks to a special rib pad constructed by the UW team doctor, Dr. Don Palmer. I missed a few practices, but I didn't miss a game.

A personal highlight was when I scored the game-winning touchdown on a long run to beat USC 6–2 during my junior season in 1935.

Our 1936 team was declared "the mightiest football team that ever wore the Purple and Gold." I led the team in scoring with six touchdowns.

We lost our first game at home 14–7 to eventual national champion Minnesota. But we recovered and shut out six teams.

The season came down to a Thanksgiving Day home game against Washington State. It was the first cross-state match-up with the conference championship and Rose Bowl trip on the line. We raced to a 20–0 halftime lead and dominated with a 40–0 win.

Washington had been to the Rose Bowl in 1924 and 1926, tying Navy in the first appearance and losing to Alabama 20–19 in the second. Needless to say, the Pacific Northwest was fired up.

The West Coast winner had the option to pick which team they wanted to play on January 1. Coach Phelan decided to play Pittsburgh. I needed 40 tickets to accommodate all my relatives and friends from Oklahoma. The game set a Rose Bowl record at the time, with 87,196 tickets sold.

Playing in the Rose Bowl was both the most exciting game I've ever played in and the most heartbreaking. We were 7–1–1 going into the game. Pitt was 6–1–1. Our national championship hopes died quickly. We lost 21–0, and Pittsburgh dominated us more than the score indicated.

After the game, I didn't make any excuses. My quotes in the newspapers stated the obvious fact: "They simply were a lot better team on that day than we were. We just weren't clicking. They smeared our plays before we could get them started. Pittsburgh has wonderful boys. It's no disgrace to have been beaten by them."

I finished my three years at Washington with 230 carries for 856 yards. A Seattle story complimented me and Haines, a hometown hero.

"Never has Washington seen a better halfback duo than By and Jimmy," the newspaper said.

The polls placed us fifth in the final voting for the 1936 season, the highest a Huskies team finished in national football rankings until the 1984 team's second place.

When I learned I was voted to the 1936 All-America football team, I couldn't sleep the whole night. I was so excited. I knew I couldn't have done it without my great teammates Ed Nowogroski (fullback), Max Starcevich (All-American guard), Jack MacKinzie (tackle), Chuck Bond (tackle), Johnny Wiatrak (center), Mitch Mondala (center), and By Haines (halfback), all seniors with me.

After the Rose Bowl, I went back to Oklahoma to see mom and friends. Twelve hours after my return to Washington, I was stricken with pneumonia and was in critical condition for several weeks. My teammates and coach gave me great encouragement, and I was ready for football in no time.

I recovered and went on to graduate Phi Beta Kappa with a degree in economics and business.

I was invited to play in the fourth annual College All-Star 1937 preseason game in Chicago, where we played the Green Bay Packers. I was joined by UW teammates Starcevich, Wiatrak, and Haines. Led by quarterback Sammy Baugh, we were the first college all-star team to defeat a pro team in the *Chicago Tribune* game.

I was recognized by *Liberty* magazine and invited to play in the Liberty Bowl (an honor as 1,498 varsity football players in 94 major colleges vote on the players) along with Bond, Haines, and Frank Peters. I was also named to the All-America Newsreel Team. Four Huskies made the All-Coast Gridiron Squad: Bond, Haines, Starcevich, and myself.

I received an offer to play for the Calgary Rugby Team. I stayed in Seattle to play and coach the West Seattle Athletic Club.

I returned to Washington as the freshman coach for the Huskies. I coached a few years and then went to work for General Insurance Company [Safeco today]. Eventually I extended my love of football by becoming a college football referee.

I officiated Pac-8, and later Pac-10, games for 25 years and made it back to the Rose Bowl field as a referee. In fact, I made one of the most controversial calls in Rose Bowl history. In the 1949 Rose Bowl, between Northwestern and California, field judge Jay Berwanger signaled that [Northwestern's] Art Murakowski fumbled the ball after crossing the goal line. I threw my hands up for a touchdown, even though he was pushed back behind the goal line. I was one of the first referees to rule a touchdown when the ball crossed the goal line. Before my call, the ball was routinely spotted where a player was tackled, regardless of forward progress. The touchdown gave Northwestern the lead, and they won 20–14.

In the 1950s I was asked to help out our armed services in the Far East and Europe running football clinics for many years.

I was thrilled to be recognized at a UW football game in the fall of 1996 as a Husky Legend. To stand on the football field after the third quarter and see my picture on the big TV and hear the fans cheer was a great experience for an 84-year-old football player. Later that year, I was honored to be inducted into the State of Washington Football Hall of Fame.

I always treasured running into teammates after our playing days. All my teammates inspired me. I summarized my time at Washington with this quote in the newspaper: "My teammates were a fine bunch of boys and I enjoyed every minute of my association with them."

Jimmie Cain was an aggressive running back who garnered All-Coast recognition besides his All-America accolades. Cain led the Huskies in scoring in 1936 with 37 points. He played in the 1937 Rose Bowl and was a part of a College All-Star team that was the first to defeat a pro team when they downed the Green Bay Packers. He is currently retired and living in Rancho Mirage, California.

BY HAINES

RUNNING BACK

1933–1936

WE LOST TO PITTSBURGH 21–0 in the 1937 Rose Bowl. Everything went wrong. I blame it on the coaches and how they handled the four tickets each player received for the game.

The coaches gathered all the tickets we couldn't use for family and friends and said they would sell them for us. Then, right before the game, they returned the tickets to us. The going rate for a Rose Bowl ticket was about $20 each. That was a lot of money in those days, considering scholarship athletes lived on $35 a month for room and board.

A few players rushed out of the locker room and tried to sell their tickets just before kickoff. I wasn't one of the them. Everyone was so upset—that was a lot of money lost. That's why we lost the game. Some players just didn't give a damn.

Los Angeles sportswriters named me the outstanding player of the game because of pass receptions I made.

The crowd of 87,196 set a Rose Bowl record at the time, almost three times as many fans as for Huskies home games [the stadium consisted of the lower bowl in those days]. I was so excited for each game. I didn't care if there was one or 10,000 fans. I just wanted to play to win. Those days are long gone. I'm 91 years old. I retired in the 1950s and haven't thought about Huskies football in a long time. Almost all of my teammates are gone now.

Running back By Haines (29) and teammates listen as head coach Jimmy Phelan holds court in 1936.

It was a wonderful thing being a Huskies football player. I came from Bend, Oregon. I didn't like the Oregon coast. I heard so much about Jimmy Phelan, the UW football coach, I wanted to play for him. So I became a Husky. I wanted to be a coach, so I studied physical education.

We couldn't play as freshmen, so I waited a year and learned the system. We used the Notre Dame system on offense. We shifted either right or left. The tailback was right behind the center and often had the ball snapped directly to him. The fullback and quarterback were up by the guards. The quarterback did a lot of blocking. The other back was out by the end. We'd just run right at them. We didn't have any trick plays.

I wasn't big. I came in 5′10″, 156 pounds. I got up to 170 pounds. I was just hard to tackle. I was shifty. In those days, our line only averaged 200 pounds, now it's 300. I played running back and safety. I ran the ball, passed sometimes, and returned punts and kickoffs.

One of the traditions then was for the students to gather on campus on Friday night before a home game. They'd have a bonfire and yell and scream to get fired up for the game. The coaches didn't want us around that, so we spent Friday night at the Sand Point Naval Station. We traveled by train, and guys passed the time by playing cards.

I hold one Washington record. In one game, I scored all the points for both teams in my junior season. We hosted Southern California for our final game of the 1935 season. On the opening kickoff, the ball bounced and hit me while I had one foot in the end zone and one foot out of bounds. That gave 'SC a safety.

I did redeem myself with the game-winning, 35-yard touchdown run (we missed the extra point). The final score was 6–2. I don't think that has happened again.

That same season I scored on a 70-yard run on the first play from scrimmage in our road win over Washington State.

The game is rough now and it was back then. We didn't have the protection they do today. Our shoulder pads and helmets were leather. We didn't have face masks. I had all sorts of accidents with my teeth and nose. Stanford had the dirtiest players ever. They'd do anything to get you out of the game. They'd get you down and slug you in the face. I came out of that game with a broken nose.

I hurt my ankles a few times, but a knee injury kept me out of three games my senior year. That cost me a lot of recognition and kept me from being a first-time All-American. I had a lot of second teams.

After the Rose Bowl, I was picked to play for the Pittsburgh Steelers. I earned the starting job, and in the first game of the season I fractured my neck. I ran into Bronko Nagurski. I tried to play in the last two games of the season, but I had to give it up. It wasn't worth it. We only received $175 a game—and we had to pay our way to and from the games.

I did coach some in Pendleton, Oregon, but was injured in a bad car accident. When World War II broke out, I enlisted in the Navy. I ended up in charge of amphibious boat landings. We landed everywhere in the Pacific, including Iwo Jima. After the war I started a shingle mill and then had a lumberyard near Sea-Tac airport. I kept buying stocks, so I came out pretty good.

I used to watch the home Huskies football games, but I haven't gone in a long time. It's too hard to walk. I still have season tickets. I gave them to the kids.

By Haines was voted the UW's most inspirational player in 1936. He played in the 1937 *Chicago Tribune* College All-Star Game.

BUD ERICKSEN

CENTER

1934–1937

Iused to sneak into Huskies games in the late 1920s. I used to go and wait with the crowd and rush the gate when it opened. Security consisted of 20 guys with paddles hitting you on the butt as you tried to rush past them. If you could escape them and make it to the seats, you were safe. I remember seeing USC come up here and scoring 20 or 30 points with ease. This created in my mind a great desire to be one of the guys on the field.

Coming out of Bothell High School, I had one college offer to play football in Ellensburg. I wanted to be Husky. So I walked on.

There were about 110 freshmen, and about 12 centers, who turned out my freshman year. Being the lightest center at 6′, 165 pounds, I got the worst equipment and least attention. A couple months went by, and I got sick of watching. We were walking up by Hec Edmundson Pavilion, and I saw an assistant coach. I walked over to him and had tears in my eyes because I was so mad.

"I came to the university to get an education and play ball, and if I don't get a chance to play, then I'm going to quit," I said.

"Okay, Bud," he said.

I didn't know whether to show up for practice the next day or not.

But the next day they put me in a scrimmage. I really looked like a wild man. I didn't really care whether I killed myself or not. I was going to make a showing and make that gosh-darn ballclub. So I made about 80 percent of the tackles and blocked well. As a result, they moved me up to the second team.

I made the varsity team my sophomore year. There were four centers ahead of me, and I was still the smallest. In the first game, against Santa Clara, I was sitting on the bench in the second quarter when I heard a coach say, "Put Ericksen out there."

It made my heart skip, and I ran out on the darn field. They had the same type of offense we did—guards pulling and center cross-blocking. I was really fast for a lineman. I knew if I could get past that center quickly, I could make some tackles. So I did get by him and nailed the halfback for an eight-yard loss twice in a row. I had a good day.

My father and mother were sitting in the stands. Someone next to them said, "Where did this guy come from?" My dad said, "That's my son!"

I earned playing time that day.

At that time, Seattle didn't have the Sonics. They had a minor league baseball team. They had a pretty good hockey team, but it was a local team. So football was really the only major sport. And basketball was quite popular, too.

I got a lot of recognition on campus for being on the football team. At the fraternity house, after the games, the girls would walk up and down 45th Avenue. After the game, there'd be a big party. I was in the Sigma Chi fraternity with two other teammates, so we had the center, guard, and tackle in the same house.

The toughest thing about football then was we didn't have face masks. Two years after I left, Byng Nixon, a tackle, started to wear a face mask. I wish I had one. We had leather helmets, and you'd get a lot of knees to the face that felt like it would cave in your head. Guys would really take a whack at you with their knees.

Coach Jimmy Phelan never gave out any compliments. The only time you ever heard from him was when you did something wrong. Sportswriters loved him all over the West Coast. Phelan knew how to work the press. He'd talk a lot with the writers but never really said anything.

Phelan wasn't afraid to be innovative. We were preparing to play undefeated "Thunder Team" California, the eventual Rose Bowl winner and national champion that 1937 season. He called us together and said, "We're

13

Bud Ericksen was an undersized walk-on center and defensive lineman from Bothell who became a starter and scored a touchdown against Hawaii in the 1938 Pineapple Bowl.

14

going to try something new on Saturday. We're going to use five down line-men." That's the first time anyone used five linemen. The linemen would just charge forward and allow the three linebackers to make the tackles.

The sportswriters from the Bay Area didn't give us a chance. We had a lot of guys from the Chicago area, so when we arrived in Oakland, the *Oakland Tribune* greeted us with: "The boys from the Chicago stockyard are in town today." The story went on to list some of our starters who didn't measure up to the mighty [California] Bears. The story said I "couldn't be the water boy for Cal's All-American center Bob Herwig." It was very embarrassing and got us motivated even more.

On the way to the stadium on game day, I started singing on the bus. Team captain Frank Waskowitz joined in, and we were harmonizing. We got the whole bus singing. All of a sudden we heard Phelan yell: "Cut out that goddamn signing! We are here to play a ballgame."

I played one of my best games that day. I saved a touchdown when I stripped a Cal runner of the ball near our goal line in the first half. I also intercepted a pass and knocked down another in the second half to help keep the score 0–0 with time running out. We drove the ball to within field-goal range with 30 seconds to play. We didn't have any more time outs, so I feigned an injury. Teammates "helped" me off the field with the clock stopped. Once I got to our sideline I started walking normally.

Phelan asked, "Are you hurt?"

"No," I said.

"Damn it, Jesus Christ, go in there and play!"

So I ran back on the field. The official asked, "Isn't he hurt?" And a teammate said, "He's hurt every game."

Well, we missed the field goal, and the game ended in a 0–0 tie, the only blemish to Cal's otherwise perfect season. I was voted player of the game.

We finished 7–2–2 and were invited to play the University of Hawaii in what they called the Pineapple Bowl. We went to Hawaii by ship, seven days going over and five days coming back. It was a marvelous trip, except when we almost lost a teammate overboard. He was sitting on the third deck and a wave washed over and sent him sprawling down the deck.

The game was a blowout, 53–13. Everyone played, and I scored my first Huskies touchdown. Our line coach always said to take care of your blocking assignment and "don't sit on your ass—get downfield and help out because you never know when something good is going to happen." On one run, I was helping out downfield when our guy fumbled. I picked it up and ran 35 yards for the touchdown.

The previous year we'd played in the 1937 Rose Bowl. I've always been very disappointed about our 21–0 loss to Pittsburgh. One of our best fullbacks cracked a rib in Santa Barbara where we practiced on a golf course before the big game.

I didn't start in that game. Phelan started a senior ahead of me. He was getting knocked over on every play. I was going crazy on the sideline. I wanted to get in there so badly. Finally, a teammate went up to a coach and said, "Get wise, put Ericksen out there."

Well, I got to play a quarter, but it didn't matter. We got whipped. I always wondered who had the courage to give the assistant coach advice during the Rose Bowl. About 60 years later, I was walking out of Husky Stadium after a game. I ran into teammate Walt Elliott, a third- or fourth-string center. I asked, "Who the hell was it that had the guts to say put me in?"

Elliott said, "I did." As a result, Elliott really never played much. I think that comment cost him playing time.

The rivalry between Washington and Washington State was just as intense then as it is now. But I think the rivalry between Oregon and us was just as strong then, too. I remember playing down there, and after the game fights broke out all over the stadium between Ducks and Huskies fans.

I earned my degree in business administration. I was invited to the play in the *Chicago Tribune* All-Star Game in 1938 and played professionally for the Redskins for two years. I served as a captain in the Army Air Corps for four years. I got married and returned to Bothell to run our family furniture business. I became a business leader, including being the executive director of the Bellevue Chamber of Commerce, a board member of Washington Federal Savings and Loan, and Bothell's mayor from 1969 to 1974. I was married 52 years and have three children and one grandchild.

I have a lot of wonderful memories.

Being a Husky was really quite an honor for me. To be on the team, and play for Washington, was reward enough for me.

Bud Ericksen was an undersized walk-on center from Bothell who became a starter and scored a touchdown on a fumble recovery in the 1938 Pineapple Bowl. He earned honorable mention All-America honors and was invited to play in the *Chicago Tribune* All-Star Game after his senior season and played for the Washington Redskins two seasons. He is currently retired and living in Woodinville, Washington.

The FORTIES

WALTER HARRISON
FULLBACK/CENTER/LINEBACKER
1939–1942

I GREW UP IN LAURELHURST, so, of course, I always wanted to be a Husky. I played at Roosevelt High School and received football scholarship offers from Washington, Stanford, Washington State, Oregon, and California. I accepted Washington's scholarship offer, and it helped that my future wife to be was going to the UW as well.

I started off as a fullback and linebacker until I hurt my knee. Then, I switched to center for my final two years. I really wasn't the best runner, but I could get 'em on defense. Defense was my cup of tea.

The first game I played as a sophomore was in our season-opener at Minnesota, the defending national champions. Minnesota was on our 3-yard line when Coach Jim Phelan put me in the game, saying, "Go out and stop them."

On the first play, the Gophers' lead blocker hit me hard. I thought he would drive me out of the stadium. He drove me back under the goal post. Rudy Mucha, our consensus All-American center whom I revered, made the tackle at the line of scrimmage from his linebacker spot. Then he came over and helped me up.

"Come on, Walt," he said. "These sons of bitches are no good. My baby could stop them." On the next play I tackled Minnesota's All-American runner Bruce Smith for a five-yard loss. "See, I told you those bastards are no good," he said. But we lost 19–14.

Walter Harrison made the unusual switch from fullback to center after a knee injury.

I scored my only touchdown my sophomore year with a bum knee. I hurt it in our game against Idaho. Injuries are always frustrating. Our team doctor, Dr. Palmer, invented a knee brace. I tried it but didn't like it much. A few weeks later we were playing California at home. We were down 6–0. I was sitting on the bench, mad. I took off the brace and threw it under the bench. Then Coach Phelan said, "You better get in there."

So I ran in without the brace. The quarterback, a fraternity brother, called my number play after play. We marched 66 yards down the field, and I scored a touchdown. Our extra point gave us a 7–6 victory. It was the only touchdown that I scored as a Husky. After the game, I had the brace in hand when Dr. Palmer ran over. "That brace worked wonders," he boasted. I didn't have the heart to tell him the truth, and he passed away still thinking that I wore his brace.

The week after my touchdown in the California game, I thought I should be a starter. So we went to Stanford for what turned out to be the showdown for the league title and a trip to the Rose Bowl. I remember vividly the day of the game. Coach Phelan called out the starting linemen. When he got to the last name, he said, "And starting at fullback, Walt Harrison." It was then that I became nervous about my first start. On the kickoff, I was in awe of the 58,000-strong crowd, which was the largest in my time as a player. I prayed, "Dear Lord, don't let them kick the ball to me!" My prayer was answered. I calmed down after the game started and played well, especially on defense.

Stanford had one of the most famous backfields at the time. They introduced the T formation during the 1940 season and were the talk of the nation. I knocked star runner Norm Standlee out of the game. I had about a dozen straight tackles, and we went ahead 10–0. Then they got me back when I reinjured my knee. The injury put me out for the season, and to add insult to injury, we lost 20–10. The team finished the season 7–2.

Coach Phelan paid me a nice compliment by saying after the game that he thought we would have won if I had been able to stay in the game. I thought Coach Phelan was one of the greatest men I knew. He was a great psychologist. After leaving Washington, he moved to San Francisco. When some of the former players were stationed there during the war, he would have us over for dinner and let us borrow his car.

Dr. Palmer performed surgery on my knee that December. He repaired torn cartilage with an experimental arthroscopic procedure. It worked perfectly, and I have never had a problem with it. It did slow me down just a bit, so I moved to center on offense.

My best defensive game we lost at Oregon State. I had about 25 tackles, and they won on three field goals on a muddy day. Their victory sent the Beavers to the Rose Bowl, which was played in North Carolina that year because of the war. However, my most memorable defensive game came against USC. Coach Phelan hated the Trojans, and we beat them three straight while I was a Husky. In a game down in California, USC tried this trick play, and they brought in a 100-yard track star. He got loose, but I caught him from behind to save a touchdown. Nobody could believe it. I loved that!

In my last two years, I averaged 56 minutes a game. I was honored to be voted the team's Most Inspirational Player in my junior year and a team captain in my senior year. I made a name for myself on defense. Coach Phelan was one of the first to use the 5-3 defense. Most other teams played the 6-2. I played on instinct and studied formations. I wasn't the fastest player, but I wasn't the slowest, either. My biggest strength was anticipating and having a quick start.

One thing I didn't love was playing without a face mask. I broke my nose so many times that I lost count. I eventually had to have it straightened out. Two guys on our team did wear "cages," and we called them the birdcage twins. Tackles Glen Conley and Byng Nixon wore glasses, so they built a cage to protect their glasses.

Even though we were on scholarship, we had to earn our room and board of $45 a month. I cleaned the stadium as a freshman. I swept and mopped the IMA gyms at 6:00 AM and later cleaned the training room.

I graduated cum laude and had to study hard to earn my degree in business. I was drafted by the Eagles and 49ers. They were paying $5,000 a year at that time. That sounded like a lot of money, but I decided not to go into professional football. I joined the Marines and was involved in the invasion of the Mariana Islands in the South Pacific.

I worked for my father after returning home and then bought a big ranch in eastern Washington. We returned to the Seattle area years later, where I was the fleet manager at University Chevrolet. My wife and I have been married for 64 years, and we have two sons, four grandchildren, and one great-granddaughter.

I have either played in or attended every Huskies home football game since 1935, except for my three years in the service during the war. I thought it was just marvelous to play Huskies football. Young kids would come up and say hello, and we received many letters from kids saying that we were their idols. I've always felt extremely fortunate to have had the opportunity to play.

Walter Harrison is a member of the All-Time Husky Team for the first 50 years and was inducted into the Husky Hall of Fame in 1999. A knee injury his sophomore year moved Harrison from fullback to center. He made his mark as a linebacker. Teammates voted him the Guy Flaherty Award. A second-team All-American, he was voted the UW Athlete of the Year in 1942 and later served in the U.S. Marine Corps, earning the rank of captain. He is currently retired and living in Bellevue, Washington.

DON CORYELL

DEFENSIVE BACK

1946–1949

I ALWAYS DREAMED OF GOING TO the University of Washington and playing football for the Huskies. I spent five years on campus and played four years and two weeks of football. I'm very proud to be a Husky and to be in the Husky Hall of Fame.

Of course I'm not in the Husky Hall for being a player. At 5′10″, 170 pounds, I wasn't that great. I played with some greats: Hugh McElhenny, Don Heinrich, Roland Kirkby, Arnie Weinmeister, George Bayer, and many others.

I just wanted to be one of the guys and make the travel squad. I loved football then, and still do. Playing at Washington gave me a taste of big-time football, and I wanted more. I coached football 35 years at every level and became the first coach to win 100 college games and 100 games in the National Football League.

While at San Diego State, we started passing so much, with new dynamic three- and four-receiver formations, our offense was nicknamed "Air" Coryell. This embarrassed me at first, but I got used to it.

It's funny how it all worked out. While playing at Washington, I didn't throw a single pass. Didn't catch one either. I played mostly on defense. I played some as a back-up running back my first three years, but mostly at the end of game when the outcome had long been decided. A rule change that allowed platooning opened up a spot for me at safety, where I earned a

Don Coryell played as a defensive back at Washington before starting his legendary coaching career that reshaped college and pro passing offenses.

starting spot my senior year. So the majority of my UW playing experience was on defense.

My first experience of playing Huskies football was a bit unusual. I graduated from Seattle's Lincoln High in 1942 with World War II raging. Like most everyone my age, I enlisted. I signed up to be in the ski troops—I've had a lifelong love of the outdoors. I was allowed to take part in spring football practices at the UW for two weeks before I went to basic training and officer's school. My first job was platoon sergeant.

I was fortunate not to see action during the war. I was moved from the ski troops to reconnaissance and later became a paratrooper. I liked the Army and the discipline. I thought of staying and having a military career. I rose to first lieutenant and executive officer of a parachute company. I thought attending the UW was more important.

When I got out of the service, I wanted to fulfill that dream of playing for the Huskies.

I returned home in 1946 and enrolled at Washington. I was a non-scholarship walk-on and made the football team. Being on the football team was very important to me. I was glad to contribute any way I could. I was given a scholarship in the spring, but they had so damn many of them at the time.

As I waited for my playing time to come, I took some forestry classes and envisioned a career as a park ranger. Unfortunately, I was dyslexic and couldn't read or pronounce the names of the trees.

I found my place in the physical education department. I loved all sports. I became the all-university light heavyweight boxing champion. I boxed a couple years and taught boxing on campus my junior, senior, and graduate years.

Being a smaller guy, I had to watch out on the field. I hit a few people, and a few hit me.

My senior year we were playing down at Cal. During the second-half kickoff, I took a really hard hit. I didn't wake up until Portland. We stopped in Portland because of bad weather, and that's the first thing I remember from the game. They put me in the University of Washington infirmary for three days. Still, I started the next game. Back then, they didn't understand much about concussions.

One memorable game was against Stanford. I was voted a captain for that game and I was really fired up. We lost 40–0.

Our coach, Howard Odell, threw the ball a lot for the times—about 20 passes a game. But I can't say I formulated my passing ideas while at Washington. Back then, it was pretty much "line up and hit somebody."

Being a Husky was very important to me. I really enjoyed my time there.

After I left Washington, I coached in high school in Hawaii for two years and then two years at the University of British Columbia.

I moved up to the next level with a job at Wenatchee Junior College. There I used the "IT" formation, what we now call the I formation. We had a 5'6" quarterback, Talbot George, from Hawaii who was very quick. I also had two fullback types. I thought we'd be a hashmark-to-hashmark team, so I put one fullback behind the other so the deep back had a good straight shot at the line of scrimmage and could get to the outside faster. Several of my Wenatchee players went on to be Huskies, including George and Bruce Claridge.

I then coached at Fort Ord, and we won the service championship. I met my best friend and wife of 50 years, Aliisa, at Fort Ord. She was in charge of the Service Club. She's also a Husky (she attended the UW three years before finishing at Linfield College, although we didn't attend the UW at the same time).

I stepped up to the small-college ranks in my next job at Whittier College. We started tinkering with new passing ideas at Whittier. Our best passer was our tailback. I shifted our quarterback out to flanker, and we threw the ball from spread formations. We led the nation in passing and total offense.

Then I was hired at San Diego State. We found we couldn't beat some teams who were stronger than us by just running the ball. I only recruited junior-college players, so we'd have all new offensive lines every couple years. If we were going to win, we had to throw the ball. It worked. We had three unbeaten seasons and one stretch when we were 55–1–1. Being a football coach in San Diego was the greatest thing that ever happened to me.

I moved on to coach at USC and then in the pros. I had fun coming back to coach at Husky Stadium a few times while I coached at USC and for a preseason game with St. Louis.

Football was an interesting path to follow and gave me a great life. Football was great to me. I had the unique experience of dealing with players at all levels. I have great memories. As much as I love football, I've managed to get by without it for 20 years now. Being a coach, you wake up every day with a gun to your head. I don't miss that feeling now, but as a coach I loved it. I really enjoyed working with the coaches and players.

Aliisa and I met wonderful people in football and successfully raised a son, Mike, and daughter, Mindy, who have been our joy. Our whole family is into sports and the outdoors. We have three grandchildren, Cutter, Kelly, and Lori—who, incidentally, was the co-captain of the San Diego State cheer team.

These days I'm back in the Northwest. Aliisa and I enjoy the quiet life in the San Juan Islands and have explored many new paths. We hike and go out on the water to fish or just cut the engine and marvel at the beauty and wildlife.

Don Coryell is one of 10 Huskies in the National Football Foundation College Hall of Fame. He is also in the Husky Hall of Fame. He is the first coach to win 100 college games and 100 NFL games. His overall college record is 127–24–3 in three seasons at Whittier College and 12 at San Diego State. He was named American Football Coaching Association's Coach of the Year four times. Coryell coached 14 seasons in pro football (111–83–1 in five seasons with the St. Louis Cardinals and nine with the San Diego Chargers). He was the NFL's Coach of the Year twice (in 1974 and 1978).

The

FIFTIES

DICK SPRAGUE

RUNNING BACK/SAFETY

1949–1952

MY UW ATHLETIC CAREER ENDED in a doctor's office in downtown Seattle after the fourth game of my senior football season.

My teammates were about to go spend the night at the Sand Point Naval Station, as was the routine before home games. The team doctor wanted to have me examined by a neurosurgeon to double-check my condition. He was concerned about my back. During the week of practice I couldn't feel my right foot, and I stumbled while I was running.

My back pain came from the previous Saturday game in which we were shellacked by Illinois 48–14. I felt like I was returning kicks all day. I got clobbered a couple times and aggravated a summer back injury I received while working in Alaska unloading trucks.

The surgeon looked me over for 15 minutes and said, "You're through playing football."

Just like that, it was over. Wow!

I had my spine fused in December of that year. During the operation they found ligaments loose around my fifth lumbar vertebra. If I had gone to Sand Point with my teammates, I would've played that Saturday and I'd probably be pushing myself around in a wheelchair. I came that close.

It was a severe disappointment. I had the honor of being the first sophomore football player at Washington to be named to the All-America team.

And I'd seen the heartbreak of missing the Rose Bowl by three yards. But I've always faced up to the old Chuck Knox statement: "You play the hand you're dealt."

The other sad part was I would've been on the UW basketball team that went to the Final Four that season. I had been on the basketball team the prior year.

I feel fortunate to have accomplished what I did. A lot of spinal fusion operations don't work. Mine did. I was able to play racquetball for 25 years afterward, and I still play golf.

I was a four-sport athlete at Gonzaga Prep in the late 1940s, where I was selected a high school all-American, all-city, and all-state in football; all-city and all-state from teams that did not make the state tournament in basketball (Bob Houbregs was another such selection); and all-city in track. I was 6'2" and lean, 175 pounds. I had a long stride and was fast. I was designated valedictorian of my graduating class and finished second that year in a national oratorical contest.

Despite being in Spokane, I had no interest in being a [Washington State] Cougar. The only game I ever saw in Pullman the Huskies won. My view was I wanted to prove I could play against the best teams in the country. I considered Washington better for that purpose. I remember the USC coach asked me where I wanted to go. He said, "Washington? Why would you want to run on that cranberry bog!"

The Husky Stadium turf had this huge crown on it. When you looked across the field from the sideline, you could only see the players from the waist up. When you ran a sweep, you'd be running downhill. It did get muddy

My mother was quite shocked I could live on my own. She didn't think I could last for two minutes on my own or find two socks that matched. She was surprised I became independent overnight. But my parents were supportive of me going off to Seattle.

Our freshman team went undefeated that year. The coaches tried me at quarterback a few weeks, then switched me back to running back. When the spring game rolled around, I was a back-up to Hugh McElhenny. I ran for 123 yards in the spring game and made a big impression on defense with one tackle.

I was at safety when McElhenny caught a pass. He was running through defenders and got loose, but I caught him from behind. Nobody could

Three-sport athlete Dick Sprague found success early as an All-American sophomore, but a back injury ended his career midway through his senior season.

believe it, especially Hugh. He went to the trainer and said, "Nobody has ever caught me from behind. Do I look injured to you?"

I felt I could catch anyone who had to carry a football.

During our game against USC my sophomore year, I proved it. The 'SC tailback busted through the line with a blocker in front. The offensive tackle reached out and grabbed my ankle, and I went down. The ball carrier went by. I got up and caught him 70 yards down field at the 3-yard line.

That play and the praise from UCLA coach Red Sanders went a long way toward my being selected on the All-America team in 1950. We had some great games with UCLA during my time. That 1950 season I stopped three UCLA touchdowns. Sanders talked me up to the L.A. sportswriters. My seven interceptions that season also helped.

I didn't get to run the ball much, playing behind McElhenny. But I did get to see one of his most amazing runs from the front row of the sideline in 1951.

Hugh caught a punt on the goal line against USC. At first the coaches were going crazy. Normally, you are supposed to let it go into the end zone. He caught it right next to the sideline, and then it was a 100-yard dash. It was the darnedest thing you ever saw [the 100-yard punt return still stands as the longest in school history].

The thing about Hugh was he had the quickest feet in the world. He could stop and start like you couldn't believe. And when he started, he would be going almost full speed again. He once said running during a football game was like running down a dark alley and sensing things coming at you from the sides. He could sense tacklers coming at him. It was unbelievable. He didn't try to overpower people. He gave with the pressure and the guys would just fall off, and he'd still keep going. Once he was in the open field they couldn't catch him.

I wasn't nearly as quick-footed. I had a long stride and looked for opportunities to cut and turn it on.

I had some memorable games returning kicks. In one game at Cal, I returned three kickoffs beyond the 50-yard line. But Cal had our number and kept us from the Rose Bowl.

My sophomore year we were 5–1 when we hosted Cal at home. We had the ball at the Bears 3-yard line, ready to score. Quarterback Don Heinrich called an audible (we called them "automatics" at the time) for a quick pass to a tight end. But the Bears tackled our end, Tracy King, and Cal linebacker Les Richter jumped over the line into Heinrich before he could find another receiver to stop us from scoring. Cal won 14–7 for our only conference loss. The next year at Berkeley, Richter kicked a 35-yard field goal in the final minutes to put the game out of reach.

My fondest memories are the friendships I had with the players and coaches. I mean all the coaches—Al Ulbrickson, the crew coach; Tubby Graves, the baseball coach; Hec Edmundson, the basketball coach. It was so much fun being around them all. Ulbrickson would hang out in the training room, chatting away with the trainers. You'd come in, and they'd throw barbs at you. Tubby was the epitome of an old Southern gentleman. The other thing I'm proud of is attaining an academic scholarship to Harvard Law School.

After Harvard, I returned to Seattle and practiced law for 41 years with Bogle & Gates. I'm semiretired now, but I still do real estate law with Kemper Freeman in Bellevue. It's rewarding to look around Seattle and Bellevue and know I had a hand in many developments, from the Space Needle to Bellevue Square, Bellevue Place, and now Lincoln Square.

I've stayed involved with the University of Washington in many ways. I've been active over the years with the Alumni Association, Quarterback Club, Big W Club, the Tyee Club, the 101 Club, and the UW medical school.

Being a Husky means being part of a dedicated group that strives to achieve excellence. Playing UW sports taught me about competition. It's rewarding and exciting when you are winning. The real test is who stands up when there is a loss and says, "We're going to get beyond this."

These days the best thing about sports for me is watching my grandkids play.

Dick Sprague became the first sophomore UW football player to earn All-America honors. He intercepted seven passes during that 1950 season from his safety position and finished his career with 13. He also was a running back and kick returner. He earned All-Coast honors. Sprague lettered in three sports at Washington—football, basketball, and track—before a back injury ended his athletic career midway through his senior season. He is currently a semiretired real estate attorney in Bellevue, Washington.

MILT BOHART

LINEMAN/LINEBACKER

1950–1953

DURING OUR SPRING PRACTICE GAME (which was held at Memorial Stadium because Husky Stadium was being resurfaced), I was playing linebacker and Hugh McElhenny came around my side. I had a great angle on him against the sideline. I had my chance to unload on him—but he just started to accelerate. He went right around me. I never touched him. That was my first impression of McElhenny—very deceptive.

My high school coach wanted me to go to Washington State College. I was impressed with Forest Evashevski, the head coach at WSC. I planned to enroll at WSC. A very close family friends, Tom Riedinger, who was a student at the UW, called and advised me that UW Coach Howard Odell wanted to talk to me. The talks resulted in a scholarship.

Being a freshman, trying to make the team, studying engineering, and being a fraternity pledge was overwhelming my fall quarter. I got by with determination and extra effort.

The 1950 season was exciting because we had a great combination in McElhenny and quarterback Don Heinrich. We went 8–2. Our only conference loss was to California, 14–7, and that kept us out of the Rose Bowl. I also looked up to Roland Kirkby and Dick Sprague, a guy who I thought was a most gifted athlete and hard worker. Dick was a very good student and played basketball, too.

In those days, players could play either offense or defense. The offensive players were specialists and didn't play defense. Defensive players, however, often had to stay late to practice as the second-team offense. That kind of torqued off the defensive players. That changed by the time I was a senior, as a new rule forced players to go both ways.

During my sophomore season, everyone was upset about Heinrich being lost for the season when he separated his shoulder on a hard tackle in practice. The crowds remained supportive. The real Huskies fan is one who supports the team whether they are in the race for the conference title or not. We were not close at 3–6–1.

Without Heinrich, everyone knew we were going to run McElhenny and lined up with eight-man fronts to stop the run.

My junior year Heinrich came back for the 1952 season, and teams knew we were going to pass. Heinrich led the nation in completed passes with 137. An 80-yard touchdown pass to George Black against Stanford is one of the longest in school history. Heinrich was not only a good passer, he was a good leader. Heinrich built confidence in the team. The excitement was back but so was the heartbreak of just missing the Rose Bowl again. Losses to UCLA and USC kept us from glory. The 7–3 season was a disappointment.

Many people pointed the finger at Coach Odell for not leading us to the Rose Bowl. We were beaten two years in a row by the California Bears' Les Richter. Then things got ugly. Odell was replaced by my freshman coach, John Cherberg.

My senior year was not a good time at Washington. It was tough for me to see Odell go because I liked him and he treated me well. I suppose a lot of people were glad to see him go. That wasn't a happy year as we went 3–6–1 under Cherberg. We didn't have much running or passing offense that year.

My highlight game that year came against USC. I played all 60 minutes of the game, which ended 13–13. I was named National Lineman of the Week by the Associated Press. It was a very difficult game. We weren't supposed to stay in the same stadium with them, but we made a good showing. They were happy with the 13-all tie.

I was chosen to play in the East-West Shrine Game and the Hula Bowl. I had a commitment to go to pilot school with the Air Force, so any professional football opportunities weren't in my consideration. I did get some recognition by being named to the *Look* magazine All-America team, the last all-star team chosen by Grantland Rice. I was equally honored to be inducted

Husky Hall of Famer Milt Bohart experienced the highs and turmoil of the UW program in the early 1950s.

into the Husky Hall of Fame in 1989. To me, the most cherished award was the Guy Flaherty Award, first awarded in 1908. It's special because neither sportswriters nor committees decide it. It's awarded by a vote of your teammates.

I flew C-118 [DC-6] transports to Europe after graduating from Washington. After three years in the Air Force, I worked for an aerospace company, designing avionics equipment for airplanes and helicopters. As a civilian, I received my rotary wing [helicopter] pilot license. In 1985 I started my own company, which designs and markets high-pressure hydraulic cylinders for use in logging, tunnel boring, construction, and oil exploration industries.

Two of my children graduated from Washington State and one graduated from Washington.

Through the good years and the lean ones during my playing days, there was still a sense of pride to be a Husky. I look back and am glad that I made the relationships I did there because I still have those friends today.

Defensive end Darold Talley is an example of Huskies friendship. He was from Aberdeen and became a successful coach at Centralia Junior College. He was a neat guy. His players really loved him. Darold was diagnosed with prostate cancer. His players set up a scholarship in his name to commemorate his success there. Once established, they had to figure out how to fund it. They had three auctions and raised the money for the scholarship.

I decided to try and get some footballs signed for the auction. I got three—one signed by UW All-Americans. One signed by players in the UW Hall of Fame. One signed by UW players voted most inspirational [Flaherty Award winners]. I was able to sign all three footballs. They did well at auction, but nothing compared to what McElhenny donated.

I called and asked if he would sign a football for Darold, if I sent him one. He said sure. A short while later I received a package from the Pro Football Hall of Fame. It was a football signed by McElhenny and 20 other Hall of Fame players.

The best part was Darold lived long enough to know the scholarship was established and funded.

To me, being a Husky is doing the best you can so you can have your school recognized, not the individual. To me, it's about the institution. I think we've gotten our priorities way out of scale with so much emphasis on athletics. We should be preparing young men to enter the business world, not the NFL!

Milt Bohart, an offensive guard and linebacker, was named to the *Look* All-America team and the All-Coast team his senior year. He was the Associated Press National Lineman of the Week, the first UW lineman to win the honor. Teammates also awarded Bohart the Guy Flaherty Award as the UW's most inspirational player in 1953. Bohart is in the Husky Hall of Fame. He currently lives in Seattle, operating an engineering company and is involved in growing sweet cherries in Wenatchee, Washington.

WENDELL NILES
PLACE-KICKER
1951–1953

THERE'S A STORY FLOATING AROUND that I wanted to be a Huskies football player so badly, I showed up at practice one day wearing my own football uniform and taught myself how to kick extra points and field goals within a few weeks.

Growing up with a famous dad in the entertainment business and making a career as a producer, I'm aware that rarely does anyone in Hollywood let the truth get in the way of a good story. But I feel I must set the record straight. I did come out of nowhere to kick for Washington, but I worked six years preparing for my chance.

I grew up in Toluca Lake, California, about five miles from the heart of Hollywood. My dad, Wendell Niles Sr., was one of last great announcers of the golden age of radio. He worked with legends Bob Hope, Bing Crosby, and Milton Berle, among countless others. But Seattle is my hometown; I was born there when my dad had taken a job as the voice of KOL radio. My grandparents lived there also, and they dreamed their grandson would one day be a Husky. So to please them, I went back up north from sunny California in 1951 to attend the University of Washington. Once there, my fraternity brothers at Phi Delta Theta encouraged me to try out for the football team.

I loved all sports and played anything and everything, even though I was small for my age. My dad didn't want me to play varsity football in high

Wendell Niles (right) and Don Heinrich enjoy a beverage at the home of Niles's famous father near Hollywood.

school for fear of injury, so I played a lot of touch football, basketball, tennis, and various racquet sports. I developed an interest in kicking the football, and thankfully, to my dad, that seemed safe enough. Like all parents who want to help their children, my father used his connections to bring some football greats to our house and work with me.

NFL star Bob Waterfield and UCLA great and first-ever Bruins All-American Kenny Washington spent a lot of time working with me on kicking. Washington's aunt worked for my mother, so he was at our house quite a bit.

I'd met many famous people thanks to my dad, but athletes awed me. I remember one incredible day: I was in the UW locker room tying my shoes, and I looked over and there was Hugh McElhenny. He seemed to me like Babe Ruth (not literally, of course, because Hugh was ripped with an Adonis body). He was the Michael Jordan of the day. To me, he was the greatest player ever. I thought that then and still do.

Then there was quarterback Don Heinrich, who'd go on to lead the nation in passing. Washington truly had the greatest one-two punch in the country, and I just wanted to hang around and make the team. I went on to lead our conference in place-kicking.

It rained during the tryout. I remember I was throwing the football around, and some of the coaches must have thought I was trying out for quarterback. Ken Roskie, an old Cleveland Browns fullback, came up to me and said, "Hey, kid, you're too small."

"I'll stick around," I said.

I played on the junior varsity team my first year. The most memorable thing about that year was standing on the sideline and seeing Heinrich take a hit in practice that injured his shoulder and knocked him out the whole year. It just about killed our coach, Howie Odell.

My sophomore year, the guy ahead of me had a full scholarship to place-kick. I didn't think I'd ever get a chance. He was great in practice but started the season making just two of 11 extra points. Out of frustration, Odell yelled my name during a game without warning: "Niles, get in there!"

In shock, I bolted out onto the field for an extra-point kick. We broke the huddle and I looked at the grass, which seemed a foot tall. For a second, I doubted if I could get my square-toe through it. I was terrified.

Then, my fear melted away with a few words. Heinrich did what all great players do: he made me believe I could be great, too. He took a knee to prepare for the snap, and calmly, confidently cocked his head back at me and said: "Come on, Wee, you can make this."

The kick split the uprights right down the middle. I went on to make my next 12 kicks in a row, setting a school record at the time. That took about five games because we didn't score a lot of points in those days. We beat Minnesota 19–13, and I made the first field goal in several years at Washington.

I earned a scholarship the next year. Kicking at Washington wasn't easy. Besides the wind in Husky Stadium, the crown on the field made kicking tough. The joke was, you'd think you were about to score, and then four guys would come over the hill to tackle you.

I had a few misses. The one that broke my heart was against 'SC. We ended in a 13-all tie. Both kickers missed an extra point that day on a wet and muddy field. I only kicked two field goals in my Huskies career, the second against Washington State College in seven-degree weather. Before the game, the *Seattle Times* called me "Golden Toe Niles."

In those days, there were no two-point conversions. You could kick the extra point or run or pass, but all three counted as one point. I ended up as the conference's eighth-leading scorer without ever crossing the goal line.

McElhenny and I share an obscure record. We combined to score the most extra points against Oregon. We made 18 extra points and beat them 63–6, 49–0, and 14–6.

Heinrich and McElhenny went on to NFL fame, and I went on to make a name for myself in entertainment and sports promotion. During my days at Washington and thereafter, Don and I were good friends right until he died.

As friendships go, you do what you can for each other when the other needs it most. Don's words of encouragement to a scrawny kid meant the world to me. Later, I returned the favor. Don battled pancreatic cancer. I did what I could to keep his spirits up. In his final weeks, I sent him a new set of golf clubs, the best money could buy, with a note inviting him to join us the next summer in Monte Carlo for our golf tournament. His son later told me that the letter I wrote and the golf clubs encouraged him so much, and that he read it every day.

I've come back to Washington periodically for home games, and my visits always bring back memories of a great period in UW football. I still have so many good friends in Seattle, like Judge Jerry Johnson, Ward Keller, Herb Mead, Coach Don James, Steve Roake, and many Phi Delt brothers. We've lost some wonderful friends, too. I greatly miss my dear friend George Strugar, the great Huskies tackle. I am currently the president and CEO of Niles Entertainment, producing television specials and doing public relations. I still reside in Toluca Lake, California, with my wife of 45 years, Nelle. Our five kids all also live in Los Angeles, and we have three wonderful grandchildren.

I've had the good fortune to meet and have my picture taken with presidents, kings and queens, top athletes, and Hollywood's most famous stars. When I was asked about my favorite picture from my days at Washington, I picked a picture I cherish as much as any I own. This one of Don and me was taken in 1951 at my dad's home in Toluca Lake. I think it captures our spirits. Hoisting a beverage, with confidence in our eyes, we were primed for our futures and eager to take on the world.

When I think what it means to be a Husky, to me, it's the memories of youth; it's special places, special games, and special people. Watching the team play, in person or on TV, always brings a smile because it takes me back. Being a Husky means making memories. It means feeling young again, when everything was ahead and anything was possible.

> Wendell Niles walked on and earned the place-kicking duties. His 13 consecutive point-after kicks set a UW record at the time. He also played tennis at the UW and never lost a conference match. He currently resides in Toluca Lake, California, and is the CEO of Niles Entertainment.

JIM HOUSTON
TIGHT END/LINEBACKER
1952–1955

MY SENIOR YEAR WE PLAYED 10th-ranked USC at home. We beat them 7–0 on a spectacular play that people still talk about today, more than 50 years later.

With just 6:20 to play, we were on our 20-yard line. Quarterback Steve Roake went back to pass. I tell everyone that he tried to throw it to Mike Monroe, but the pass was short. So I ran over on a crossing pattern and caught it. I ran about five yards before a USC halfback got a hold of one leg. Our other tight end, Corky Lewis, came over to block someone. As I was about to fall on the 45-yard line, I lateraled the ball to Lewis. He rumbled toward the end zone, 55 yards away, with USC's fastest player, C.R. Roberts, gaining ground from behind. Roberts caught Lewis near the goal line, but Lewis fell into the end zone for the game-winning touchdown. It was quite a thing.

That game and that play was the highlight of my football career. It was a big win and a dream play for a guy from a small town in eastern Washington.

I graduated from Prosser High School, the class of 1951. We had a graduating class of 68. Prosser High has a remarkable football tradition now, but it didn't when I played for the Mustangs.

In those days, everyone played on both sides of the ball. I played end on offense and linebacker on defense.

During my junior year in high school, I was selected on the first-team all-state football team. And that included a trip to Seattle to watch the UW spring game. So that was my introduction to the University of Washington. I decided that was where I wanted to go, so it wasn't very hard to recruit me.

I could have gone to Idaho on a football scholarship. I had opportunities to go to Oregon or Oregon State. But I wanted to go to the big city and be a Husky.

I played end the entire time I was at Washington. I wasn't big enough, and I wasn't that fast. But I was a good linebacker and not bad offensively. My last year as a Husky there were 600 minutes of football, and I played in 500 of them.

I came in at 180 pounds and I left weighing 195 my senior year. Today they wouldn't even look at me. I wouldn't be big enough or fast enough. Prosser High School probably wouldn't even look at me.

I wasn't overwhelmed when I first arrived. Nobody, in those days, was that big. George Strugar and Fred Robinson were the two biggest linemen, and they weighed 245. There were no 300-pound guys in those days. George was 6'4" and Fred was only 5'11".

When I arrived at Washington, Howard Odell was the coach, and he came out of the Ivy League. His ideas of training and getting in shape were pretty meager compared to Jim Owens's reputation. When John Cherberg took over the next year, he brought in a staff of former pro players. He brought a much higher level of training. John brought a version of hard-nosed football.

It wasn't very exciting in terms of football. My sophomore year we won three games, the next year just two. My senior season we won our first four games, then dropped four of the next five. But with a couple of breaks, we could have been 7–3. But that's just the way it goes, you know. That's football. That's why I don't bet on football games.

I did have a couple of memorable moments. In our Minnesota game in 1955, I intercepted a pass and ran it back 54 yards. I was named the Associated Press Lineman of the Week for that game. I also scored on a 24-yard interception against Oregon State that year.

It wasn't a great time in history for Washington football. There was a big scandal involving illegal payments to out-of-town players. After our season-ending victory over Washington State, about 30 players met with Athletics Director Harvey Cassill to complain about Cherberg's bad temper and

Jim Houston, involved in one of the most famous plays in UW football history, became Washington's first Academic All-American in 1955.

propensity to berate players and coaches. Cassill fired Cherberg, who retaliated by revealing that boosters, through the Washington Advertising Fund, illegally paid UW football players. The whole thing blew up, and it was a mess. Cassill resigned, and all Washington athletic teams were placed on two years of probation. An investigation by the Washington state legislature discovered 27 football players received an average of $60 per month more than the allowable $75.

I never received extra money. It went mostly to players from out of state. Unfortunately, I got caught up in it as a casualty. I was selected to play in the Hula Bowl and the East-West Shrine Bowl, but was never invited to play by the coaches because of the scandal. Nobody from Washington was invited. But it did happen. That was the lowlight of my Washington experience.

Despite our record, I had a great experience from my standpoint.

My father had been killed in a plane crash when I was 14. I didn't know up or down when I went to college. I studied engineering because it seemed like a good thing to do. Being a football player was a great experience.

I was a fairly good student and belonged to a fraternity. I experienced the best of academic brotherhood and football brotherhood. It taught me so much about how life really is and how life really works. The coaches we had taught me about hard work, and if you wanted to be good, you had to work hard to be good.

And I had, at the time, natural abilities that would get me by. I had a good pair of hands. I'd been quite a good baseball player, which was good for a receiver because I could keep my eye on the ball. But a lot of life lessons that have helped me get where I am today, in terms of the business world and all the other things I do, I learned at the University of Washington playing football. Had I not played football, I don't know where I would have ever learned those lessons. So, from my standpoint, it was a very, very good experience.

One of the greater prizes from my days as a Husky was meeting my wife, Jackie Lee, at Washington. I met her when a football teammate introduced us. George Strugar was a real character. So one day he said, "Jim, I know this beautiful girl. She's Miss Washington and she's dying to meet you." He told her that I had seen her and was completely taken with her in the worst way and so on and so forth.

George kept after us about it. Finally, we agreed to go on a blind date. We met at a reception at her sorority. And that's how we met for the first time. We've been married 50 years.

After college, I went into the Air Force and spent my time in an office building in Baltimore. Jackie Lee and I were married while I was in the service. We moved to Vancouver, British Columbia, after I got out of the Air Force and spent most of our time between there and Palm Springs.

Jackie Lee and I moved to Canada in 1958 to go into the real estate development business. We carried on that business for 35 years in various locations in Canada and the U.S. We also were involved in a number of other businesses: the Red Robin Restaurant franchise for all of Canada; the Rocky Mountaineer, an excursion train that runs in the summertime in the Canadian Rockies; and a wind energy business in Italy. Those businesses have been sold. We still have a water treatment business based in Denver, Colorado, and a gold mine near Laughlin, Nevada. I also spend a lot of time coaching non-profit organizations. I am a director of the University of British Columbia Property Trust and the University of Washington Real Estate Foundation. In Palm Springs, I am a trustee of the Eisenhower Medical Center and the McCallum Theatre, and an unpaid consultant to the local food bank and the Palm Springs Art Museum, to name some of them. We have three children and seven grandchildren. In 2001 we moved from Vancouver to Palm Springs permanently.

About five years ago, the University of Washington Athletic Department was raising funds to improve their athletic facilities. Jackie Lee and I decided to participate. If you look at the rose garden, you'll see it's named the Jackie Lee and Jim Houston Plaza. It's a football pass away from Husky Stadium, home of so many memories.

That was so much fun that we decided to include the University of Washington in our estate plan, and we are now presidential laureates of the University of Washington.

It's amazing how so many fans remember certain college games. I have a friend who is on the board of the Eisenhower Medical Center with me and he went to Colorado. He still talks about the Colorado vs. Washington game in 1953. He talks about this play and that play. And I couldn't even remember that we played Colorado when we first met. But he's still playing these games, all these years later. It's just an interesting phenomenon.

Throughout my business career I can't tell you how many times people asked me about "the Pass."

I'd have people tell me, "I was there at that game." And all they want to do is talk about that damn pass in the most unexpected places.

The exclusive Bohemian Club in San Francisco sponsors a two-week camp called The Grove. It's a gathering of the world's rich, famous, and powerful. You'll find presidents, CEOs, celebrities, and athletes. One year I was invited to attend the prestigious meeting of 2,600 guys. So one of the activities was skeet shooting. I was wearing a UW hat, and this guy walked up to me and asked if I went to Washington. He was a Husky, too. I introduced myself.

"Jim Houston?" he says. "Aaagh! The Pass! I was there!"

So a lot of people remember that. It's one of the most remarkable things that has ever happened to me. We're coming on to 51 years, and they still talk about this damn pass. The fact that I was involved is not the important part, it's just the fact that people remember something like that. I recently gave a luncheon talk to a group of fraternity brothers from that era. I titled it, "How Husky Football Prevents Alzheimer's" and gave them seven incidents that had occurred in the last five years where the subject of "the Pass" had come up.

Jim Houston was Washington's first Academic All-American (1955) and an All-Coast player the same year. His catch and lateral for an 80-yard touchdown tied for sixth among the longest touchdown pass plays in UW history. Houston led the Huskies in receiving his senior year with 16 receptions for 149 yards and one touchdown. He currently lives in Palm Springs, California.

47

STEVE ROAKE

QUARTERBACK/TIGHT END

1952–1955

I GREW UP IN BARRINGTON, ILLINOIS, a suburb of Chicago. I played football, basketball, and track. I was all-state in football and basketball and fortunate enough to be named to the high school all-America football team. I was the only player from the state of Illinois to be named to the first team, which gave me a great deal of national exposure.

I received scholarship offers from most of the major colleges in the United States, plus appointments to both the Naval Academy and West Point.

Dr. Alfred Strauss was a famous surgeon in Chicago who had played football at the University of Washington, and he helped direct outstanding football players from the Midwest to UW. He contacted a prominent booster for the UW, Torchy Torrance, and told him to come back to Chicago and talk to me. Torchy came to Barrington with his son, John, and was a very charismatic and charming person who was able to convince me and my parents that I should visit Washington.

I took a visit to the University of Washington and fell in love with the mountains and the water, plus Howie Odell's offense featuring Don Heinrich throwing the ball and Hugh McElhenny running it.

I came out as a 6'1" end, but after I got here the coaching staff needed a quarterback, so they switched me. I played on the freshman team my first year, like everyone did. Then, right before my sophomore season was about to start, I tore ligaments in my knee. I sat out that year of football, but my knee recovered quickly enough that I was able to turn out for basketball. I made the team, and that year we went to the Final Four.

I came back the next year and played quarterback. My junior year I switched back to end. Sandy Lederman was the quarterback. We had worked out together quite a bit. By the third game I was one of the leading receivers in the nation. Then Sandy broke his leg and was out for the year. Bobby Cox came in for him. Cox liked to throw the ball deep to Dean Derby. I think I only had a couple of balls thrown to me the rest of the season.

In the spring, Jim Sutherland became the quarterbacks coach. He asked me if I would like to switch back to quarterback. I did and had great spring practices. Cox decided to transfer to Minnesota, and I became the starting quarterback. We opened the 1955 season beating Idaho 14–7. We traveled to Minnesota and shut them out 30–0 in front of 58,000 fans. I played both offense and defense in those days. As a safety on defense, I contributed with a couple of interceptions, including one in the end zone. I've never heard 58,000 people be so quiet. After the game, Cox, who had to sit the season out for transferring, came up to me and said, "Jeez, maybe I made a mistake." Well, he went on to a successful career and earned All-America honors, so I think he made the right decision.

We came back home and beat Oregon 19–7.

49

Then Southern California came to town on one of those rainy days in Seattle. 'SC athletes just hate those days. We slogged around back and forth between the 20-yard lines. Finally, in the fourth quarter, we had a third-down play on our own 20-yard line. I went back and threw a pass, and Jim Houston caught the thing. As he was being tackled he lateraled to Corky Lewis, and the play went for 80 yards and that was the ballgame. We won 7–0.

People really started to get excited about our 4–0 start. Head coach John Cherberg got a little too excited, and a little jealous. I think he was afraid that Sutherland was going to get the credit for our success because people were talking about Sutherland being the mastermind of our offense, which he was. Cherberg became paranoid. They had a confrontation, and Cherberg told Sutherland to "stay away from the quarterbacks, I'm gonna handle the quarterbacks."

Well, the players felt it was Sutherland who was telling us how to win games. So we'd sneak out on Friday night before a game and go to Sutherland

and talk strategy. So Sutherland would say, "Okay, here's what you gotta do…" and he'd lay out a game plan.

At the time, quarterbacks were allowed to call the plays, which made games a lot more fun for me. The coach might send in a play every now and then, but 90 percent of the time the quarterback called the plays.

The conflict between the coaches caused a lot of tension. Cherberg was the type of coach who would berate you in front of the team if you made a mistake. You'd feel embarrassed for the guy. He treated me okay, but I remember one time he came up to a guy and stomped on his foot with his cleats. Jeez, I mean it really hurt this guy. Most of his torment was psychological. He'd get into a rage over the smallest things. He'd go off if someone had an extra dessert during dinner. He made you nervous because you never knew what to expect. A lot of people thought he was great, but they didn't see the dark side of him.

So, after Cherberg took the offensive reins, we lost to Baylor, tied Stanford, lost to Oregon State, and lost to Cal. The Oregon State loss was really a bummer because we had them beat. We'd be down on the goal line and fumble or something. Several times we couldn't get it across and lost 13–7.

Next up was UCLA, with the season slipping away. We had a big meeting before the game. We basically told ourselves to "forget the coaching turmoil and let's go out and play for ourselves." UCLA was favored to win that one by quite a bit. We ended up losing 19–17 on a field goal in the last 18 seconds. That was probably the best game I ever played. I had a couple of touchdowns and earned Conference Player of the Week honors, which is pretty good when you lose. It was just a terrific game.

We ended the season with Washington State at home. It was another gray day, and the field was a quagmire. Credell Green, who was a halfback for us, ran for 258 yards (the third-most rushing yards by a Husky in a game), living up to his nickname "Incredible" Green. We beat Washington State badly that day. So we went out on a pretty positive note despite our 5–4–1 record.

After the season, the pressure built to oust Cherberg. *Seattle Times* writer Hy Zimmerman called and said he was working on a story. I said I was graduating and didn't want to get involved in all of this rebel stuff. I wanted to stay out of it. But Zimmerman said, "You gotta make a statement."

The thing that changed my mind was how Sutherland was treated. Sutherland had said he would defuse the tension by leaving the UW to get a job

Steve Roake played tight end and quarterback and was involved in one of Washington's most famous touchdowns.

elsewhere. Then Cherberg decided he had to blame somebody, so he blamed Sutherland. He said Sutherland was the guy who masterminded all of this dissension, which was not the case at all. Then Cherberg turned around and fired him.

Sutherland came to me and said he wanted to clear his name so that he would be able to get another job and asked if I could make a statement. So I called Zimmerman, and a story came out from the players' side. I think that kind of tipped the scales and people said, "Wait a minute, maybe we should make a change."

The next year, Darrell Royal came in as the coach. Royal looked at our films, and he reportedly said, "If I had that team, we'd have been in the Rose Bowl." We really had a lot of talent. We ran the split-T that year. That was a really great thing for me because it had an option-type deal, and I was always good at handling the ball. I wasn't a pure passer, but I could throw the ball, and I could run the ball. I would have loved to play for Royal.

I graduated in 1955, and, having gone through the Navy ROTC program, I went to Pensacola, Florida, to go through flight training. I heard when Cherberg was fired, and it was a bittersweet feeling because it kind of cut off my ties to the program a little bit.

In Pensacola, the admiral knew I had played college football and asked me to play for the Navy team. I think we won six games against other military bases, which made the admiral happy. It also enabled me to have my first choice of duty after completing flight training. That turned out to be flying single-engine jets off aircraft carriers in the Pacific for three years. After leaving the Navy, I worked for General Dynamics in San Diego for several years before becoming a commercial airline pilot with Pan American World Airline. I spent 25 very enjoyable years flying around the world before retiring in 1991.

Huskies football has always been near and dear to my heart. In the days before the NCAA ruled that alumni could not contact potential recruits, we used to help Jim Owens and Don James in their recruiting efforts. It was a lot of fun talking to potential recruits about the advantages of attending the University of Washington.

I must say one of my most pleasant experiences was getting a phone call from my old friend, Tracy King, the Alumni Association president in 1985. He told me I was being inducted into the Husky Hall of Fame. When I asked him what for, he said because I was a member of the 1953 Huskies basketball team that went to the Final Four and took third place in the NCAA Tournament. It's funny how nice things like that happen when you least expect it.

I will certainly never have any regrets about coming to the University of Washington. I made a lot of lifelong friends during my four years there. No matter what happens, I will always bleed purple!

Steve Roake was inducted into the Husky Hall of Fame as a member of the 1953 UW basketball team that finished third in the NCAA Tournament.

LUTHER CARR
RUNNING BACK/DEFENSIVE BACK
1955–1958

THE BEST THING I CAN SAY ABOUT my football career at Washington is I missed the Rose Bowl by one year.

The truth is I had a miserable college football career. We had three coaches in four years.

The controversy was highly destructive. Frankly, there wasn't much good football played while I was at Washington. There were too many off-the-field activities. It was a very difficult period for the UW program and for me.

When I entered the program we had a team-mutiny controversy with the head coach, John Cherberg, who was fired. The next year, Darrell Royal coached us to a 5–5 season before leaving. And the third year, we had Jim Owens. By then, my career was over.

Oddly enough, the year after I left, the Huskies went to the 1960 Rose Bowl. We didn't even feel like we contributed to the foundation of the turn-around. Still, I'm glad I attended the university. I firmly believe that going to a school where you are working is a real benefit. But beyond that, my tenure was highly frustrating. I had high hopes coming out of Lincoln High in Tacoma. But I guess it was not meant to be.

I had a few highlight games I was satisfied with. Probably the most exciting for me was in my sophomore year. I came off the bench, and on my first varsity carry, I ran 75 yards for a touchdown. That was exciting.

The next time I touched the ball, there was a problem on the exchange from the quarterback to me. The ball bounced in the air, and a defender caught the ball in mid-air and ran for a touchdown. We lost 13–7. Can you believe that? Two touches, two touchdowns for two teams.

That made me the goat of that game. I barely survived the embarrassment. The only salvation was that it wasn't a good handoff. I either ran wide or he was too narrow. Whatever the cause, instead of a handoff, the quarterback pitched the ball to me. I wasn't expecting a pitch and lost control of the ball. When you are building, as you say, those things happen.

The greatest run I ever made was a screen pass I caught against Oregon in Husky Stadium. I had fabulous blocking by my teammates. I think five or six Ducks put a hand on me. I zig-zagged all over the field for a 60-yard touchdown in our 6–0 win. It was a really gratifying run. It took a long time and a lot of people had a shot at me. Fortunately, I was able to make them miss and break a few tackles.

I led the team in rushing as a sophomore in 1956 with 469 yards and five touchdowns. If we passed 10 times a game, that was a lot. We had an experienced, good team. The only thing we lacked was a quarterback. Our starting quarterback was injured, and we were playing with a sophomore. They called my number quite a bit.

55

Another memorable play was watching a run by teammate Jimmy Jones. He knocked out two Illinois players on his way to a touchdown. Jimmy was a tough runner. That 28–13 victory was a hell of a game.

Another game that stands out is when we played at Stanford. Their quarterback was probably the leading passer in the nation. The previous week UCLA beat Stanford. And Royal said, "Hell, why don't we use the same defense UCLA used and do the same things that they did?" And we did. And we beat them. That was a hell of a deal.

We had many frustrating games. I suppose the most frustrating game was against the Minnesota Gophers my junior season, the first for Coach Owens. We went back there and they were rated No. 1 in the country. They were undefeated, and Bobby Cox, from Walla Walla, was the quarterback. Bobby was an all-everything player. They chewed us up 46–7 and outclassed us. It was the longest game we ever played. It was a long season. After opening the season with a 6–6 tie against Colorado, we lost the next four games on our way to a 3–6–1 record.

Running back Luther Carr has some fun posing as a quarterback for the annual staged "action" shot. Carr had one of the most improbable starts to his UW career.

We did get some payback my senior year by beating Minnesota 24–21. That was good. But as a senior, I didn't make significant contributions as Owens was building for the future with young players.

That same year we were playing Ohio State in Columbus. Every time we got down inside the 20, we were penalized. We actually beat those guys that day, even though the scoreboard said we lost 12–7. That whole season Owens played mostly sophomores, which helped the program the next year. We won only one conference game.

I have to say I didn't agree with many of Owens's decisions or his coaching style.

Owens came in and made a statement the first day of practice. He frankly killed his team in those days, in my opinion. The guys lost all confidence in him for that. We stayed out about four hours practicing. You don't do that. He would end the practice with wind-sprints.

Customarily, we would sprint 100 yards at the end. He kept saying, "Do it again. Do it again."

We'd say, "What are you talking about?"

I guess we didn't do it to his satisfaction. He finally made us run a hill, which was in the stadium at that time. Good God, man, we scrimmaged that day and had drills. We were just bone tired. I'm sure there were some who quit each day. I was there on a scholarship and quitting was not part of my interest.

As for my impression of Coach Owens, let me speak for myself. I didn't have a high regard for him. First, I didn't know him. Secondly, he wasn't too personal. And some of the things that caused his demise were exhibited when he first came. I, frankly, thought he was a racist coach. He put all the black players he had in two positions in the backfield. I felt that any one of us could have started.

And by putting us all at two positions, you see, he was assured of having a non-black player in the backfield. And you know, I came from a school where the name of the game was "win" and use the best players you have. And I didn't feel that he felt that way.

57

The good thing about Owens, for me, was that it became apparent that I wasn't going anywhere in the sporting world. We had a losing team. And he didn't use me to maximize my ability. So I immediately knew that I had to make a wall of sunshine and take advantage of my academic career. I had a free education and there is something to be said for that. I tried to turn a negative into a positive. The training I had in my field was steady and it helped immensely. I was successful in business. I had a good career.

I got my degree in zoology. I didn't do anything with that. Yet I went into business and spent my working years in the investment business, real estate, and construction. It's good that I went here because people remembered my name and that gave me an advantage in the business world—I had something to initiate conversations with.

I worked for Urban Industries. We did more than 3,000 housing units, worked on I-90 construction and Seattle Convention Center projects, which I'm very proud of.

I can thank the UW for my family, in a way. One son is a football coach in Montana. He graduated with honors. In fact, all three of our kids attended college.

You see, I met my wife at the UW and got married during my senior year. I've been married 48 years. So, overall, it was a win-win. In the final analysis, I won by playing football at Washington. The standing in the community has been immeasurable. It's a segment of my life I'm proud of. I met an awful lot of fine people I would not have met had I not gone there. I'm glad I'm a Husky.

Luther Carr was a versatile player who could run, catch, and return kicks. He led the Huskies in rushing in 1956 with 469 yards and five touchdowns. He led the team in receptions in 1958 with 14 catches for 238 yards and one touchdown. His 14.9 yards per punt return in 1956 ranks fourth-best in Huskies history. He is currently retired and living in Seattle.

The

SIXTIES

CHUCK ALLEN

GUARD

1957–1960

ICAME TO THE UNIVERSITY OF WASHINGTON from a small coal-mining town called Cle Elum. It was about 70 miles east of Seattle.

I was just one of the many incoming freshmen, the first recruiting class of Coach Jim Owens. I remember calling Coach Owens right after the Washington High School East-West Game in Spokane. I told him I wanted to be a Husky and asked if the scholarship offer was still open and would he have a locker available for me? He said yes.

What he didn't tell me was when I got to the UW, there were 150 other guys. They came from all over Washington, Oregon, Idaho, Montana, California, and far-off places I'd never heard of.

There were fraternity flag football enthusiasts, gym rats, and some upper campus guys who had played some high school football. They wanted to see if the new coach would give them a shot to show their best stuff. Most didn't last long. Day after day their numbers dwindled.

I was fortunate to have had a good coach at Cle Elum named Frank Mataya. He had been a four-sport star at Washington State College. He taught his players sound fundamentals in blocking and tackling. I felt this helped me to survive the early training as a lineman.

Freshmen did not play varsity in 1957, but we did scrimmage them, and as I recall, we held our own. We heard rumors of the famed death march, as the press called it. This involved the varsity players only. The coaches reportedly

Chuck Allen always felt his mission was to be involved in football. Being an All-American guard at the UW was just the beginning.

ran them before, during, and after practice. They ran them 'til they dropped. We were told many quit and some who didn't wished they had. To my knowledge, no one died, but it sure sent a message to all players.

If the Huskies lost a game, it wouldn't be because of a lack of conditioning. The players who survived this rigorous training earned respect from the coaches and us younger players. I remember guys like George Pitt, Jim Heck, Carver Gayton, Mike McCluskey, Ed Peasley, and others. We bonded with these guys.

Coach Owens and his staff taught mental toughness as well as physical toughness. If you could convince yourself you were as tough or tougher than your opponent, you would have a big edge.

Coach Owens brought with him an excellent staff. Chesty Walker was the winningest high school coach in Texas. Tom Tipps had coached with Coach Owens at Texas A&M. Most of my training was under him. Coach Tipps was like an army drill sergeant. He could look you in the eye and you better not blink. His stare could go right through you. He could chew you out so badly and you felt so low, but he knew how and when to bring you back up.

This was a sign of a good coach. Coach Norm Pollom was an outstanding high school coach in Washington, and players worked hard to earn his respect. Two other assistants, Bert Clark and Dick Heatley, had Oklahoma and Air Force backgrounds, and fine coaching credentials.

Everything they did was to turn the Huskies into a good football team. Guys cussed at them at times, but later most realized we were like kids who didn't appreciate parental directions until we realized it was the team that was important, not individual accomplishments.

They not only taught us football skills, they thought us values of life, like courage, honor, respect, commitment, and perseverance.

When we were sophomores, I think eight or nine starters were from our class. We showed that Owens's brand of football was going to be hard-nosed. They kept stressing that toughness was a quality of the mind.

We learned to dismiss small injuries, bumps, and bruises. Sometimes you had to play with pain. Mental toughness was definitely part of the program. One player we all respected was running back Don McKeta. He was older, having been in the service, and also played junior-college ball before becoming a Husky. He was smart, but "Grandpa" was tough, too. He played most of the Huskies-Cougars game our senior year with a half-dollar-sized, L-shaped hole in the back of his calf, caused by being cleated. Lesser players would have left the game, not Don. When the plane got back to Seattle, Bill Kinnune, a fellow lineman, and I took Don to the hospital for stitches. I think Bill and I felt worse than Don just watching him get stitched up.

If there was a turning point when we believed we could be a good team, I'd say it was our 12–7 loss to Ohio State in 1958. We felt we played a heck of a game. Although we lost, we felt we gave them a good butt-kicking.

Coming home on the plane, the press was excited and impressed. They stated that this game, this effort, was the best a Washington team had played in a long time. They knew and we knew we were on the right track to becoming a good football team.

We played a lot of close games with our two 10–1 seasons. Different players played big roles, but basically we won as a team. I didn't have many moments of personal glory, only one in the UW–Colorado game. I fell on the football in the end zone on a kickoff for a touchdown. It was definitely more luck than skill.

All memories of the Rose Bowl were good. I think half of Seattle wanted to go to the game. People were so excited. The Huskies had not been to the Rose Bowl since 1944 and had never won.

The team stayed in Long Beach for pregame training. The town practically adopted us. We had a huge Christmas party. It was very family-oriented. The team went to dinner at Lawry's The Prime Rib Restaurant. The Huskies got there early and began eating. The Wisconsin team marched in looking brash and snickering at us. They looked big, tough, and mean, but we were not awed. We were confident. What was the final score? 44–8 in the Huskies' favor. They didn't know what hit them.

We had some close games our senior year. Every team wanted to knock off the Rose Bowl champions. Quarterback Bob Schloredt got hurt during the season, but the team rallied around Bob Hivner, and he led us to another Rose Bowl. We faced Minnesota and outlasted them 17–7. It was a great era to go through. Our 1959 and 1960 teams and the Rose Bowl wins proved to be a turnaround for West Coast football.

I left the university with a degree in business administration. I played nine seasons with the San Diego Chargers, two with the Pittsburgh Steelers, and one with the Philadelphia Eagles. A knee injury helped end a 12-year career. Coach Owens asked if I might be interested in being a linebackers coach. I accepted it, but told him that if Seattle got a pro franchise I would try to get involved.

Moving a family of five around the country to pursue a college coaching career did not appeal to me. I had already had a taste of that in 12 seasons with the pros. When Seattle was awarded an NFL franchise, I spoke with Herman Sarkowsky, part owner and acting GM for the Nordstrom Group. He told me they might have something available and to hang loose. Four months later, I was hired to be a pro scouting director and, along with Mark Duncan, be responsible for the supplemental draft.

I'm sure it helped to have John Thompson, the former Huskies publicity director during the Rose Bowl years and right-hand man to NFL Commissioner Pete Rozelle, as the new franchise general manager. There were a lot of Huskies connections within the Seahawks organization.

It was exciting to be involved with all aspects of a new sports franchise, but that is a different story for a different book.

We are all faced with many decisions in our lives. One of the best I ever made was to attend and play football for the University of Washington. I am also fortunate to have married a wonderful woman, who has been my wife for 46 years now. We have five great children, all who graduated from college. Four are married, and we are blessed with 10 grandchildren.

It is said that to achieve happiness in this life you must find your mission. I've always felt that mine was to play and be involved with this great game of football. It can teach us many of life's lessons. I have always had a good life with many things to be thankful for.

Even now, with knee and hip replacements, back surgery, and what feels like a 90-year-old ankle, I can still hunt, fish, read books, be involved with my grandkids, watch the Huskies beat the Cougars in the Apple Cup…and remember how good it feels to be a Husky.

Chuck Allen is in the Husky Hall of Fame and the San Diego Chargers Hall of Fame. He earned All-America honorable mention honors in 1959 and All-Conference honors in 1959 and 1960 as a guard. He played 12 seasons in the NFL (nine with the San Diego Chargers, two with the Pittsburgh Steelers, and one with the Philadelphia Eagles) and spent 20 years in management with the Seattle Seahawks. Before joining the Seahawks, he coached two years of Huskies football. He is currently retired and enjoying family, hunting, and fishing in the Northwest.

BOB SCHLOREDT

QUARTERBACK/
CORNERBACK/PUNTER

1957–1960

THE SPORTSWRITERS ALWAYS WROTE that I was Washington's "one-eyed quarterback." It made for a good story because it was true.

The press had some fun with it. There was a cartoon in the newspaper when we went to the first of back-to-back Rose Bowls that showed me with a patch over my eye, like a pirate. Truth is, I never wore a patch.

I did lose the sight out of my left eye when I was five, growing up in Wyoming. I lit a firecracker and dropped it in a Coke bottle, then put a small rock on the top to see how high it would go in the air. A piece of exploding glass permanently damaged my lens and left a scar on my cornea.

I grew up with one-eyed vision and got used to it. I boxed, played football, baseball, and basketball, and was all-conference in the three team sports my senior year in high school. I never thought I was handicapped until I came to Washington. I wanted to be a dentist and studied pre-dent at the UW. I got halfway through until I learned my lack of depth perception would prevent me from ever being a dentist. But as far as playing football, or other sports, it wasn't a problem for me. I just had to turn my head back and forth a little more than the next guy to see the whole field and not get blindsided.

My vision didn't stop colleges from recruiting me, except for Air Force, which wanted me until they found out. USC, UCLA, Washington, and

Bob Schloredt, the one-eyed quarterback, led Washington to back-to-back Rose Bowl victories.

Oregon recruited me. Deciding where to attend college was a tough choice. My family moved to Oregon when I was 10, and I played high school ball in Gresham. Our team finished second in the state when I was a junior, and I was an all-state quarterback my senior year. My high school coach was an Oregon grad, and there was a lot of pressure on me to be a Duck. I had a really hard time deciding.

But after visiting Washington and meeting Coach Jim Owens and Chesty Walker, I felt at home. My dad was a coach and a schoolteacher, and going to Washington meant it was close enough for him and my mother to see me play.

By happenstance, the all-state quarterback in Washington that year, Dave Gross, went to the University of Oregon. When we played each other, it made for good newspapers articles.

I came in as Jim Owens's first recruited class. You had to show you could be really tough in Owens's practices. In those days, the coaches had the freshman practice for an hour before the varsity, and all the varsity coaches would be out coaching the freshman for the first hour. When they saw the talent our freshman team had, Coach Owens had a hard time getting the assistant coaches to the varsity practice because they wanted to stay and work with us.

There were 11 freshman quarterbacks that year, and all were good athletes. I never did feel intimidated. I was 6', 195 pounds, and a tough defensive cornerback, which is where I first got attention. The running backs weren't that big then, maybe 165 to 175 pounds.

We had to play both ways by the rules of the day, so you if you were good enough to play on defense, coaches found a place for you on offense. Defense was the focus. I was a good quarterback, too, but never had to throw the ball that often. I passed when I had to, but I ran belly options and rollouts. I rolled out to run, and if a receiver broke open, then I passed it. My passing game came along in the next couple years.

Because of injuries I got my first start as a sophomore. I was told five minutes before our 1958 game at Ohio State that I would be the starting fullback and linebacker. That proved to be the only time I played those positions in a game. The Buckeyes were the No. 1–ranked team in the country, and we only lost 12–7. We felt we could stand up to anybody after that game. But we were a young team and made mistakes that killed us throughout the season. We finished 3–7. Our only conference win was against Oregon.

Many sophomores got a lot of playing time that year. The substitution rule then said that you could come out of the game once during the quarter, but if you came out a second time, you had to wait until the next quarter to get back in. If you were a starter, you played a lot. Another interesting thing about the rule was coaches often substituted a whole unit at a time. Our first and second teams were the Purple and Gold teams. So if the first team needed a break, coaches would yell, "Gold team in!" So fans would see 11 new guys take the field. Our first two teams were pretty equal talent-wise, so there wasn't a drop-off. That also made it easier to keep track of who had been in and out of a quarter.

I also punted. Owens put a lot of emphasis on the punt team. Field position was an important part of his game strategy—keep the game close, wear the other team down, and knock their ass out in the fourth quarter. We did a lot of conditioning by practicing punts. I had a pretty good punt average. I'd kick the ball high to prevent long runbacks, but I had some long ones, too, including five in my career that went more than 60 yards.

My junior year we put it all together. We stopped making mistakes. We thought we were as good as anybody we played.

I became the first-team quarterback my junior year when starter Bob Hivner hurt his finger in our season-opening win against Colorado. We were 4–0 until we lost to USC 22–15. We beat Oregon that year 13–12. I intercepted a pass from Dave Grosz to prevent the Ducks from scoring in the final minutes. I'm proud I never lost to Oregon in my four seasons as a player.

On Saturdays, we were the only game in town, so businesses would shut down for home games. Washington had not been to the Rose Bowl since 1944, so when we clinched our invitation to the 1960 Rose Bowl, Seattle went nuts. It was very exciting. There were signs all over the city.

The Big Ten had dominated the Rose Bowl until our two wins [losing only once in 13 games against the Pacific Coast Conference], so we were an underdog even though we had a 9–1 record. Our opponent, Wisconsin, was bigger and stronger than us. We ran belly options and rollout passes to start the game. When we got them worried about our outside attack, we went inside with traps and quick-hitting plays to help neutralize their size advantage.

That year we put in a pass against Utah that worked well, so we called it the "Utah special." We had two variations of it, so I could roll to the corner and run or pass to that side or stop and throw back to the other side of the football field. We had some big plays with that in the Rose Bowl.

We got ahead early, 17–0 in the first quarter. George Fleming contributed 10 of those points with a 36-yard field goal and 53-yard punt return for a touchdown. Another long punt return by George set up a touchdown just before the half when Lee Folkins made a fingertip catch from me for a 23-yard touchdown to put us up 24–8 at halftime. We shut out the Badgers in the second half for a convincing 44–8 win. Four lost fumbles by Wisconsin really helped us. Fleming and I shared co-MVP honors.

What a great year it was. I just felt very fortunate to be playing at Washington and being the starting quarterback. I was flabbergasted when I was named to the All-America team and to be mentioned in the same breath as Fran Tarkenton at Georgia and Bill Kilmer at UCLA.

Expectations were very high going into the 1960 season. Owens's staff had a way of breaking you down and then building you back up mentally. When I came back that fall, I was listed as the number-three quarterback on the depth chart. I didn't say anything about it—just worked my way back up to starter.

On October 3, 1960, I became the first UW player to be on the cover of *Sports Illustrated*. I think I contributed to the so-called *SI* jinx, because I broke my collar bone two weeks later in our fifth game against UCLA and missed the second half of the season. Our only loss of the season, to Navy on a last-minute field goal, came two days before the *SI* story.

We had some other key injuries that year, but the second-team guys stepped up. The UW promoted our top seven linemen that year, called the Sturdy Seven. Of those seven, five missed at least two games.

We won a lot of single-digit games in 1960: beating UCLA by two, and one-point wins over Oregon and WSU.

We again went to the Rose Bowl at 9–1 and were underdogs. This time we faced Minnesota, which had been voted the national champion for the 1960 season. Back then, they voted on the final polls before the bowl games.

Because of my collar bone, I knew I wasn't going to be the starter in the Rose Bowl. I was sitting in the lobby in a hotel down in Long Beach the night before the game. Coach Walker came walking right by. He stopped and said, "Don't worry about it, Bob, you're gonna be playing. You're gonna get in soon."

I did get into the game in the first quarter, completed my first pass, and helped us drive to our first touchdown. The Gophers were also big and strong. We ended up having a tough time in the fourth quarter. They moved the ball down close to our end zone in the fourth quarter, and we held them at the 2-yard line. We ran three plays, and I had to punt out of the end zone.

For a couple years, I'd stay after practice to work on my punts. Many days I'd envision myself punting out of the end zone in the Rose Bowl.

So when I actually had to do it, I told myself, "I've done this before, now is the time to remember how to do it."

The punt went 55 yards, and we held on for a 17–7 win.

I was named MVP again as I scored on a quarterback sneak and tossed a short pass for a touchdown. The unsung heroes were really Don McKeta, Ray Jackson, and our two All-American linemen, Roy McKasson and Kurt Gegner.

Now, we can argue we were the national champions that year because we beat the No. 1 team in the last game of the year. We didn't think that way after the game, but in recent years we've felt, as a team, we didn't get the credit we deserved.

I went and played with the B.C. Lions in the Canadian Football League a few years before returning to the UW, where I was an assistant coach for Owens from 1963 to 1974.

Being a Husky is about heart and guts all rolled into one. You take pride in what you accomplish as a team. I've stay connected to many of the guys I played with and coached. We experienced unique moments together. The camaraderie we had, and still have, is very special.

Bob Schloredt was a triple-threat quarterback. He could run, pass, and punt, and was an outstanding defensive back. He was voted into the National Football College Hall of Fame, the Rose Bowl Hall of Fame, and is in the Husky Hall of Fame. He was the co-MVP of the 1960 Rose Bowl and MVP of the 1961 Rose Bowl, and was an All-American in 1959. He also won the Voit Memorial Award in 1959 as the outstanding West Coast player. He is the UW's third all-time rushing quarterback with 782 yards. His career 9.19 yards per pass (1,195 yards on 130 attempts) is most in Huskies history. His 57-yard average on six punts in the 1959 game against Colorado is a school record. Schloredt's career-best 70-yard punt ranks fifth for UW. He is currently semiretired and living in the Puget Sound area.

GEORGE FLEMING

RUNNING BACK/ DEFENSIVE BACK/PLACE-KICKER/ KICK RETURNER

1958–1960

THE 1960 ROSE BOWL put me on the map. It was my highlight game of my Huskies football career.

I was a versatile player, and it showed in that game as I accounted for 272 yards of total offense, set a record, and was named co–Most Valuable Player of the game with Bob Schloredt. It was a childhood dream come true.

What's remarkable is 10 minutes before the game I wasn't sure if I would play or not.

During the week before the game, I smacked knees with teammate Don McKeta during practice. My knee was heavily bandaged. I limped around all week. We went out to warm up for the Rose Bowl, and I still wasn't sure if I'd play. As we jogged off the field to the locker room, Coach Jim Owens asked me, "Can you go?"

"Try and keep me out of the game," I said.

I set a record for punt return yards with 122, including a 53-yard touchdown return and a 55-yarder that set up a touchdown. I had about 80 yards in kickoff returns. I had a 65-yard reception and kicked five extra points and a 36-yard field goal. I rushed for only five yards, so it's a good thing I played on special teams.

A lot of my relatives were at the game, which was great. My high school football coach was also there to see me shine. That meant a lot to me.

Playing in the Rose Bowl is what I dreamed about while playing football in Texas during my youth.

I went to high school in Dallas, Texas, at Booker T. Washington High. I hoped I could play for Ohio State, Michigan State, USC, or UCLA because during that time they were in the Rose Bowl quite a bit.

I was fortunate to be all-state as a quarterback my junior year and all-state as a halfback my senior year.

I had always gone back and forth to California because some of my relatives moved there during the war. Before I went to high school, I went to L.A. and stayed a year with relatives. I'd always go back in the summer or during Christmas. When I got to be a senior, I went out to visit during Christmas. One of my aunts worked for a UCLA alum. She told him about me, and he helped set up a meeting with the Bruins coaches. We didn't have video to show in those days, so I brought my scrapbook. The coaches read through my newspaper clippings and said the Bruins were interested in me.

72

Many in my family wanted me to go to an all-black college. I wanted to go to UCLA. I'd always been a really good student. You needed a 3.5 grade-point average as an out-of-state student to get in to UCLA in those days. I had a 3.3. I petitioned, but they wouldn't let me in. They advised me to attend East Los Angeles Junior College. I went there and played ball with future Husky Ben Davidson. After five or six games, I did pretty well statistically. But a knee injury made me miss our last four games.

After I got injured, the UCLA coaches stopped coming around. I asked my East Los Angeles coach, What's going on? He said the Bruins' staff thought I wasn't durable and they lost interest in me. My coach convinced me the UW was a team that was building, and I'd have a chance to start right away. I said I'd go and visit the campus. I wasn't that hot on the Huskies because they had running back Luther Carr. We called him "Hit and Run" Luther Carr. I saw him run all over UCLA when they played in L.A. I said, "Where I am going to play?" because Luther Carr played left half, my same position. I didn't want to sit on the bench.

I asked when the Huskies last played in the Rose Bowl. When they said 1944, I swallowed hard. About four or five different people started games at left half that year. They convinced me I might get an opportunity to play. Still, I wanted to play in the Rose Bowl.

George Fleming (25) could do it all on the field as an all-purpose player—running the football, defending, returning kicks, and kicking field goals.

I came up in February and practiced in the spring. The team had gone 3–6–1 that fall, so they were trying a lot of folks. Many of Owens's coaches were high school coaches from Texas. They had a system that would wear you down, and many players were reluctant to buy into it.

We played at Ohio State my sophomore year. We weren't supposed to be on the field with them. They beat us 12–7 with a blocked punt. We got off the plane on Sunday and went right on the field, and they ran the hell out of us for hours. Just punished us. I was never at the breaking point, but there was a point where I thought, "I'm not sure I'm going to stay here."

There were some other players, who are well known because they were successful, who almost left the team, too.

There wasn't much winning my sophomore season. The Huskies were 3–7. I think I started maybe two or three games. It was a bad situation.

Players told the captains, you better talk to those coaches because this isn't going to get it. They'd treat us like high school kids. You might be watching basketball practice or be at lunch, and the coaches would walk right by you and not say anything to you. It was like "us vs. team." It wasn't a good situation.

After our captains went in and had a talk with the coaches, then they started to treat us like humans. They'd come over and talk with you during chow time and say, "How are you guys doing?" You started to feel like a part of a team. And we began to feel like we liked these guys. And then in 1959 we started winning and we starting thinking, "Let's go out and win it for the Big Guy [Owens]." Then we started developing an *esprit de corps*.

We played the wing-T, or split-T. The fullback and quarterback did much of the running. Owens prided himself in having two teams almost equal. So even starting halfbacks didn't get many carries. The most I ever ran in a game was 10 times. That's the way we did it.

Maybe one of the reasons some of us didn't play as much is because in those days they had what we called "stacking." We had four to six African American ballplayers at left half. Almost all of the white guys were at right half. That limited our opportunities. If you screwed up, you had to go to the back of the line.

I had a good relationship with Chesty Walker, the backfield coach, and we could talk candidly. I asked him, "What in the hell is going on?" He had the nerve to tell me, "Black guys run better from the left half because you are going to your right."

That year Don Clark played at Ohio State and went to the Rose Bowl and was an All-American playing at right half. Excuse me, Coach? That was the excuse given.

With that said, I still believe they coached us well. We out-conditioned people. It was tough. It's a lot easier to complain when you're losing. When you're winning, people buy in and say, "Maybe they got something here."

One of the reasons we were successful my junior year is because the last three games of 1958 they started eight to 10 juniors and sophomores. When we came out in 1959, we were ready.

Our turnaround was dramatic. We went from 3–7 to back-to-back 10–1 seasons and Rose Bowl wins. My senior year we won three or four games with less than two to three minutes to play. We could be three touchdowns behind with a minute to play, and we still thought we could win. People were having heart attacks in the stands because of our comebacks. In fact, when we played WSU in 1960, it went out over the news wires that the Cougars had knocked us out of the Rose Bowl before we came back and won.

I saw myself as not great at many of the things on the field but very good at a lot of them. Some people thought I was one of the most versatile players at Washington. I wasn't the fastest guy in the world, but I was quick and had moves. Defensively, I wasn't the hardest hitter, but I was very good at defending against the pass.

After we flew back from our first Rose Bowl win, a big crowd met us at the airport. There was a big rally on campus. Since Schloredt and I were co-MVPs, we attended a lot of banquets. A helicopter picked us up on campus and took us down to Tacoma to talk to the troops.

The following summer, Schloredt, McKeta, and I were hired by Rainier Brewery to be sales representatives. We made sales calls throughout the West Coast. Everyone wanted us to have a beer and talk football. That fall I reported to camp overweight. Schloredt and McKeta had bloated up, too. The coaches didn't want us getting big heads about our first Rose Bowl win, so they didn't start the first-string players until the third game.

75

That third game cost us a national championship. We played Navy at home and lost 15–14 on a field goal. But we could've won the game in the first half. We were faced with a fourth down a few yards from the goal line just before the half. I was motioned to go in and kick a chip-shot field goal. For some reason, Coach Owens called me back, and we went for the touchdown. We didn't get in. So if we would've kicked the field goal, we would've won. It was a real disappointment for us. I took it hard.

The 1961 Rose Bowl was anticlimactic for me. I didn't get to play that much. The newspapers were saying, watch this Fleming guy because he does this and that. I remember getting hit low and coming out. Everyone thought I was hurt, and I didn't get back in much. I wasn't hurt. I did have one big punt return, and I set a Rose Bowl record with a 44-yard field goal. When I went out to kick it, the Minnesota players were laughing, thinking I didn't have the range. I boomed it. It would've been good from 55 yards out.

I enjoyed kicking. I kicked straight on, and teammates called me "the Toe." Most of my kickoffs went into the end zone.

A couple other memorable kicks came in a come-from-behind win over Oregon State, 30–29 on an extra-point kick, and our 10–8 win over UCLA on a fourth-quarter field goal. Whenever I kicked, I always remembered what Coach Tom Tipps said: "Keep your head down and don't look up, and let the crowd tell you if you made it."

I missed a few. My junior year I attempted eight field goals and missed two. We didn't kick field goals much. One was from about 50 yards, and the other I shouldn't have tried because my knee was injured.

One of my worst moments was in the 'SC game up here. I had a fumble that didn't help us, and we lost. I think I might have dropped a punt once or twice, too. For anyone who is realistic with themselves, you have to admit there are times when you lose your confidence. The question is how fast can you bounce back.

In 1961 I was the second-highest draft choice from our team when the Oakland Raiders of the American Football League took me in the second round. Chicago also took me in the sixth round of the NFL draft.

I played one season for the Raiders then sat out a year because of a contract issue. I then played two seasons for Winnipeg in the Canadian Football League before an injury ended my football career. Between CFL seasons I returned to school to complete my degree in business administration. I did economic development work at U.S. West and then became director of government relations with the Seattle School District and later for King County. I represented Seattle in the Washington state legislature as a state representative and senator for 20 years, rising to the number-two spot in the senate for eight of my last 10 years. I played a role in establishing our state's Martin Luther King Jr. holiday.

There's no question being a Husky helped me win elections by having the name familiarity. More people remember me for football than for being a senator. Sports and politics can both get rough. It's a learning process, and it helped to have councilman Sam Smith as a mentor. Even though you run as an individual, you can't do it on your own. Teamwork is really helpful.

In 1980 I was inducted into the Husky Hall of Fame, and in 1998 I was a Husky Legend. Those were tremendous honors.

Being a Husky meant a heck of a lot. There's a lot of spirit with the Huskies. One thing our Rose Bowl wins did is turn around football on the West Coast. The Big Ten had really been sticking it to us for a long period of time. We prided ourselves in our system—our hard-nosed football.

George Fleming is in the Husky Hall of Fame for being one of the most complete football players. He could run, catch, defend, and kick. He was named co-MVP of the 1960 Rose Bowl with 272 all-purpose yards, a punt-return touchdown, five extra points, and a field goal. His punt-return average of 40.7 yards on three returns (122 yards) remains a school record for a single game. He set a Rose Bowl record in 1961 with his 44-yard field goal. He was named to the All-Conference and All-Coast teams in 1960. Fleming played in the Hula and All-American bowls and the Chicago All-Star Game. Fleming's career punt-return average of 12.6 yards ranks number four in UW history. He played one season in the AFL with the Oakland Raiders and two seasons in the CFL with Winnipeg. He held the AFL record for longest field goal with his 54-yarder and set a CFL record with his 55-yard field goal. He led the CFL in scoring (135 points) in 1963. *Columns* magazine named Fleming one of the top 100 most famous, fascinating, influential UW graduates of the century. He is currently retired and living in Seattle.

DON McKETA
HALFBACK/DEFENSIVE BACK
1958–1960

My first trip to the Rose Bowl, I was a spectator. I sat under the scoreboard on the top row and watched Oregon play Ohio State. What a great game—Oregon lost 10–7. My thoughts ran wild—what a great show—it would be awesome to play in the Rose Bowl.

This was a long way for a young man to go, to get to college from a small coal mining town in Wood, Pennsylvania, where I never saw a football game until the eighth grade. I saw my cousin play, and that was it. I never saw a uniform until I was issued one at Robertsdale High. I had no idea what to do with it. Robertsdale High was eight miles from our home, and after practice Bob Price and I began our walk home, hoping for a ride. Those winter nights were so cold. Robertsdale High School had a great reputation as a football power—of the 150 boys in school approximately 100 turned out for football—I was the starting quarterback as a junior and starting halfback my senior year. During the Claysburg game, I broke out on an 80-yard touchdown, and there was Dad waving a $5 bill as I returned to the bench.

After high school, I was 16 and went to work for a construction company in Allentown, living in a boarding house for one-and-a-half years before going to work for the Philadelphia Electric Company as a lineman for another one-and-a-half years. Then I joined the Navy in 1953 for four years. While in the service, I had the opportunity to attend many schools. I chose

Don McKeta entered the UW program as a 22-year-old junior-college transfer in his sophomore year and was twice honored with the Guy Flaherty Award as the Huskies' most inspirational player.

the Aviation Electronic Technician School in Memphis. After completion I was transferred to VR–5 Moffett Field, in Mountain View, California.

Playing football for three years in the Navy gave me a lot of exposure— we played the JVs from San Jose State and Stanford, plus all the military bases in the area. Playing service ball, I received a lot of recognition. I was selected to the All-Service Team. I received attention from colleges, and three professional teams inquired about my future.

I was discharged in June of 1957, and a decision had to be made regarding my future. My coach, Joe Moore, and I spent many hours discussing pro versus college. I decided to go to San Jose City College for one year and then look at my options. I had a very good year at SJCC, and many colleges contacted me inquiring about my plans.

In 1957 Coach Moore saw the Huskies play California and stated, "Don, you better take a good look at the Huskies; I like what the coaching staff is building." During my service years I had flown into Whidbey Island Naval Station and onto Kodiak and Adak, Alaska. One of my ambitions was to enjoy boating and fishing, and I loved the islands, the city, and the campus.

I arrived in the summer of 1958, and our sophomore year was not the most productive. Our record was not impressive at 3–7. But as a group we knew we had to pay the price for greatness. Our coaching staff was very hard-nosed—we never received a compliment, regardless of our accomplishment.

The next season was a great year. We made it to the Rose Bowl! It was a dream come true for the 48 members of the Huskies football team. The score: UW 44, Wisconsin 8. The highlight of the game—all of our teammates played in the game. Seeing all the happiness along the sideline and in the locker room was worth all the hard practices. Frustration of losing as sophomores had come to an end. We won the biggest prize in college football—winning the Rose Bowl, the granddaddy of them all.

The 1960 season proved the most challenging. As a group, we were committed to repeat the 1959 season, never realizing all the obstacles that lay in front of us. Everyone wanted to beat the Rose Bowl champs. I can't express what I had witnessed during our senior year—overcoming all the injuries that the team sustained through the course of the season. I know this was when the foundation of the great Huskies tradition of paying the price was born— all the sacrifices that were made by so many to make our dream come true. Our coaches preached that—the mind will always quit before the body—a quitter will never win and a winner will never quit. Yes, we overcame many adversities—but you had to be there to realize the contribution that our linemen and their understudies made to the success of the 1960 season. They are Pat Claridge, Lee Folkins, Barry Bullard, Tim Bullard, Dave Enslow, Chuck Allen, Bill Kinnune, Ray Mansfield, Dave Phillips, Kurt Gegner, John Meyers, Stan Chapple, Roy McKasson, Dick Dunn, and Jim Skaggs. The linemen were the ones who were responsible for all of us to accomplish our goal and go on and win the second Rose Bowl against Minnesota 17–7. We all are so proud of our accomplishments.

Looking back over three great years, I have many great memories of different plays, the fellowship we developed as teammates. I have great respect for our coaching staff for their high standards and the ability to evaluate our talent. Our trainers—we had two—they were the greatest.

My most cherished awards and memories are when my teammates voted me the inspirational award [Guy Flaherty Award] my junior and senior years. My teammates selected me to be the co-captain in the Wisconsin and Minnesota Rose Bowls.

On the plane back from the USC game, Chuck Allen and Bill Kinnune approached me and gave me a small box. I opened it and there was a small spark plug inside—they stated, "Don, this is what you are to this team"—this is one of my most cherished trophies.

Coach Owens signed his picture, "Don, you are one of the select few that always played the game the way it was meant to be played—Jim Owens."

In 1990 the *Tacoma Tribune* readers voted me on the All-100-Year Offensive Team.

In 1998 the All-American Football Foundation awarded me the Unsung Hero Award for the 1960 season.

I had the great honor of being inducted into the State of Pennsylvania Hall of Fame. Mother, at the age of 90, walked me to the podium, and as we walked, with tears in her eyes, she looked at me and said, "Son, I love you." That moment will live with me forever.

Don McKeta's hard-nosed style and leadership inspired his UW teammates. He was voted the Guy Flaherty Award as most inspirational player for the 1959 and 1960 seasons. He was named to the All–Pac-8 team in 1959 and All–West Coast in 1960. The *Seattle Post-Intelligencer* named McKeta the Sports Star of the Year in 1960. The All-American Football Foundation awarded McKeta its Unsung Hero Award. He is currently retired and living in Sequim.

BEN DAVIDSON

LINEMAN

1959–1960

IWAS A SLOW STARTER when it came to football. Growing up in East Los Angeles, I didn't play football until I went to East Los Angeles Junior College. I ran track and played basketball in high school. My mom was a librarian, and my dad a policeman. The joke in our house was, if you didn't read, you were going to jail.

I owe my football career to Clyde Johnson, a 6′6″ All-American lineman who played a few years for the L.A. Rams. He coached at East Los Angeles Junior College and convinced me to play football. My 6′7″ size attracted attention.

The University of Arizona, along with a few other schools, recruited me. Part of the Wildcats' pitch was that Nogales, Mexico, was right down the road from Tucson. I was also thinking about Fresno State, as it was not too far from home.

Then, Coach Johnson called me in his office one day. He said Coach Jim Owens was in town and would like to take me to lunch. I was impressed because it was a free lunch.

My mom grew up in Missoula. When I was younger, our family took a trip to Montana and we went through Seattle. I remembered it being a sunny day. I had visions of crystal blue sunny days all year round. The air was foul in L.A. in the 1940s and 1950s. So I asked Coach Owens how the air was in Seattle.

"Fresh air," he said. I found out it's fresh because it rained every day.

My mom was impressed. She was pushing for Seattle. So I decided to be a Husky. The UW athletic department sent me a plane ticket. I went to the airport and immediately cashed it in and kept the money. I got some boxes, packed my clothes and wrapped them up in string, got a one-way Greyhound bus ticket, and headed north. When I made it to Seattle in the winter of 1958, one of my first sights was a huge building with lights on it—Sea-Tac Airport. I got to the bus station in Seattle and checked into the Virginia Street Hotel. The next day I called the athletic department and talked to George Briggs. He said, "Why didn't you tell us you were coming?"

Transferring from a semester to a quarter system, I had fours weeks with nothing to do. They put me up in the YMCA. Another fellow, in same situation from Long Beach, and I ended up in a boarding house near St. James Cathedral. I got a job in a commercial shipping yard. I got soaking wet daily and caught a bad cold, but I saved about $400.

Then school started. I took up wrestling at the UW. I did well. I won the Northwest Olympic trials and went to the national Olympic trials before losing. My ambition as a kid was to run hurdles in the Olympics. I thought the next best thing was wrestling. I was just bigger and tougher than most. I had visions of going into TV wrestling.

There were rumors of how the football coaches would run you to death. Coach Owens made a statement of toughness with his relentless conditioning. Half the 1957 team quit before spring practices.

I was still pretty incompetent at football. I was big and could run, but that's about it. I started on the fourth team. We had purple for first team, gold for second, orange for the third string, and then green for the fourth string. We called ourselves the Green Weenies. I ended up starting a game that year due to injuries to guys ahead of me. I saw my first action at Colorado. That was one of only two starts at the UW. Back then, it was one platoon. Starters played on offense and defense.

I bounced between second, third, and fourth teams. One of my problems was I didn't get enough to eat. Mom sent me $60 a month. My room and board, tuition, and books were paid by my scholarship, plus I got $15 a month. We had to work for that $15, too. I showed up every day at Hec Ed to fold clean towels. I could knock off three dryer loads pretty fast for 50¢ a day. At lunch we'd get one sandwich, and nobody was going to give me their meal. They were hungry, too. I'd get a fourth meal at Dairy Queen at night. Back then, the thinking was they wanted lean, hungry players. I was bigger and burned more calories. My senior year I showed up in shape at 260 pounds. After two weeks, I was down to 240. By the end of the season, I was down to 225. I was worn down.

I picked two great years to be a Husky, with back-to-back Rose Bowl victories. We went to the 1960 Rose Bowl and beat Wisconsin 44–8. We were gross underdogs. They wrote a funny article in the paper. I remember their saying we were small and slow and didn't have a chance. We were all looking at each other saying, "We're not that slow." And I wasn't that small. When the things were over, Wisconsin scored at the end of the game. We "squeaked" by the mighty Badgers.

Coach Owens called me in before my senior season and said, "Ben, we'd like you to not play this year and then play the year after." Redshirting wasn't too common then. He did say I'd probably be an All-American and high draft choice and make more money if I stayed the extra year. I wanted to get on with my life, so I didn't redshirt. I ended up being a second-stringer my senior year, but things worked out okay.

We only lost two games while I played for the Huskies—to USC in 1959 and Navy in 1960. We beat Minnesota 17–7 in the 1961 Rose Bowl.

I still have lifelong friends from my two seasons with the Huskies. I had a great time playing there. It was a great start for my life. I got in a few plays in both Rose Bowls. I can't say I remember making any memorable hits. The one play I remember most is watching Lee Folkins make a fingertip diving catch for a Rose Bowl touchdown. That was a spectacular catch.

Back then, there were a lot fewer pro teams and two leagues—the AFL and NFL. I wasn't drafted by the AFL. The day after the NFL draft, I got the morning newspaper and turned to the sports page.

Being a pragmatic guy and knowing I was a second-stringer, I started looking for my name from the bottom up. I thought this wasn't good when I got to the 10th round and didn't see my name. I thought I was going to have to get a job. Then I got to the fifth round, and I didn't know what I was going to do. I majored in geography and had no ambition to teach.

All of sudden, there it was: Ben Davidson, New York Giants, fourth round. I was the highest of all UW draft choices even though I was only honorable mention All-Coast. It was pretty bizarre. Being the third-best end and tackle on the team wasn't so bad.

I live in San Diego and feel badly I haven't returned to Washington as much as I would like. I played in 17 consecutive UW alumni games, and we

Ben Davidson never became a starter at Washington but was the highest Husky drafted in 1961 by the NFL and went on to a 12-year pro football career. He later found fame as an actor.

won two of them against the varsity. After a few years, we formed a last-man club and each put in $10. Quite a group of us would come back. Our alumni game was the first football contest in the Kingdome. But then Don James decided to end that tradition.

I played 12 years in professional football. Coach Owens prepared me well. He was a disciple of Bear Bryant. I would say his coaching style would not play these days. You couldn't do that to people anymore—things like no water during practice. I always thought his strong point was his discipline. They'd break you down and build you back up. I was traded to Green Bay my first year, and Coach Lombardi had a reputation for being tough. I figured if I made it through Coach Owens's summer workouts, it would be no sweat to play for Lombardi. That proved to be true.

After football, I dabbled in several businesses while being an actor for 19 years. I made far more money acting than playing football.

UW boosters called on me once to help recruit a player. They had me recruit one fellow while in Oakland.

"You want to know about the weather in Seattle? Well, it rains a lot," I told him.

He didn't want to hear that and didn't go to Washington. That was the end of my recruiting days. They didn't ask me to help anymore.

I had a great time at Washington. I made lifelong friends, even though I was only there two years. I met my wife in an accounting class at the UW. For our first date we took a bus to downtown Seattle and had dinner at a Mexican restaurant. She knew she was in for it when she had to eat this weird, hot food. We've been married 44 years. Several teammates attended my wedding and three were in it.

"Big" Ben Davidson became a star after his playing days at Washington. He made only two starts while a Husky, both due to injuries to players ahead of him. Davidson played 11 years in the NFL and AFL with the New York Giants and Green Bay Packers in 1961; the Washington Redskins from 1962 to 1963; and the Oakland Raiders from 1964 to 1971; he also played with the World Football League (WFL) Portland Storm in 1974. He had acting parts in seven movies and 27 Miller Lite "Tastes Great, Less Filling" TV commercials. He is currently retired, living in San Diego, and traveling extensively with his wife.

CHARLIE MITCHELL

RUNNING BACK/
DEFENSIVE BACK

1959–1962

THE THING MANY PEOPLE DON'T REALIZE is the Big Ten dominated the Rose Bowl for a decade before we won back-to-back Rose Bowls in 1960 and 1961. The Huskies brought toughness and respect back to West Coast football. We were part of a history-making team. It brought pride to our league.

Under today's postseason voting system, we would have been Washington's first national championship team in 1960. Minnesota came into the 1961 Rose Bowl ranked No. 1 in the country by three of the four major polls. We were as high as No. 4. Associated Press had us at No. 6. The crazy thing about it was the polls were out at the end of November, so they didn't take into account the results of the bowl games. If they had a poll after the bowls, we would have been No. 1 because we beat Minnesota 17–7.

My parents and brothers came down from Seattle for the 1961 Rose Bowl, along with a lot of friends. I had lots of relatives in L.A. We went to an aunt's house after the game. Everyone was really proud. It was very exciting for everyone. Everyone bathed in the joy of a lifetime.

Without a doubt, my greatest thrill at Washington was playing in the Rose Bowl. Being a sophomore, I could hardly sleep the night before the game. I couldn't help but be nervous before the game.

I got to play quite a bit in the 1961 Rose Bowl as the backup to George Fleming. Everyone was very excited and happy about it. It was a hard-fought game. I did well and had some good runs. I believe I had an interception, but I didn't score. I had an opportunity with a ball thrown my way on offense, but we didn't connect. The key to the game was we got ahead in the first half. They had a talented, bigger team. We were wearing down in the second half.

That was unusual because we were always the better-conditioned team. I thought all teams worked as hard as we did.

I didn't know how hard we worked until I was a senior and went to several college all-star games. I played in an all-star game in Chicago, pitting college all-stars against the NFL champion. We played Green Bay with Paul Hornung and beat them! I also played in the Hula Bowl and the East-West Shrine Game. During practices guys were in sweats. I said, "Wow, this is good." Players from other teams said they practiced in sweats all the time. We

Charlie Mitchell (21), a Husky Hall of Famer, was a durable two-way starter and displayed breakaway talents as a running back and record-setting kick returner.

didn't. Ours were always hard-nosed with tackling during the week. I think that's the reason those Huskies teams were really good. We might not have had the most talent. We had the right attitude.

We practiced so hard we didn't have time for much else. We got hazed a little as freshman, but we were so tired after practices we didn't have a lot of time for that. We won so many games in the fourth quarter. We out-conditioned you.

We ran the T formation—right and left halfback and a fullback. The fullback and right back were more for blocking. The left half would carry the ball most of the time. The fullbacks ran straight up middle. Our senior quarterback, Bob Schloredt, was deft at faking. We ran far more than we passed. When we did pass, we were very effective because everyone would sneak up to the line to stop the run.

Our only loss of the 1960 season came at home against Navy, 15–14. It was just one of those games. We knew we should have beaten them. They kicked a field goal with 14 seconds to play. A guy named Joe Bellino had a good day against us. He went on to win the 1960 Heisman Trophy. I remember they used a lot of trickery.

I started my sophomore year with a bang. In our second game, against Idaho, I had an 85-yard touchdown run in a big win. I also had an 85-yard kickoff return for a touchdown later in the year.

Even though most of our starters were seniors, we thought we would go back to the Rose Bowl, but we never did.

My junior year we finished 5–4–1, but three plays kept us from the Rose Bowl—a blocked punt at California led to a loss; a fourth-and-inches at the Oregon goal line that came up short led to loss; and a 50-yard touchdown run called back by penalty in a 0–0 tie to USC.

My senior year we lost to USC to keep us from returning. That was probably the most disappointing game I remember. Being second in the league didn't get you anything.

I had fun returning kicks and punts at Washington. During my last three years, I was the kick return leader (my 32.6 average is a UW record), including a 90-yard touchdown return against UCLA in 1961. My 11.4-yard average for punt returns ranks sixth in Huskies history. At 5'11", 185 pounds, I was running for my life.

Growing up in Seattle and attending Garfield High, I wanted to stay close to home and be a Husky. In high school, I got to see Huskies players up close.

We used to play touch football against Huskies stars at Washington Park during the summer.

I had a great time at Washington and feel blessed to have had the athletic ability to play in college and in the pros. More importantly, the UW was the first step in my educational journey. I was a high school scholastic all-American. I received my UW degree in history education. A decade later I received my master's and then 10 years later my doctorate.

After playing at Washington, I played five seasons with the Denver Broncos and one year in Buffalo. After my playing days ended, I spent time in government [assistant to the governor of Colorado and affirmative action administrator for King County] and education. I started my education career at Seattle University as the director of the Northwest Assistance Center and Minority Affairs. I was dean of students and later the president of Seattle Central Community College. Now, I'm the chancellor of Seattle's five community colleges, serving 55,000 students.

I've been married 31 years to my high school sweetheart, Nancy. We raised two great kids and have two granddaughters. I've been involved in the community in many ways. I've served on a dozen boards, including the UW Tyee board of directors.

To me, being a Husky means learning life lessons. Playing football had a positive impact on my life and has a lot to do with leadership. It teaches you how to work with a team and within a team concept. It teaches you how to go through adversity when you're behind or playing in adverse conditions. A lot of my leadership style and attributes today I learned playing football.

Being inducted into the Husky Hall of Fame was very important to me. I was very honored and pleased to be selected and included with all the Huskies greats that came before me.

Charlie Mitchell was a durable two-way starter who thrilled Huskies fans with his breakaway running abilities. He was named to the All-America and All-Conference teams in the 1961 and 1962 seasons. He had the seventh-longest run in UW history with a 90-yard touchdown against UCLA in 1961. His kickoff-return average of 32.6 yards is a UW record. His career punt-return average of 11.4 yards ranks sixth for Washington. Mitchell played six seasons in the NFL with the Denver Broncos and Buffalo Bills. He is currently the chancellor of Seattle's community colleges.

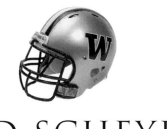

ROD SCHEYER

LINEMAN

1959–1962

W̲HAT BEING A HUSKY MEANS TO ME now is I have a lot of great memories. I still have a number of Huskies friends and teammates who get together periodically. In fact, about a half-dozen of us got together at a teammate's house close to Husky Stadium. We gathered before and after we beat Fresno State in 2006. We agreed it was the best 2–1 team we've seen in years.

I can empathize with the UW teams the last couple of years and how difficult it is to lose. Playing football at Washington was a great experience for me. Even though we didn't lose many games while I played—just seven—we had some real heartbreakers.

And if I could've caught a couple of passes, we might have won a couple more.

I decided to be a Husky despite the fact my father, a former Bremerton High football coach, played football at Washington State.

My dad played in the first Huskies-Cougars game in which the winner went to the Rose Bowl. In the 1936 game, Dad says he remembers seeing a big hole on the first play and watching the Huskies back run for a touchdown and not seeing a white Cougars jersey the whole play. Washington won 40–0 and went to the Rose Bowl.

My junior year at Bremerton East High was the first season for UW Coach Jim Owens. Those first few seasons under Owens were rough. They went

3–6–1 and 3–7. Still, I wanted to be a Husky. I had watched Don Heinrich play high school football for my dad and go on to be a Huskies legend. My dad didn't have any problem with it. He felt I should make up my own mind. He said he didn't want to influence any kids on where they should go because if they didn't like the school, then they might blame him.

I played tackle at 6′2″, 215 pounds. Coach Owens was defensive-minded, so the coaches placed you at your best spot on defense and then stuck you wherever you could fit in on offense—since we had to go both ways in those days. I played defensive right tackle, which in today's terminology would be right end, and on offense weak-side tackle, which meant the side the end was split out.

My freshman season I hurt my knee. The Huskies' 1959 team was great—10–1 with a huge win over Wisconsin in the 1960 Rose Bowl. I watched the game from Bremerton with a cast on my leg, recovering from knee surgery.

I sprained my ankle badly in the middle of the next season. I did get to travel for our Rose Bowl return. We stayed out in Long Beach. The practices started out like two-a-days. They were really torture. I thought I was going to die because I was out of shape. The game was a lot of fun, though, a 17–7 victory over Minnesota for another 10–1 season.

I had been to the Rose Bowl as a spectator. Dad always wanted to go, so we went and saw California play Iowa in 1959. Looking up into the seats from the field was a new perspective. A view I figured I'd see one or two more times.

But we didn't make it back to the Rose Bowl my junior or senior years.

Both passes I dropped were from my defensive position. My junior year we played in Berkeley and it was about 100 degrees on the field. A lot of guys had trouble with the heat. My backup got sick during pregame drills, so I played the whole game. In the second half, there was a deflected pass at the line, and the ball fluttered right in front of me. If I had caught it, nobody was in front of me for an 80-yard touchdown to tie the game. But I couldn't hang on. We lost 21–14. I think it was Cal's only win that season. I doubt I would have been able to run the 80 yards, anyway.

I played 445 minutes that year [about 44 minutes a game], the most of any Husky that season. I'm told first-unit players now play about 20 minutes a game. We played both ways and all the special teams.

My other big chance to score a touchdown came against Oregon State at home. I had a chance to intercept a pass on the goal line. If I could've held

Lineman Rod Scheyer decided to be a Husky with the blessing of his father, who played for Washington State.

on, one step would've been a touchdown. That was kind of embarrassing. We lost 3–0.

Despite our unimpressive 5–4–1 record, we were actually one game away from a third-straight Rose Bowl. That's because Washington State, Oregon, and Oregon State were not in the Athletic Association of Western Universities [forerunner of the Pac-8]. We were 3–1–1 in conference play, beating UCLA and tying USC (0–0 no less). We finished second. So that Cal loss cost us dearly.

I was named co-captain my senior year along with Bob Monroe. We lost just once—14–0 to Southern Cal. The Trojans had a terrific team, undefeated national champions.

I played in the Senior Bowl, but that's where my playing days ended. My UW degree was in accounting. I found work with General Electric in the tri-cities for several years, then returned to the Puget Sound and worked 35 years for Boeing. I've been retired six years.

My dad's Huskies season tickets were passed down to me. I enjoy going to the games. I don't remember much of the hard work and sweat. It's fun to go back in the stadium and relive the days I was on the field. The memories are sweeter as the years go on.

Rod Scheyer overcame injuries early in his Huskies career to earn honorable mention All-America honors and All-West Coast in 1962. He was named the UW's Lineman of the Year as a senior and played in the Senior Bowl in 1962. He is currently retired and living in Puget Sound.

NORM DICKS

LINEBACKER

1959–1962

Senator Warren G. Magnuson always had this advice for a politician: never get introduced at a sporting event because people will always boo you.

I had been asked several times to return to Husky Stadium and stand on the field at a home game to be honored as a Husky Legend. I heeded the Senator's advice a couple years. Then they called one year, a non-election year, and I finally agreed.

As the stadium announcer, Lou Gellerman, read off my accomplishments as a player, the stadium crowd listened intently. When Gellerman described my last play, he finished by saying it helped the Huskies "win the first Apple Cup!"

I didn't hear a single boo. I violated the good senator's rule, but it helps when you get lucky to win an Apple Cup.

The 1962 Washington vs. Washington State game was billed as the first Apple Cup. We had two ties that season with just one loss, to USC, the eventual national champion, which knocked us out of the Rose Bowl race. So all us seniors knew the Apple Cup was our final game.

We were at Joe Albi Stadium in Spokane. Late in the game, it was tied 21-all. Coach Owens called me over before I went out to my linebacker position on defense. "Dicks, I can't stand another tie," Owens said. "Go in there and get the ball back."

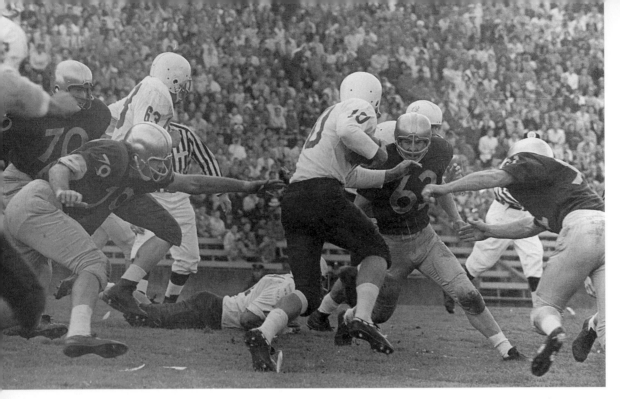

Norm Dicks (63) led the Huskies in tackles his junior and senior years, and was carried off the field after he helped the UW beat Washington State in his last game.

WSU quarterback Don Matheson threw a flat pass, and I intercepted it and ran it back to within field-goal range. That interception was my last play as a Husky. Our field-goal team came in and kicked the go-ahead points. We kicked off to the Cougars and tackled the quarterback in the end zone for a safety and a thrilling 26–21 win. My teammates carried me off the field.

Decades later I attended a WSU game at USC. I ended up sitting next to Matheson. He couldn't believe it. I introduced myself, and he said, "I've been having nightmares about that pass for years!" We had a good laugh about it.

I have many friends who happen to be Cougars. One is V. Lane Rawlins, WSU's recently retired president. He told me he always wanted to see that 1962 game. One year, he came into my office with a picture of my interception he had made from the game film. The next year he gave me a DVD of that first Apple Cup. And to make me feel even better, he took out the Cougars' touchdowns.

As a Huskies middle linebacker, and considering the Cougars' 21 points were the most we gave up that season, not seeing those scores was much appreciated. It was fun to watch on DVD.

The only thing I'd rewind about playing at Washington was I wish we had the two-platoon system when I was there. I was a much better defensive player than offensive. Still, by rule, we had to go both ways, so I played center and guard on offense. It was tough. Washington's program was tough, extremely difficult.

I remember *Los Angeles Times* sports columnist Mel Durslag said the Huskies were the toughest, nastiest team on the West Coast. The way the Huskies decided who starts, he wrote, was to throw raw meat on the floor, and the first 11 guys to ask for toothpicks get to start.

The start of my Huskies career was a golden time for Washington as my freshman and sophomore seasons we won back-to-back Rose Bowls. All freshmen were required to play on the freshman team the first year, but they took us down to watch the Rose Bowl from the sideline.

My sophomore year was disappointing. I thought I deserved more playing time.

So I talked with my dad about my frustration and told him I felt like quitting. My dad said, "You never quit anything in your life. Hang in there. Things will get better." They did.

My junior year I earned my first start—on the road against Illinois, second game of the season. We won 20–7, and it was probably the best game I ever played. I had 13 tackles, 12 assists, and two interceptions. The two picks weren't that impressive, considering I fumbled away one, and the other was on fourth down, and it would've been better if I just knocked the ball down. Still, I consider it my top overall performance. I started the rest of the games during my UW career and led the team in tackles in 1961 and 1962.

Speaking of interceptions, I got my first during my career as a sophomore in our 34–0 win at Southern Cal, in the wettest game I've ever played in. I got in late in the game. On my first play I intercepted a pass.

My senior year I dropped one pass from Oregon State's Heisman quarterback Terry Baker. Our linebackers coach had drilled into us that if we take three steps back and two steps left, Baker would throw the ball right to us linebackers. Well, on one play, he hit me right in my hands. The ball bounced off my hands, hit my chest, and fell in and out of my hands again. After that, coach thought I needed to work on catching the football, so I spent some time in practices with the tight ends. I guess the extra practice paid off in that last Cougars game.

Playing football at Washington was an incredible experience. I'm glad I stuck with it. I look back on it as one of the great experiences of my life. I still have a lot of friends who were teammates. I thought the coaches were outstanding.

I received my Juris Doctor degree from the University of Washington School of Law in 1968 and later that year joined the staff of Senator Magnuson. I served as legislative assistant until 1973, when I became the senator's administrative assistant. I resigned from that post in early 1976 to begin what was a successful campaign for Congress in Washington State's Sixth Congressional District. I have been reelected in every election since that time.

Over the years, a lot of teammates have stopped by my office in the other Washington. Coach Jim Owens came in once as a lobbyist for a Texas company. I was honored to see him. I've been able to help some teammates along the way—thankfully nobody has asked for anything I was uncomfortable doing.

Being a Huskies football player prepared me in many ways for being a congressman. You learn to keep fighting even when things look bad. You learn about toughness. You learn it takes teamwork to get things done, and you learn about competing against another team. You learn persistence.

How do I feel about being a Husky? Anyone who comes into my congressional office in Washington, D.C., knows instantly. On my desk rests a Huskies football given to me when I was honored as a Husky Legend.

On my walls are pictures of Husky Stadium and my last play as a Husky.

98

Norm Dicks led the Huskies in tackles in 1961 and 1962. He was an All-Conference Academic selection as a senior.

JIM LAMBRIGHT

LINEBACKER

1960–1964

WELCOME TO LIFE. That's what Huskies football said to me for 35 years. In my five years of playing and 30 years of coaching football at Washington, I lived it all—a knee injury, being at the Rose Bowl but not playing, All-Conference honors, returning as a coach, a 1–9 season, racial tensions, more Rose Bowls, a national championship, being hired and fired as head coach. Nobody said anything was going to be fair. What I gave Washington was my all, and I never quit.

It all came full circle the fall of 2006 when I was inducted into Husky Hall of Fame to join about a dozen of my players and teammates. It took my breath away and was a tremendously emotional thing for me—a great honor.

I signed my letter of intent out of Everett High the year Washington won the 1960 Rose Bowl. I was one of 110 new players who reported my freshman year in the fall of 1960.

I was a fullback and linebacker at Everett and a hard worker. It took three years to prove I wasn't a recruiting mistake. I played on the freshman team and was thrilled to take part in Rose Bowl practices and watch from the sideline as teammates won a second straight Rose Bowl.

I put Jim Owens and his staff on a high pedestal. I bought into their brand of football and never ever even thought of quitting. Of my 110 classmates, about a dozen of us graduated in four or five years. I stayed five. If I had quit, then I would've had to figure out how to pay for school. Nobody in my family had ever gone to college, and they didn't have the money to send me.

Owens's program was a survival thing. They didn't want anyone in the program who wasn't tough enough to win games in the fourth quarter. With limited substitution, you were conditioned to play the entire 60 minutes. No water was allowed on the practice field. It was considered a sign of weakness.

My sophomore season, I blew out my knee in practice and sat out the season. By the time I completed my second year, I knew I wanted to teach and be a coach.

I finally got to play my fourth and fifth years in the program.

I had been in the system long enough. They found ways for me to fill in. I played fullback, wide receiver, and inside and outside linebacker. I understood the system. I even started as a wide receiver against Air Force. I caught a few passes that year.

My junior year I came close to realizing a dream of playing in the 1964 Rose Bowl. There were two guys ahead of me. I knew we were going to have to beat them big for me to get on the field. I didn't get in during our disappointing loss to Illinois.

My senior year the NCAA changed the rules to allow the two-platoon system. That allowed me to concentrate on playing defense. It was a significant change for the Huskies program. We had one of the best defenses in the NCAA, as far as scoring and rushing statistics, but we couldn't score enough points.

I played outside linebacker as a senior. I was listed at 6'0", 190 pounds. I was never over 5'10", 175.

Three memorable games my last season were against Cal, Oregon, and USC. I had good games as far as tackles and sacks against the Bears and Ducks. It was fun. I was starting the whole time. I had chances to do a lot of blitzing from the outside. I knew the game and how to play it. In the Trojans game, I split my eyebrow open before the half. They stitched me up, and I played a solid game in the second half. I believed I was elected team captain for all three of those games.

One of my favorite Huskies traditions while I played was the Purple Helmet Award, which Owens started. In those days, we had two helmets—the gold issued to everyone and the purple for the toughest players, as voted by the coaches. When you'd come running out, the people in the stands got used to seeing new purple helmets. It became a thing to guess when a player was going to get his purple helmet.

Jim Lambright always showed enthusiasm for Huskies football as a player and during 30 years on the coaching staff, including six as the Huskies' head coach.

The highlight of my senior seasons at Everett High and Washington was being voted the inspirational award by my teammates. Being named to the All-Coast, All-Conference, and honorable mention All-America college teams was a reward for perseverance.

I earned my teaching degree and got a teaching and coaching job at Fife Junior High. An eighth grader from my PE class grew up to be the president at the University of Washington. Mark Emmert and I use that for introductions at banquets. I then spent four years at Shoreline Community College.

Coach Owens had an opening on his staff and invited me back. To be hired back by the coach I played for was a dream come true. The 1969 season was no dream—just one win. We had a racial revolt, and we went through sensitivity training as a coaching staff. It was quite a way to be introduced to college football coaching. The next year Sonny Sixkiller jumped in, and we turned it around.

To coach with Owens gave me a new viewpoint. When I came back, I was able to realize what a warm person and great teacher he was to work with. He demanded a lot out of his coaches, but after a win you might be swimming in his pool until 4:00 in the morning celebrating.

Being on his staff helped me understand the hard work and distance the coaches kept from the players and the image I had of him. It was extremely hard working as a coach for him, massive hours. He taught you how to succeed. It was six years of learning how to coach and recruit. The best thing that helped me as a coach was my teaching degree and wanting to be a teacher. Most of Owens's coaches who taught me were trained teachers. My last season with Owens I was promoted to defensive coordinator, which was a challenging reward. Jim Owens will always be a close friend.

Then Don James was hired, and I made the jump to his staff. Working with Don taught me the importance of organization and vision. He had a pyramid of objectives and always at the top was a national championship. Don did a great job of motivating his players and coaches.

Reaching that pinnacle of success with the 1991 national champion team was the ultimate. A defensive mindset change three years before played an important role in producing Washington's only perfect season [12–0].

Arizona State came to Seattle in 1989, and we couldn't stop them. They could've run and passed for 700 yards. We didn't have an answer. When the defensive staff met after the game, we took a hard look at what we were doing and came to the conclusion, with Don's approval, that we needed to be more of a disguise and attacking defense.

We changed the whole defense that weekend. When players came in for their Sunday meeting, they were shocked when we went down a list of position changes. We said, "Okay, you're moving from here to there."

We changed from an odd to even front. We had two games left in the regular season. We beat Oregon State 51–14 and Washington State 20–9. When we played WSU, we doubled our number of sacks for the season.

Our new scheme got national exposure in the Freedom Bowl, where we dominated Florida 34–7 and limited Emmitt Smith to just 17 yards—an impressive feat considering he's the NFL's all-time leading rusher. That kind of got our new defense rolling.

When a quarterback came to the line, we didn't want him to know what was coming. We had enough people on the line so that if they made a mistake, we could always rush one more than they could block. The quarterback was putting himself at risk if he couldn't get out of a call. We attacked to gain a numbers advantage. This put the game into the hands of the linebackers and safeties and took it away from the quarterback.

No matter how good the scheme and philosophy, you need the players with the talent, strength, and speed to execute the plan. We had the athletes.

In the next two seasons it was common to hold opponents to negative rushing yards most of the game. In 1990 we held teams to 15.3 points a game. Our 1991 team held seven teams to single-digit scoring, including two shutouts, and gave up only 9.6 points a game.

What does it mean to be a Husky? I guess the thing that jumps out to me is the level of commitment and dedication that they taught me when I was a player, which I hope bridged into my coaching and my players. You take great pride. You practice so hard that when you play a game it will be easier. You get an up-tempo of running and hitting that are essential to a winning mind-set.

In the armed forces, you are taught that there is a bond so strong you would die for someone rather than leave him unprotected. I'm not sure how many people would understand it. I know those who have fought in war understand it. I know I understood that level of commitment as a player and a coach.

Jim Lambright waited three years for his chance to play. He made the most of his opportunities, earning All-Coast and All-Conference honors as a senior linebacker. He was also named as the Guy Flaherty Award–winner in 1964 as the team's most inspirational player. Lambright played five seasons and was a member of the UW coaching staff 30 seasons, including six as the head coach from 1993 to 1998. UW teams were 44–25–1 under Lambright and went to four bowl games. He is currently retired and living in the Northwest.

DAVE KOPAY
RUNNING BACK/CORNERBACK
1961–1963

ONE OF THE MOST MEANINGFUL THINGS to happen to me as a Husky came long after I was a co-captain of the 1964 Rose Bowl team.

The spring of 1976 the UW alumni football game was held in the King-dome. It was the first football game played in the Kingdome and the last year former Huskies played against the UW varsity. I had finished my nine-year career in the National Football League as a journeyman running back for six teams. I was eager to play in a football game one last time.

The previous December, 1975, I read an article in *The Washington Star* newspaper with the headline, Homosexuals in Sports: Why Gay Athletes Have Everything to Lose. I called the writer, Lynn Rosellini, daughter of former Washington governor Albert Rosellini, and she wrote a follow-up article about me two days later, making me the first professional athlete to openly talk about being gay.

The article caused a national firestorm of condemnation to link sports and homosexuality. My father threatened to kill me. My outing kept my brother, Tony, from becoming head football coach at Oregon State. I received death threats warning I'd be shot if I played in the alumni game. I wasn't going to back down.

So I came back to Washington not knowing how my teammates and fel-low Huskies would react. It was amazing. Rick Redman and others voted me team captain of the game! Everyone embraced me with open arms. They collectively said, "We don't give a damn if you're gay; you're a Husky." It meant everything to me.

The word "competition" comes from the Greek derivative of a word that means, "to seek together, to reach beyond." And that's exactly what I was doing when I spoke out about something as private as my sexuality. I was reaching beyond myself, and as a result became a public figure. I wrote my autobiography, *The Dave Kopay Story*, in 1977, and the book became a *New York Times* best seller.

Being a Husky and playing UW football shaped me and gave me courage for my journey to truth.

My family was from the South Side of Chicago, where everyone was either a White Sox fan in the spring or a Bears fan in the fall. We moved to North Hollywood, California, when I was 10 and life centered around St. Patrick's Church. My older brother and I would often serve as altar boys for Sunday mass, and Dad would usher. I grew so fast that my knees struggled to support my body. I prayed to be healed. The doctors called it Osgood-Schlatters disease. They wanted to keep me in casts, and said only if I stayed away from all sports and did little kneeling then maybe we could avoid the casts. I convinced my parents I would do just that. Of course, I didn't. But when my parents found out that I'd forged the permission slips I needed to participate in sports, they looked the other way.

105

I quickly discovered being successful in sports led to being popular. I couldn't understand why all my dreams and fantasies centered around my buddies. I decided that to please my folks and to cure myself I would enroll at the Claretian Jr. Seminary to study to be a priest. As I matured, my knees grew stronger but so did my desires and fantasies about the fellow seminarians. Although I was a favorite of the headmaster and became the youngest infirmarian they ever had, I thank God that I never experienced any sexual abuse. I did feel an uncomfortable closeness that both scared and excited me. But even with all my prayers and acts of contrition I wasn't getting any relief or success in dealing with my deep secret. I decided to transfer to Notre Dame High School. There I immersed myself in the sports and the competition I so loved. I became the school's only three-sport letterman, in football, basketball, and track. I surprised myself by making the all-Catholic team and then did better than average on the college boards.

106

Dave Kopay overcame losing his starting position and personal struggles to be voted co-captain for the 1964 Rose Bowl team.

I was offered athletic scholarships to Cal, Stanford, Marquette, and an alternate appointment to the Naval Academy—but no scholarship to the one school I really wanted, Notre Dame. I wound up at the University of Washington when Marquette dropped their football program after my freshman year. My brother, Tony, was on the UW football team, and I saw them beat the giants from Minnesota in the 1961 Rose Bowl.

When I arrived on campus, right away I got a big rush from a number of fraternities. The fact that I was a halfback on a team that just had been to the Rose Bowl seemed to get everyone's attention!

I joined Theta Chi and loved the praise of my fraternity brothers for being on the football team. I fell in love with one fraternity brother and didn't understand it all and was scared to death by it. We both ran away from it. He ran away from it his whole life.

We went on double dates with girls to the movies and drank beer. To my teammates and fraternity brothers, it looked like I was a tough jock who had his shit together, but on the inside I was an angry and confused man. My fraternity brother and I never talked about our feelings for each other. Our sexual feelings were only expressed after we dropped our dates off and drank enough to forget about what we did. Or at least pretended to forget.

In 1961 I was either first or second string and playing both ways. Tony was mostly playing on the second and third string. As a younger brother, you always want to beat your older brother. I was overachieving, but he really was much tougher than me. He motivated me. If I whined, he'd always tell me to get my ass out there. I started three or four games.

We finished 5–4–1, but each of our four losses were by seven or fewer points.

My junior year, however, I lost all my credibility as a football player and confidence in myself. I guess the coaches thought I wasn't tough enough. And I wasn't. Coaches moved me to defensive tackle and offensive guard or tight end and down to third string. My 6′1″, 210-pound size was good for a running back, but on the line I got the hell beat out of me for a year. I didn't even letter.

We had a great team that year, going 7–1–2. We lost the wrong game, to USC 14–0, to keep us from the Rose Bowl. We were crushed.

When you get pushed down like that, you learn a lot about yourself. I had to learn to be the tough guy that I naturally never was. I fought back. I vowed

107

to myself that somehow I would get back on top. My senior year I moved back to running back and defensive back. I played for 48 out of 60 minutes and led the team in minutes played. I led the team in receiving with 13 catches for 190 yards (we didn't throw much).

Our 1963 team showed character after losing our first three games. We beat the teams we needed to and earned a Rose Bowl berth despite our 6–4 record. We beat 'SC 22–7, and I was the Player of the Week thanks to a key interception.

It was a magical time and a terrible time, too. Before our regular-season finale with Washington State, President Kennedy was assassinated. Officials moved the game back a week. Football was almost a release to get away from the horrible sorrow you saw on TV.

It was very special to play in the Rose Bowl, having lived so close, yet so far away from the stadium. I was elected as a co-captain along with John Stupey. It was very exciting. It was a dream come true, but the Thursday before the game I separated two ribs at practice and could hardly breathe without intense pain. Because of that, I wasn't available to play my normal amount of time against Illinois.

I did score the first points of the game with a seven-yard touchdown run in the second quarter on a great pitch from our quarterback and a terrific block from Ron Medved, who knocked Dick Butkus on his ass. I practically walked into the end zone.

Unfortunately, we lost power runner Junior Coffey to a broken ankle during bowl practices, and then Douglas was injured early in the game. Douglas ran the ball quite a bit and was a very inspirational player. It might have been a different story if he played the entire game. We were moving the ball with him. The air came out of everyone when he went down. We lost 17–7. It took me many years to get over that loss. I missed being named Seattle's Man of the Year in sports by one vote.

I wasn't drafted by any pro football teams, so I poured myself into making it as a free agent. My sexuality was a motivating factor to prove I was equal to the next guy and to show my fraternity brother and special friend that I could do it. I had to show I was tougher than anyone. I played nine seasons in the NFL.

I had the privilege to spend two seasons in Washington, D.C., under Coach Vince Lombardi.

Living in D.C. and playing for Lombardi and the Redskins changed my life! Lombardi was often philosophical about life. Everyone always remembers him saying, "Winning isn't everything, it's the only thing." I never heard him say that. What I did hear him say over and over was, "The quality of one's life is in direct proportion to one's commitment to excellence." If you do your best, never slack off, and never give up, you'll come out on top. Also around that time I read a definition of what it meant to be a man. It went, "A man is someone who accepts the responsibility of what he does, what he says, and who he is." It was like hearing Lombardi talk. I certainly wasn't ready to come out, but I was getting there.

It was only a year or so after I was no longer playing and five years since Lombardi's death when I just happened to be back in D.C. and saw the headline in *The Washington Star* that would change my life.

That article, while not naming him specifically, was all about my ex-teammate Jerry Smith, who was still playing tight end on the Redskins. He was quoted anonymously as, "a closeted homosexual NFL player" and was not identified by name, position, or team. But by the description of his scarred hands, I knew it was Jerry. My feelings were very complex — very confused and conflicted. But even more than all that, reading that headline I felt betrayed. Often Jerry and I discussed our dilemma. We even discussed writing a book together and telling the world the truth. We laughed and spoke of setting the record straight, so to speak.

We had both gravitated to Martin Luther King Jr. and embraced practically everything he had to say. We both looked to a day when we too would not be judged by our sexual orientation but by the content of our character. But deep inside, and putting myself in Jerry's place, I knew why he chose to stay in the closet and remain anonymous. He was "Mr. Touchdown." He was the Redskins' star and held NFL records that were only recently broken. And he was still playing. But I wasn't playing anymore. But more than that, I needed to find my integrity. I needed to stand up and be a man. Be that man who accepted the responsibility of who he was and what he did.

I called Lynn Rosellini and said we needed to talk. And talk I did.

After Lynn's article about me came out, *The Washington Star* had never before received such criticism and hate. But all I had done was to speak openly and honestly! The next year I wrote *The David Kopay Story*, which expanded on that theme of honesty. All those years of lying to my friends, lying to my family, and most importantly, lying to myself were wasted history. I felt like I just climbed out from under a rock, and a huge burden had been lifted, and the freedom and exhilaration I felt were just like hearing the national anthem right before the kickoff at a ballgame!

It's been 32 years since I first spoke out and 27 years since I first went to work for my uncle Bill at Linoleum City, a flooring store here in L.A. that specializes in supplying flooring for the entertainment industry. He knew I would have the queer eye for the straight folks and could figure out the needs of all the production designers and set decorators that came into the store. I have made a good living and live well in a very nice house in Larchmont Village. I am a spiritual person who happens to be gay. I have continued to speak out on gay issues.

I really love the University of Washington. The university has given me so much self-esteem and personal growth, I wanted to give back when I retired. That's why in 2007 I gave $1 million to fund the David Kopay Endowment for gay, lesbian, and transgender students. I'm very excited about creating a legacy that will live on and help those who need it.

Going through the ups and downs at Washington helped me for life. Being a Husky now means everything to me. It was a life-forming experience and it continues to be. It helped build character in me and helped me face some of the demons I needed to face. Seattle was a very accepting place in those days, and, hopefully, still is. I'll probably retire and move back to Seattle. The UW has shown great humanity and has been an incredible force in the U.S. and the world.

Dave Kopay was named to the honorable All-America team in 1963 and was voted co-captain for the 1964 Rose Bowl. He led UW in receiving with 13 catches for 190 yards in 1963. He played nine seasons in the NFL with the San Francisco 49ers (1964–1967), Detroit Lions (1968), Washington Redskins (1969–1970), New Orleans Saints (1971), and Green Bay Packers (1972). *The Dave Kopay Story* made the *New York Times* best-seller list for 10 weeks in 1977 and was chosen by the American Library Association as suggested reading for all high school kids in the same year. The book is in its third printing. He is currently a salesman and buyer with a flooring company in Los Angeles.

RICK REDMAN

LINEBACKER

1961–1964

WHEN IT CAME TIME TO DECIDE on college, I was pretty sure I would go to Notre Dame. I was attending Blanchet High after moving from Maryland to Seattle in 1957. Notre Dame offered me a scholarship in my junior year, and it made sense to go there.

Until, that is, my stepfather, John Sellen, told me that if I made a name for myself in Seattle and stayed here it would probably change my life. So I reconsidered and took a hard look at the UW. I watched their practices and saw how Jim Owens was developing the program. I really liked his style. I committed to Washington in August before my freshman year.

When I got to the UW, the freshman didn't practice until school started, and I watched a lot of the varsity's two-a-days. We had a lot of good guys in my class, and there were a lot of guys who were still there from the Rose Bowl years. My sophomore year, I was playing with those guys. I wasn't really intimidated, though it was certainly a step up from freshman ball. There was always tough competition, and there was a physically demanding side of practice that made this team different. I never thought of quitting, though we certainly had some guys who did.

My freshman team didn't win a game. We only played four games. We played Oregon State in our last game. We had a terrible first half; we couldn't tackle anyone. At halftime, the freshman coach yelled at us and said we ought to just go out and have a tackling practice. Someone in the back of the room yelled, "Yes!" So we went out during halftime and had tackling practice while waiting for the Beavers to come out. At least they didn't score in the second half.

We weren't really worried about wins and losses as freshman because the whole emphasis was on learning the system.

Classes weren't too difficult for me, though sometimes I'd have a class with a professor with whom I didn't get along. But, for the most part, I was a pretty good student. My first couple quarters I got ahead of the curve. I joined a fraternity, the Theta Chi house.

During my sophomore year I got to play quite a lot at linebacker and guard. The guy in front of me was a senior, Dave Phillips. He was one of those veteran tough Huskies who was effective and got the job done. My first game we played Purdue and tied them 7–7. I was in the right place at the right time—their running game was geared around a lot of fullback runs up the middle. I ended up having a really good game, and I was Conference Player of the Week in my first game. I moved up the next week to being the starter. The week after, however, I was back down to the second team, as Dave was on my heals, and I needed to understand how to be consistent in my play. There were a lot of things like that during my sophomore year. I actually only started about half of the games. The guys ahead of us were seniors, so they'd survived long enough to earn playing time. Phillips made me a better player. He pushed me to be better, and everyone did that to each other. The competition within our team made us better players. All of the Owens teams during that era always said they couldn't wait until Saturday, because it was going to be the easiest day of the week. They wouldn't get hit nearly as hard as they did during the regular practices.

112

That 1962 season we were 7–1–2. Our only loss was to Southern Cal, 14–0 in the Coliseum. The Trojans won the national title that year.

We were waiting for USC the next year, and the coaches and field crews did a pretty good job of slowing the field down. We blocked a punt on the first series that got the snowball rolling, and beat them 22–7. They had all their guys back from the year before but obviously did not like the soggy turf that we had waiting for them.

I think my play was a little bit of everything, I was able to anticipate and read things quickly. I was fortunate to meet some people who taught me about visualization and how to slow the game down. Through mental preparation, I was able to be better prepared for the games on Saturday.

My junior year started off really badly. We lost to Air Force, Pittsburgh, and Iowa. That 0–3 start was a horrible experience. The anguish and sadness in the locker room after that third game propelled us to a new commitment and a great week of practice. After we lost that third game, we could've beaten anyone that next week. We took out our frustration on Oregon State, winning 34–7. We ran off three more wins and then beat Craig Morton and Cal 39–26. We scored every time we had the ball, except once, all on long drives. The game was never in doubt, but Morton led a couple touchdown drives.

The coaches were so mad that we let them score so much on us that the next week we went down to the lower field where it was muddy, and they killed us running on that horrible field. We went down to UCLA and had no legs. We were all out of gas and lost the game 14–0. We came back, and Owens flipped the whole team, so the starters were second team and second team were starters, with the exception of Steve Bramwell, who was the only one to play really well. On Friday of that week, President Kennedy was assassinated, and now we were knocked down to second team for two weeks since the games were canceled. I was supposed to get married the next week after the last game, so I had to move the date up to Thursday and get married on Thanksgiving. Two days later we played Washington State. By the time the second team went in, we were foaming at the mouth. When we got into the game, we kicked the dog out of 'em. I think the score was only 16–0, but it was like a 35–0 whipping.

Even though our overall 6–5 record wasn't that impressive, we won the conference championship and with it a trip to the Rose Bowl. The Rose Bowl was a good trip. We went down there and represented the university well. We went to Disneyland and all the places they take you to on those trips. My wife came down with the rest of the wives just before Christmas.

As a team, we weren't that big compared to everyone today. It's such a specialized game today, where most players are in one position their whole life. You couldn't be 320 pounds and go both ways and play the whole game. I was 6', 215 pounds, and considered average size.

We lost to Illinois because our quarterback Bill Douglas got hurt early in the game. They had a really good team. If we had been able to get some points early, it might have been different. Our back-up quarterback had been out all season with mono, and we just didn't jell after Bill went down.

Losing the Rose Bowl was tough to swallow. I didn't have that great of a game. It was one of those games that just went by. We didn't get the job done.

I was an All-American that year. I was going to all these All-American events. A lot of those took place between the Washington State game and the Rose Bowl. I made three All-America trips back East, including being on *The Ed Sullivan Show.*

All I remember is coming back from one of those trips, and Tom Tipps, my linebackers coach and the defensive coordinator, was mad because someone quoted me as saying that Illinois was too slow of a team to keep up with us in the upcoming game in the Rose Bowl. He sat me down and really chewed on me for about 15 minutes. I tried to tell coach what I really said, but the damage was done and he was sure that the article would make it to the Illinois locker room. Dick Butkus had been on all of those trips with me, as he was their center and I was our middle linebacker, so he came after me quite a lot.

Every once in a while I'll get a signature request with a photo from that game. It's taken from the backfield of Illinois and I'm right in front. Dick's butt is in the foreground, and I always say, "Send it to Dick Butkus, you want his autograph, not mine." I get one or two autograph requests in the mail a week, and I sign those. Typically, the requests are from guys who are my year or younger, trying to get something for their kids. I've always been amazed at how many people are into collecting autographs, but I am still honored that they are still asking.

During my senior year, the college rules on substitutions changed, and I played primarily defense. That season we lost to Air Force 3–2 in our opener. The next game was a 35–14 win against Baylor. They had Larry Elkins, an All-American wide receiver playing for them. He later played for the Houston Oilers in the AFL, and he'd always complain about how hard he got hit in the tunnel going to the field at Washington. He'd always say "hardest hit I took all day." When we were in the pros, the people who did the photographs for bubblegum cards accidentally switched my face with Elkins's on the cards one year, and I was always kidding him about how much better I looked than him.

Bill Douglas tried to come back our senior year but never regained the form that he had before his injury. Bill was a really good leader and quarterback, and guys just loved being in the huddle with him. He exuded confidence. Without him, we really struggled and couldn't find our rhythm. There was a lot of controversy that year, though I think we led the nation in defense against the run, holding opponents to 64.4 yards per game. We also

Linebacker Rick Redman, in two Halls of Fame, is the only Husky to be twice named a consensus All-American.

led in covering punt returns at 2.7 yards. Of course, my friends say that was because of my short punts, about which I can't argue.

When I played at Washington, all our games against Northwest teams were low-scoring affairs. We had a whole bunch of knock-down, drag-out games. We had some great battles with the Oregon schools and the Cougars.

I had a couple memorable plays against Oregon State to stop touchdowns. They were driving and were inside our 20. We called a blitz. I came right through and took the handoff from the quarterback before the ball carrier got there. On another play, their quarterback, Terry Baker, who won the Heisman that year, broke loose on an option and was almost gone, but I ran him down from behind and saved the touchdown. I'm not sure where that speed came from.

My senior year we played Washington State in Spokane, and Clancy Williams, their All-American tailback, needed about 75 yards to break the all-time WSU rushing record that his cousin, George Reed, had held. He was really good, and Coach Tipps put some blitzes in to get into their back-field. I had about six tackles for losses. Clancy was so upset. After about four of them, he got up and threw the ball down, saying, "Where in the hell are you guys coming from?" We won 14–0, and George kept his record.

During that game I had a record on my mind. I really wanted to try and break the record for longest punt that was held by Bob Schloredt at the time, but it never happened. On my last kick in college, we were backed up pretty good on the Cougars' frozen field, and I sliced it, trying to kick it so hard. The ball looked like it was going to go out of bounds, so the return guy just let it go. I think that the ball landed after about 30 yards and then went straight down the sideline for about another 29 yards. It finally tumbled out of bounds after 59 yards, just two yards short of Bob's record, but not a bad final punt.

The worst punt I ever had was on my first kick during a varsity-alumni spring game the first year that Don James was here. We played the first game ever played in the old Kingdome. I had actually retired from pro ball and wasn't planning on playing, but the alums didn't have a punter, so they asked if I'd just do the punting. I think it went seven yards. And I think I held the record for the shortest punt in the Kingdome for a number of years. I topped that in the pros, however. We were playing an exhibition game in Rice Stadium before they moved the goal posts to the back of the end zone, and I was in the end zone punting. I punted the ball, and it hit the goal post and went out for a safety. The bad thing is that after that, I had to go kick it again from the 20, since it was a safety.

One of my favorite games was the East-West Shrine Game in 1965 after my senior year. My wife was expecting and had stayed home. I got a message when I was boarding the bus to the game saying that she was going to the hospital. I came back into the locker room after pregame warm-ups and was told I had a son, Scotty. I was feeling about four feet above the ground during the game, and I played really well. I had an interception and made some great plays against Roger Staubach, and we won the game. Those are some nice memories.

Probably the most unpleasant memory was a pain in the neck. I had a really bad pinched nerve in my neck for almost the whole time that I played in college. Outside of that, I didn't have many injuries. The brand of football that Owens taught was to punish your opponent with your helmet. It eventually took its toll on almost every team we played. Between tackling and blocking, we wanted to wear them down. Our coaches did a great job of teaching the fundamentals of inside-out tackling, of always keeping leverage on the runner and breaking down before you made contact—making sure that you delivered a blow by going up through the ball carrier's numbers and chin. When you see guys missing tackles now, it's because they haven't been taught these same fundamentals, or they're trying to take someone's head off and overrun the ball carrier. You don't see the same type of play. That and drive-blocking contributed to my pinched nerve.

The physical side of Washington was harder than in the professional ranks. The mental side was much more challenging in pro ball. I played 10 years, nine seasons with the San Diego Chargers and one in Portland with the old Portland Storm team in the WFL, that's the "we'll finance later" league.

There are a couple of Huskies teammates I play golf with every year, but a lot of those old friendships don't need the contact because we can get together and have things be the same as they were when we played together. There's a bond there because of what we endured as a team while playing at Washington. I can't say I have those same feelings for guys in the pros because it was like you survived with UW guys. It gives you a perspective of who you and your teammates truly are.

The guys who inspired me most were the guys I played behind at the UW. The ones who were in two straight Rose Bowls. They set the bar for how you played the game and how you conducted yourself on the field, whether is was during a game or at practice.

Being a Husky in the 1960s was about the whole aura of playing under Jim Owens and his staff. What you had to go through and how you played and how hard you could push yourself. That taught me how to compete really well. You had to compete every day, at every practice. No one would just show up. What I learned playing at the UW helped throughout my whole career and still is paying dividends today because I run into five people every day who want to talk football or are interested in talking to me about our business because they still remember my playing days. It never leaves you. Developing leadership skills takes previous success to build one's self-esteem, and the UW football experience helped give me the confidence to take on anything.

When I first got out of pro football, I was wondering if I was going to be able to get the same highs that I did when I made a great play or experience the thrill of running out of the tunnel. The wins in business are just as rewarding, and the team concept is just as important.

I've now been the chairman of Seattle's Sellen Construction Company since 1992. When I hire Huskies, it's because it just happens that way. We always try to hire the best talent we can find, and there aren't many ballplayers who major in construction. One exceptional talent was former UW tight end and team captain Scott Greenwood. He worked with us for 14 years before tragically dying far too early from cancer.

We aren't going out there looking for athletes, but I like to hire them because I believe they have an edge in how they like to compete. If they can put together their life skills as an athlete with life skills they need in business, they can be effective.

My stepfather was so right about advising me to stay in Seattle. Being a Husky has opened many doors. I'm very proud of all we have accomplished at Sellen. There are too many construction projects to list, but going down to Pacific Place and seeing the smiling faces on kids at Christmas makes us feel good. We did the Washington Mutual Tower, and it's a great part of the city's skyline. It's great to work with the people involved. We're doing the Olympic Sculpture Park for SAM [Seattle Art Museum] right now, which will be a great new public place for the city. We do a lot of work in the health-care community, and you cannot help but be inspired when you work with people who are carrying out the missions at places like Children's Medical Center and the other great health-care providers in the Puget Sound region.

Rick Redman is one of only 11 Huskies inducted into the National Football Foundation College Football Hall of Fame and is a member of the Husky Hall of Fame. He is one of 18 UW players to be named consensus All-American and is the only Husky to be so honored in two seasons. He was named on All-America teams three seasons. Redman averaged 12–15 tackles a game from his linebacker position and averaged 37.6 yards in 134 career punts. *The Detroit Sports Extra* named Redman the Lineman of the Year in 1963. Redman played nine seasons in the NFL with the San Diego Chargers and one in the WFL with the Portland Storm. He is currently the chairman of Seattle's Sellen Construction.

BILL DOUGLAS

QUARTERBACK
1961–1965

INJURIES ARE PART OF FOOTBALL, and sometimes luck doesn't always go your way. Our 1964 Rose Bowl team experienced both, and I was a casualty of unfortunate timing.

I was the starting quarterback for our January 1 game against Illinois. We lost starting running back Junior Coffey to injury during practice before the Rose Bowl.

Coffey looked like a freight train. He was big. I liked him a lot. He was a great football player, a guy you wanted on your side. He was a great athlete. So when he went down, it was a blow to our team. I was worried whether or not we were ready as a team to play Illinois.

I was All Conference as a junior, and I came into the Rose Bowl with more passes and more passing yards than any Huskies quarterback since Don Heinrich. We didn't throw much in those days, so that's not saying a whole lot. We ran an option offense.

In those days there were no other bowl games on the West Coast. So we dreamed about going to the Rose Bowl. It was probably bigger then than it is now, in some respects.

We were driving on the Fighting Illini on our first possession and ready to score. Then everything changed. I got hurt on the first drive, if you can believe that. It happened on an option play on the 3-yard line. The blow to

120

Bill Douglas led the Huskies to the 1964 Rose Bowl as an option quarterback but was hurt early in the game.

my knee knocked me out of the game, and my replacement didn't have much playing experience. We lost 17–7.

It took a long time to heal. It was pretty disappointing to work all those years to try to get to the Rose Bowl and then get hurt on the first drive. It was very devastating.

I didn't even want to play football as I grew up in Wapato, which is near Yakima. I actually wanted to play basketball rather than football.

I knew about the Huskies because I had two older brothers who went to Washington. I favored the Huskies over the Cougars.

When I arrived at Washington, the Huskies were coming off two Rose Bowl wins. We had a really strong recruiting class. There were about nine quarterbacks recruited, so there was a lot of competition on the freshman team. I wasn't sure how well I'd fit in.

I did fulfill my dream of playing college basketball by making the UW team my freshman year. But I felt my best chances were on the football field, so I only played basketball one season.

I was an option quarterback. We ran a lot of options and rollouts, and I enjoyed running the ball. My sense is that I was pretty good running the ball and just an average passer.

My sophomore year I was thrust into the spotlight early in the season. The senior quarterback got hurt in the second game of the season. I ended up starting by default.

When you become the starting quarterback, you are treated differently in practice. Nobody wants to hurt the starter. I gave All-American center Ray Mansfield a scare. He was a friend of mine and a good guy. One day at practice, I was on the punt team in front of the punter. Ray broke through up the middle and just rolled me over. They had to pick me up off the ground. Ray ran over and said breathlessly, "Billy, Billy, are you all right?"

I did okay in my sophomore year. We only lost one game—that was to USC, and they were national champs. We lost 14–0, and we didn't play very well. My inexperience probably hurt us a little.

They didn't have any other bowl games if you finished second in the Pac-8. It was the Rose Bowl or nothing. To miss going by one loss was tough to swallow. I guess being named to the All-America team helped a little.

Our 1963 season started slow, losing our first three games, before winning six of our last seven. So we actually had a pretty good season and earned our trip to Pasadena.

My knee injury in the Rose Bowl destroyed my ACL. They tried to fix it, but it didn't work. I struggled with nerve damage. I had a "drop foot," where I couldn't raise my foot for six months because of nerve injury.

I studied accounting and finance. I was fortunate to be named a national scholar athlete. I wanted to graduate on time, so I did not consider holding out a year. I had to wear a brace, which limited my flexibility and didn't allow me to be my best as an option quarterback. In hindsight, I probably should have sat out my senior season because my knee was not quite ready.

I started the first two games. I had limited mobility, and I needed to be mobile. We lost games early in the season, so a change was made, and I watched most of the season from the sideline. We ended up having a great season, beating all the California schools.

For me, despite my injury, I was excited to be a Husky and have a chance to play. I had a great experience playing. I liked playing for Jim Owens, and it was really exciting to be a Husky and play in Husky Stadium.

Except for my one injury, my football career was terrific. It helped me make a lot of friends at the UW and in the Seattle area, and it helped me learn to compete on the field and in life.

Bill Douglas was named to an All-America team his sophomore year. He was named a National Football Foundation Scholar-Athlete. His 509 rushing yards rank sixth-most for a Huskies quarterback. His 8.4 passing yards per attempt in 1963 is the second-highest in UW history. He is currently in the fruit-growing and -packing business and building materials business in Yakima.

STEVE BRAMWELL
KICK RETURNER
1962–1965

I WAS A SKILL PLAYER PLAYING IN THE WRONG ERA—a time when players had to go both ways.

At 5'8", 140 pounds, being physical was a big challenge for me. It was a stretch for me to play anywhere on defense.

Being an incoming freshman was a transition year. The UW had unlimited scholarships for freshman. So we had three or four freshman teams that would sometimes play the sophomores. There was a transition period for our bodies to change and to pick up college football. Huskies football was a big deal.

I played running back, or wingback, and cornerback. Where I felt most at home was returning punts. Returning kicks gave me a chance to get on the field. There were no restrictions on special teams. I'm grateful Coach Jim Owens emphasized kick returns.

My sophomore year I was able to run back a few kicks for touchdowns. My first touchdown was against Air Force on a 90-yard kickoff return. It was an interesting year.

I had nightmares before games about muffing a punt catch. I was very anxious before games. It always took me a while to settle down. Against Oregon State it was a windy day, and I misplayed a punt. It went off my shoulder pad. I went back eight yards to pick it up and raced down the sideline for a 92-yard return for a touchdown. So when I got graded on the play, I got a minus for dropping it, a minus for not falling on the ball, and a plus for a touchdown. So I got an overall minus score. And they weren't that happy since I broke two key rules. Punts were short back then, they didn't want the ball carrier running around. The whole idea was field position. I think they saw that we had some potential for the kick-return game, so they did well to adjust and kick away from me.

I seemed to see the field well. I would see openings, and I had a natural way of cutting back. I was aggressive mentally. I tried to use the quickness I had to make things happen more quickly. I didn't have blazing speed. In those days we were timed in the 50-yard dash. I ran it in 5.1 seconds. We did a lot of up-the-middle returns and then broke outside. I realized I had to beat the first couple guys and then pick up blocks.

When it came to returning kickoffs or punts, I hated the punt returns but was more successful at them. Husky Stadium was a hard place to play because in those years we had some bad weather. I really liked the short kickoffs because they gave me a chance to penetrate, but long ones were just too hard because there were so many people. I think it was more challenging to do punt returns, but I was more suited to do that.

We got on a roll and went to the 1964 Rose Bowl. The thing I remember is the practices in L.A. were hard because the smog was so bad. Our quarterback, Bill Douglas, got injured on the second series. We lost the game. With him, we would've won it. We were a physical team with a lot good players.

Illinois had a decent player named Dick Butkus, known as the meanest, nastiest, fiercest linebacker ever. We crossed paths a few times during the game. I ran a counter-reverse and deked him and got a 15-yard gain for a first down. I came back in later for a run. I was running down the sideline and he came roaring over. He was a mauler back then. So after the tackle, he told me never to do that on television again. I was able to get a long punt return in the Rose Bowl but didn't score.

That was the last time the rules were geared to Jim Owens's brand of football, because after that players could specialize on offense or defense.

My junior year we played two-platoon football. That was a stretch to that system. I don't know if they made the switch like other teams did. You had to put more emphasis on scoring points. They used a power-I and a wing-I. I had to block against big guys, and offense was frustrating for me. We didn't throw the ball a lot, but it was enjoyable to play, and I appreciated being a Husky.

Steve Bramwell played at 140 pounds and made his mark on the field as a kick and punt returner, then returned to the program as the team doctor.

125

We didn't do too well that year, as I recall. We had great linemen that year and we were first or second in defense in the nation. We lost a couple games early and lost our way out of the Rose Bowl race early on. We didn't do well offensively.

We could play with anybody, though. Those were all good memories. I got to play in the Rose Bowl and beat 'SC a couple of times. Speaking of USC, when we lost to them at home, I fumbled twice. I almost ran one back, but they stripped it at the last second.

I think the discipline I learned helped prepare me for the future. Committing yourself and working hard all the time carried over to other disciplines. I think it was a great place to develop commitment. They didn't ask us to work out all year round. We were playing basketball and skiing in the winter. It isn't like today where they have to lift weights every day. We didn't do a lot of speed and agility drills that developed speed.

I really didn't think about playing college football until our Bremerton High team won the state championship. I had opportunities to play at Stanford, Washington, or Air Force. I wanted to go into medicine. My dad was a doctor.

I always got the best grades during football season. I was more disciplined. The winter is usually when my grades slipped. We had some other guys who were doing medicine. Some guys went to medical school and a couple guys to dental school. There was a large group of people interested in professional schools. There was a focus on school that was good. We had lab conflicts with practices, but our coaches were good about letting us miss practice if it was necessary.

Playing football at Washington was a great opportunity. There were a lot of things I learned as a player to help me become a doctor. It certainly puts you in a category of high expectations—being at the university. The discipline certainly helped. One of the biggest things was learning to immediately recover from mistakes. There are going to be things that aren't going to turn out very well and you have to recover. You know, like dropping a football in Husky Stadium and recovering helps establish that. Being able to have a positive response to a negative outcome is something a doctor needs.

After I became an orthopedic doctor, I focused on sports medicine. I was the UW team physician for about 20 years. I was able to give back a lot of what I took as a player. I was able to donate back a lot of my knowledge to help the team. I was able to do things in orthopedics that weren't conceivable. I was able to transfer what we learned from athletes to the natural population. A lot of things have been figured out for surgical and recovery techniques by seeing results of extremely dedicated and fit patients—UW athletes.

Steve Bramwell was named an Academic All-American in 1965. He is the UW's all-time leading career kick returner with 1,532 yards in three seasons. Bramwell averaged 31.1 yards on 21 kick returns in 1963, most in a Huskies season. His career average of 26.9 yards per return ranks second in UW history. Bramwell returned 61 punts for the Huskies, and his 11.9 average ranks fifth. His 92-yard punt return against Oregon State in 1963 is the second-longest ever by a Husky. He is currently an orthopedic surgeon in Kirkland.

DAVE WILLIAMS
TIGHT END
1963–1966

I FLEW UP FROM MY HOME IN ARIZONA to Seattle to stand on the field at Husky Stadium as a Husky Legend during a 2005 game. I was honored. But I wondered who the old guy was on the big screen. The best part was the Huskies won.

Forty years before, in a 1965 game against UCLA, the Huskies lost 28–24, but I caught 10 footballs for 257 yards and three touchdowns—all for school records. My single-game reception-yard record still stands.

A decade later I was the first Seattle Seahawk signed in the fall of 1975. A track injury kept me from ever playing a down for the Seahawks. Steve Largent showed up, and they gave him my jersey, my locker, and my number. I tell my grandkids I'm not in the NFL Hall of Fame, but my jersey is. It just has another name on it.

Coming out of Lincoln High of Tacoma, I almost went to West Point. I decided to stay in the Northwest. It came down to Washington and Oregon. When Coach Jim Owens came to my house to take me and my parents out to dinner, he drove up in a 1963 Impala convertible. That did it. My parents said, "This is cool."

The Huskies program was the toughest brand of football, and I wanted to prove I could play for them.

The hardest part was getting used to the system, the sophisticated offense, discipline, and mental toughness. Sure, I felt like quitting. I got the crap beat

Dave Williams, a tight end, set a single-game receiving yardage record in 1965 that still stands.

out of me. It's a gut check and a confidence check. It's not meant for every-one. If you make it through, good for you. You developed a lot of mental toughness. When I made it to the pros, it was much easier.

They called summer practices "death marches." For some, it was. For me, it was relative. I was running track as well. I had to get used to contact, but the cardio wasn't hard for me. We'd do 120 up-downs (jogging, drop to the ground, then up to jogging), and that was nothing. We'd get heat exhaustion in 70-degree weather. It was tough. When I went to college all-star games and heard what other teams did in practice, I realized people didn't under-stand how hard we worked.

I had a great season on the freshman team. My sophomore year was lousy. That bothered me. I focused on indoor track and got my confidence back. I was having trouble adjusting to what they really wanted. I could run all day. I could catch the ball. But I wasn't a terribly good blocker.

The drill I found most interesting was the challenge drill. You'd get three cracks at a guy, and he'd get three cracks at you, blocking and defending, to decide who moves up or down the depth chart.

The life lessons I learned without a doubt helped me be a successful pro player. When I saw a pro player who didn't want to play because he tweaked his ankle or dislocated a finger or broke a nose, I just wanted to say, "Get your ass back out there." That's what the game is all about—you play hurt and you get mentally tough. I think those are important lessons in life.

I broke three ribs in our Air Force game my senior year. The next six games were hell. I couldn't stretch for the high ball. The trainer, Bob Peter-son, made a fiberglass brassiere for me to wear to protect my ribs. That was hard. I made some catches, but I was ineffective.

By today's standards, I was a tight end for the Huskies, unless we went to a spread formation, where I was a flanker. We had to throw more because we weren't able to dominate other teams the way Coach Jim Owens liked to do.

My freshman year we were still going both ways. My sophomore year we switched to playing one position. It was a tough transition for the Huskies. Before the platoon change, it was about physical conditioning. Washington wore down a lot of teams in the fourth quarter.

My breakout game came my junior year against Idaho. The Vandals were ahead with 1:34 to play. They had never beaten us, and we were embarrassed. I wasn't starting, but I had caught some passes. I had worked on the scrub teams for two years. Quarterback Tod Hullin threw it to the end zone, and I went up and got it over my shoulder for a touchdown. That started us both on a roll.

What being a Husky meant to me was a sense of accomplishment. I felt blessed to play, to have a scholarship at one of the finest schools in the country, and to play under Owens. It meant a lot. I'm very proud I wore the purple and gold.

I also loved track. It was hard my first two years to run track and play spring football. My last two years I was allowed to miss spring ball and focus on track. I loved my experience with track and field, and I think it helped me be a better football player. I ran both hurdles, both jumps, and both relays. I also threw shot and disc. I was in the 1964 Olympic trials. My dream was to make the Olympic team as a decathlete, but I fell short.

I was drafted by the Cardinals. I made it to the playoffs three times and lost every time. When I look back on my pro experience, I'm grateful I was able to live the dream for 10 years in the NFL and WFL.

There were a lot of high moments. We weren't entertainers; we were a bunch of characters. We were still well-disciplined players. We didn't get paid much but didn't care about that. I also played for the Chargers and Steelers.

My knees were shot when I retired in 1976. I had both replaced in 1991. I took my competitive spirit into the real estate business, where I managed property leasing and operations for real estate trusts.

Dave Williams earned second-team All-America honors and left the UW as a record-setting tight end. His single-game receiving mark of 257 yards still stands. His 10 catches in a game, three touchdown receptions in a game, and 10 touchdown receptions in a season all set records at the time.

MAC BLEDSOE

LINEMAN

1964–1967

WHEN I WAS IN HIGH SCHOOL, about ninth grade, is when Jim Owens started taking the Huskies to the Rose Bowl. I became enamored with the University of Washington Huskies football team about that time because the whole state was talking about the team.

I still have a paper on which I wrote a set of goals for my life at that time. Listed in my top 20 goals was the goal of playing football for the UW. That goal-setting exercise taught me the power of setting goals as I wound up being captain of the Huskies football team during my senior year in the 1967 season.

My dad was a Cougar. Even though Dad did not play football, he was about as proud of Washington State University as anyone ever could be. My dad was a great role model for me. When I was recruited, he said, "Where I went to school should have nothing to do with where you go. You go to the place that's best suited for you." Later on, that made it much easier for me when our sons came along and they were trying to make the decision about where they would go to school.

Back in 1964 Bert Clark was the coach at WSU. He came to our house to recruit me and offered me an illegal scholarship. He set a grant-in-aid scholarship on our dinner table and crossed out "one-year renewable" and wrote "four-year contract." My high school coach had done a very good job of preparing me for the recruiting process, and I knew that what that coach had done was outside of the rules.

That said to me, "If this man would change the rules for me, a high school recruit, then he would probably change the rules for anything!"

When I took my official recruiting trip to the University of Washington and met Jim Owens, that sealed the deal for me. To this day, I think Coach Owens is one of the most principled and most honest men that I, personally, have ever been privileged to know. I'd count him among the top six most positive influences in my life. (I'd throw Coach Owens in with my dad, Stu; Alden Esping, our YMCA leader; Buck Minor, the cowboy on our ranch when I was growing up; and Stub Rowley and Arch Andreotti, my high school football and track coaches.) Man, I have been blessed by being taught by some of the most amazing men.

Back in those days, college teams were basically able to offer as many scholarships as their alumni would pay for. Today schools are limited to about 15 scholarships a year. My freshman class had 134 guys on scholarship. Back when we were being recruited, if they had to sort all of us down to 15, I'm pretty positive that I would never have received a scholarship offer. It seemed that the strategy back then was to recruit anyone who could walk and chew gum. Then when they got us on campus, they would make practice so hard and make the experience so brutal on us that many would quit. Then they'd have a bunch of really tough guys left with which they could build a football team.

I'd say wanting to quit was part of the daily activity after our very demanding UW football practices. Many days we all walked off the practice field saying, "I don't ever want to go through that again!" It seemed that every day of freshman football another player or two would leave the team. *However, I must make it clear that I would NOT trade that extremely challenging, sometimes brutal, and terribly difficult experience for anything in the world.* In my life, I've never met another challenge that has come close to matching that experience; making it through a season of Huskies practices was a life-changing experience for me. Some people called 'em a "death march." We even sometimes called practice just that…and some days we called the experience names you wouldn't want to print in this book. Now, believe me, I know that what we endured was nothing compared to what some of our armed forces have faced down through the years as they fought to defend our freedom, but it was still plenty tough. Some days we might lose as much as eight to 10 pounds during a particularly strenuous practice. Most of that lost weight was pure sweat.

A combination of things made those practices tough. Many days we'd practice three hours, going after each other in full-out contact. The practice schedule, posted on the bulletin board prior to practice, might call for an exercise period followed by two hours divided into seven or eight 15-minute periods, and then what we, not so affectionately, called the "question-mark-period." We all knew that "question-mark-period" was of unlimited length, and we knew that the better we practiced, the shorter it could become. Conversely, if we had a bad practice, we knew all too well that the "question-mark-period" could extend into something we would definitely regret.

When we saw that infamous period on the bottom of the practice schedule, we would gather together and vow to have a good practice. It didn't always work.

At other times, a coach might just shout to the manager who was timing the periods right in the middle of practice, "Start the clock for this period over!" And what had been scheduled for 15 minutes could suddenly extend to 26 minutes or more.

Then there were the challenge drills where a player might move up or down one or even two teams in a practice depending on the outcome of a head-to-head and one-on-one competition. There was not one player on the team who was secure in his position more than a day away from a game! You had to show up for each practice ready to defend your right to a position on the team.

Once we had completed the scheduled practice, we'd have to run 15 to 20 sprints ranging in length from 10 to 100 yards. Then, before you could leave the field, you'd have to gut it up and say, "I'm going to make it through this," because after all of that, you'd have to run until you won your group. The fastest guys got to leave earliest. We often joked that we liked the games so much because they were so easy compared to the practices.

During the summer two-a-day practices, it seemed like a couple guys quit almost every day. I remember one time that a junior-college transfer was still running after I showered and was on the way to dinner. I never saw him again!

The last day that we ran into Husky Stadium—for the Apple Cup our senior year—I believe that there were only six or eight guys from my freshman class of 134 guys on scholarship and 13 walk-ons, who were actually in uniform that day. I think that there were 11 or 12 of us still on the roster, but a number were injured and were not suited for the game. It is my recollection that Mike Maggart was the only walk-on from our freshman class who made it through to that game. Some had redshirted and returned for one more year, but not many of us actually made it through four full years.

I played tight end and linebacker as a freshman. My sophomore year was the first year of the new rule allowing unlimited substitution, meaning we didn't have to play both offense and defense anymore. I stuck with offense and moved to the position of tackle.

I personally feel that the rule change to unlimited substitution started to make it difficult to win with Jim Owens's philosophy of playing football. He believed that he would teach his players a simple offense and a basic defense and go into every game able to execute that scheme to near perfection. By this disciplined approach, his teams would keep games close until the fourth quarter when his players would then "out-tough" opponents because we had worked harder and been through more in our extremely tough practices. His philosophy was to keep it close until the fourth quarter and then beat them with guts, determination, and conditioning! It was a simple but effective approach, which worked very well when the opposing teams could not substitute a completely new team to give players a rest. Coach Owens's approach did not work nearly as well when bigger and faster players on many of the other teams got to go to the sideline and get a rest every few plays. When players started playing just offense or just defense, and every player became very specialized, to a great extent, it negated the element of conditioning.

When players didn't play both ways, it just became much tougher to wear them down. The winning in the Huskies program slowly started to slip. I was so sorry to see it happen because Jim Owens's method had been a very satisfying way to play football. It was fun to play games when you just knew that the teams you were playing could not keep up with you for all four quarters. It was satisfying to look at the player across from you and see quit in his eyes.

I started the second game of our sophomore season when we went down to play Baylor in Waco, Texas. Getting to start that game was kind of a fluke because I had been the third-team tackle at practice on Monday, but the two

Mac Bledsoe, one of a half-dozen Huskies players from his 134-member freshman class who stayed through his senior year, says surviving UW practices was a life-changing experience.

guys ahead of me were injured during that week, so I got to start the game in their place. I count that day to be among the most memorable experiences of my life. I was the first guy from our class to earn a starting position. I was pretty proud of that, and luckily I was able to hold onto that position for the rest of that year. I certainly was not going to go to practice and give it up easily.

During that sophomore season we also played UCLA in Husky Stadium, and when they came to town they were ranked No. 1 in the nation. We beat them! It think it was my first game in Husky Stadium as a starter.

I'll never forget that day, and I get tears in my eyes just thinking about that wonderful experience—of running into Husky Stadium as a starter. My parents had come to that game and were in the stands to watch me play. All through high school, my parents had thought I was too skinny to play football. That mindset all started when I was three or four years old. I had a vitamin B deficiency, which caused me to wake up one morning, unable to get out of bed. My parents panicked, thinking I had polio, and that really scared them because my father's sister, Ann, was paralyzed by polio when she was 15. All through junior high school and high school, I had to plead with Mom and Dad every season just to get to turn out for sports.

When I ran out of the tunnel and into Husky Stadium that day, I was unabashedly crying. I looked up in the second deck where I knew my parents were sitting among that wall of cheering fans. I ran out shouting, "Look down here at your skinny son! I'm starting this game! I'm playing against the No. 1 team in the nation! I'm doing this, even though you never thought I could!"

It was so much more than a football game for me. It was the first time I was able to say to myself with complete confidence: "Maybe you can accomplish something big in your life." And to top it off, we beat the Bruins that day.

I give 90 percent of the credit to Jim Owens for that experience. He was so dedicated to fairness that if you achieved something with him as your coach, you knew that you had earned it and that you deserved it!

As a perfect example of how practices could go beyond the norm, during my senior year we actually scrimmaged on game day, before the Cal game down in Berkeley. Normally, we'd arrive to a stadium at around noon for a 1:30 game. And, there we were that Saturday, at the stadium at 11:00 AM going full tilt against each other in a scrimmage. I remember the Cal players asking us, "Hey, what were you guys doing out there so early?"

In terms of "life's lessons learned," those lessons of toughness learned as a member of those Huskies teams were unrivaled. I've been asked many times, "Who was the toughest player you played with?" To me, I always have felt that honor went to UW All-American Tom Greenlee. He always played with great leverage. Hitting him was like hitting a brick wall. He went on to play in the NFL with the Chicago Bears as a backup to Gale Sayers.

My contact with most "old" Huskies from my era really dried up after the annual alumni game was canceled. I played in every single one of the University of Washington's alumni football games, including the last one. I played in the first one as a freshman and the last as an alumnus of some eight or nine years. I even flew home on leave from the Army to play in one of the games. The first football game played in the Kingdome was the very last of the games between UW alumni and the Huskies varsity. My claim to fame from that last game was that I made the first official tackle in the Kingdome. I made the tackle on the opening kickoff. That was Don James's first year as head coach of the Huskies, and he decided to end the tradition after that year.

Other than my first start, the most memorable game was a victory over Ohio State, in our junior year. We played the Buckeyes in Columbus that year and beat them in front of more than 100,000 partisan Ohio State fans. They were one of the top-ranked teams in the nation that year, and we beat them at their own game, running the ball for more than 250 yards that day.

I used to get up every morning before a road game and find some place to get my cowboy boots shined. Before our game at Ohio State, I was down in the hotel barbershop getting my boots shined when I overhead a Buckeyes fan sitting in the barber chair getting his hair cut. With his head down he was saying loudly to the whole room, "Who are we playing today, Washington? Who have they played? What are we doing playing a nothing team like them?" he said.

When he looked up and noticed me sitting in the shoeshine chair wearing my team blazer, he asked if me if I was on the Huskies football team. After I said, "Yes," he sized me up and asked, "What position do you play, wide receiver?"

When I told him I was an offensive tackle, he kind of stifled a guttural laugh. I was certainly not as big as the typical Big Ten offensive tackle.

Trying not to be rude, he asked, "Well, do you play much?"

"Well, sir, I'm starting today, and I anticipate playing most of the game when we are on offense," I answered.

"Well, what's your number, son?" he asked, again belatedly trying to be polite.

"I wear No. 73."

"I'll be watching you, kid." And rather insincerely he wished me, "Good luck against our Buckeyes."

In the mail at the Graves Building on Tuesday or Wednesday, a couple of days after the game, there was a letter addressed to: No. 73, Husky Football Team. The letter read:

Dear Mac Bledsoe, No. 73, Husky Football Team,

   Boy is my face red. I'm the guy who was in the barber chair Saturday morning. I was the fellow getting my hair cut. I'm embarrassed about treating you in a disparaging manner and disrespectful manner. I will never badmouth a UW Husky Football Team again as long as I live!

   By the way, I'm the pastor of the Columbus First Presbyterian Church located here in the University District and I will always remember the way your team played!

I showed the letter to Coach Owens, and he got quite a kick out of it!

In that Ohio State game, Donnie Moore had gained most of his yards running off tackle behind my blocks. I was playing against a big defensive end, who couldn't seem to get low enough to defend himself against my low-drive blocks. Like we used to say back then, "I owned him" all day long. That was a huge victory for Jim Owens because his team had beaten the premiere "three yards in a cloud of dust" program at their own game on their own field.

Coach Owens had grown up and played in Oklahoma, and the Big Ten was his idea of the best football in America. I believe that in his mind we had passed the test of playing with the best! It was the first time I ever saw him really celebrate a victory. He came into the locker room with a cigar in his mouth. He announced what a great victory it was, and he handed out a victory cigar for everyone.

Somewhere, stored away in a trunk at my house, I still have that letter from that pastor. Stored along with it, in a plastic envelope, is the "victory cigar" from Coach Owens! That cigar might be one of my most prized possessions.

The biggest controversy during my time at Washington surrounded that same running back, Donnie Moore. The week after the Ohio State victory, Coach Owens kicked him off the team for breaking a team rule.

Coach Owens made his rules very clear at the start of each season. One rule prohibited players from even being in a bar.

The week after Moore ran for 200-plus yards in our huge victory at Ohio State, for which he was named the *Sports Illustrated* Offensive Player of the Week, Owens confronted Moore about reports that he had been in a bar. I admired Donnie because he told the truth to Coach Owens. But honesty did not affect the outcome for Donnie.

I played with Moore later for two seasons with the Seattle Rangers. Donnie told me Owens basically asked him, "Where you in a bar?" And Donnie said, "Yes, I was." I think he hoped the rules would be bent for him because he was a star, or that maybe he would receive a warning and a second chance.

Donnie told me that Coach Owens very simply told him he would have to find another place to play football until next season. Donnie never returned to play football for the Huskies.

I cannot speak for anyone else, but, for me, Coach Owens's action in enforcing the rule with Donnie Moore said that I was playing for the most fair and honorable coach. He didn't bend his rules for anyone, not even a superstar. I admired Coach Owens even more for taking that very unpopular stand.

Later many people tried to make that suspension into a black-white issue. I never could see it as such, and I do not believe that Donnie saw it that way, either. Donnie Moore was without a doubt the best pure football player whom I ever had the privilege to play with. He was clearly the most talented player on our team. I thought it took amazing courage and integrity for Coach Owens to take that stand and apply his rule, while knowing it would hurt our chances of winning. It's my observation that many modern college football coaches would have swept it under the rug, but not Coach Owens. At that point, I'd have gone to hell for Jim Owens. When the chips were on the table, he was very predictable—he was going to do what was right, honest, and fair. He was going to do exactly what he said he was going to do…even if it was difficult. He was a man of integrity who was willing to make a decision based upon principle rather than on what was expedient.

I was a graduate assistant in 1968 and 1969. During the fall of 1969 the varsity went 1–9. Along with the difficult days on the field, Jim Owens was starting to come under fire for racial issues. I had no idea where that was coming from. In our sophomore year, I roomed with Davey Dinish, one of many African Americans on our team, and he was one of my best friends on the team that year. Maybe I was blind to the racial issues, but I don't think so; I was pretty close to Davey, and he never mentioned any issues to me. When the racial charges finally hit the papers, I was in the Army at Fort Eustis, Virginia. My folks sent me some articles, and I couldn't believe what I was reading. I felt that Coach Owens was one of the fairest men that I had ever met.

The most frustrating loss during my time as a Husky was in our junior year against the University of Southern California down in the Los Angeles Coliseum. In the fourth quarter of that game, we had the ball first and goal at the 5-yard line. If we had punched it in for that score, we would've won the game, placed first in the Pac-8, and gone to the Rose Bowl. Going to the Rose Bowl was one of my dreams in becoming a Husky. It was so disappointing that we did not make it, but with the perspective of years, the importance of winning wanes and the importance of lessons learned grows in my mind.

140

It took me a few weeks to get over my final game as a Huskies player—a 9–7 loss to Washington State. We drove to the 18-yard line in the final minute of that game but missed a field goal that would have given us the victory. Everyone walked off the field after the game thinking, "My gosh, was all this work worth it?"

I have never been a person who focuses totally on winning and losing. I had some big wins and some big disappointments while playing Huskies football, but I now know that the most valuable lessons I learned came from a commitment to the *attempt* to win while operating inside of the very strong moral structure that Coach Owens created.

I went on to a teaching and coaching career at five high schools in eastern Washington. There was one lesson I learned while playing football for the Huskies that I always shared with my players: "One of the great things about football is that the game isn't for everyone! Not everyone is cut out for this tough and challenging game. You must be tough to play the game well. It will hurt sometimes. If you want to be successful, you are usually going to be extremely uncomfortable during the period of preparation. However, if you are tough enough to play the game well, you will learn some wonderful lessons from this game!"

Both of our sons, Drew and Adam, were highly recruited high school quarterbacks. Whenever a coach wanted to have dinner with them, we always insisted that the coaches have dinner at our house. We did this just so our sons would be in their own comfort zone and not the coach's.

The night Don James came to Walla Walla for his official visit with our oldest son, Drew, I was rather surprised by his actions that night. He was scheduled to arrive at our house for dinner at 6:00. He called 15 minutes after the time he had been invited to arrive, and said he had accepted a dinner invitation with a Huskies alumnus in Walla Walla. He said he'd come by after dinner, which he did.

When I told my family what happened, I watched Drew's face. Coach James had just stood up Drew's mother, and I could tell that this did not sit well with our son. At that moment, I pretty much knew that our son would not follow me to the University of Washington. My gut feeling that night proved to be true.

I told both of our sons exactly what my father had told me when I was being recruited; they should both make their own decisions about where to go to college. They should pick the school that best fit them and that where I went to school should have little if any effect on their decisions.

My loyalty to the University of Washington and what it means to have been a Huskies football player doesn't have much to do with a mascot, a building, or even the institution in general. My loyalties from my experience at the University of Washington are very specific: *my loyalty is to the people who were there who influenced my life!* My loyalty is to my teammates. Especially, my loyalty is to Jim Owens, and to the many men on the Huskies coaching staff like Don White, Bob Monroe, and Mel Thompson.

Looking back, it seems odd to me that in all of the many classes that I took over my five years as a student at the University of Washington, not one professor had anywhere near the impact on my life that the football coaches had. Not one professor even attempted to touch my life away from the time I was with them in the classroom. Not one professor touched my life with anything that could approach the way that Jim Owens touched me. He may have been very harsh at times, but he was always extremely fair and honest with me, and with the rest of the team. He challenged us all to see what excellence we could find in ourselves. He challenged me in a way that few people have ever challenged me. He taught me integrity by allowing me to watch him display his integrity at very tough times.

Husky football was one of the most important periods of development in all of my life. I will forever be thankful for having gone through every single minute of that difficult experience.

Mac Bledsoe was voted as a UW team captain in 1967. Currently he is the president and founder of Parenting with Dignity, a parent education curriculum designed to improve the lives of children by promoting and teaching effective parenting skills to parents all across America. He has written two books on parenting and has been featured on ABC's *20/20*, NBC's *Today Show*, and numerous national broadcasts focusing on the Parenting with Dignity curriculum that he and his wife of nearly 40 years created together from their experiences as classroom teachers.

The SEVENTIES

CALVIN JONES JR.

CORNERBACK/KICK RETURNER
1969–1972

I HAD THIS VISION that I wanted to dot the *i*.
I wanted to be a star running back in the I formation. I broke O.J. Simpson's Bay Area high school touchdown record of 16 touchdowns in a season. I scored 23 as a junior and 19 as a senior at San Francisco's Balboa High School.

I watched as O.J. dominated as a running back with the Trojans, and I wanted to go to USC and take over for O.J. I had one problem. I was really small—5′5″, 155 pounds.

The coach at City College recruited me. I told him boldly, "I'm going to USC to dot the *i*." He said, "Calvin, you're not 6′2″, 190. You're 5′5″. That's going to be a long shot."

I graduated from high school during mid-term in January. I wanted to start college right away. Only a couple schools were willing to admit me at mid-year. I considered Berkeley, Washington, and Washington State. My father was the pastor at Providence Baptist Church in San Francisco for 28 years. I didn't want to be a pastor. I wasn't sure I'd be that good.

I seriously considered going to Cal and hanging out with the hippies. The whole scene mesmerized me. My mother wanted me to stay in the area and play at Cal because then I could come home on the weekends. I decided to go to Washington.

Calvin Jones Jr. dreamed of being a Pac-8 running back but instead became an All-American cornerback. He left the UW because of racial tensions, yet returned in hopes of being part of the solution and was voted the Guy Flaherty Award as most inspirational player by his teammates.

It worked out pretty well. The UW coaches put me in at defensive back in spring drills. I had good training in high school, so I adapted well. I thought defense would be temporary, and when they saw my ability they would put me on offense. After spring practices, I was told I would be a starting defensive back my sophomore year. But I was still dreaming of being a running back.

All freshmen played on the freshman team. They had me returning kicks and punts. On the first kickoff, at Washington State, I let the ball go over my head and bounce into the end zone. I didn't realize that was a live ball. I forgot to down the ball. The Cougars rushed down and fell on it. I looked at the scoreboard, and it was 0–7 with 15 minutes still on the clock. That wasn't a very glorified start for the star who was going to dot the *i*.

I got in a few times on offense as a running back that year, but not many. That was a great disappointment. I begged them to let me play running back so I could show what I could do. The highlight of the year was when our freshman team scrimmaged the varsity to a tie.

By my sophomore year I grew to 5′7¼″ (although I was always listed at 5′9″) and gained about 10 pounds. I did become a starting cornerback, as predicted, and returned kickoffs and punts.

My sophomore season my success on the field continued as I earned an All-America honorable mention and All–Pac-8 first-team honors. But I was faced with a dilemma.

The racial tensions on the team had reached a breaking point. At the end of the 1970 season, four black underclassmen felt we needed to make a statement by announcing we would not return to the UW program. Our sophomore season, Mark Wheeler, out of Seattle Prep, after having a great game against Michigan State University, was not given much playing time and was criticized after the game. Many of the black players felt it was discrimination. Mark quit the team early in the 1970 season. As a group, it was decided the black players would boycott the Huskies football program. Things happened during the 1970 season that we felt showed things were not improving.

Because I was the only African American starter, many of my black teammates advised me to stay. I can tell you all those who boycotted loved the UW. We felt we weren't being treated fairly and it was time to protest and raise consciousness. I felt it was important to support my brothers, even though things were going well for me. It was a heavy time—over the years we discovered black players felt they never reached their full potential in football under Jim Owens's administration.

In the summer of 1971, I decided to enroll at Long Beach City College so that my completed classes would not prevent me from playing at Long Beach State College that fall. By going to community college and getting my academic credits, I would not have to sit out a year from playing football, according to NCAA rules at the time. I realized later that, by going to school at Long Beach City College, it also enabled me to return to the University of Washington and participate in my junior season in 1971.

In the spring and summer of 1971, with all the negative publicity, the UW administration investigated our protest and made some changes. Several new black staff members were hired, and athletics director Joe Kearney hired Don Smith, an African American, as assistant athletics director. Coaches were made aware of our concerns and took sensitivity training.

Coach Owens and Don Smith flew down and asked me to consider returning to UW and promised I would be welcomed back. They said I could be part of the solution. As I thought about it, I believed I could help the cause and be part of the healing process, not only for the football team, but for the whole school. Some of the black students thought I was an "Uncle Tom" and had sold out. Some of the white students felt I was a troublemaker, and my wife and I received some threats over the telephone. Still, I felt there was a sincere commitment being made by the athletic department and necessary changes were being made.

147

Quarterback Sonny Sixkiller burst into the picture, and he was a phenomenon—it was a joy to watch him play. If that ball he threw hit you in the chest, it hurt. Even watching pro quarterbacks, I couldn't think of anyone who threw a prettier pass. He could throw a rope.

Upon returning to UW, I started at the left cornerback position and returned punts. I played alongside Bill Cahill, and we were a tag team in the defensive backfield and on punt returns.

After my senior year at UW in 1972, I was drafted in the 15th round by Denver's John Ralston, who remembered me as a sophomore when he was the Stanford coach. I played in the NFL for four years.

Being a Husky meant several things to me. It was a joy to play in a top-notch program. After going to the pros, I realized each step of the way I was around good coaches and good teammates. It was such a joy to see the program turn around from a 1–9 season to a pair of 8–3 seasons with Sixkiller.

The ultimate dot of the *i* came during the 1978 Rose Bowl. I was part of Seattle's flagship radio broadcast team as a color commentator. There was Warren Moon throwing a touchdown pass to Spider Gaines. I felt our boycott demonstration came to fruition when I saw the touchdown. It showed the Huskies were able to change and adapt, athletically and interracially. I thank God, to be honest with you, I had a chance to share in that transformation. And now, with Coach Willingham, I'm amazed we've really moved to a color-blind approach, where whoever can play will play. We all can see, in the end, all people benefited and, above all, the UW benefited.

Calvin Jones Jr. was named to the Associated Press All-America first team in 1972 and earned All–Pac-8 and All-Coast honors three straight years. He was UW's Most Valuable Player and won the Guy Flaherty Award as a senior. His career average of 12.7 yards per punt return ranks third in UW history. His 596 punt return yards ranks 10th. Jones played four seasons in the NFL with the Denver Broncos (1973–1976). He is currently the pastor of Providence Baptist Church in San Francisco.

SONNY SIXKILLER

QUARTERBACK

1969–1972

Had it not been for the encouragement of several varsity players, I might not have thrown a single pass for the Huskies. I seriously thought about transferring during the winter of my freshman year.

When I arrived at Washington, Coach Jim Owens went from a balanced offense to the wishbone. That fall I played on the freshman team. I did well and proved I could pass. But I thought to myself, "What the hell am I doing here? I don't run the wishbone." Funny thing was, I probably ran it the best of our quarterbacks in practice.

Things were not good at Washington. There was unrest. During one of our freshman-team study sessions, we were told to go down and wish the varsity good luck as they boarded buses to go play UCLA. We went and quickly realized something was wrong: no African American players were on the bus.

I thought, *Wait a minute, I don't see any black players.*

What?

They're not going?

The African American players boycotted the game in protest of inequities in the program.

That really affected some of our black freshman players. We didn't know what was going on.

Quarterback Sonny Sixkiller electrified Huskies fans for three seasons during a period when the Northwest needed something to cheer about.

Then the Bruins showed no mercy and ran a trick play while up 20 points. The 57–14 loss infuriated all of us, like salt in a wound. The season ended 1–9, the only win coming against WSU in the last game.

That winter I got the vibe that I wasn't the favored guy, even though I had success with the change of the offense my freshman year. The coaches favored another guy, Greg Collins from California. He was a little bigger than me, which wasn't saying much, considering I was 5'11", 172 pounds.

In fact, I heard a story that Owens questioned my height while recruiting me. I played in southern Oregon for Ashland High, the last town along I-5 before you hit California. I was an all-around athlete. I played football, basketball, and baseball. I threw about 15 touchdowns my senior year. Earl Nordtvedt, an ex-Huskies baseball player, watched me play and sent film to

Coach Owens. Assistant UW coach Bob Schloredt came down, met me, and watched some film. He came down a couple times to watch me play basketball. I guess I convinced him of my athletic ability.

On his final trip, Owens came down with Schloredt to meet me in person. As they walked out of my home, Owens turned to Schloredt and said, "Hey, is this kid going to grow?"

"I don't care if he does or not. He can throw the ball," Schloredt said.

The older UW players, guys like Du Cornell and Bob Burmeister, kept telling me not to make a decision until after the spring practices. So I decided to stay until spring. Turns out Collins got hurt in the spring game. I played three quarters of the game and opened some eyes. I won the quarterback job in fall camp, and Owens decided to scrap the wishbone experiment and open up the offense.

The first game of the 1970 season was electrifying. Completing a pass was enough to get the crowd excited. On the third play of our first drive against Michigan State, I ended up running for a lot of yards. A couple plays later I threw a touchdown pass. It happened *boom, boom, boom.* You wouldn't believe how loud it was. When the day was done, our 42–16 win over Michigan State put more offensive points on the scoreboard than any Owens team in the past nine years.

A couple games stood out that year. One was our nationally televised game against Stanford and Jim Plunkett. We were in a position to beat Stanford but lost. Still, it was an exciting game.

The other is the Apple Cup in Spokane. The wind-chill factor was minus 20 degrees. It was the coldest game I've ever been at or played in. It was marred by overexcitement. Some guys from both sides got thrown out. I got my first taste of the rivalry.

Playing UCLA at home was sweet revenge as a sophomore. We were up by a sizable margin, and Coach Owens called for an onside kick. I remember being on the sideline and everyone was whispering, "We're going to onside, we're going to onside."

When we got it, UCLA coach Tommy Prothro angrily threw his hat on the field. I'll never forget the sight—the wind taking it and rolling it around on the turf. We were having a ball with it. Touché! If you do it to us, we'll do it to you. We won 61–20.

One thing I remember about the game, they had a quarterback named Dennis Dummit.

Yell king Robb Weller had a microphone, and he was yelling all game: "Fumble Dummit, damn it. Fumble damn it, Dummit." He kept mixing up the words. It was great because we were kicking their butts. I remember standing behind the bench and listing to him. It was the best thing ever.

No other Huskies team had really thrown as much as we did. In all but one game, we scored at least 22 points and had games with 43, 56, and 61 points. Our 334 points were the most in a Huskies season. That year I won the Sammy Baugh Trophy as the passing champion, based on completions per game.

There were a lot of things going on in society and Seattle. Boeing had huge layoffs, so unemployment was high. It was the beginning of Indian fishing rights becoming a big issue. And, of course, there was Vietnam and racial tensions. Everything was negative. I think because of all that, our football team was a ray of hope…something positive for the region.

Everywhere I went, I was a magnet. My family would come up for the games. We'd go out after the game, and I couldn't get a burger. Everyone was pretty nice. They just wanted to be around us.

It was a tough time, to be honest. One lucky thing for me was meeting Professor Nathaniel Wagner. He was doing some pregame and postgame psychological tests on players. I took some classes from him. He befriended me and helped me through the process of understanding my role, as not only a football player, but being a Native American. I didn't grow up on a reservation. I never really considered that as being a real issue until I came up here. You have the football thing and ancestry rolling around in your head, and then you have to deal with school. I'd sneak on campus and sneak off. He helped me keep everything in perspective.

People ask me all the time, "What were the most exciting games you played in?"

I'd have to say it was our Purdue home and away series. The lead changed hands a couple times in our first game. We won in the last two or three minutes on a pass to Tommy Scott. The defense made a key interception to hold on 38–35. It was a very physical game. The next year was in West Lafayette, Indiana. The hostile crowd threw ice cubs on us. Option quarterback Gary Danielson ran for 200 yards but had a touch of the flu and couldn't come out in the second half. They played their second-team quarterback, and he made a couple of mistakes. Next thing you know, we won 22–21.

A memorable game my junior year was back in Illinois. Their grass was three feet high. We were used to that, coming off turf. It was tied 7–7. I got hit from behind while throwing, and they intercepted and took it back 98 yards to go up 14–7 just before the half. We ended up winning 52–14. We had a few games where we just opened it up.

We lost a heartbreaker in Oregon. Dan Fouts wasn't an everyday starter yet. We were up 14–0 and inside the 10 going for another score. Our tackle was flagged for lining up in an illegal formation. Next play we fumbled, and they scored. They turned the tide and went ahead. We got the ball back, with not much time left and moved the ball down the field. We ended up with a field-goal attempt inside the 20. Steve Wiezbowski kicked it over the upright, and they ruled it no good. We lost by two points.

Whether we won or lost, I felt Owens and his staff were tough on us. We strapped it on three days a week with full contact during the season. I felt they never gave anyone a break. They were tough, but they were fair, in my opinion.

Nobody ever wants to lose his last game. So losing my last Huskies game to the Cougars was regrettable. They were a good football team, though. We knew going in that Jim Sweeney was a tough coach. We were out of the Rose Bowl race and weren't allowed to go to any other bowl, so it might have crept in that the game really didn't matter. It was a dreary day. We went ahead, but then the wheels fell off in the second half.

153

In sports, you have to have a short memory when you lose. Every quarterback gets booed. It's part of the game. You have to take the good with the bad.

Opposing teams had some fun with my heritage. They'd do Indian war dances and whoop it up. Some players would take it to a different level. I took it personally, but I didn't worry about it. You can't get yourself involved in that kind of taunting.

I was honored to be on the cover of *Sports Illustrated* on October 4, 1971. I really didn't want to be singled out at the time. In retrospect, it's a great honor to be one of two Huskies on the *SI* cover (Bob Schloredt was the other). The publicity was crazy as I was on the cover of seven national magazines, including *Boys' Life* and *Street and Smith*.

We did get tired of the media using the Indian nomenclature. They'd call me the "Cherokee Chucker" or worse. Our captains wrote a letter to all the local sportswriters, asking them to stop.

In another show of team unity, fellow Huskies co-captain Bill Cahill and myself, along with our teammates' encouragement, decided to take issue with the purple helmets awarded to players giving 110 percent. We told the coaches it wasn't fair certain people got the helmets when we felt everyone was giving their all. So my senior year we all wore purple helmets.

In my three varsity seasons we were 6–4, 8–3, and 8–3. We didn't play in the Rose Bowl, but there is a lot of pride in how we turned everything around to get the program back on the positive side. Thanks to everyone who played on offense, including great receivers like All-American Jim Krieg, Tommy Scott, John Brady, and Ira Hammon, I left with Huskies records, at the time, for career passing yards with 5,496 and 35 touchdowns.

After my Huskies career, I got an opportunity to spend six weeks in camp with the 1973 Rams. One in a million guys have that chance. I played two seasons in the World Football League in Hawaii. So I'm not bitter about not having a long pro career. I did get the chance to be in a classic movie, *The Longest Yard*.

Now I'm still involved in sports through broadcasting and working for ISP Sports, which has all the marketing and media rights to UW athletics. I'm still happily married to the woman I met in college, Denise, and we've raised three kids. I live a few miles from Husky Stadium and get to watch home games on the sideline when not doing games for Fox Sports.

I consider myself an ambassador of the UW. People know I'm a Husky and respect that. I still get letters all the time. I get an *SI* cover to sign every month in the mail. I get touching letters from young Native Americans all over the country.

I'm very lucky to have had a scholarship to go to the UW and be a Husky. Being a Husky means being proud of your school. I'm very proud to be a Husky and wear purple. My biggest pet peeve with Huskies parents is when they have kids go to other schools and they wear the colors of their kids. I say be true to your school, just like the old Beach Boys song.

Sonny Sixkiller was inducted into the Husky Hall of Fame in 1985. He earned All-America honors in 1971. His 5,496 passing yards (fifth all-time) and 35 touchdowns were school records when he left. Sixkiller's 16.41 passing yards per completion for a season still ranks number one in school history. His career average passing yards per game of 196.3 ranks second, along with his average passing yards per attempt in a single game (23.0). He is currently a Fox Sports broadcaster and associate general manager of Washington ISP Sports Network. In 2002 he wrote a book, *Sonny Sixkiller's Tales from the Huskies Sideline*.

BILL CAHILL

DEFENSIVE BACK/
KICK RETURNER

1969–1972

THERE WAS SIGNIFICANT POLITICAL TENSION during the years I played at Washington—on the campus and around the country. All the news seemed horrible. Vietnam. Protests. Kent State. Racial unrest. Antiestablishment turmoil. Heavy duty stuff was going on.

There were problems inside the program as well. There was a very real pressure on players to use their football notoriety to make a statement about the issues of the day. Everyone had an issue.

My freshman class watched from the stands as the Huskies went 1–9. The low point was a 57–14 crushing by UCLA in Los Angeles in which the African American players did not make the trip. The day-to-day tension was very palpable. Everyone's nerves were on edge. This was way bigger than football.

Quarterback Sonny Sixkiller and my class came of age in a hurry.

We had a real good group of players, starting with Sonny. We had a great turnaround for Coach Jim Owens toward the end of his tenure. For three years, the 1970–1972 seasons, Washington football brought everyone in the Northwest something to cheer about. And something to laugh about, at times.

We had a nationally televised game on Halloween. Back in those days, there were very few games televised nationally, about one or two a week. So being on TV was a big deal. I found out the offense was going to be introduced on TV before the game. So I talked Coach Owens into letting me be introduced as well to represent the defense because I was the co-captain. He said, "Okay." My defensive teammates started teasing me big time—Why was I being introduced and not them?

So to make up for it, they persuaded me to wear some Halloween fangs that one of the players had in his locker for my close-up on TV to get a laugh. The offense lined up for the introduction, and I was the last one. Behind me stood Coach Owens, who had no idea what I had up my sleeve.

Sixkiller was right in front of me and, of course, he got a huge applause. Then it was my turn. I had slipped on the fangs without Coach Owens noticing. I stood on the X marked on the ground and looked up to the camera that was about in the 10th row up behind the bench. I dropped my jaw to show these big old fangs. It was a bit of a tricky maneuver to do it without looking like a fool. I crack up when I think about how much time I spent in the locker room, in front of the mirror (instead of warming up for the game), to make sure it had the right effect. And it worked! Everyone started laughing, and the cameraman nearly fell off his chair. The laughter spread across the stadium. I could "smell" Coach Owens fuming behind me. I ran out as fast as I could before he could say anything to me.

156

That era was Robb Weller's heyday. He wasn't just a "yell king." He was a professional comedian. He became a national TV entertainer. He was hilarious. He would do a Johnny Carson–style monologue at the start of every game. There was a whole bunch of times that we'd be out there warming up and we'd hear this tremendous laughter coming from the student section. We'd gravitate over to the sideline and get involved in this whole comedy show that was going on over there. Absolutely hilarious.

He had a couple of famous incidents against UCLA (remember they stomped on us the year before when we were short-handed) where he cranked up the fans to get UCLA to fumble. And they did! Their quarterback was Dennis Dummit. Robb got a cheer going that was something like, "Fumble, Dennis, Dummit. Fumble, damnit, Dummit. Fumble dammit, Dennis you Dummit!" And he would come up with things that were just on the edge of okay. The student section had tricycle races, which were a hoot. There was always something going on. It was wonderfully distracting.

One of the best things about those teams was the humor we had. We had some absolute comics each year. It was just funny to be around these guys.

Bill Cahill had the intensity to be an All-American defensive back and record-setting punt returner, yet he found ways to break the social tensions of the early 1970s.

We could really roast each other and make light of situations that were pretty heavy. We had the biggest mistake award (what we called "The Chump of the Week") every week. It's difficult to communicate in words, as it was a strange kind of black humor that paradoxically built up teamwork. We did have a tremendous amount of healthy laughter happening all the time that I truly believed helped us win. The fun and high performances really went hand in hand.

I got my chance to play as a sophomore in 1970. That team was probably one of the most exciting teams Washington had because we turned it around so fast. There were a core of seniors who were the strength, some key juniors, and a whole host of young, inexperience sophomores. We were smaller and faster, so they opened up the offense, and all of a sudden it just got exciting.

I was recruited as a wide receiver from Bellevue High, where I played running back. I was small, standing 5'11" and weighing just 170 pounds. I was a Huskies fan growing up and went to a fair number of games. The stadium was always such a great place to go.

I was not highly recruited by any stretch. I think Stanford was probably my first choice, but they didn't offer me anything. Then I was going to go back east to Princeton and do the Ivy League thing, but that didn't pan out, so Washington was the choice.

The comeback wins are what really stick with me. Our home game in 1970 against UCLA was a comeback story. After the troubles of the year before, it was so sweet to trounce them in Seattle 61–20. Everybody played well. Second- and third-stringers were in there making touchdowns.

Then we beat WSU big [43–25] to finish 6–4. It was probably as fun as it gets. It all turned around. We were actually only one play away from going to the Rose Bowl that year, had that one play gone our way. There was a lot of excitement for a lot of people.

My junior year we went 8–3, with all three loses in the conference. Again, we were just a couple plays away from greatness and a bid to the Rose Bowl. We put up a lot of points, 65 in our opener and 38 or more in five games. But we lost to Oregon by two, and the killer was a 13–12 loss to Southern Cal that cost us the Rose Bowl.

The 1972 season produced another 8–3 season and more heartbreak with road losses to Stanford and USC our undoing. The Trojans went undefeated, one of those all-time great USC teams.

Back in those days, it was a huge deal to have "big hits," the kind of tackles and contact that exemplified giving it everything you had. The Trojans were famous for their student body left and right. They had these huge linemen leading the play. I was the weak-side safety, and we had to take on those pulling linemen a lot. On one of these plays, I was coming from the weak side, and it was a strong-side sweep. The running back was getting ready to cut right up off of the tackle. The guard came out, and the running back didn't see me. I was going full speed and must have been just slightly behind the guard, because the 'SC runner turned up the same time I turned up, and we collided head on. He went spinning backward, and I spun around three times myself, recoiling from the impact. The ball went flying out of bounds. It was one of those big hits that defined what Huskies defense was all about, and helped set the bar for more.

The passing offense with Sonny caused a buzz on its own. Our defense, however, brought our own brand of thrills.

We had a small, quick secondary. Our whole defense was actually very undersized, but we were fast. We ran the entire defense like an offense. We loved to see the defense on the field because we planned on scoring. We were always looking to create fumbles and force interceptions.

One thing we did very well was our punt return. The defensive coordinator and former All-American quarterback, Bob Schloredt, engineered an elegantly simple and effective return scheme. The anticipation of a great punt return flowed into third down. The fans would get excited on third down because they knew that on the next play we had a chance for a wild play on a punt return.

Our returns were designed to go up the middle 80 percent of the time. We were targeting to get 15 to 20 yards. Calvin Jones and I were back there returning punts, and both of us could break for a score at any time. So we worked on it quite a bit.

When a team is not doing well, you sort of cringe when it's third down. When we got them in third down it was, "Yahoo! Here we go! We're going to get the ball in a second."

I believe we still have the highest average for punt returns in the record books. It was one of those things that was catchy. Everybody got excited. Whether we played offense or defense, it was just a matter of how quickly we were going get the ball back.

And, really, that's what it means to be a Husky, to me—that mindset of tough Huskies defense.

Going against Sonny in practice was always a challenge. He'd throw perfect spirals on a rope. He had one of the best-looking passes I've ever seen. And he can still throw! He threw harder and more accurately than any quarterback I've ever faced. He could just fire that thing. He was a quarterback with a linebacker's mentality. His toughness was incredibly inspiring.

Another thing that marked our era was the purple helmets. It wasn't so much of a gimmick, but it was a motivator. If you're giving 110 percent play in and play out, they'd change your helmet to solid purple. Players would flat put it out there every play to get one. And when the crowd would see somebody new getting one, they'd get excited.

It was great when you had a hard hit, since the paint would come off to show your "stick marks." For us defenders, being a Husky meant everybody runs to the ball; there are a lot of helmets on the ball; you're always moving forward, never on your heels; you never quit. You learned that was the best way to play.

After my senior year, the New Orleans Saints drafted me. I bounced up to Pittsburgh and then landed with Buffalo for a few years. It was a great experience. I went on to get involved in some small business entrepreneurial adventures before working for Boeing, where I have been for the last 20 years, working in operations, labor relations, and leadership development.

Having the experience of working with a high-performance UW team, and fitting in with a team, prepared me well for business. I learned how to come forward when leadership is needed and how to back off when somebody else is taking the lead. It taught me how to be a team member and work for the bigger goal and support that with my own performance. I experienced the camaraderie of a high-performance team and how to interact with team members with trust, respect, and love. And, perhaps best of all, I learned how to have a laugh every now and then.

Bill Cahill earned All-America honorable mention honors and a National Football Foundation Scholar-Athlete Award in 1972. He was a Pac-8 All-Academic selection in 1970. He holds school punt-return records for average per season (16.2 yards per attempt in 1971) and career (13.6). His 49 career punt returns ranks 10th at the UW. He had a three-year NFL career with the New Orleans Saints, Pittsburgh Steelers, and Buffalo Bills. He currently works for Boeing on the new 787 Dreamliner program and started The Champions Group, a management consulting firm linking health and fitness systems with world-class profitability.

DENNIS FITZPATRICK

QUARTERBACK

1971–1974

M Y WIFE, KAREN, WAS TREMENDOUSLY supportive my junior year when we won only two games and my senior season when we won five.

When you are down and not doing well, and there's the pressure for the Huskies to win continually, you have to surround yourself with a core group of people who believe in you and help you not quit. As a quarterback, you have to be a leader even when everyone else is down. A lot of people give up during the middle of a losing season. People will go through the motions, even coaches, and I thought it was my responsibility to be the quarterback and be the leader.

So much of the game is mental and emotional. That's something I had to learn. The other guys are just as strong and quick as you, and they watched you on film. It's all the same, and it's even ground. It boils down to mental strength and emotion. Coaches have so much of an influence on a player— more than they get recognition for—when they instill confidence and a safety net.

Players aren't going to make every tackle, do every assignment, so you have to have a comfort level with your coaches where you know you're not going to be taken out. We needed a lot more of that in our time period. We weren't winning very much, so we didn't have much consistency between our quarterbacks.

One week it was me at quarterback, the next week it was Chris Rowland. There were times when I was on the field, and the next series he was going to be in. So that made it tough. That was the condition the program was in, the coaches just wanted to win.

I was recruited by most of the colleges in the Pacific Northwest and Notre Dame. I went to a Catholic school, Gonzaga Prep, in Spokane. My vision all along was to travel to Seattle and play in Husky Stadium. It was just something I always wanted to do. WSU was really after me. I heard all the mystique about the Irish, and I knew in my heart I wasn't going to Notre Dame, even if they offered me a full scholarship. So I basically had my mind made up that I was going to go to Washington and be a Husky.

To go and see a game in Husky Stadium and to see the Huskies come out of the tunnel made me think that Seattle was just a fantastic city. I figured my parents and my friends in Spokane would be able to come over, so there were a lot of reasons to come to the UW.

My wife, who was my girlfriend at the time, ended up going to the UW, and we got married in my sophomore summer in 1973. We have three daughters, and two have gone to the UW.

162

The magnitude of 60,000 people, playing the top teams, and everyone wondering if you're good enough to make it as a starter puts pressure on you. There is an intimidation factor because these coaches are so dedicated and you have to rise to another level. Then you have the college education system, and there's so many things going through your mind. It's hard to adjust. Then people wonder why so many freshman athletes drop out—it's because it's so hard to adjust.

My sophomore year, I was redshirted because Sonny Sixkiller, Greg Collins, and Mark Backman were in front of me. I guess a lot of people remember me because halfway through my redshirt year Sonny and Greg got hurt, so the coach asked me to come off my redshirt.

Sonny just took me under his wing, and he would take time with me to tell me I was throwing off my left foot, or whatever I was doing wrong, and really went out of his way to help me. We had a really good relationship, and there's a bond between Sonny and me.

The first game I started was against USC in the Coliseum. They were ranked No. 1 in the nation and considered one of the best USC teams of all time. We lost 34–7. Sonny came back, and we won three of our last four to finish 8–3 in 1972.

Quarterback Dennis Fitzpatrick ran Jim Owens's option offense and still holds the UW record for most rushing yards by a quarterback in a game.

In 1973 and 1974 I started most of the games but alternated some games with Chris Rowland.

I was an option quarterback. I was very quick on my feet and a pretty good thrower. Robin Earl was a very good power runner, and a lot of people concentrated on him. I'd give him the ball a lot, and it worked really well for the option as a decoy.

My junior season was forgettable, with just two wins. In our second game, I did have my career-longest pass. I remember it was to Scotty Phillips, who was a small receiver. I threw it before he cut, and it was just perfect. I read the defense perfectly and threw it perfectly, and he ran for a 73-yard touchdown against Duke.

Our first Pac-8 loss came in the fourth week against Cal in a wild 103-point game, which we lost 54–49, if you can believe that score. One especially tough game was our 58–0 nightmare at Oregon. We didn't beat a single Pac-8 team that season.

My senior season we improved to 5–6. I had some memorable plays and games.

Midway through the season we put together back-to-back great performances. We avenged our shutout from the year before with a 66–0 payback victory over the Ducks.

Then we beat UCLA, ranked 18th at the time. Our team put it together, and I was the conference player of the week in those two games.

My final game as a Husky was a victory on the scoreboard and in my soul. So many players work hard four or five years and don't have a memory of a game of their life. My final game was my best. We ran all over the Cougars in a 24–17 season-ending win in Pullman. I set a record for most rushing yards by a UW quarterback with 249 yards. I was the national Player of the Week.

That was a nice honor and it felt good, but people forget that. What I can feel so good about is winning the Guy Flaherty Award my senior year. To inspire people around me is what's most important to me.

One guy who inspired me was linebacker Dan Lloyd [the UW's number-three all-time tackler with 502 total tackles]. I love Dan Lloyd. He came to play every day in practice. He had passion and was a spark—a very good player. A week after the season ended, we met at the Olympic Hotel for our banquet.

There was so much talk during the season over whether or not 1974 would be Coach Jim Owens's last season. Owens was larger than life for so many people. He walked on water from his house to the stadium! He was a very good-looking, intense, and charismatic man. When he announced his retirement at the banquet, we were like, "Oh, my goodness, the legend Jim Owens isn't going to be at the head of the program anymore." With our record, it was pretty much expected, but just hearing the good-bye was historic.

When you're winning, it's so easy. When you're up against the wall, that's when you find out what's inside of you. I had to do that for three years as a Husky because the program was on the way down—until Don James restored the program.

What does it mean to be a Husky? To be a Husky stood for resiliency, being very passionate for what you believe in, and being classy. Being a Husky was to have class. I feel so great to tell someone I'm a Husky. It's more than just winning.

I do get to see Huskies every now and then as the general manager of the Beverly Hilton Hotel in Beverly Hills, California. I see Sonny Sixkiller a lot when he's down here, and many Huskies teams have stayed at our hotel. Seeing the purple and gold always brings back good memories.

165

Dennis Fitzpatrick was voted the Guy Flaherty Award for UW's most inspirational player and the team's scholar-athlete in 1974. His 249-yard rushing performance versus WSU in 1974 stands as the most by a UW quarterback in a game and ranks fifth all-time for all rushers. His 697 rushing yards is the most in a season by a Huskies quarterback. Fitzpatrick's 854 career rushing yards is second only to Marques Tulasosopo. He is currently general manager of the Beverly Hilton Hotel.

RAY PINNEY

CENTER

1972–1975

IREMEMBER MY FIRST TRIP to play UCLA in the Coliseum. It's a pretty awesome venue. It was November, and they crushed us. After the game, it was sunny and the palm trees were out. We were waiting for the bus. All the UCLA players were walking out, and they had all their girl-friends hanging on them. It looked so attractive, glamorous, and sexy living in L.A. I turned to my friend and teammate, Chris Rowland: "Hey, Chris, we went to the wrong school." We had a chuckle about that.

I really don't think I went to the wrong school.

When I was a kid, my dad took me to Huskies games every now and then. I was impressed by the huge stadium and good football at various times. Being a homegrown kid (Shorecrest High), I wanted to be a Husky.

I came to Washington to play center. At 6'4", 215 pounds, I was smallish compared to linemen now. I'd look at all the other players coming in, and they looked like giants. I thought, "Oh man, there's no way I'm going to hold my own with these guys."

I played on the freshman team. I treated football like a job. I was very focused. It was uncommon for freshman to play on varsity. Dan Lloyd was the only freshman who played on varsity from our class.

I remember distinctly my first freshman game in Pullman. We lost. I didn't have any fun. It was a long bus ride home. I thought of quitting the team. Then we won our next four games and ended the season with a win over the

Ray Pinney was the first of three UW centers in the 1970s who went on to successful professional careers.

167

Cougars at Everett Stadium. We celebrated at the Crew House as it was just as important as a varsity game to us. Being on the freshman team was a very positive experience.

I was fortunate to be at the right place at the right time. The Huskies came off a pretty good year in 1972, Sonny Sixkiller's senior year. A lot of seniors graduated. There wasn't a lot of senior leadership in 1973. We had a strong freshman class, and a lot of us started our sophomore season. I got a chance, and things just started clicking. I won the starting job and kept it until I graduated.

My sophomore year we played USC at home. I went out on the kick-return front line, closest to the football. I was 10 to 15 yards from USC players. They looked completely different than the guys on our kickoff team. They were lean and athletic, like greyhounds. After they kicked off, I dropped back to my position to block, and half the guys were already by me. I thought, "Oh man, this is D-1 football." It was very memorable.

Unfortunately, the 1973 season wasn't memorable for fans. We lost to Hawaii, were 2–9 overall, and winless in the Pac-8. We were still a respected program, but we had a crummy year. We knew we were good. It just didn't show.

Coach Jim Owens, "J.O." as we called him, was very charismatic. A big physical presence. He was kind of intimidating. There was a lot of respect and reverence.

My senior year Don James took over the program. The philosophy was different. With James, everyone had to earn his job. If you were a starter the year before, you weren't guaranteed a job. There wasn't a lot of complacency. You could feel a sense of urgency.

The thing you don't hear about James was that he brought in a very good staff. About four or five of those guys—Jim Mora Sr., Bob Stull, and Ray Dorr—went on to become head coaches themselves. Later on, there was a tough transition from his first coaching staff. UW lost a lot of good coaches, and it was no coincidence that they had some less productive years.

People forget we almost went to the Rose Bowl that first year with James. We needed to beat Cal and we would've gone to Pasadena. Dan Lloyd got an interception and was tackled at the 20. We just needed 20 yards. But we couldn't score. We finished 6–5, a relatively good year for Coach James's first year.

The Apple Cup was a crazy game. We were down 27–14 and came back. I was snapping the ball on the kick to put us up again 28–27. Our kicker was Steve Robbins. My view made it seem like it was a close kick. I looked up and thought, "Oh, he missed it." Then I saw the referee put up his hands to signal that it was good.

I'm still close to several teammates, guys like Chris Rowland, Paul Strohmeier, and Joe Simmons. They were teammates and frat buddies. There's a strong camaraderie that goes on after football.

Ray Pinney began a tradition of Huskies centers who went on to successful pro football careers. He was named to All-America honorable mention teams and first-team All-Conference and All-Coast teams in 1975. Pinney played 12 pro seasons with the NFL's Pittsburgh Steelers and the USFL's Michigan Panthers and Oakland Invaders.

MIKE BALDASSIN

LINEBACKER

1973–1976

M Y DAD TOOK ME TO MY FIRST University of Washington game my sophomore season at Wilson High of Tacoma. I was blown away by Husky Stadium. The crowd was incredible. When I left the stadium, I whispered to myself, "I'm going to come back and play on that field someday."

None of the big schools recruited me. They all thought I was undersized to be a Pac-8 linebacker at 6′1″, 180 pounds. I signed a letter of intent to play at the University of Puget Sound and figured my dream of playing in Husky Stadium wouldn't come true. I was grateful someone wanted me.

That August I played in the high school all-star football game. I had worked out really hard over the summer and gained about 25 pounds. The other team had a huge quarterback named Robin Earl. He and I went at it all night. I opened some eyes. After the game, representatives from the UW, WSU, Arizona State, and Oregon State were saying, "We want you; come to our school." It was overwhelming.

I took a trip to ASU, but in the end I knew there was one place for me. I signed my letter of intent to the UW on a Friday, and the next they handed me pads for our first day of summer practices. I met Huskies coaches for the first time that day.

The first guy I saw in the locker room was fellow freshman Mike Rohrbach. He was the only guy who said anything to me. All the other guys were like, "Who is this guy?" He came up, shook my hand, and introduced

Linebacker Mike Baldassin was a last-minute signee—the day before summer practices started—and made the most of his chance, becoming the UW's sixth-leading tackler.

himself. I knew who he was because he was an all-state linebacker. I used to read about him all the time in the paper. That's how our friendship started, and we remain best friends to this day.

I didn't worry about trying to impress people my first season. I put blinders on and just wanted to make the team and not embarrass myself or my family. I must have done well. Within weeks, I was on special teams and in the middle of the Huskies pack running into the stadium. I played in our 1973 home opener against Hawaii. We lost by three points, but I was in heaven. Dad, who had coached me in youth football, basketball, and baseball, was of course in the stands watching that day. I later told him about the promise I made to myself.

"Dad, it's because of you that I'm here at Washington," I told him in a moving moment for both of us.

I played special teams and got in a few games at linebacker. There were rumors that Coach Jim Owens might retire, but nobody knew if they were true or not.

We improved to 5–6 my sophomore year. I started my first game in our season finale against Washington State thanks to an injury to Dan Lloyd. I didn't understand the rivalry until I got there. It's like life and death. I was so excited to be able to play. I had a good game with 15 tackles. We ended up winning in Spokane. We found out later it was Owens's final game, and we all understood the significance.

Owens was so big and tall—a walking legend. I was intimidated by him. He had a reputation for being a tough guy, but he really was a nice guy underneath.

I was pumped up for my junior year when Coach Don James arrived. Everyone was asking, "Who's Don James?"

The only thing we knew about Kent State, where James coached the previous season, was from the tragic 1970 shootings of four students by the National Guard.

When James arrived, it was quite a change. He was much more disciplined than the relaxed style of Owens. The intensity level at practice was 1,000 miles per hour. James had a totally different approach. We older guys weren't sure if his system would work.

Compared to Owens, James was tiny physically. But I was more afraid of James than Owens. I got nervous just walking by his office door. You knew if you screwed up you'd pay for it. He didn't really yell at the players. He'd yell at the coaches in front of the players. Then the coach would in turn yell at you.

The Oregon bus story illustrates the mental power James had over us.

We drove two buses to the Oregon game his first season here. I was on his bus. James always sat in the first seat and insisted his be the lead bus.

On the way, the second bus passed us. James told the driver to catch up and pass. The driver said not to worry, he'd take care of the bus.

James started getting angry.

"You catch up to that bus!" he yelled.

"Relax!" the driver shouted back.

Everyone on the bus went silent. We didn't know what was going on. Then James leaned up to the driver and whispered something in his ear. The driver pulled the bus over to the side of the road. We sat there for a half an hour. Finally, a new bus driver arrived and took us the rest of the way. We were petrified!

Either James fired him on the spot or he quit. Either way, it made an immediate impression and brought new meaning to the phrase "my way or the highway."

When I look back, I now know why he did things the way he did. It's what we needed. When I left football and got to know James away from the field, I found out he is the sweetest guy in the world. That whole fear thing was an act to keep us in line.

James changed Owens's pro 4-3 defense to a 5-2, which meant we had two inside linebackers over the guards. My first big game was against Alabama, a 52–0 loss. I didn't start, but it was about 100 degrees, and our guys were dropping all over the place. I got in and made 20 tackles. After that, they started me the rest of the year.

I was always lighter than other guys. I knew I had to play with different things. My tools were quickness and intelligence. I studied the game really well and was taught by really great linebackers coaches. If you do the technique right, if you stay low, are quicker, and get to the right spot with angle and leverage, you can beat bigger guys.

I had many other run-ins with Robin Earl, who at 6′3″, 245 pounds, was an insane Huskies runner to bring down. I made sure I was a lot lower than him when I ran into him.

One of the hardest guys to bring down, however, was Joe Steele, who came in my senior year. He could put a lick on people. He wasn't very big, but there was something about his leverage and explosion just before contact.

My senior year we finished 5–6. Our defense had a lot of talent. I have a favorite picture of me in a huddle in 1976. Turns out six of us played in the NFL: Michael Jackson, Nesby Glasgow, Charles Jackson, Dave Browning, Doug Martin, and me.

That season I broke my ankle in the third or fourth game, although I didn't realize it was broken at the time. The trainers taped it up every day as tight as possible and sewed on extensions that turned my low-cut shoe into a high-top shoe. I'd ice it before every practice and game, so I couldn't feel anything for a while. I thought I'd sprained it, and I wasn't going to miss my senior season over a sprained ankle. But it really killed me.

I went on to play almost three seasons for the San Francisco 49ers, which happened to be my favorite childhood team. When I took my first physical, they x-rayed my ankle and said, "We see you broke your ankle, how's it doing?"

Playing in pain is a mindset. My close friends on the UW team, including Rohrbach and Jeff Leeland, had what we called "toughness tests." We were the original Jackasses. If we had a video camera back then, we would've made millions. We'd hold dumbbells from above a chair and drop them on our guts. We'd eat lizards raw or go to the beach and eat sand crabs. If we were walking along and someone pointed to a worm on the grass and said, "Toughness test," we had to eat it.

When my career ended with the 49ers, I called Coach James and asked if I could help coach when I returned to complete my sociology degree. He welcomed me back. While at the Crew House for dinner, I met an All-American rower, Mary, who caught my eye. She was making extra money by serving food. I'd intentionally spill milk so I could talk with her. We eventually married and have four kids.

I was a police officer for 10 years in Oakland before returning to Tacoma, where I'm a teacher at Bellarmine Prep and member of the football coaching staff.

Being a Husky exposed me to my inner character—what it takes to reach your dreams. When you're in that competitive arena, it tests you to the core. You learn about perseverance and endurance.

Being a Husky is a privilege. When you love something, you want to give your best and achieve your fullest potential. You never know where it's going to go, but I'm grateful to have been part of something big, to make an impact is really special. I look back at the 180-pound high school guy who showed up on campus the day of practice, and I just have to think there was an angel looking over me. I feel very lucky.

Mike Baldassin became the UW's third-leading tackler since 1967 by the time he ended his career. His 386 career tackles now ranks sixth. His 200 tackles in his senior year ranks fourth-best in a season. Teammates voted him the Guy Flaherty Award as the team's most inspirational player in 1976. He played three seasons for the San Francisco 49ers. He is currently a teacher/coach at Bellarmine Prep.

MIKE ROHRBACH

LINEBACKER/SPECIAL TEAMS

1973–1977

L IKE ALL PLAYERS ENTERING THE HUSKIES football program, I had dreams of Huskies greatness. Rose Bowl rings. Starting. Tackles. Record books.

Growing up in Seattle and playing at Ingraham High, I wanted to be Husky as long as I wanted to play football. It all started when my grandfather, H.W. "Zip" Neuman, took me to my first Huskies game when I was eight. That's all I thought about after that…someday playing for the Huskies!

We'd have family football games in the backyard, and we all impersonated the Huskies greats of my time.

After five years in the UW football program, I started a grand total of one game. I scored one touchdown. You won't find my name in the Huskies record books.

Some might say I didn't live up to expectations of being a recruited high school "star." My dad always said if you give your all and do your best, then no one can be disappointed in you. Yeah, my dad was a big fan. My mom was real supportive, too. My grandpa loved Huskies football as well.

Sports, and life, are like that. You never know where your path will lead and how one day can be a defining moment.

Looking back, I wouldn't change a thing.

I'm most proud of the fact I survived the Huskies program.

I've been on the UW sideline 23 years, counting my five playing years and every year since 1989, up until the 2006 season. I have a national championship ring, four Rose Bowl rings, and 13 gold "Bowl" watches.

My favorite is the 1978 Rose Bowl ring. It's a good conversation starter to share with people what I do now, and I feel I truly earned that one through the blood, sweat, and tears of being a player.

I almost didn't survive. I think quitting goes through every player's mind from time to time. At that level, the stress of competition wears you down. It's such a transition from high school to college. The program is so demanding. Yeah, I'm not ashamed to say that I considered quitting early on. But, I just felt God had me there for a higher purpose than just being a linebacker.

I put my time in on the "hamburger squad," otherwise known as the scout squad. The coolest part about the hamburger squad is we imitated players on the other teams. In my first couple years, we'd wear the 'SC colors in practice the week before we played 'SC, and I was No. 41, James "Sweetwater" Sims.

I took a lot of hard hits in practice. But the most painful hit came from little, tiny receiver Scotty Phillips.

I didn't see him coming on a play, and he put his helmet right in my sternum and pancaked me. Knocked the wind out of me. The guys grabbed my belt, lifted me up so I could get a gasp of air. I was on my back, and Scotty, who was such a good buddy, came over and said, "Whoa, I'm so sorry."

"I forgive you," I uttered. "Just don't let it happen again."

It was my fault. I committed the number-one sin for a linebacker. I didn't keep my head on a swivel.

I didn't redshirt my freshman year in 1973. It was the first year freshmen could play varsity. My redshirt year came just before my senior year. I blew out my ankle before the spring of 1976. It was a freak thing. I was wearing experimental football shoes, I was just working out, and *snap!*

I really wanted the chance to play my senior year with my good friend Mike Baldassin, a fellow linebacker from Tacoma. We'd become tight. We were looking forward to playing side by side together our senior seasons. I didn't know if I'd ever get back on the field. Doctors said I might never play again.

I think the best thing about my whole playing experience was the friendships I made and the teammates I played with. I played with some great athletes. Some great guys. Warren Moon, Blair Bush, Dan Lloyd, Ray Pinney, Charles Jackson, Michael Jackson.

Mike Rohrbach, the inspirational leader of the 1978 Rose Bowl team, returned to be the spiritual leader as the team's chaplain.

There was one guy whom I got off on the wrong foot with. Don Wardlow really didn't like me because I'd hurt one of his buddies in a high school game the year before. And he thought I was a cheap-shot artist. He really didn't like me, yet we became pretty good friends, so that was kind of neat. I made some great friendships with a lot of really good guys.

The friendships started right away. I lived in the Crew House my first quarter of school. Those were some fun times, bonding with the other freshman. You know, to this day, when I hear the song "Summer Breeze," I think of a guy, our 6′5″ safety Alex Simpson, from California. He was always playing that song full volume. To this day, I'll hear that song on the radio, and I'm immediately back at the Crew House sitting in the sun on my little lanai with Alex "A.T. Kaboobie" three doors down, playing that song.

Every team has its great nicknames. I was "Rohr." We called Dave Stromswold "Rug" because he was covered with hair. I remember coming out of the locker room with him after a game and introducing him to Karen Riemcke, a UW basketball player who became my wife.

"Karen, I want you to meet my good friend…Rug," I couldn't remember his real name because that's all we called him.

We had some other good names. Al Burleson was "the Mad Hatter" because he always had a hat on. Kenny Conley was "Fly." When Warren Moon first became a Husky, we called him by his real first name, Harold. Whenever I see him I always call him "Harold." He just kind of laughs.

What an honor to have played with a Hall of Fame guy like Warren Moon, who was a great leader, an amazing guy, great football player, great friend, great human being.

Watching him taught me a lot about leadership. Surprisingly, so did sitting out my senior year with an injury. It was a tough year, but I kept my spirits up. I learned how you don't have to be a "star" to be a leader. My teammates voted me a team captain my second senior season in 1977.

That year I played a little at linebacker in our first game of the season against Mississippi State, which we lost. I started the next week, against San Jose. As a team, we had a real poor performance. We won but weren't playing very well. The coaches started making some changes, and I was one of those changes. The guy who stepped in for me, Bruce Harrell, went on to make the sophomore All-America team, so how could I be bitter about that?

He was really a good, fine player. But, for me, by that time having hurt my ankle and being told that I may not ever play again, just going back out there, being in a position as a captain was a real thrill. I was just honored to wear the purple and gold and be part of something.

I still played some linebacker as the second-string guy. It wasn't always garbage time. Football is football. Whether you're up or down, whether it's the fourth quarter or the start of the game, you better be ready because it's crazy out there. You never know how it could go down.

I was on a lot of special teams. It was still real intense. Coaches loved my enthusiasm for special teams.

During the 1975 season, linebackers coach Skip Hall put me in charge of pumping up the special teams. He named us the RTKs: "Rohrbach's Trained Killers." And we had a pretty good unit. Guys just flew around. Good guys. And, yeah, it was fun.

I scored my only touchdown on special teams. In 1975, against Stanford, we blocked two punts and ran both back for touchdowns. I ran one back, and Steve Lipe ran the other one back. Spider Gaines blocked them both within 55 seconds, and we scored two touchdowns. I thought I had *both* touchdowns. Spider's second block almost bounced into my arms, but at the last second went sideways to Lipe. I think we blocked 11 kicks that year.

So I took pride in being a special-teams player. My most meaningful hit came on a kickoff. My grandpa and my parents loved going to Huskies games. I always knew where they were, and I'd always look for them to let them know I appreciated their support. My parents always encouraged me to keep fighting.

One year, my grandpa was very sick in the hospital. We were going down to play at UCLA. Before we left, I told him, "Gramps, I'm gonna get a tackle for you on the opening kickoff."

Well, I got the tackle on the opening kickoff! We got back into town really late. I went straight to the hospital in Ballard. I snuck into his room. He gave me a big hug and said, "You got the tackle for me!" You can't measure how cool that was.

The 1978 Rose Bowl was definitely amazing. I had a local TV cameo whooping it up on a roller coaster ride at Disneyland. We went down two weeks early, and they took us everywhere. They treated us like kings.

My spotlight play was the coin flip. As a captain, I walked out with Warren Moon, Blair Bush, and Dave Browning for the ceremonial event. I've watched every Rose Bowl since, and every time they show the coin toss, it's exciting, having been there. I relive those moments every year.

Beating Michigan was great, but it was sweet to see my roommate and high school buddy have one of the best hits I've ever seen in football on a Rose Bowl kickoff. Jeff Leeland lit up Dwight Hicks, the All-American safety. To this day it is the greatest hit I have ever seen on a football field.

My defining play, which received national attention, was taking a knee.

It happened after that 1975 Stanford game when I scored a touchdown, but that wasn't it. The "play" needs a little setup. The summer before, a number of Huskies players, Mike Baldassin, Jeff Leeland, Kevin Richardson, and I, were part of a summer huddle leadership staff for the Fellowship of Christian Athletes Conference in Ashland, Oregon. Several Stanford players were there, too. We all became good friends during that week, ministering together and working out together. We talked about getting together on the field after our game in the fall.

Even though we blocked those two punts, Stanford came back and won 24–21. After the game, a bunch of us were walking off the field, Stanford guys and Huskies guys from that Fellowship of Christian Athletes group. I don't know which guy said it, but we were standing in the end zone, and one of the guys said, "Hey man, let's have a word of prayer."

And we just knelt down and grabbed hands and prayed. *Seattle Times* writer Georg N. Meyers saw it and wrote a story about me scoring a touchdown and having two trips to the end zone—one to score and one to pray. A lot of wire services picked it up, and the story went nationwide.

That story got written up in a pastors' example book for preaching, the examples of camaraderie and prayer.

I'm not saying that it was the first time guys ever did that, because it might have happened way before that, but it was one of the earlier times when guys specifically knelt and prayed with their opponents.

The prayer was basically thanking the Lord for the privilege and opportunity to play the great game of football and to compete against each other and to honor and glorify the Lord.

I still take a knee after UW football games. I've been the team chaplain since 1989, through 2005. I am currently on a two-year sabbatical so that I can attend our son Chris's games at Central Washington University.

Yeah, I wish my career had been different from the standpoint of games started, tackles, and all that stuff. But in the final analysis, I wouldn't trade it for anything. I went through the transition between Coach Owens and Coach James. I guess the thing I am most proud of is finishing strong, being one of the guys left standing at the end.

Mike Rohrbach started only one game and scored just one touchdown in his five-year playing career at Washington, but he was elected as a team captain by his teammates in his senior year, 1977, and became an inspirational team leader as a second-string linebacker and special teams player. He has been the team chaplain since 1989.

BLAIR BUSH
CENTER
1974–1977

I WASN'T VERY BIG MY SENIOR YEAR in high school for an offensive tackle and defensive end at 6′3″, 220 pounds, so USC and UCLA weren't interested in me.

Being from Southern California, that was disappointing. But the Northwest schools and Colorado were interested in me. I liked Jim Owens, the campus, and the city quite a bit. I decided this is where I wanted to be.

I grew up watching USC and UCLA, so I wasn't all that familiar with Washington, except for the greats, like Hugh McElhenny and Sonny Sixkiller. So I came up not knowing as much about the program as if I had been a local kid.

My first year at Washington I played offensive guard. I was going against a defensive lineman named Dave Pear—a damn good player, who ended up playing about six years in the NFL and going to a Pro Bowl. Going against him opened my eyes. I knew I had to get a whole lot better, let's put it that way. He was a senior, and he taught me a lot.

Being a scrub team member going against the first-team defense, he man-handled me pretty well.

The summer two-a-days weren't that tough for me. I always stayed in shape and wasn't one of the big fat guys. It wasn't like a Marine boot camp or anything. But, from what I've heard, Coach Owens had mellowed some.

I was blissfully ignorant. To me it was just a challenge, and I was a competitive guy. I didn't like to get beat, so I just worked harder and concentrated more.

I got onto the field once my freshman year as a member of the kickoff return team. I missed blocking my assignment all three times, so I didn't get a chance to do that again. But it turned out it was Lester Hayes, so I don't feel too badly about those misses. Nobody else could catch up with him either.

It was a ball just to be on the field, though. Probably the highlight of that year was when Coach Owens and Coach Tony Kopay felt sorry for me, so they let me make the trip down to USC. That was neat to go back home. I didn't do anything but stand on the sideline. I had a great seat.

I used to be an usher in the Coliseum. Somebody at my high school had some connections, so about eight of us ushered USC games my junior and senior high years to earn a little cash. So it was extra special for me to just be on the field.

Coach Owens retired after my freshman year. I was disappointed because I really respected and admired the man. He was one of those people who just walked into a room and had a presence. I liked him. He always talked to my parents, said "Hi" to me, asked me about school, and knew my name. He seemed to have an interest in me—which was pretty cool for a freshman.

So Coach Don James came in. He was a little bit detached and let the coaches do the touchy-feely things. There wasn't much of that from the assistants either.

That first summer under James was a Marine boot camp. Owens decided to retire when he knew he was handing the next guy a reasonable team. So our senior and junior classes were really strong. The sophomore class was a little weaker, and then the freshman class was the last recruiting class from Owens—my group was pretty weak. So Don came in with some tools, with some really good players like Scotty Phillips, Robin Earl, Ray Pinney, and Al Burleson. He had a whole bunch of competitive players.

In our first meeting with James, he made it very clear that we were going to spend time in the weight room. We were going to get in shape, and we were going to do it his way or we weren't going to get on the field. He came in with a very mature group of coaches—a whole bunch of experienced coaches. He basically said, "Sign up or sign out."

It was not a warm and fuzzy place. But then again, college football isn't warm and fuzzy. I was moved to a backup center behind Ray Pinney. I started

Blair Bush was an All-American center and senior leader for the 1977 team that marked Don James's first Rose Bowl win.

learning the position as quickly as I could. I played special teams. I just tried to learn as much as I could. But I knew I wasn't going to get on the field.

I played on special teams and got in a few plays at the end of games.

Learning the center position didn't take long. It's just making sure you get the ball to the quarterback. I'm sure the ball ended up on the ground during practice, which is not unusual with young quarterbacks and young players trying to learn a new program. Coaches get a little upset when the ball ends up on the ground on that exchange.

When you think about Coach James's first recruiting class, it had to be one of his best at Washington. He signed Warren Moon, Michael Jackson, Dave Browning, Antowaine Richardson, Nesby Glasgow, Spider Gaines, and Ronnie Rowland. It was an exceptional class of guys who went on to play in the NFL. I think I was the only guy out of our recruiting class who started.

I finally earned my chance to start as a junior.

We started my senior year 1–4. People forget that. It was quite a turnaround. We were pretty close to realizing Don James's nightmare of having a good team for the first two years and then falling apart the third year. We were on the edge of doing that.

Then we beat Oregon 54–0, and everything changed. It all just came together. The team looked very weak, and then, all of sudden, two or three guys had an "ah-ha" moment and we started playing like a pretty good team. Or we just got damn lucky. I'm not sure which one it was.

When Coach James came in, he wanted to play his guys. So he sat senior Chris Rowland and put in Warren at quarterback. Chris was a very good quarterback, but he wasn't going to be around that third year when James needed an experienced quarterback. So James invested in the future, and it was a hard deal for some of the guys.

I was pretty good friends with Warren and hung around him some. He was then, and is now, a very strong man emotionally and mentally. I don't think I could have handled the pressure and criticism the way he did. He took some hard physical, mental, and emotional shots. There were a lot of people saying awfully nasty things about him. So it must have been very hard for a 19-year-old kid to stay strong and focused.

It didn't matter to anyone on the team that Warren was black. It's one great thing about sports—especially team sports, when you have such a big team like a football team—players are just players. It's just Warren. It's not white

Warren or black Warren, it's Warren. But it was a big deal for an awful lot of people sitting in the stands.

After we turned our 1977 season around, that whole stretch drive to the Rose Bowl was great. When a team comes together like that, it's a blast being a part of the experience. To go down to Pasadena and get ahead early and beat a team that was better than we were was as good as it gets. I wish we hadn't made it close at the end.

I think it really helped having a coach who had been around some big programs and assistant coaches who had been in many different places under many great coaches. It wasn't a surprise for them. They knew how to handle it, and because of that I think they were able to call on their vast experiences.

If Don had a young, inexperienced staff and it was their first time in a bowl, it probably would not have turned out as well.

Playing in the Rose Bowl is a different experience. You have extra time to prepare, so you are rested and fresh. The extra weeks of preparation makes you more focused. Not many people get to compete in front of 105,000 fans and a national TV audience. It's a wonderful experience.

I was playing against a guy who I think was either a freshman or a sophomore, a guy named Mike Trgovac, who ended up being a very good player. He played a little bit of pro ball, and he's defensive coordinator for the Carolina Panthers now. When I was playing, we used to razz each other a little bit about that game. The Michigan center was Walt Downing. We were two of the All-American centers that year. So it was kind of fun to have one of the other top centers in the game.

Being named to the All-America team was never really a goal of mine or something I focused on. I remember a conversation I had during spring drills of my junior year. A mentor of mine, John Meyers, who helped recruit me and played nine years of pro ball himself, said, "Hey, Blair, some friends of mine in the NFL think you're gonna get drafted pretty high."

It was the first time that anybody in the world had ever mentioned something like that to me.

"What are you talking about?" I said.

The program wasn't that type of a program that it turned out to be later, where guys had that kind of expectation of turning pro. I think sometimes, in a great program, the top guys expect to be drafted, and then they start getting distracted. Being drafted was not the expectation with any of us.

I was fortunate to play 17 seasons in the NFL. I think the great thing about sports, at any level, is that it teaches you humility. It teaches you that if you work hard, good things happen. It teaches you that teams are a lot better than individuals.

Seeing good leadership and Don James's organizational skills made it a very positive experience, not only during it, but on looking back on it. The lessons you learn are very valuable.

I played five years in Cincinnati, six years for the Seattle Seahawks, and finished up with three in Green Bay and three with the L.A. Rams.

Returning to Seattle to play for the Seahawks was a real blessing. It was a very enjoyable period. Fortunately, we had kind of the same track as I had with the Huskies. Mike McCormack came in and then hired Chuck Knox. They made four or five trades, and all of a sudden we started having some success. Then we got in the playoffs, and that was a fun thing to be around.

After my NFL career, I coached for three years with the Carolina Panthers, and then returned to Seattle and became a partner in a couple of businesses. Some good experiences and some disappointing experiences, just like football.

I really like to follow the UW program. I hope people will continue to take a longer-term perspective on things. Programs have their ups and downs. I see some huge similarities between Tyrone Willingham and Don James in terms of organization and focus, and they know exactly what they want to see on the field. I'm confident fans are going to see more great things.

Blair Bush quietly anchored the 1977 offensive line and was one of three Huskies named to All-America teams. He was also selected to the All-Conference and All-Coast teams his senior year. Bush was the Huskies' top scholar-athlete in 1977 and earned an NCAA post-graduate scholarship. Bush played 17 seasons in the NFL with the Cincinnati Bengals, Seattle Seahawks, Green Bay Packers, and Los Angeles Rams, and was named to the University of Washington Centennial team. He currently manages National Medical Management in Bellevue and lives on First Hill with Rachel, his wife of 28 years. They have two children: Madison, 21, and Clayton, 18.

WARREN MOON

QUARTERBACK

1975–1977

I WANTED TO PLAY QUARTERBACK. Being black, that was a problem in the 1970s.

I dealt with death threats before high school football games and being left off the Los Angeles area high school all-star game.

Several Division I schools liked my 6'2", 195-pound size, if I would be willing to switch positions. But I wanted to play quarterback.

I played a year at West Los Angeles Junior College. I had a good season. My coach wanted to keep me another year and told recruiters not to touch me. I took matters into my own hands.

My J-C roommate, Leon Garrett, was eligible to be recruited. I played piggyback with some teams who were interested in him. I started to send out letters and got some film out of our library. I was very proactive.

I sat down with my coach and had a heart-to-heart conversation. I felt like I was ready to take the next step. I explained my goal was to play in the Pac-8. Then I got his blessing. I learned a valuable lesson. If you want something, do it the right way.

Garrett ended up going to Washington. I took a recruiting trip to Seattle and fell in love with Washington. The environment was different than anything I'd ever seen. Fresh air! I wanted to compete and have the opportunity to play quickly.

Warren Moon's three seasons at Washington didn't go smoothly for the future NFL Hall of Fame quarterback. But they ended with a Rose Bowl victory over Michigan.

I was aware there were some racial problems in the athletics department. But I crossed paths with Cliff McBride, a black quarterback Jim Owens had recruited and who had played. I thought, *He's here and he's playing*. Don Smith, a black administrator in the athletics department, made assurances. Coach Don James assured me I'd get a fair chance to show my talent.

My first season I beat out popular returning quarterback Chris Rowland and then lost the job to Chris during the season.

I knew everything going on wasn't my fault. I learned lessons about my position. If you're not performing at quarterback, you're going to get a lot of the blame. I had never been benched, so that was tough for me to take. James felt we needed some type of change, so I went along with it. I kept working hard. I felt my work ethic and talent level, once given the starting nod again, would win out. I felt I'd get another chance through the grading system they used in practice.

My first two years with the Huskies were tougher than I ever expected.

At one point, Coach James called me into his office and said he would stick with me as the starter because he felt I was the best at the position—no matter how much pressure or criticism he faced. He wanted me to know I had his confidence. I'll always respect him for that.

The height of the criticism came my junior year when I lost track of downs. We were playing at home. It was a two-minute drill right before the half. I completed a pass to my old J-C teammate, Garrett. I thought it went for a first down, but it was short. I wasn't aware it was fourth down. I threw the ball out of bounds to stop the clock. It was my fault for not knowing it was fourth-and-one. Everything was so hectic. It was totally my fault.

I heard a lot of boos those first two years, but that was the loudest.

My girlfriend at the time and friends heard other things in the stands besides boos. They'd be sitting in the stands and almost came to blows because of things being said about me. I knew some of the criticism was because I was quarterback. It's one thing to boo because someone is not playing well, it's another to boo and say things because of the color of my skin. I didn't read the papers. I isolated myself.

There were days I thought about saying, "I'm out of here." My mom talked me into staying. She wasn't sure about my going to Washington because the racial things she'd heard about scared her. She said, "This is the decision you made for the right reasons. This is just what you have to deal with in our society."

I had a couple of host families I met and who helped me. I'm grateful to all of them. One family I grew especially close to, Willie and Thelma Payne, lived near Lake Sammamish. That was my getaway place. I lost my father at age seven to heart and liver failure. Willie became a father figure. It felt like a different world to be that far away from campus. It was nice to get away from school and fans. When I felt stressed, I'd sit with Thelma on their couch and lay my head on her lap and weep. She comforted me and told me to breathe deeply and think of the ocean, the beach, or anything relaxing.

One memorable game came at the end of my sophomore year when we came from behind to beat Washington State 28–27 at home to finish with a winning record at 6–5. I came off the bench and threw a long touchdown pass to Spider Gaines. Then WSU got a little greedy, and Al Burleson intercepted a pass and took it back 80 yards for a touchdown. It was an exciting win and good to send the seniors off with a win. But I wasn't overly encouraged by it. As I said, it was a rough year.

The game that turned the program around, in my opinion, was our 54–0 shutout of Oregon after our 1–3 start during 1977, my senior season. After that game we put it together, winning seven of our last eight games.

Still, we had to wait for the outcome of the USC-UCLA game. We needed UCLA to at least tie the Trojans for us to go to the Rose Bowl. I was watching it in a hotel suite with other Huskies alums. It was quite a celebration. I usually don't like watching games with people because I'm really watching and studying the game. When UCLA kicked that field goal for the victory, it was the biggest relief.

It was so great to return to L.A. to prepare for the Rose Bowl. I had my high school and J-C coaches come by. We got a lot of rain in those few weeks. We kept moving practice sites. One day we practiced on a parking lot.

Our confidence level grew every day. I had no doubt we'd win even though we were huge underdogs. One thing I liked about James was his consistency. You knew what you were going to get. There were no rah-rah speeches. The best speeches were on Thursdays.

When we arrived at the Rose Bowl on game day, I got a chance to say hello to Mom and my sisters outside the stadium at a tailgate party.

I was loose on the field during warm-ups. I didn't get nervous until we came out as captains for the coin flip. It was a picture-perfect day. Chills came over my body. It was one of those moments where you try to take in everything. I got caught up in the pageantry. I made sure I got myself together before kickoff.

I thought we had a good plan against Michigan. My only problem was I wondered if we could handle them physically. We methodically moved ball down the field and scored the first touchdown of game. I felt we were quicker. We knew it would be quickness versus strength.

When Spider caught that touchdown pass and ran into the end zone wall, I was really worried about that. I ran down to see if he was okay. I don't think he was the same that day after that. That took our aggressiveness away, and we got conservative.

I was disappointed we didn't help our defense down the stretch. Our defense made some big plays.

I heard about getting the MVP award of the game back in the locker room. It was a surreal feeling. It was special seeing my family afterward and knowing how proud my mom was.

I never envisioned what happened after the Rose Bowl. I thought I'd start hearing from teams and be invited to combine workouts. But I didn't get any NFL attention. I started hearing teams wanted me, if I would switch positions. It was very discouraging. I wanted to play quarterback.

The knock on me was that I didn't come out of a pro-style offense. They didn't think my arm was strong enough. They thought I was too small. The real reason was the NFL wasn't ready for a black quarterback.

So I went to the Canadian Football League and won five straight Grey Cup titles before finally getting my chance in the NFL with Houston. I threw for more than 70,000 yards and 400 touchdowns during a 23-year pro career.

After finishing my NFL career, I've tried to help the UW program any way I can. As you're going through it, you are just trying to survive. It's not until you look back that you understand. I had no peers to discuss it with. Unless you're a quarterback, you don't understand. That's why I tried to talk with Isaiah Stanback. I wanted to make sure I was there for him. I've told all those guys, whenever they want to talk, to have a sounding board, feel free to call me.

There has been healing. I've had grown men, with tears in their eyes, apologize for things they said about me from the stands of Husky Stadium.

Being a Husky means much more now than it did then because we established a legacy. Coming off some subpar seasons, the first recruiting class of

Don James took a while, but we turned it around in the third year and then we were off and running. I think all the guys who played when I did are proud of what we did to start a legacy.

I'm proud that I survived and didn't break. All of us during those first three years with Coach James went through tough times. It was not easy on anyone. But we all survived and ended up on top. The success of our 1977 team changed the whole direction of the program.

Warren Moon is the first black quarterback and third Husky to be inducted into the Pro Football Hall of Fame, joining UW players Hugh McElhenny and Arnie Weinmeister. He is also in the Husky Hall of Fame. Moon was named the MVP of the 1978 Rose Bowl and co–Pac-10 Player of the Year in 1977 with Stanford quarterback Guy Benjamin. He earned the Guy Flaherty Award as the Husky's most inspirational player in 1977. Moon's 71-yard touchdown run in 1977 against USC is the longest by a UW quarterback. His two interceptions in 122 attempts in 1975 is the lowest interception percentage in a UW season. Moon ranks 12th in UW history in career passing yards, with 3,465 yards in three seasons. He threw 20 touchdowns at Washington. Moon played pro football in the CFL with the Edmonton Eskimos (1978–1983), and in the NFL with the Houston Oilers (1984–1993), Minnesota Vikings (1994–1996), Seattle Seahawks (1997–1998), and Kansas City Chiefs (1999–2000). Edmonton won five straight Grey Cup titles with Moon. He was a nine-time Pro Bowl selection. He threw for 70,553 yards and 435 touchdowns in 23 pro seasons. He is currently a football TV commentator.

MICHAEL JACKSON

LINEBACKER

1975–1978

WHAT I AM ABOUT TO SAY WILL SHOCK some people, but it is how I feel today. Looking back, the one thing I know is this: if I could change my life, I never would have played sports. I regret playing because of the physical pain I have to deal with now.

I truly believe my life could have been what it is without sports. I was smart enough to get an education and earn a scholarship through academics rather than sports. I have that regret. I think that the best athletes are born. It is sad to say I was born to play football, and I wish I hadn't been. When I look at today's athlete, I think the difference between me and a lot of athletes today is I was the one who wanted it. My parents never pushed me toward sports. I walked through that door. It was always my fault I was playing sports.

Since I can't change the past, I still appreciate the opportunities and friendships football gave me.

Growing up in Eastern Washington, I was a Cougars fan. I hated the Huskies. The first football game I attended was an Apple Cup. Sonny Sixkiller was the quarterback, and I hated him, too. I do not know why. All I wanted to be was a Cougar or go to Notre Dame. When I was in high school, Jim Sweeney was the WSU coach. He came to my house in Pasco to recruit me, and he told me I was not good enough to start as a freshman. My dad was really offended by that statement. At that time, Washington was changing coaches and had just hired Don James.

He came to the airport in Pasco. Coach James never made it to my house. He stopped at the airport on his whirlwind tour to meet other recruits. He met my family, and we talked for about 40 minutes. He said I would have a chance to play and compete as a freshman. He said things that made sense. He was interested in our getting an education and being competitive. He seemed honest. My parents and I were very impressed with him. After that, there was no comparison, and I did not take any other trips. I was honored he thought I was good enough to have an opportunity to play at Washington. Coach James made a real special effort to show me that he was a man of his word.

So I went to Washington and got an opportunity to play right away through the attrition of injuries to Danny Lloyd and Mike Baldassin. In the first two weeks I was there, they went down, and it gave me an opportunity to play early.

The first practices were quite scary to me. I was recruited as a safety and running back. I never played linebacker until I went to Washington. I was what they called a "pretty boy." The first day of practice, I was the fifth-string safety. I did not think this was going to be fun at all. We played an undisciplined defense at Pasco. My first practice, I did not know where to line up or how to line up. I did know how to hit. I did not know the techniques of football. I came in weighing 205 pounds.

I was fast. I did not want to hit anyone, especially the linemen. I had never seen lineman 290 pounds before, and the speed of the game was intimidating. Coming to Washington, you felt like an 18-year-old boy going against 21-year-old men. I was scared to death.

I was used to the heat in Pasco. This was cold, being in Seattle in the summer. The hardest thing for me was trying to remember the plays. In high school, I played freestyle and I would just go to the ball. To learn why it was important to keep your left arm free and hit with your right arm did not make sense to me. It was tough to learn those techniques. Over the course of four years, I learned the reason for that.

Quitting is something that never entered my mind. This was something I wanted to do for myself. My parents did not want this for me.

We started two-a-days and went two weeks straight. In the third week, the linebackers started getting hurt. Don James sent a graduate assistant to me

194

and asked me to play linebacker. They needed someone to play on the scout team. I got in there against the number-one offense, against guys like Jeff Toews, also a freshman. I remember being run over by these guys. I was like hamburger meat. They just kept pounding on me.

I wish I could remember who the graduate assistant was because he helped me stand up to the pounding and he stuck with me. He said, "You have to stay here, you can't run out of the way."

After being pounded so much, you just get so angry, and I said to myself, "Okay, now it's time to be a man and take this pounding and give it to him." On one play, I remember a lineman took off to run me over. I'd had enough, and I floored him. After that, I said to myself, "Okay, I can do this. I'm as tough as anybody."

I knew I needed to be aggressive in practice to get a chance to play in a real game. I was not the strongest guy, but I was fast. I could use a lineman's weight against him and sidestep him at the last second and get around him. The coaches started watching this, and somehow word got to James that he should watch this guy going against the number-one offense and making them look stupid. I could catch any of the running backs from behind. I was doing some remarkable things.

195

Our first game was against Arizona State. I didn't make the travel squad, so I went home to Pasco and listened to the game on the radio. I heard three linebackers went down in our 35–12 loss. On Monday, James was pissed off that we had been beaten up, and he was disappointed in how our team performed. He told the team some changes would be made. The next thing I knew, he called me into his office. He said he saw what I was doing in practice and wanted to move me to linebacker. I said, "I'm a running back and safety." "I told you when I recruited you I'd give you a chance to play," he said. "Here's your chance. Do you want to do it?"

He let me take that day to think about it. Being a second-team linebacker meant I might get in the game. So I agreed to change positions. I started learning the first-team plays. Our next game was against the Texas Longhorns and Earl Campbell, in our home opener. As luck would have it, Danny Lloyd went down in the first quarter and No. 5 got called on to go in and be the defensive signal caller! I did. I had learned the signals and concentrated on the game and did really well.

After that, it is history. I was a starter the rest of the way.

To be on the field that first home game was huge to me. I had never seen so many people. It was probably the best feeling of my life. It happened so fast. It was that overnight success everybody wants, but they do not see the sweat and effort it takes to get there. It was a dream come true. Campbell knocked some stars into my dream. That guy was a train. One time we met head to head. We both went down, and neither one of us got up.

I knew my biggest attribute was my speed. I was a bright athlete, and it was easy to pick up the plays and signals. I knew I would be able to stand in there, *mano a mano*, and take it to them every play. I also knew nobody could block me. I would hit a guy straight up a couple times, and then after that I'd go around them.

I got hurt in the Alabama game. I did not stop a blocker who was trying to cut block me, and he caught me from behind, clipped me, and rolled over my ankle. They were the fastest bunch of guys I had ever seen. Their linemen were just as fast as our running backs. They flew around the field. It was 21–0 when I got hurt, and we lost 52–0. We were outmanned.

I was out three weeks. I came back and played some special teams. The WSU game that year was the most unbelievable game. We thought the game was over. Then, being a freshman, you don't realize how important that game is for the rest of your life. It was rainy and wet, and we wanted to go home.

Moon made that great play to Spider, and Al Burleson intercepted that pass. That really solidified our team for the next year.

Sophomore year was my second worst year of my life. I had all this experience I was bringing to the game. I started thinking a lot. Every game it got worse and worse. I made mistakes I didn't make the year before. I was thinking more than using my talent. I hated that whole year. It wasn't me playing football.

My junior year was our Rose Bowl year. Things did not really look good after the first four weeks. Moon was a senior, and we had all these returning starters. We were the team to beat in the Pac-8. We believed it and forgot to play like it. We started 1–3. We played like a bunch of sorry slugs.

After that third loss, James came back and just pounded us to death in practice. There was never anything good said to us. I remember we were all talking about the Rose Bowl, and Coach James said, "I don't want to hear the 'Rose' word in your mouth ever again." This was right before the Oregon game. We were so mad at each other, Oregon didn't have a chance. We

Michael Jackson, Washington's all-time leading tackler, preserved the 1978 Rose Bowl victory over Michigan with a late-game interception on a play he dreamed about the night before.

massacred them. They took us starters out by halftime. We won 54–0. We could have beaten them 100–0.

That put us at 2–3. We started thinking we could be good, but we could not say it anymore. That Oregon game changed our careers, literally, and I think that game changed Huskies football because we turned into men. We turned into a real good team.

It was a learning period for every one of us. We clinched the Rose Bowl the week after the Apple Cup. 'SC had to beat UCLA because we had beat 'SC. I watched it at home with my parents for Thanksgiving.

The Rose Bowl was better than I thought. When we found out we were going to the Rose Bowl, the natural reaction was to think we arrived, that we had accomplished our goal. We didn't care that we were big underdogs. We were the best in the Pac-8. Winning and losing didn't matter. I was going to be able to say I'd played in the Rose Bowl.

We went down two weeks early. We heard the hype about Michigan. We had lost to Minnesota and somebody else Michigan had played. They said we did not stand a chance against Michigan. We thought, "We're at the Rose Bowl. Who cares? We're at Disneyland."

For me, the Rose Bowl was Disneyland. We ran into the Michigan players a couple times. There was a lot of sizing up going on. They were a huge team, and I know they didn't think we were any good. I think two days before the Rose Bowl we started to believe we could win this game. The coaches were always trying to keep us loose and enjoy the game and get the job done. Something happened in practice. You could see that the team was getting serious about the mission we were on. We started practicing like we were going to beat them. Then we jumped on them early. We thought, "This is going to be easy, this is going to be fun."

At the end, we ran out of gas. They were storming back on us, and it was 27–20 with maybe two minutes left. We were tired. Our offense wasn't moving the ball, and the big boys in blue were coming at us. Fortunately, I made an interception on the 3-yard line.

Michigan quarterback Rick Leach started rolling out. The coaches had told us we wanted to make him throw the ball. We didn't think he could beat us through the air. I stayed back long enough to make him run the ball, then he started coming toward the line. I was behind the running back he was throwing to. He saw me come in and wanted to dump it over my head. It bounced out of the hands of the receiver and onto his head, and I got it. I saw it happen in slow motion. I tell everyone I dreamed it the night before. I dreamed I would be caught in that position on a rollout, but I would wake up before I knew what Leach did with the ball.

We got to be a tight team because of what we went through the first four games. We got to be a team that only depended on ourselves. We were only as good as our weakest member of our team. I know that was the best team I ever played on, in terms of camaraderie. That includes pros, college, high school, and little league. I have played on more talented teams. But our dedication was so intense. I believe championships are won on dedication. I have never seen any group of people more on the same page as that team.

After that third loss to Minnesota, we all let our pride go and said, "Let's do this together." It's something that was never spoken. The captains did not harp on us, but they pulled us together, and in the same yoke, we went forward in unison. It was the greatest feeling in sports that I have ever had.

I would say the Rudy of that team was Jeff Leeland. He really was. I think Mike Rohrbach was our Rudy, too. He was a captain and he lost his starting job. Everyone wanted Mike to have an opportunity to play in that game. He was such a spiritual leader for the team. He found a way to contribute to the team off the field. He was not the most talented, but everyone liked and respected him. We went nuts on that hit by Leeland. We were dominating that game. When you do something like that, it's, "We're manhandling you now."

My senior year was so disappointing. The most disappointing thing, for me, was Tom Flick, when he broke his jaw. I loved that guy. He was the heir to Moon. You need a good quarterback to be a championship team. Joe Norman, who played for Indiana, broke Tom's jaw. I was teammates with Norman later on with the Seahawks, and I always hated him for that. When Tom went down, junior-college transfer Tom Porras came in, but he wasn't the quarterback Flick was. We were 7–4, second in the Pac-10, and didn't go to a bowl. We didn't know the Cougars game was our last game. It was the end of a long ride. It was wonderful. I knew I had an opportunity to go on. For a lot of guys, it was their last game. Selfishly, you start to go into a cocoon and take care of yourself. I am still friends with a bunch of them. Those are my guys. Doug Martin, he was the defensive tackle in front of me. He was so big, he was double- and triple-teamed. He always says he made me. It might be true.

I am different than all of the other guys I played with. I truly believe I would have made as close of friends doing something else besides sports. I don't know what I missed out on if I had been into my academics. I got a degree in drama. When I came to Seattle in 1975, I was a reserved, shy guy, if you can believe that.

I think the most courageous thing I saw was watching what Warren went through, being a black quarterback at that time. Warren came into a situation that was not admirable—coming off the Jim Owens era, when you had the boycotts of Huskies football and black folks did not want their athletes to come here. I was told not to come here because Owens was still here. They had Chris Rowland as the starting quarterback, and Moon beat him out. Then Moon threw the ball out of bounds on fourth down—hell yeah, they were going to boo. However, I would also say Don James was courageous, too. Don took a lot of heat. It takes a lot of strength for both guys to stay together and have faith in Warren's talent. And for Warren to never lash out against the crowd and to take that booing. I think those were the two instances of courage I saw.

Don James's life was a speech. The way he carried himself and the way he treated us. He was like a surrogate dad to me. He has such a special place in my heart. He taught me the value of time. When our meetings started, if you were on time, you were late. Things started on time and ended on time. Time is important to us. He was always shaping us to be contributing human beings, to be men. I think, for the most part, everyone who played for him while I was there turned out to be okay.

I got along great with Coach Lambright. A lot of people didn't like him, specifically the black players. Everyone thought he was a redneck. Some thought he was racist. I never saw that. Lambo took me under his wing and taught me how to be a linebacker. I didn't know how to be a linebacker. I was one when I left there.

I am always critical of people who make sports life or death. It is not that important. I think life teaches life lessons, not sports. It is difficult for me because what I think of sports now. Did I learn anything from sports? I do not know. It showed me I could live with pain. Maybe I cannot differentiate between life and sports anymore.

In my eight years playing with the Seattle Seahawks, I played against one fellow Husky. I went against Blair Bush, and he still could never block me. I always wanted to play against Warren, but I never got the chance. I believe we could have shut him down. He was with Houston, scoring 35–40 points a game, but I knew his tricks.

Maybe if I did not play eight years in the NFL I would view sports differently. I had five knee surgeries while playing for the Seahawks. That is where the pain jumps in there. It is a different game. In college, you want to win and get to the next level. In college, there is just this enthusiasm that pervades everything you do. You want to please that crowd. You are being paid by the food you eat, the friends you meet in college, and getting an education. You're not tainted. In the pros, you lose your perspective. It is all about money. After my third year, I held out because I wanted more money. That is when the game changed for me. I was being paid more than most people, and I was holding out? There was something wrong with that. Football wasn't fun anymore. I went through my first divorce then. But life changed for me. I started thinking about retirement.

I bought Huskies season tickets last year, the 1–10 season [2004]. I do not think they want me back. I have not told this to anyone but a few select people, but there were years I rooted against Washington. That's because I had two boys who should have been recruited by Washington. But they didn't go there, and that hurt me. I have a big opinion of myself. I look at myself as a Huskies legend. My kids should have had the opportunity to play there just because of what I had done there, because of the records I still hold today. It bothered me to no end.

201

I certainly did not push my two boys into sports. I did the opposite. I told them not to play sports. They chose to play, anyway, and both earned football scholarships. My oldest, Chris, played at UCLA until he blew out his knee in his third year. My youngest, Justin, went to San Francisco City College for two years and then got a scholarship to Utah State. He wanted to go pro. He had some injuries and finally gave up football and went back to school to get his master's degree.

When Chris was at UCLA, I could have cared less what Washington did. I would wear UCLA colors in public. I even rooted for the Cougars during the Apple Cup. It was a thrill to be honored as a Husky Legend during a game. Ironically, it was against UCLA, so my Chris got to come out on the field, in uniform, with my wife and me. It was really cool. I chose to do it that game because I wanted to show everyone my son did not go to Washington. In addition, I wanted people to be upset. I had talked to Bob Toledo the night before and told him I was going to be honored. I asked if it was okay if Chris came out with me. I was bitter until Justin graduated from Utah State, and then I went back home to the UW.

I renewed my season tickets, and I am hoping only the best for them now. I met Coach Willingham, and I like him very much. I hope he is as good as he has been elsewhere.

I will probably have both knees replaced in 10 years. I have pain in my feet, my shoulders, my arms—everything hurts but my head and my heart. I think it was the turf. I think most of my problems came from the Kingdome. That turf was on top of cement. I would say playing football was worth meeting all the guys and friends I have made in the game, but it was not worth the money. There is no amount of money they could pay us.

I will say being at Washington was the greatest time of my life. That's then. And I have to live with this pain and understand where this pain came from. The stadiums were full. The educational experience was world-class. The friends I met there, and the friends I still have, will always live in my heart. This was the greatest time in my life. There was nothing, ever, ever, no experience, except when my kids were born and when I married my wife, Kathy, that compares to what I experienced at Washington. I am so appreciative of the love and warmth I felt from Huskyville. If all I ever did was play Huskies football and get my degree at Washington, then I would have had a wonderful life. And I have had a wonderful life. I hope it is one of several crowns. Having walked through that tunnel and experienced the cheers, and the people I met there, I will never forget it.

Michael Jackson holds the UW records for most career tackles (578), most in a season (219), and most in a game (29, twice). He was voted to All-America teams, All–Pac-10 Conference teams and All-West Coast teams in his junior and senior seasons. Jackson won the team's Guy Flaherty Award in 1978. Jackson played for the Seattle Seahawks from 1979 to 1986.

NESBY GLASGOW

CORNERBACK

1975–1978

GROWING UP IN CALIFORNIA, my dream was to play football for USC. But I was one of those guys out of high school who didn't have all the things colleges look for—size (170 pounds), height (5'9"), speed (40-yard-dash time of 4.5 seconds). The recruiting process was interesting. My best recruiting trip was to the University of Hawaii.

I always made mature decisions at a young age. I realized I wouldn't be able to study if I went to Hawaii. They wanted me as much as any other. They did anything they could to get me to go there.

The reason I became a Husky has a Bruins connection. Jim Mora Sr. recruited me while on staff with UCLA. Then he left to join Don James at Washington as the defensive coordinator. So he thought I might be worth giving a scholarship to. The UW offered me a scholarship, and I accepted.

The UW was a great opportunity that allowed me to grow up, meet a lot of people, and see a different part of the country.

I only knew one person at the UW. Antowaine Richardson and I played youth football together, and we played in the same high school league. I knew I could turn to him and rely on him.

I arrived in Seattle a couple days before summer practices. I never had any doubts in my mind. That's how I approach everything. I believed I would fit in and would compete and succeed. I wasn't going to go into a situation intimidated. I still viewed it as football, and by that I mean ever since I was 11, 12, 13, I still had that same butterfly feeling before the first hit.

One of the things I knew was a benefit for me was the coach I played for in high school, Ralph Bidal. He prepared us for college by teaching us everything about our defense. Not just the position. We played match defense, where I'd match up with their best player. So sometimes I was strong safety, sometimes I was corner. This gave me an advantage because a lot of the other freshman weren't used to the different defenses the UW was running. I felt even if I didn't have a physical edge—in most cases I did—I had run cover-2 and other defenses that other freshman had never run before. This gave me a mental edge over others.

My goal that first year was to make the travel squad. I ended up winning a starting job at the end of my freshman year because of an injury to Frank Reed. When Reed was ready to return, Coach James decided to stay with me as the starter, even though it was unfair to Reed.

It was an awkward time in the program. The upperclassmen felt on-guard. Coach James has always been pretty straightforward. If you ask a tough question, he'll give you a tough answer. Everybody was ready to throw us under the bus. We played harder and got better. The Pac-8 got a little crazy that first year, and we almost went to the Rose Bowl.

It was not a big surprise to me that year that I was able to transfer my play in high school to college. Playing in the football league I did, there were so many guys going to D-1. When I was in high school, I believed I was going to be able to make the transition to college.

Coach James did one thing to punish us, and this is how I knew we were pretty good. He had the freshman go against the varsity. It was a very physical game for both sides. We were giving as much as we were getting. It got so competitive, he had to blow the whistle.

There was a play when I hit fullback Robin Earl so hard he had to take his helmet off and get some breathing space. That's the kind of energy at the point of attack I could muster up to win the battle. I've always had that knack. It's kind of uncanny, but I've been able to run into bigger guys and walk away.

My sophomore season was a tough year for me. We were up and down and up and down. The only thing we did was beat Washington State. All my years of football, that year's losses have dwelled on me. Our loss to Cal hurt the most.

Cornerback Nesby Glasgow had the talent and confidence to return kicks and punts and become an All-Conference defender.

We felt and believed we had enough talent to go the Rose Bowl, regardless of what people said. That's what we believed, and that's how we played.

My junior year, I earned the punt-return duties and finished the year as the leading punt returner. Returning punts is nerve-wracking, but I always could focus. I could have a storm coming, and I could still catch it by just focusing. My best punt return went for 73 yards down the Stanford sideline.

We felt destined to go to the Rose Bowl, and it worked out for us. For me, in particular, that was a childhood dream come true. I would always go to Disneyland and I'd see the champion teams visiting Disneyland. I wanted to do that. It was a childhood dream come true to go to Disneyland as a team with the Huskies.

I knew our chances of beating Michigan were pretty good. At Disneyland, most of them wouldn't talk to us. Most of their players were just uptight and standoffish. We were confident in our game plan and knew we could shut them down with Spider Gaines on the outside.

The best thing about the 1978 Rose Bowl was winning it. It was such a great memory. To be such a big underdog made it important.

Our defense had two key interceptions at the end of the game to protect our 27–20 victory. I had one and so did Michael Jackson, who was a close friend, apartment roommate, and future Seahawks teammate. Jackson saved a touchdown with his interception at our own 3-yard line. My interception came on the last play of the game. Michigan ran a similar play before my interception. When they came back to the same play, I decoyed, read the play, and pounced on the ball. I lured their quarterback to throw the ball to that receiver and then picked it off.

Other than the Rose Bowl, the other vivid memories are the rivalry games, the importance was shown to me my freshman year against WSU. When you only have a little hope and you turn it around and win it, those are the ones you remember the most and stick in your mind. Whether it was me making a defining play or a teammate, I always hold onto those games.

My senior year was disappointing. We lost too many close games—three of our first five by a total of 13 points. My high school coach always said champions win close games. If we found ways to win those first few games, we would've been champions. Our only Pac-10 losses were to UCLA [season opener] and USC as we finished 7–4.

That left my personal record of playing against 'SC at 2–2. I was happy about that.

Even though I broke my ankle in the Senior Bowl, the Baltimore Colts drafted me. They called me up and said they'd drafted me. They said they didn't expect me to play my rookie season. I said I was going to try to play. And I ended up starting my rookie year.

The Colts released me in 1988, and I became a Seattle Seahawk. I had just built a house in Kirkland. When the Colts released me, it was okay. I felt it was good timing for me to return to Seattle.

I've always looked at football as the greatest team sport in the world. It really takes more than one individual. You have to be accountable and a part of the workforce. The dedication to the team inspires each individual. There's a will to be successful, for not just yourself, but for everyone working.

To me, being a Husky means toughness. Even when I got to the pros, other players would always say they hated to play us because we were always hitting hard to the last whistle. Football is a tough game, and we played very physically. We wanted to be known as a tough physical team. It wasn't just us saying that, it was our competitors saying that.

207

An example of that came in a game against Minnesota. An offensive lineman knocked me down. Doug Martin picked me up and said that doesn't happen on this side of the ball. I ended up knocking out two offensive linemen. We didn't have to have the coaches chew me out for that, it was our own players. The players got to control the football field, and not look to the coaches. Our toughness came from within us.

Nesby Glasgow played bigger than his 5'10" stature. He earned All-America honorable mention honors in 1977 and Pac-10 All-Conference recognition in 1977 and 1978. Besides being a durable cornerback, Glasgow's 98 career punt returns is tied for third all-time in Huskies history, while his 100 career kick returns rank fifth. His 73-yard touchdown return against Stanford (1977) is the 11th longest for the Dawgs. He was drafted by the Baltimore Colts and played 14 seasons in the NFL with the Baltimore Colts (1979–1983), Indianapolis Colts (1984–1987), and Seattle Seahawks (1988–1992). He is currently the senior VP for Northwest Real Estate Consultants, Inc.

JEFF LEELAND

SPECIAL TEAMS/
OUTSIDE LINEBACKER

1975–1979

SOMEWHERE ON A HIGHLIGHT FILM of Huskies football there is a tackle I made. Some call it one of the best hits in Huskies history.

It really wasn't one of my most violent hits—I cracked my helmet once on a tackle against Arizona (I still have that helmet).

I just happened to be in the right place at the right time, and it happened to be on the big stage of the 1978 Rose Bowl.

I was on the kickoff team, and in the first half I met Dwight Hicks as he jumped over a pile of players on a kickoff return. I accelerated, put my face mask in his chest, and flattened him to his back. It didn't decide our win over Michigan, but some say it helped set a tone.

The main reason I was on the field that day was because of teammates, like Mike Rohrbach and Mike Baldassin, who encouraged me not to quit. I felt like hanging up Huskies football so many times. Starting off as a walk-on, I felt like a nobody and endured the disrespect of even team equipment managers to be on that Rose Bowl field. I was no blue-chip recruit…I didn't have ideal size or speed. What I had was heart and a willingness to run through a brick wall for the team. About 15 years after my Huskies playing days, my teammates rallied for me about a mile northeast of Husky Stadium.

I played high school football a few miles north of Husky Stadium at Ingraham High. One of five boys, my older brothers played basketball. I started
playing football at age nine. I was a late developer—smaller and slower than
I wanted to be. But I wasn't afraid to hit.

I played defensive back as a junior and outside linebacker my senior year in
high school. We went to the playoffs that year. Being 5'10", 170 pounds, I did-
n't attract much attention. Pacific Lutheran University wanted me. My brothers went to PLU. As much as my dad wanted me to go there, we couldn't
afford it.

Assistant Coach Jim Lambright asked me to walk on at Washington. My
Ingraham teammate, Mike Rohrbach, a year ahead of me, was a Husky. I was
thrilled and honored to be asked.

The day before fall camp started, Coach told me the Crew House and team
were too "full." He said I ought to sit out the season and turn out that spring.
I was crushed. They didn't even want me to practice!

It was the first time I'd missed a year of football. I joined a fraternity and
met people, but I was a drifting ship that fall of 1974.

After the Christmas break, Don James was hired to replace Jim Owens. I
was invited to join the winter conditioning program. That spring I was the
fifth-string cornerback. I ran the 40-yard dash in five seconds and could
barely bench 200 pounds. As a walk-on, it was tough because of how few
looks or opportunities I got in practice. During drills, the first-string got four
plays (what we'd call "reps"), second-string got three, third-string got two,
fourth-string got one, and fifth-string got in every other fourth-string rep.

That was four weeks long, six days a week. Then we capped it off with the
spring game. I got stuck in for a series in the third quarter. Denny Fitzpatrick
was the alumni quarterback. I was playing corner. It was third and eight, and
Denny bootlegged out to my side. He likely had the option to throw, but I
think he saw me and thought he'd just tuck in the ball and run me over for a
first down. We had a train wreck on the sideline a yard short of his goal. I
jacked him, but it knocked me silly. I heard the crowd go "Whoa!" I didn't
even know where I was for two hours. It was the first time at Washington
anyone gave me a glimpse of respect. It was cool after that. Guys on the team
started recognizing me as player who had the heart to be a Husky.

Even by my sophomore year, Coach James's second season, I didn't get to
suit up for the games. I watched from the stands with the redshirts. I played

209

Walk-on Jeff Leeland (13) stands over Michigan's Dwight Hicks in the 1978 Rose Bowl after his memorable mid-air hit flattened Hicks on a Huskies kickoff and set a tone for the game.

J-V and was on the defensive scout team. It hurt because I wanted to play so badly. New recruits fresh from high school came in on scholarship and were put in front of me. It angered me. I felt I had paid my dues. But I had to play for a different reason. I played for my friends and my God. I learned to play for the scoreboard in my heart—to be the best I could be.

After my sophomore season, I asked to meet with Coach James. I had utmost respect for Coach. His program was based on sound principles, hard work, and integrity. You could trust him. I asked what I needed to do to play. He said I needed to gain 20 pounds, get my strength up, and get my 40 time down.

I immediately started eating four meals a day. I ate so much food. I worked hard in the weight room and in sprint drills. In four weeks I gained 20 pounds. By spring I was ready to go. I benched over 300 pounds, weighed 195, and ran a 4.7-second 40. Fortunately for me, sophomore All-American strong safety John Edwards—the guy in front of me—was sidelined with a chronic ankle injury. I got my chance and did well in spring football. I made the varsity team as a back-up defensive back and special-teams player.

Shortly after spring ball another problem arose. My dad's business struggled, and paying for college was a growing challenge. UPS [University of Puget Sound] offered me a scholarship. In early June of 1977 I went to Coach James's office and told him I might have to transfer for financial reasons. In James's system, being second-string meant you were eligible for a scholarship. Coach James met with the other coaches and offered me a scholarship the next day. I was ecstatic!

That 1977 season started off as a disaster. We were 1–3 before conference play. I didn't play a lot, either, except for special teams. At that time we had an award called the "Will Breaker." It was a helmet sawed in half and put on a plaque. If you had the big hit, they'd hang it on your locker for a week. I won it for a hit in the Washington State game. I'd call it a "snot-bubbler." That season, and team, was special—we miraculously rallied to represent the Pac-8 Conference against Michigan in the Rose Bowl.

Despite being on scholarship, I was still dressing in the walk-on locker room. I'll be honest, I battled with pouting and jealousy. I felt like I was contributing, but there were a lot of newer guys getting it better than me. The freshman recruits would come in and be treated with a red carpet. A graduate assistant told me once I had a lot of heart, but "you just don't have the talent to play at this level." It burned me and made me want to prove him wrong.

Sometimes it was petty things that got me fired up. Like in the locker room just before the Rose Bowl game, many defensive backs, backs, and receivers got cool-looking towels with a Dawg logo to wipe their hands off. I didn't get one. Even to the equipment managers, I was a second-class citizen. I was selfishly upset and felt disrespected. I didn't really care that it was the Rose Bowl. When I got a chance to hit someone, it all came out.

We'd scored a touchdown and a field goal. Pete Tormey and I were wedge-busters. But Michigan's front lineman in the middle would come after me every kickoff, rather than dropping back. So I had to dodge the guy first, which delayed me, so I wasn't in the first wave downfield. That put me in position to nail Dwight Hicks mid-air as he jumped over a pile of people.

I always thought that when you pay the price, eventually it will pay off. We won the Rose Bowl, got a watch and ring, and I felt I contributed to the team. When we had our banquet, they played the highlight film and showed the hit.

I got a standing ovation from my teammates. It got me choked up.

212

My senior year, I was about 6', 195, and played special teams and nickel defense—alternating in against passing teams at outside backer. They moved me up to the varsity locker room that year. I even ran for a touchdown at Stanford after scooping up a blocked punt and going 22 yards for the score. I never was considered a starter, though.

But the hit was my career highlight.

After I graduated, I became a high school PE teacher and coach. At our 10-year Rose Bowl reunion in 1988, my wife, Kristi, and I sat at a table with Warren Moon, who had just signed an $11 million contract with Houston. I was the defensive coordinator at Omak High. I asked Warren what he wanted to do after the NFL, and he said he thought about coaching high school or college football. I thought that was cool. I thought to myself, *Here's a guy who just signed an $11 million contract, and he says he wants to do what I'm doing.* I told Kristi on our way home that night that I felt like a rich man.

When you do what you're supposed to be doing, and you do it with all of your heart, the status and recognition don't matter. Every Division-1 team needs its stars and first-teamers. But, maybe more important, it also needs the inspiration of contributors who challenge those on first string to sell out for the team, too.

I played with a lot of guys who played with a lot of heart. We loved each other. That's what gives you the edge. We changed Huskies football. It was the start of the Don James dynasty. It was rooted in friendship.

Years later, in 1992, I drove by Husky Stadium for six months straight on my way to Children's Hospital, where my baby son, Michael, fought for his life. Doctors said he had weeks to live and needed a $200,000 bone-marrow transplant to survive a rare form of leukemia. Our insurance refused to cover the operation

A junior high student of mine named Dameon—probably the most picked-on, underdog-type kid in my school—heard about our predicament and gave his life savings of 12 $5 bills to start a school fund to save Michael. Other kids joined in. Word spread. My Huskies teammates and the community rallied for us. Tom Flick, his wife Molly, the Rohrbachs, the Baldassins, and many other Huskies reached out to us and donated to Michael's fund as well. In four weeks, $227,000 was raised to cover the life-saving transplant. Michael is a now a healthy teen. Dameon became a hero.

God gives us ultimate strength, which is His love. He also gives us opportunities to exercise faith and give of ourselves for one another, despite how low we feel. Driving by Husky Stadium is still a reminder of that for me.

213

In 1995 I wrote a book about Michael's miracle: *One Small Sparrow: The Remarkable Drama of a Little Boy's Fight for Life…and the Compassion That Continues to Save*. The book helped to launch a kids-helping-kids organization called Sparrow Clubs USA (www.sparrowclubs.org), which has raised millions to support children in medical crisis—and to help kids in schools across the nation to become heroes like Dameon.

Jeff Leeland, an invited walk-on, was voted the team's most inspirational J-V player in 1976. He later earned a scholarship and lettered two seasons. His kickoff tackle in the 1978 Rose Bowl is considered among the top plays in Huskies history. Leeland coached high school football for 15 years. His is now founder and executive director of Sparrow Clubs USA based in central Oregon, where he lives with his wife, Kristi, and their five children.

ROBERT "SPIDER" GAINES
RECEIVER
1975–1979

I T WAS AN UNBELIEVABLE FINISH that got us into the 1978 Rose Bowl. That was a hell of a great experience. It was one of my best games, too—four catches for 122 yards and a touchdown. All Huskies who watched that game remember my touchdown because I caught it and ran smack into the corner of the Rose Bowl concrete wall.

When I caught the touchdown early in the third quarter on a 28-yard pass to the corner, I was trying to slow down once I caught it. And then the dude tackled me. That's why I fell into the wall. If he hadn't tackled me, I would've been fine. You know, he tripped me up. That's when I cracked into the wall.

They had padding right at the bottom of the wall, but I missed the padding.

The impact busted open my elbow, and it swelled up. I needed six or seven stitches, and then they wrapped it up really good. But I couldn't lift my arm. I couldn't squeeze my hand to catch the ball. So I only had one arm. I didn't even think I was even going to play after that.

Coach James asked me, "Do you want to play?"

I said, "Yeah," and he said he needed me out there to keep the defense honest in the second half.

I'm proud of myself for going back out there to help out any way I could. It was a great day for all Huskies.

Robert "Spider" Gaines played one of his best games at the 1978 Rose Bowl, with four catches for 122 yards and a touchdown.

The reason I became a Husky can be traced to an assistant coach under Jim Owens. I had 30 or 40 schools after me during my senior year at Richmond, California. I had my eye on Southern California. I ended up coming to Washington because assistant Mike Keifer talked me into it.

He came to my high school my senior year and got into a big argument with my high school coach about what was best for me. He made me feel Washington really wanted me even though the coaching staff was changing under Don James.

There was so much rain the first three months I was in Seattle, and I wasn't playing. I was like, "I'm out of here." I called my mother and told her

I was ready to leave. She said come on back and run track, but she encouraged me to stick it out. I decided to stay.

One day in practice my freshman year, Coach James asked me if I had ever tried blocking punts. I said I had in high school. So he put me on the punt-coverage team against Stanford. That started my career. I got two blocked kicks that day, both returned for touchdowns.

No, I didn't know right away Warren Moon would lead us to the Rose Bowl and go on to be a Hall of Fame quarterback. I didn't know too much about him because he was from a junior college. He threw some interceptions and was having some problems. But it was good to see a black quarterback in those days. I knew he had the potential because he was big and strong, and I'm so glad he stayed.

Capping my freshman season with the 78-yard, game-winning touchdown catch in the 1975 Washington State game gave me a lot of confidence.

The spring going into my sophomore year, an injury set me back. It was really hard for me because I was getting ready to play in the first football game in the Kingdome [the UW alumni game]. I had won the position but then threw my shoulder out and had to watch them play at the Kingdome. It was really hard. I was starting to make my mark. They knew that I could play and knew that I had ability. But it was a pretty good sophomore year.

My junior year we started slow. It took Warren and I a while to get that connection, but I started every game. I guess we started clicking. I ended up leading the team in receiving with 34 catches for 782 yards and seven touchdowns. That was my best season.

My senior year was really frustrating even though I earned All-America honorable mention. If Warren would have come back, we would've been undefeated because we had everyone else coming back. We just weren't very experienced at quarterback, and that hurt us. It wasn't the same.

My favorite route to run was the post corner. I could get downfield with my speed. When I ran the post, I'd fake like I was going to the post and then back it outside and run right past the defenders.

Some could argue that my school record eight career receptions of 50-plus yards and my school-leading 23.6-yards-per-catch career average made me one of the school's big-play receivers. My career 17 touchdown receptions still ranks third in school history. I had big dreams of making big plays in the pros, too.

But I didn't really get a chance in the NFL because I got hurt my first year. I went to Green Bay and got released. I went up into the Canadian Football League and played about three or four games. Then I got in a big argument with the coach and got released. So I kind of bounced around for a couple years and didn't have an interest in playing anymore.

From there I got involved in some things I'm not proud of. I made some mistakes. I found that the Huskies football coaches, players, and fans were a forgiving family. A newspaper story came out about how I lost my way with drug and alcohol problems.

Coach James called me up and asked how I was doing. He encouraged me to come back to school and be a running backs coach. People really tried to rescue me. But I ended up messing that up and getting myself back into a little trouble. I just wasn't ready. So I left school to look after my family.

But I finally got it right. I returned to school and got my degree in sociology in 2006. I'm very proud of that accomplishment.

I've talked to the UW freshmen football players about when you become a Husky, if you get in trouble, the whole university will get in trouble. I'm glad to be back. I'm doing great now. I'm taking care of my child and working with kids as a counselor. Maybe I'll be a high school coach someday.

217

I've always been proud to be a Husky. I came to a program that was in a lot of disarray, and I think I was one of the characters on the team who helped James turn around the UW program. I'm really proud that we got to, and won, the Rose Bowl. After that, people started respecting the Washington program. We started getting really good recruits, and then we became a great powerhouse and a national champion. I think everyone from that time feels like we were pioneers of the program down the right road.

What does it mean to be a Husky? Like the Dawg, you've got to have heart. That's how I'd summarize it. Being a Husky was about having heart, being tough, and being strong for life.

Spider Gaines earned All-America honorable mention honors in 1978. He was the biggest big-play receiver in Huskies history, as his career average of 23.6 yards per catch (1,651 yards on 70 receptions) is a team record. His eight career catches over 50 yards is also number one in school history. He is currently a youth fitness trainer and counselor in Seattle.

TOM TURNURE

CENTER

1975–1980

HAVING BEEN BORN AND RAISED in the shadow of Husky Stadium, I guess I always wanted to be a Huskies football player—so did all my friends. My grandfather and uncle had both been Huskies athletes, but I wanted to be the first Huskies football player in the family.

I played linebacker and tackle at Roosevelt High. I had decent size, but I wasn't a blue-chip recruit by any means. I had offers to play at a few junior colleges. Fortunately, my coach put in a good word for me with UW assistant coach Jim Lambright. His response was: "Well, we encourage him to walk on, but we're not going to give him a scholarship."

A chance is all I wanted. I was told not to turn out until school started, but knowing I'd really be behind, I made an appointment with Coach Don James and introduced myself. I told him it was my dream to play Huskies football and make a difference in the program.

I was allowed into the first practice and quickly learned there is a two-class system—scholarship players and non-scholarship players. As a walk-on, I started at the bottom of the food chain. During summer practices, I wasn't even allowed to eat lunch or dinner with the team in the Crew House. Fortunately, my parents lived in Portage Bay, so I could go home for lunch.

One hit changed my status. In our first scrimmage, I had this great hit and stuck this guy so good. At the Monday meeting, Coach James made me stand up and gave me the "Best Hit" award. I could hear guys say, "Who the hell is this?" Needless to say, after that I got to eat lunch and dinner with the team.

For walk-ons, practices are the games. I didn't even suit up for games as a freshman. I spent many practices scared to death. Everybody was so huge and strong. I guess I was just crazy enough to think I could do it and didn't give up. I managed to prove myself on the scout team.

Fall practices are chilly, dreary, and you're out there in the glare of stadium lights getting your butt kicked by juniors and seniors. Pretty soon, you're running every play because other scout team players are injured or have quit. You just try to survive. The coaches recognized that kind of passion, that desire.

By spring training we were out of centers. I was asked if I had ever played center. "No, but I'll play it," I said. By the end of spring, I had earned the back-up center job. At the time, Coach James gave a scholarship to players who made the second team. So I went in to see Coach James about my scholarship. "Well, you know, I don't have one to give you," he said. I could have been bitter. But I understood it wasn't personal. I learned right there that D-1 college football isn't just a game, it's a business.

Learning to play center wasn't easy. The key to being a good center is taking that first step at the point that you're snapping the ball. To be able to do that and get the ball in the right spot and into the quarterback's hand was incredibly difficult. That first six-inch step gives you an advantage over the nose guard, who doesn't know the snap count. A lot of guys still make the mistake of snapping the ball and then taking their step. Getting that first step right took hours of practice. I started snapping left-handed because that's my strong hand, but quarterbacks are used to right-handed centers, so I switched to my right hand. That was kind of a double whammy.

Centers have the thankless job of snapping on field goals, extra points, and punts. Centers don't get any attention unless they screw up. My goal was to be invisible. I didn't want anybody to see me out there. I knew if they saw me, it meant I had made a mistake. I didn't wish anybody ill will, but if somebody was going to make a mistake, it was going to be the holder or the kicker. It wasn't going to be me.

One thing Coach James did that I thought was really smart was working on special teams with the whole team watching. He'd stop practice for special teams. He'd have the whole team surrounding us. Coach James would be unmerciful. If you had a low snap, he was all over you. I think it was probably easier doing it in games than in front of Coach James. I remember once

Walk-on Tom Turnure (56) switched to the center position at Washington, earned the starting job, and went on to a successful NFL career.

I put two snaps low in practice. Coach James came up to me and said, "Tom, put the ball anywhere but on the ground this time." The next play I almost hit the guy's head. I was determined it wasn't going to be on the ground.

My sophomore year, I was voted Most Improved Lineman. That next fall Coach James gave me the scholarship.

My junior year, we beat the University of Oregon in Oregon 54–0. That was my first start ever at guard. I played guard the whole game. It was a blast. After that I didn't play much guard or center, only special teams. I recall one game in which I stood out, for better or for worse, and that was the Syracuse game. I was on the kick-return team. It was my job to intimidate the kicker by trying to hit him after the kick. One kick I was offside and caught him good. I hit him so hard he was lying on the ground, flopping around like a fish. Everyone in the stands went ballistic. I almost caused a riot. Everyone was yelling, "Kill 56! Kill 56!" I was No. 56.

We lost to Syracuse and then lost to Indiana. I have never run so many 100-yard sprints in my life. Coach James just ran us to death. One of the worst things was to have Coach James talk to you when he was up in the tower. You had to screw up badly for him to talk with you. If he called you to the tower, you knew you were in big trouble. He was like a CEO out there. He really didn't have communications with players other than the captains during games.

I did get to play a lot of special teams and got a nice hit in the Rose Bowl. One of my Rose Bowl memories consisted of throwing up all night after the "Beef Bowl" at Lawry's The Prime Rib. I ate four or five pounds of prime rib. I ate myself sick.

Compared to professional football, college football was definitely more fun. My senior year was amazing. I went on to play pro ball. I played eight seasons professionally, six seasons in the NFL in Detroit and two in the USFL.

My wife, Terri, and I returned to Seattle after my NFL career. Following my father, I went into the commercial insurance business, and in 1997 I started the firm Turnure & Associates, LLC. Recently I sold my company to Seattle Financial Group, a long-time family-owned company offering a mix of financial services. I have twin daughters, both juniors in the business schools of the University of Washington and Northeastern University in Boston.

I'm in my fifth year as a Tyee Club Advisory Board member. I will become chairman next year. It's exciting to see how much energy these people have for the program. I've always known the coaching side, but to see the administrative side has been a learning experience. To see the quality of people who are involved, especially now, it's pretty interesting.

I remember seeing the big-time Huskies supporters hanging around at practices and games. As a player, I would sometimes wonder if they had any other interests. The thing I didn't realize is that these people are helping recruit and giving millions to the program. I don't think we do a good job of showing the players that it's not all just about them. These people just love Huskies sports.

I enjoy supporting the program and giving opportunities to kids. I think the kids are really taking advantage of it, better than they ever have. I mean, look at the grade-point averages and graduation rates.

Being a Husky means something to me every day. It's a heritage that's just unique. It's one of the most elite fraternities you can be involved in. I work in sales now and I am always surprised that people still remember my name from football. Often I run into old teammates and friends who want to talk Huskies football.

Recently, we had about 150 former football players come back, and it was like we were long-lost brothers. We shared an experience that was unique. I believe we are better people because of it.

Tom Turnure became the rare walk-on who worked his way up to be a UW starter and NFL player. He earned All-America honorable mention in 1979, was named to the All–Pac-10 and All-Coast first teams, and was the UW's Outstanding Lineman that year. He was voted Most Improved Lineman his sophomore year. He was the 57th player picked in the 1980 NFL draft by the Detroit Lions. Turnure played eight seasons of pro football, six with Detroit and two in the USFL. He is currently the president of the Seattle Insurance Group.

RONNIE ROWLAND

RUNNING BACK

1976–1977

Although I broke O.J. Simpson's single-season high school rushing record with over 2,000 yards rushing my junior year, I wasn't highly recruited.

So I basically just bummed around a year in my Hayward, California, neighborhood, hung out with the fellows, and took odd jobs. Then one day my former high school coach called me out of the blue and saved me, because I was headed in the wrong direction.

He had a new coaching job at San Jose Community College and asked me to come and play for him. I was reluctant and out of shape but decided to take him up on his offer.

I remember the team conducting a week of three-a-day practices. It was tough, and I was not in good shape. I remember straining both my groins, but as time went on, I began to get back into the groove.

I did not play the early part of the season, and it wasn't until the running back ahead of me was ejected from the game for fighting that I got my opportunity. I entered the game and scored twice on long runs and won the game for us. The rest, you could say, is history. We went on to become conference champs, and I was named all-conference and all-American and went on to back-to-back 1,000-yard seasons.

I was highly recruited by many schools but liked what I saw at Washington with new coach Don James going into his second season. James liked to run the ball, so I figured the University of Washington would be the best place for me. My first spring game was very successful, as I ran for five touchdowns and got everyone's attention. I also seemed to bond with several guys from the Bay Area, including Spider Gaines, Lance Theoudele, and Jeff Toews, which made my transition even better. As a junior-college transfer, I felt I was mature enough and ready for the academic and athletic obligations that the UW had to offer. I was ready to go.

I earned the starting tailback spot alongside fullback Robin Earl for the season opener. We started off well, as I rushed for 184 yards in my season debut. Unfortunately, our season did not go well, and we ended with a 5–6 record. It was strange to hear the fans booing us. Going into our final game with Washington State, I needed 196 yards to become Washington's first 1,000-yard rusher since Hugh McElhenny 26 years earlier. I broke off a few long runs, including a 59-yard touchdown, and knew I was getting close to the 196-yard goal. Then, with about 15 seconds left in the game, I heard the stadium announcer say I had 999 yards. Unfortunately, the Cougars had the ball deep in their own territory, so I figured I was going to come up one yard short.

But then Jack Thompson was sacked in the end zone for a safety, and the Cougars had to punt the ball. Coach James instructed Nesby Glasgow to fair catch the kick and leave enough time for one more play—a dive over left tackle Jeff Toews, who later told me he had never blocked so hard in his life. I gained three yards to finish with 1,002. It was an accomplishment for the entire offense. Robin had about 150 yards that day, as well, to finish with 963 for the season.

That off-season proved to be a bad one for me. I sustained a stress fracture in my ankle while playing basketball and was placed in a cast for six weeks. During the summer I hurt my back working for a furniture store. I came into the next season unprepared to start, so highly touted Joe Steele stepped in and did his thing. He was a good back, and I enjoyed watching him run. But being on the sideline wasn't much fun. I went into Coach James's office during the season and asked what I needed to do to get my job back. He said, "Keep working hard." So I did. Our 1977 team (with the help of UCLA) won our conference and accepted an invitation to play in the Rose Bowl.

Unfortunately, Joe Steele was hurt in the game, and I played the majority of the time, so it worked out. In two seasons I was a 1,000-yard rusher and got a Rose Bowl ring. It was a great career, and I wouldn't change it for anything.

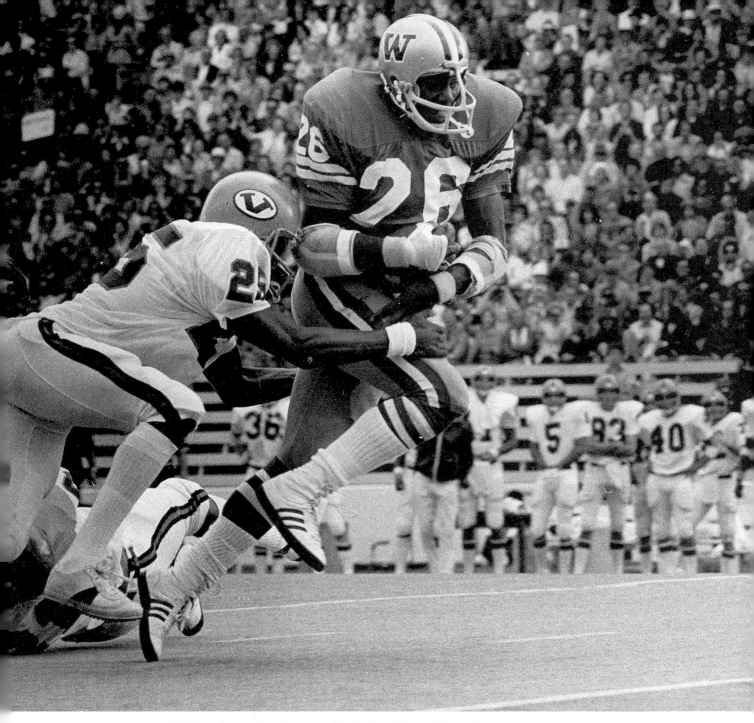

In 1976 Ronnie Rowland became the Huskies' first 1,000-yard running back since Hugh McElhenny accomplished the feat 26 years earlier. Rowland went on to play several years in pro football.

I played a short time in Kansas City with the Chiefs and in the Canadian Football League with the Calgary Stampeders and the Hamilton Ti-Cats, where I was all-pro. At the end of my career, armed with my UW degree in sociology, I returned to the Northwest and entered law enforcement as head of security at Edmonds Community College for 10 years and also at the Snohomish County Jail as a counselor. I'm currently director of security at the Westin Hotel. I'm married with three kids.

Huskies football and Don James taught me discipline that I still use today. I like to have things in order and have a plan. Coach James had our practices down to the second and made sure everyone was on the same page.

Today, I currently serve on the board of the Big W Club in order to stay involved with the program and mentor student-athletes to excel, stay focused, and plan for the future. Anything I can do to give back to players is a bonus for me. Plus, once a Husky, always a Husky!

Ronnie Rowland became the first UW running back to break 1,000 yards rushing in 26 years when he totaled 1,002 yards (which ranks 11th all-time for a season) in 1976. He played several years of professional football with the NFL's Kansas City Chiefs and the Canadian Football League's Calgary Stampeders and Hamilton Ti-Cats. He is currently the director of security for the Westin Hotel.

BRUCE HARRELL

LINEBACKER

1976–1979

F OR ME, BEING A HUSKY MEANS having very close ties to Seattle and the community. It means having a strong sense of pride and tradition that comes with this program.

I didn't really plan on going to the University of Washington initially. I played at Garfield High and thought about going to school out of state. But after my recruiting trips and discussions with Don James, he really convinced me that the UW was the best place for me, given my long-range goals in politics.

I played right away. I was on special teams as a freshman, so I wasn't really presented with the redshirt choice, and that was fine with me.

My first time on the field was against Mississippi State. I remember how big everyone seemed on the field. I remember the fans and Husky Stadium, and it was a rush. In that first game, on the first play, I broke the wedge as a member of the kickoff team and made a tackle. It was a great feeling.

My freshman year was the first time I remember not playing a lot. I was talking about this just recently while talking with teammate Michael Jackson at church. I was talking about how I sat on the bench and hated to see my team losing and not being able to do anything about it. It was a tough first year, yet it was a great learning year.

Mike Baldassin and Michael Jackson were starting inside linebackers, so I didn't become a starter until well into my sophomore season. Linebacker

Mike Rohrbach got hurt in the third or fourth game. They went through some other guys until I eventually got my chance.

Interestingly, Rohrbach had a big influence on me. His locker was right next to mine. He doesn't even know this since I haven't talked to him in a long time, but seeing him live his Christian faith really changed my life. He and I were in the Fellowship of Christian Athletes group together.

One game during my sophomore year stood out. Against Oregon I had a bunch of tackles, an interception, and a couple forced fumbles. I finally believed I got to show what I could do out there. I personally had so much fun that that was one of my most memorable games.

I had good lateral movement, speed, quickness, and I wouldn't let anything stop me from finding the ball. Michael Jackson taught me how to read the linemen and how to anticipate plays. I learned from him how to take on a guard who weighs more than me. To do that you have to hit him quickly and get under him and disengage quickly. Strong arms help a lot, or as the kids say, "strong pipes."

Playing in the 1978 Rose Bowl was probably the best experience I had. The camaraderie, excitement, and the magnitude was so great. I recently talked to a guy who went to Michigan, and our kids go to school together. He said he remembers the game vividly because he drove from Michigan to watch that game, and he was surprised to hear I played. The whole city seemed behind us.

My mother and father stayed with Quincy Jones while they were down there for the Rose Bowl. It was cool because he gave me an autographed album saying good luck for the game. Turns out I had the most tackles in the Rose Bowl that day.

Warren Moon was always a class act. He was a strong leader but not overly forceful or boastful. He always had a strong presence and helped our team tremendously. Spider Gaines overcame many of his challenges and has an amazing story. He showed that if you keep trying and work hard, things can work out. He was phenomenal at catching the ball. Doug Martin is one of my best friends. A lot of us during that era would stay in contact with Doug because he has always been well grounded. The other day he and Mark Lee, another Huskies great, went fishing and invited me. They joked that I took a salmon pole to fish for crappie. I told them I will use any advantage I can to catch more fish than those guys.

Bruce Harrell, a homegrown linebacker from Garfield High, earned All-America honors on the field and in the classroom.

Our whole 1977 team received a Rose Bowl ring and a Rose Bowl watch. I gave the watch to my dad. He wore that watch all the time, and I never realized he wore it that much until he died with it on, and I removed it for his burial. I treasured my Rose Bowl ring, but now it's at the bottom of Lake Washington. I would only wear it on special occasions, but for some dumb reason I wore it waterskiing. I put on some suntan lotion before I went into the water. After waterskiing, I realized it fell off.

Going into spring practices for my junior season, Stafford Mays was a big recruit from a junior college as a linebacker. He was big and quick. So the word was, there's this guy who was coming to take my position. We were playing basketball, and I remember he couldn't play very well, but he could dunk and was kind of showing off his powerful dunking abilities. Once we started playing football, he wasn't a fit for the middle linebacker position, so they switched him to nose guard.

Today I would tell him that he was supposed to take my position, but he wasn't good enough! Our sons went through kindergarten through fifth grade together. On the orientation for kindergarten, I saw him from the back and elbowed him hard and said, "Excuse me!" He was ticked and turned around to see who this idiot was. He smiled, and after years of not seeing each other, he was happy to see me. So now we run into each other often, and he remains a good friend.

My junior year was a disappointment because we didn't repeat as conference champions.

My senior year was more positive since we went to the Sun Bowl. We were 10–2, so we had a good year. The Sun Bowl was a great experience. When Joe Steele got hurt, we were devastated. He was a strong, silent running back. I felt horrible since we had played in high school against each other and had grown as athletes together. My last game was extremely emotional. After the game, I went to a private bathroom stall and thought about everything in my career. I cried privately. At that point, although I most likely had an opportunity to play in the NFL, I knew I was entering another phase in my life and didn't want to go to the pros.

I majored in political science and went right to law school at the UW. I'm a successful attorney and have a great family and my health. I am now entering local politics in Washington, which has always been my goal. Since I'm an attorney, I've been involved in a lot of different things with the UW. I've represented probably more than 20 Huskies, several Seahawks, and several coaches at all levels, including the pros. Sometimes it's pro bono, sometimes not. I used to speak to the players during two-a-days to make them think about consequences of their actions as student-athletes. I enjoyed that.

Being a college athlete helped me become a better scholar, person, husband, and father. It kept me disciplined. I had a trial two weeks ago with limited time to prepare since I took it on for a family who could not find a lawyer. It was regarding the death of their son. I stayed focused and did what I had to do. I didn't have the opportunity to just sit back; I had to go after it. Being an athlete allowed me to have that confidence. As a politician, I will attack Seattle's problems with the same focus and drive.

Bruce Harrell earned All-America honorable mention and All-Conference honors in 1979, and made the Academic All-America first team in the same year. In addition, he was the National Football Foundation Scholar Athlete of the year. Harrell received an NCAA post-graduate scholarship in 1980. Harrell's 375 total tackles ranks eighth in UW history. He is currently a defense attorney in Seattle.

DOUG MARTIN
DEFENSIVE TACKLE
1976–1979

I WAS RECRUITED BY ALL THE PAC-8 SCHOOLS and didn't know anything about the University of Washington when I took my recruiting trip.

The day I arrived, it was rainy. I fell in love with it. I went to high school in Fairfield, California, and didn't really like the heat. The coolness of the Pacific Northwest was cool with me.

I also became part of Coach Don James's second recruiting class because I saw I had an opportunity to play defensive line right away.

It was an opportunity to get away from home and grow and use my wings to fly. I didn't know anyone in the Northwest. It was challenging the first couple of months here. Everything was new to me. Being in the program, we made friends and felt like comrades going through training camp.

One thing that weighed on me was the unknown. Would I be able to live up to the hype? I was one of the top recruits. I didn't want to let anyone down. I overcame it all.

I came in and was physically equally matched. I never feared the contact. The training itself was hard. I'd never experienced two-a-days and never experienced the type of drills and workouts we did. At times, I didn't think I was going to make it. I pushed myself to the limit and gave it all I had.

I earned a starting spot as a defensive tackle in the second week of the season and started all four years. The thing that impressed me was coming out

Doug Martin (73) decided to enroll at Washington to get out of the Fairfield, California, heat. Martin put the heat on offenses, as the defensive tackle recorded the third-most tackles by a lineman in Washington history.

232

of the tunnel—the sounds and the roar and vibration. Every time I think about it I get goose bumps.

I think for the most part everyone respected each other. I lived on campus two years and enjoyed it. I was impressed by the mutual respect of the students on campus. In my development, Washington exposed me to different cultures. I was surprised to learn recently just how stressful it was for Warren Moon to be a black quarterback at Washington. Warren never showed any signs of stress to his teammates. I know he was going through some tough times, but he never showed it. At that time we were just having fun and playing ball, not concerned about trailblazing. We were concerned about our performance on the field.

I seemed to play my best games against 'SC and UCLA.

The 1978 Rose Bowl was a highlight, even though I personally had an average game. I remember the big plays by Michael Jackson and Nesby Glasgow on defense. It was a nail-biter to the very end. We were such underdogs. There was nothing but confidence. I thought we went in prepared to win, not just prepared to participate. Our game plan was the big difference. We knew what we were capable of doing. The offense really helped take the pressure off the defense.

I went on to a 10-year NFL career with the Minnesota Vikings. Huskies teammate Mark Lee and I became best friends. He played in Green Bay. He likes to tell people that I never talked to him during the season, before or after games, because I was so competitive. We go fishing every now and then. I love steelhead and salmon fishing.

After my football career, I returned to the Pacific Northwest with my wife, Audrey, and two sons, Kyle and Corey. I've been an entrepreneur, owning restaurants and real estate. Most of all I've tried to be a good husband and father.

To be honest, my body right now is in a great deal of pain. I'm in therapy for many aliments. Seems like every part of my body is in a world of hurt. I'm lucky. I'm still able to walk. I enjoyed the game of football. It's the price you pay. It's brutal on your body.

For me, being a Husky meant pride and responsibility. I'm proud to say we started to do some things on the national level while I was there. I played 10 years in the NFL, but I've never been in a organization as thorough and organized as Don James's staff. Playing at Washington reinforced the principles of being a responsible person. It's helped me through my professional and family life.

233

Doug Martin was a two-time All-American and was twice named to the All-Conference team as a defensive tackle. His 323 career tackles rank third in Huskies history among linemen. Martin played 10 NFL seasons with Minnesota. He is currently an entrepreneur living in Woodinville.

JOE STEELE

RUNNING BACK

1976–1979

I HAD AN UNUSUAL RUNNING STYLE. A Seattle sports columnist, Royal Brougham, once said I looked like an airplane landing without the front landing gear. I don't know where it came from. I loved playing wide receiver before my Blanchet High coach moved me to running back as a sophomore in high school.

My forward lean as I ran became an effective style. I was big for a runner at 6′4″, 215 pounds. I was a slasher, always moving forward. I had some ability to make a few moves and make people miss. But the way I ran, I was a big target and susceptible to rib and hip injuries.

In my four seasons at Washington, I ran the football 676 times, more than any other Husky up to that time. I finished with 3,168 rushing yards, also a record. Both are still second only to Napoleon Kaufman's totals.

My last play as a Husky, I didn't even touch the football. That one play changed my life. From there, I took a different direction.

Coming out of high school I had many paths to consider. Our Blanchet team won the state football title my junior year, and we won 26 games without a loss or tie from sophomore year to senior year. I topped many recruiting lists. I had some interest in going out of state. I took a recruiting trip to Nebraska and had plans to visit Notre Dame, prior to deciding to stay at home and be part of Don James's second recruiting class. Fortunately, a lot of great local talent decided also to stay home and became Huskies that year.

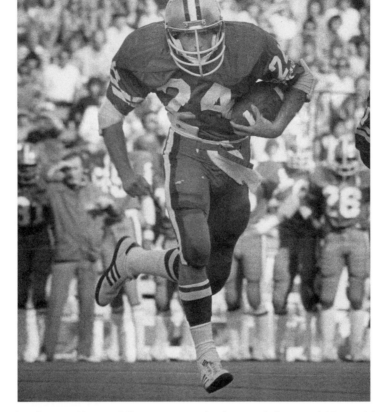

Joe Steele's forward lean while running packed a punch for would-be tacklers, as he set UW records at the time for rushing touchdowns and most yards rushing in a season and career.

When I ran in high school, I had the speed to take the corner on a sweep and cut behind people without anyone else to worry about. The biggest difference I found in college was the speed of the backside pursuit.

On one of my first sweeps in summer practices as a freshman, I felt the speed of defenders. I got around the corner and let a few guys go by and all of a sudden guys on the backside were on me. Antowaine Richardson buried his helmet in my ear hole and said, "Welcome to the Pac-8." I was a tall, lanky kid. The juniors and seniors were chiseled men. I heard, "Who is this Steele kid?" I remember the intimidation factor of the older players.

Even though we had formidable runners in our I formation with Ronnie Rowland and Robin Earl, I still was able to play quit a bit for a freshman and gained about 500 yards. Rowland became the first 1,000-yard runner in 26 years, and Earl had 963 yards in 1976.

I had a lot of respect for Ronnie. He had a great junior year. Coach James had the first- and second-string players room together on the road. That summer I worked hard in the weight room and got stronger. My sophomore year I became the starter and Ronnie, a senior, the backup. It wasn't always the most comfortable environment to room together, but our competition made both of us better players.

I believe 90 percent of being a running back is athletic ability. Different from most positions that can be learned and are very mental, the running back position and especially the I-back position is very natural. You need to learn the blocking schemes over time, but often you can play and perform well early by purely "running where they aren't." My first UW running backs coach, Ray Jackson, was a great technician, and I learned a lot from him. He taught the mental side of running. Garfield's Al Roberts came in my sophomore year to coach running backs. He was always a rah-rah, in-your-face guy and an enthusiastic motivator.

I didn't need a push because we had such talented runners while I was at the UW—after Ronnie Rowland and Robin Earl came Ron Gipson, Rob Smith, Toussaint Tyler, Vince Coby, and Kyle Stevens. You had to compete or lose your job. James was up front about that and would always play the best player.

In 1977 we started slow but turned it around to earn a Rose Bowl date with Michigan.

Our team was led by five or six seniors, including Dave Browning, Cliff Bethea, Mike Rohrbach, Blair Bush, and Warren Moon.

I had a ton of respect for Warren. He was like a dad, an older guy you looked up to. He had his challenges his first two years, but by the time he was a senior he had it down with great leadership skills. It didn't matter to any of us whether he was white or black. He knew the game. I was surprised when he didn't get any opportunities out of college in the NFL and had to go to Canada. It was great to see when he did get his chance, he made the most of it.

My most memorable home game was the Southern California game my sophomore year. It was cold and rainy. We were competing for the Rose Bowl, although we were long shots. We took it to them. Warren had a phenomenal game, including a long breakaway touchdown run, and we played well defensively. That told a lot about that team that year, delivering a message to all what the Huskies would be in the future years of the Don James era.

I got hurt on the third or fourth play of the Rose Bowl with a helmet to the hip and ribs. I had a bad hip pointer and severely bruised some ribs. After that I would always play with double hip pads and a rib protection jacket. There is pain and there is injury. This was pain. Pain in the ribs and hip pointers are things you can play through. I went into the locker room, came back out in the third quarter, and went back in to finish with 75 yards rushing as we increased our 17–0 halftime lead to 27–7 going into the fourth quarter. Our defense held on for our 27–20 victory.

In 1978, my junior year, I broke Hugh McElhenny's single-season rushing record by four yards with 1,111. We had some success but didn't go to a bowl. We did take care of the Northwest schools, which was always a goal to help recruiting.

My senior year we had a lot of fun. I came into the season in incredible shape. There was a lot of talent on that team with guys who were mentally very strong. James was always able to get the most out of his players. We had a good year going at 6–1 when we played UCLA in week 8 down in Los Angeles.

In the second quarter Tom Flick called a 47 blast reverse. The 47 blast was the fullback leading the way through the 7 hole and I followed. We'd run it a thousand times. So instead of handing me the ball, Tom faked to me and flipped it to the flanker going the opposite direction. The UCLA linebacker thought I had the ball. When you are faking a run, you overact a little. If I had the ball, I probably would not have gotten hurt.

The Bruins helmet smashed against the inside of my right knee. The impact blew up three ligaments and ripped away my hamstring from the back of my knee as it rolled up to my buttocks. I rolled around on the field in excruciating pain. Everyone knew it was serious.

Two guys carried me off the field, and the sideline doctor examined my knee. My leg could open up in an L shape. I was immediately carted off to the locker room. I flew home with the team and had season-ending surgery the next day. The surgery was successful, but I was on crutches for the remaining games, including an exciting 14–7 Sun Bowl win over Texas. Being around great family, teammates, fans, and supporters with good hearts and souls helped me move through all of this.

The Seattle Seahawks drafted me despite my knee. I rehabbed hard, and by training camp my knee was as strong as ever. My straightaway speed was coming along, but I didn't feel like I could cut the way I did before. The funny thing about an injury like that is you can recover, but you never forget what that pain was like and what that hit was like. Until then I'd never experienced that. I never felt I could run with reckless abandon anymore. So I was done and I knew it.

That one play changed my life overnight. Looking back, I grew so much from that adversity. I was able to make it through thanks to family and friends and people who loved me before I was an athlete. It was tough, very challenging.

When your dreams end like that, you have two choices: get up and go in a different direction or become self-destructive. I finished up school at the UW and got my degree in political science and pursued a career in business.

Coach James always expressed that you learn more through the adversity you experience in life than by being on top of the world. I utilized the same lessons I learned from James, Lambright, Roberts, and my teammates, just in a different way and redirected my energies. I married my high school girl-friend, Lisa Fitzmaurice, who also went to the UW, and we've been together since. We live in Kirkland and have two children. I've stayed in the Seattle area, which I love, and I am in the real estate business. For 25 years I worked in the commercial and corporate brokerage and service provider industry and recently began working on my own account in the real estate development industry.

Joe Steele ended his Huskies career as the school's leader in single-season rushing yards (1,111), career rushing yards (3,168), career rushing touchdowns (32), and career carries (676). His career yards and touchdowns still rank second. His career average of 81.2 yards per game ranks third. His five career runs of longer than 50 yards is tied for second. Steele was named the *Seattle Post-Intelligencer* Sports Star of the Year in 1979. He currently lives in Kirkland and works in real estate development.

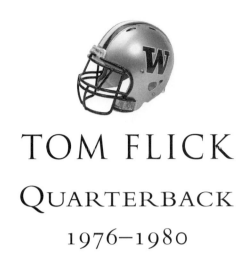

TOM FLICK

QUARTERBACK

1976–1980

Becoming a Husky provided a pathway for me to grow from a teenager to an adult and cement in my life the valuable lessons of responsibility, integrity, and discipline. We often bandy about such words in our everyday language, but during the five years I spent at the University of Washington, I appreciated the opportunity to be held accountable for my success or failures and to learn the importance of leadership, teamwork, and excellence.

I also witnessed the power of personal and collective vision to create change. When I entered the program, it was Coach Don James's second year at Washington. The football team had not been to a bowl in 12 seasons. When I left, in five seasons we went to two Rose Bowls and a Sun Bowl. I saw firsthand the foundation of a new era in Huskies football, and I am grateful to be part of that.

The lessons learned have stayed with me. I use them today as a husband, father, and businessman. Even though I played football in the NFL for seven seasons, I consider my Huskies experience to be the most valuable in shaping and influencing my life.

When I was in youth football, our little league teams would occasionally visit Huskies practices. I attended as many Huskies games as I possibly could as a kid. It's hard to believe now, but my mom allowed me to go to UW games by myself as a young boy. She would drop me off on game day and then pick me up after the game.

Tom Flick earned the respect of his teammates and others, being named team captain, most inspirational, and Pac-10 Player of the Year his senior season.

The NFL played exhibition games at Husky Stadium before the Seahawks came to Seattle. When they did, I would show up bright and early at Husky Stadium the day before the game and wait for the teams to arrive. Then I'd walk up to the equipment manager and say, "I'm the kid who won the radio contest to be your ball boy for the weekend." (There really was no radio contest.) So I warmed up Hall of Fame quarterbacks Joe Namath, Dan Fouts, and Terry Bradshaw all at Husky Stadium. Coincidentally, I eventually became Dan Fouts's backup in San Diego with the Chargers.

I had always wanted to be a Husky since moving to the Seattle area. I took recruiting trips to Oregon and WSU, but my mind was made up. I canceled my other visits to Stanford, Colorado, and ASU, and in the spring attended Huskies spring practices and meetings with the quarterbacks, and began my relationship with quarterbacks coach Ray Dorr.

My first practice was a bit overwhelming. During a full-contact drill with the interior line, I was to hand off to mammoth Robin Earl, our 6′5″, 250-pound fullback. I placed the ball deep in his stomach but didn't get my hand out in time. Earl's powerful arms clamped down on the ball and my arm, dragging me like a rag doll into a pile of linemen in the hole. After the play, I was the last to get up, and Robin looked down at me, shaking his head, and said, "Stupid freshman!"

241

As freshmen we were housed in the dorms before school started. The rest of the team and upperclassmen roomed at the Crew House. It was an eclectic group of young guys from all over the country who would form the foundation and future success of Huskies football under Don James. I remember Greg Grimes, our strong safety, would walk into everyone's room before bed check and say, "I'm Greg 'Mr. Wonderful' Grimes. Just call me 'Mr. Wonderful.'" Then he'd knock on the next door and say the same thing, and you'd hear him go down the hall into every room introducing himself. A bond formed with fellow teammates with each passing day.

I remember meeting Lance Theoudele, who grew up in the rough parts of San Francisco. Our lockers were next to each other. I remember one of the first things he said to me: "I don't like white people, and I just wanted you to know that."

Surprisingly, despite this introduction, over the course of our years as teammates, we became respected friends, which has taught me that we're more alike than different once you get to know one another.

During training camp we had evening team meetings, led by Coach James, and as camp progressed we all began to get a sense that we were part of something bigger, something special. By the end of summer practices, we were a team. We were the Huskies.

I didn't think I would be a starter as a freshman. Junior Warren Moon was our number-one quarterback, and upperclassmen Duane Akina and Larry Worman were listed number two and three, respectively. I was number four on the depth chart. I moved up the depth chart as the season progressed and saw my first varsity action as a freshman against WSU in the Apple Cup. That's the game in which tailback Ronnie Rowland surpassed 1,000 yards rushing for the season and senior fullback Robin Earl was just shy of 1,000 yards. We had a comfortable lead when Coach James put me in.

"Use up the clock," he said.

"Got it, Coach," I gushed.

I went in and ran a play. Earl jumped up and said, "Huddle up…quick, everybody," and then grabbed my jersey and in a menacing voice demanded, "Call my number!"

"I'm not supposed to!" I said back.

"Then call timeout and save time," he said.

So I called timeout. I walked over to the sideline, and Coach James stood there, shaking his head. I told him what had happened, and he simply said, "Tell Robin to be quiet."

I went back out and ran out the clock.

During spring ball in my sophomore year, everything began to click. I was elevated to number one on the depth chart. But a week after that, during a Saturday scrimmage, Kyle Heinrich, our All–Pac-10 free safety, exploded on me while I was running the option. I ended up with a separated right shoulder. I was out the rest of spring ball and fell to third string on the depth chart in the fall. Warren had a great senior year, and since I wasn't needed, I sat out the season and saved a year of eligibility. I still traveled with the team and went to the Rose Bowl and shared the thrill of beating Michigan.

The next year the Huskies signed Tom Porras, a junior-college all-American from Los Angeles. We were neck and neck, competing for the starting job, and they gave Tom the nod to start against UCLA on opening day. I was hugely disappointed. Tom quarterbacked most of that season, and I was rotated in during second and third quarters to get game time. Tom blew out his thumb at the end of the season, and so I started against WSU, my second

Apple Cup. That's the game Joe Steele ran for 197 yards. I added a couple of touchdown passes, and we won 38–8. We were a very talented team but underperformed, finished 7–4, and didn't get to a bowl.

My junior year, Tom and I battled again. Tom played the first four games and then hit a tough stretch against ASU. They finally inserted me into the lineup the next week against Pittsburgh when we were behind at the half. We rallied and I played well, yet we still lost. I knew one thing, from that point forward I was not about to give up the starting job—I had waited too long for this to come. We went on a tear, winning four of our last five games, culminating in a 14–7 win over Texas in the Sun Bowl.

Winning a bowl game is an awesome experience. But beating the Long-horns, who think football was invented in Texas, was extra special. The worst part about that season was losing our star tailback, Joe Steele, to a knee injury against UCLA. Joe and I were roommates. Our girlfriends, Lisa and Molly, who became our wives, were best friends. When Joe went down with his injury, all of Seattle mourned. Just a side note about my wife, Molly: we met in high school as sophomores when I was trying to make my high school var-sity team. She went on to become a Huskies cheerleader, so she's seen me through it all.

243

About a week before two-a-days started my senior year, my father, who was a test-pilot, crashed on takeoff during a test flight. I remember I was working a youth football camp with Chuck Nelson when my dad's co-pilot showed up. I knew something had gone wrong. I rushed to Harbor View Hospital where Dad was clinging to life. His body was shattered, eventually held together with screws and plates. Entering my senior season, my father's health weighed heavily on my heart.

Every year the West Coast sportswriters visit each Pac-10 school during summer practices and then predict the finish of each team. My senior year, the Pac-10 writers rated us to finish seventh in the conference. I remember telling the media I thought we'd win the Pac-10 title, and I told the team that, too.

I had a great group of people as teammates. I like to call our team that year a "legacy team," and that season, a team predicted to take seventh by the sportswriters of the West Coast finished 9–2 as Rose Bowl–bound Pac-10 champions. In all the years of football, I look back on those days as the most fun I have ever experienced playing sports. It's what college football, or any sport, should be about.

My most meaningful game came in the middle of the season. We played at Stanford and won 27–24 in the closing moments on a last-second Chuck Nelson field goal. That was the first time my father was able to attend a game after his plane crash in the summer. Still in a body cast, he watched from behind the goal post midway up in Stanford Stadium in a section for people in wheelchairs. On our final drive with just over a minute to play, I could see him straight ahead of us in the stands. As we drove down the field in the hurried atmosphere of running the two-minute offense, I would look up and see Dad cheering us on. Winning on the last play is always a rush, and winning like that on the road is even better. The locker room at Stanford is a good distance from the field. So before I went to join my teammates, I gave my helmet to Tony, our equipment manager, and went into the stands in uniform and pushed my father in his wheelchair out of the stadium. It was a poignant moment for me and a cherished memory, as Dad passed away four years ago on Father's Day.

Another memorable game came against Arizona, where I suffered a concussion early in the first quarter. Despite being knocked out and missing a couple of series, I came back in and completed 15 straight passes and three touchdowns, moving us closer to the Pac-10 title. Then we beat USC in the Coliseum, the first Huskies team to do that since 1964. At the time, they were ranked No. 1 in the nation with the longest winning streak to date. That was a sweet victory.

Our last regular-season game came against the Cougars at WSU, my fourth Apple Cup. Even though we won that game 30–23 and I passed for over 300 yards and three touchdowns, I started slowly, going 0-for-4 with an interception. I remember a 65-year-old Cougars fan making a serious effort to heckle me from behind our bench area. After my third touchdown, I walked over to him, smiled, and said, "It's a great day for football, don't you think?" He didn't respond.

Given the preseason predictions by the media and then earning an invite to the Rose Bowl as Pac-10 champions was enormous. My second Rose Bowl trip was much different now being the starting quarterback and team captain. Sadly, losing the Rose Bowl [23–6 to Michigan] was a huge disappointment. Two controversial fumbles didn't go our way, including one near the goal line. We had the talent, the tools, and the opportunities, but we simply failed to capitalize on them to win the game.

I'm fortunate to have played under Coach Don James, whom I consider the finest coach I have ever played for. Though at times he could be intimidating as he climbed his coaching tower to observe practice or meeting with him in his office, he was always fair. His method of teaching was to coach his coaches who, in turn, would communicate to the players. Given his success, who would argue with his system?

My position coach, Ray Dorr, was the finest, most meticulous, most prepared position coach I have ever played for. If you talk with Warren Moon, Tim Cowan, Steve Pelluer, Hugh Millen, or Chris Chandler, they will all say the same thing. It's amazing how many incredible quarterbacks came out of the Huskies program under the tutelage of Coach Dorr. Ray played such a big part in our success.

After the 1981 Rose Bowl game, I went on to play in two postseason all-star games in San Francisco and Tokyo, Japan. I didn't get home for a few weeks, and when I did I went to Tubby Graves at nights to work out, thinking I'd have the weight room to myself. One evening I walked into an empty weight room and headed to a back room where the Nautilus machines were stationed and was surprised to see Coach James working out. I jumped into the machine next to him and we started to talk.

It was a much different experience this time now that my eligibility was over and I was heading into the NFL. It was a friendly, open conversation about my family and how my mom and dad were doing, and my recent travels to Japan. Our relationship seemed at that moment to instantly transition from player and coach to respected friends. I see Coach and his wife, Carol, at church on most Sundays and always enjoy the moments when we bring each other up to speed on the happenings of our busy lives.

Since leaving the NFL in 1989 after seven seasons, I have been traveling the country as a corporate speaker, keynoting conferences and special meetings for companies like Starbucks, Microsoft, Ritz-Carlton Hotels, Merrill Lynch, and Shell Oil, to name a few. And what do I speak about? Leadership, teamwork, and managing change effectively...all the things I learned while growing up playing football and honing my skills as a quarterback. And most everywhere I go I am still recognized as a Husky.

I organize my schedule so I can attend the UW homecoming game almost every year. I always look forward to going on the field at halftime and participating in the tradition of standing with past letter-winners from all sports and connecting our UW blankets. The team reenters the field by running through our "tunnel" of history. I mingle with familiar faces and briefly catch up with old friends. The time is always too short for these reunions, but it's a tremendous recharger of my spirit and brings back waves of memories. What does it mean to be a Husky? For me, each year it means a little more.

Tom Flick was elected team captain by his teammates, who also awarded him the Guy Flaherty Award as most inspirational player. He was the Pac-10 Conference Player of the Year in 1980 and led the Huskies to the 1981 Rose Bowl. He shares the Huskies passing record for career completion percentage (.597, tied with Damon Huard) and owns the highest completion percentage record for a game (.941, 16-for-17 vs. Arizona, 1980). Flick's career passing efficiency (130.01) ranks second at Washington. He ranks in the top 10 of most UW passing categories. Flick played seven seasons in the NFL with the Washington Redskins, New England Patriots, Cleveland Browns, and San Diego Chargers. He is currently a corporate speaker. Since 1989 he has delivered more than 2,500 presentations and speaks to 70,000 people each year on high-performance strategies for leadership, teamwork, change, and personal growth.

MIKE LANSFORD

KICKER

1978–1979

I HAD THE PRIVILEGE OF BEING THE FIRST scholarship place-kicker at Washington.

After graduating from Arcadia High, I traveled through Great Britain playing soccer, then enjoyed two successful years at Pasadena City College, during which we won the national junior-college championship, played in the last Junior College Rose Bowl, and I was named J-C all-American. I was recruited by many universities. Washington was in town playing Michigan in the Rose Bowl, and through my former Arcadia High teammate, Chris Linnin, we made contact.

I didn't need too much persuading after that. I immediately fell in love with the University of Washington.

I came in the same year Chuck Nelson walked on. Chuck and I would cross paths again in the pros.

The worst thing about kicking in Husky Stadium is the swirling wind. It was a challenge. The winds were a true test of a kicker's physical and mental abilities.

Don James's special teams were second to none. Unfortunately, in my debut game for the Dawgs, we lost to UCLA due to a special-teams mistake. In one of the wettest games ever played, the Bruins' Kenny Easley (a future All-Pro) blocked a punt and recovered it in the end zone to beat us.

Like all athletes, I had my own pregame routine. It was a way to deal with the inherent pressure of the position. I'd pick out something behind the uprights and draw an imaginary line and follow through to that spot.

We didn't have many games come down to a final kick. I can only recall a game at Stanford that came down to a last-second field goal from 25 yards.

I established one kicking record at Washington. I was perfect on PATs for [at the time] a Pac-10 record—73 of 73 attempts. I was also part of a consecutive PAT string that spanned a couple years. Due to transferring from a J-C, my career at the UW seemed all too brief.

It was a great time in my life. I left home for the first time, and that meant a ton for me. Friends I made at Washington are still lifelong friends, the closest friends I have. I'm a passionate Huskies fan.

While at Washington I kicked with a shoe. That changed in the pros.

That two-inch tee made all the difference. I was drafted by the Giants and was cut in two weeks. I ended up kicking line drives up my center's and guard's backsides. I couldn't get the ball in the air without the tee. The 49ers picked me up and also cut me after two weeks. I was determined to figure it out. The next season the Raiders gave me a chance before cutting me in two weeks.

A blister proved to be my breakthrough. One day I was working out with former New York Giants and WSU Cougars kicker Joe Danelo. I kicked so much, I developed a blister. I didn't want to stop, so I took off my shoe. Without cleats, I was able to strike the ball lower to gain the trajectory I needed. Without the blister, I would have never considered kicking barefoot. My family thought I'd lost my mind. From that day on, I kicked barefoot.

A Husky helped save my career. George Strugar, a UW lineman in the mid-1950s, gave me employment when I needed it most and organized a tryout with the Rams my third year out of college.

Chuck Nelson went on to be an All-American kicker. Seven days before the 1983 NFL draft, Chuck came to visit me. I helped him adjust to kicking off the ground. Then, unbelievably, the Rams drafted Chuck to take my place. I needed knee surgery that season. Chuck struggled a little. I came back at the end of the season and kicked a 42-yarder to send the Rams to the playoffs. After that next training camp, Chuck left the Rams and went on to a successful NFL kicking career with the Buffalo Bills and Minnesota Vikings.

Chuck and I remained friends throughout. Competing daily against such a talented kicker helped me develop as a top NFL place-kicker.

Mike Lansford never missed an extra point at Washington in 73 tries. He kicked soccer-style with a shoe in college before changing to barefoot-style during a successful NFL career.

I played nine seasons for the Rams, became an All-Pro, and was the Rams' all-time leading scorer [now ranked second behind Jeff Wilkins], played in nine playoff games, and was 15-for-15 on game-winning, last-second field goals.

Today, I'm still in Orange County, I'm a partner in Global Outsourcing, and I'm raising three teens with my wife, Jill. I also work with young kickers.

The decision to attend the University of Washington was one of the best (and easiest) decisions of my life. A beautiful campus, top football program, and great friends were part of my experience at the UW.

Mike Lansford never missed an extra point in 73 attempts during his two seasons with the UW to set a Pac-10 record at the time. He went on to a nine-year NFL career. He ended his career as the Los Angeles Rams' all-time leading scorer. He was Mr. Clutch, making 15-of-15 of his game-winning field-goal attempts in the NFL. He was an NFL All-Pro kicker in 1989. He is currently living in Anaheim and running payroll and insurance businesses.

The
EIGHTIES

MARK STEWART

LINEBACKER

1978–1982

I'VE BEEN A HIGH SCHOOL FOOTBALL COACH now for more than 20 years. I've been the head coach at Renton, Garfield, Highline, and Meadowdale high schools. During that time, I've had one player earn a scholarship playing football at Washington and a couple walk-ons.

That just shows you the long odds playing football for the Huskies and how special it is when you do.

Still, I think the biggest things about being a Husky, for me, are getting my degree, the people I met, and the connections I made. I can't say enough how big it's all been in my life and for what I do today. I feel very happy with what I do every day, teaching in high school.

I didn't even think about going to college until the spring of my junior year. I had just won my league's 100-meter championship, and a California Bears coach asked me my plans for college. My family didn't have anyone saying, "You need to prepare yourself for college." I started getting recruited because of my size and speed.

I grew up in San Jose. Seeing the Huskies in the 1978 Rose Bowl put them on my radar.

I didn't know what to expect when I took my recruiting trip to the UW. They drove me from the airport to Bellevue and then across the 520 floating bridge to see Husky Stadium from the water. At the end of the trip I knew

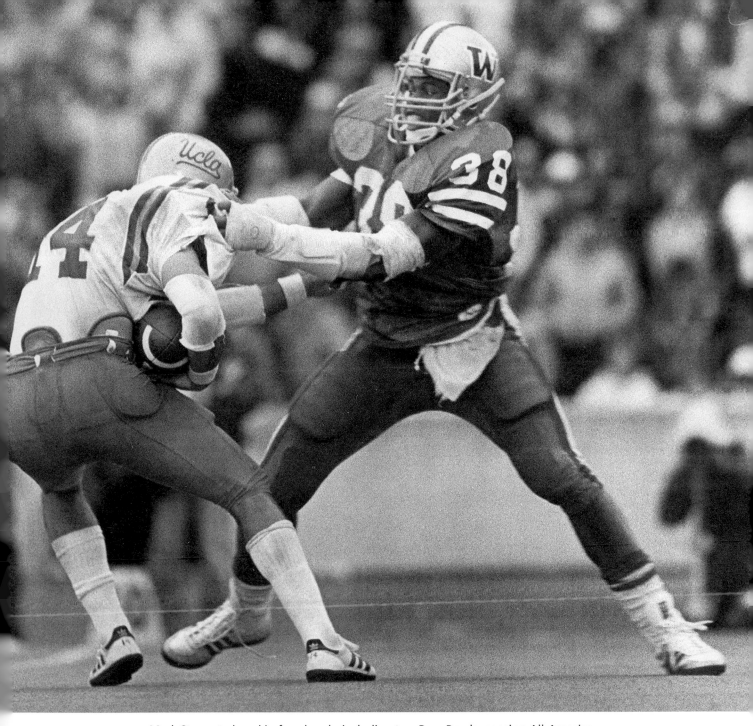

Mark Stewart played in four bowls, including two Rose Bowls, earning All-America honors for his play two times, and Academic All-America honors for his chemistry studies.

I wanted to come back. It was everything—the water, the city, the atmosphere, Coach Don James.

My first scrimmage was about survival. I didn't understand how to play linebacker at the Pac-10 level. The veterans just lit me up. I was just a blocking dummy. I didn't know where to look, and guys were blindsiding me. I didn't make a single tackle. I redshirted my first year and learned the ropes on the scout team.

School was a tough adjustment. I wasn't prepared for college classes. I got a 1.6 in my first class, Psychology 101. It was tough. I ended up doing pretty well, though. My biggest goal was to be successful on the college campus. I figured if I stayed at the UW, I wasn't going to waste my time and walk away without a degree. So I took advantage of tutors for athletes and studied hard. I got a B.A. degree in chemistry and teaching certification. I taught high school chemistry for 10 years and now I teach physical education.

Senior tight end Scottie Greenwood often lined up across from me when the varsity played against the scout team. He took the time to pull me aside and gave me points on what I needed to do to get on the field in a real game.

I played in my first game my second season, against Oregon. I was the fifth linebacker. The guy ahead of me blew some assignments, so I went in. I made some plays. That year I started a couple games and played in six or seven. A couple articles were written about me. The coaching staff had a grading system. You got a plus for a great play, a check for an average play, and a minus for a negative play. I was grading out well.

My sophomore year, an injury to fifth-year senior Antowaine Richardson opened the door to a starting spot. I was one of the first big linebackers at 225 pounds. I started three games. Then Richardson was ready to return. I was doing so well, they couldn't deny me. Instead, linebackers coach Skip Hall told me before our ASU game that I would start, but because Antowaine was feeling better he would take my spot when ASU lined up without a tight end. I watched the ASU film, and that was the only formation they ran. I did start, but after the first defensive play, Antowaine ran in. I only played one play all night. I was pissed off. I learned I needed to be patient and wait my turn. Antowaine and I are good friends to this day, and he jokes how there was no way a sophomore was going to take his place.

The four years I played we had great success, going to four bowls, including two Rose Bowls, and winning three. My greatest game has to be our

UCLA game my senior year. I had 22 tackles and five sacks. They had a small tight end, and I got after him. They kept running the ball at me.

No question the toughest loss was that 1982 loss in Pullman that kept us out of the Rose Bowl. I thought we played horribly. I still get a pit in my stomach when I think about it. I went out with our one-point Aloha Bowl victory over Maryland. We finished 10–2, which was excellent. But our two losses were to teams with losing records.

It was a special time to be a Husky. What Moon and his teammates broke out, we helped continue. It was hard for people to come into Husky Stadium with our tough defensive football. Being in the chase year after year…that made it exciting.

I played a couple seasons with the Minnesota Vikings and with Winnipeg in the CFL. I was a 'tweener. In the pros, I needed to be a 250-pound defensive end. I was stubborn. I wanted to stay at linebacker. I thought about college coaching but wasn't interested in all the recruiting. I always loved the high school level. I love the Northwest and am very happy I'm here.

Being a Husky means being hard-nosed. It's special. It's not just given to you. You have to earn it. You have to challenge people. When teams played at the UW, they knew they'd been in a ballgame.

255

Mark Stewart was a two-time All-American outside linebacker. His five forced fumbles in 1982 is a school record for a season. His five sacks against UCLA in 1982 is tied for the UW's single-game record. Stewart's 49 career tackles for losses ranks third all-time for the Huskies, while his 339 tackles rank ninth among UW linebackers. Stewart also was honored for his academic success as a member of the All–Pac-10 All-Academic team and a national Academic All-America team. He is currently a high school football coach at Lynnwood's Meadowdale High.

RAY HORTON
CORNERBACK/RETURNER
1978–1982

I REALLY WANTED TO GET AWAY FROM Tacoma and play out of state, just like my two brothers, who went to play football at Oregon and Oregon State.

I wanted to go to Arizona State. Frank Kush coached the Sun Devils at the time. I took a recruiting trip to Tempe, but I never got a chance to talk to Coach Kush. The assistant coach who showed me around kept calling me "Roy." I corrected him a few times. Finally, I just went with it. I didn't have a great impression of the place I wanted to go. My decision of where to go became easy minutes after landing at Sea-Tac.

I had visited Washington a few weeks before. The trip was okay. As I was coming down the escalator at Sea-Tac from my Arizona trip, UW assistant coach Al Roberts was going up the escalator. He saw me and said, "Ray… Ray Horton!"

From that second I wanted to go to Washington. They knew my name. Done deal.

I graduated early from Mount Tahoma High and took part in Huskies spring football practices. I played defensive back. It was eye-opening.

In one of the first practices, Coach James was on the field watching a special-teams drill. He usually watched practices from his tower. He was standing behind the field-goal kicker. I was on defense and came around the end to try and block the kick by diving flat-out and landing on my belly. So

256

I was on the ground thinking to myself what a great effort I'd just made. James walked up and said, "Get your ass off the ground!"

When James came to my house, he was a very pleasant man. He was very engaging with my parents and me. I thought, *What a great guy this is.*

So after he yelled at me, I thought, *Is this the same guy who was in my house two months ago?* It shocked me. I knew this was business then. I was not in high school anymore—not in "Kansas" anymore.

Those 20 spring practices were especially difficult for me. I was the only new guy. I didn't have any orientation. Everyone knew the program but me.

Everything came at me pretty fast. I didn't understand what I was supposed to do on defense. I was making mistakes. One of the coaches yelled, "If you don't know what you're doing, get out!"

"If I don't learn, how am I going to get it?" I responded.

From that point on, I knew I had to study. I had to learn the system. I had to know it better than anyone.

By the time summer practices started, I had a huge head start on the other incoming freshmen. Not only did I know what I was supposed to do, I knew what everyone on defense was doing, too.

I redshirted my first season. It helped me mature and learn how to become a college football player. It would have been hard for me to compete at 18, let alone at 5'10", 170 pounds. I got to see Kenny Easley and Ronnie Lott from the sideline. Watching them was amazing.

I played behind Nesby Glasgow and Mark Lee my redshirt freshman season. I was the third guy in the nickel package [five pass defenders]. I also returned punts. I remember my first play on defense. The wide receiver hit me right in the mouth. I thought, "Oh, boy, you have to play now."

We went to the Sun Bowl and beat Texas in their backyard. It was an awesome way to cap my redshirt freshman year by playing on Christmas Day.

My sophomore year, I had an injury to my knee, and it made me think about what I wanted to do if I didn't have football. I didn't know if football was for me. On a whim, I took the Seattle Fire Department written and physical tests. I passed. I was called in for an interview. I remember two key questions the interviewer asked.

The first was, "What would you do if you were a Seattle fireman and ordered to go into a building you knew was unsafe?" I said, "I'd go in

257

because I would trust that the commander wouldn't send me into a situation I couldn't handle." I still don't know if that was the right or wrong answer in his eyes.

Then he asked, "What would you do if offered the job?" I told him I'd make that decision if offered the job.

In the meantime, I told my high school coach, George Nordi, that I was considering the fire department. He said, "I'll whip you up and down the street. You have a chance to play in the NFL. How many people have that chance? You can always become a fireman later."

I never had to make the decision. I never got a return call.

The personal highlight of my sophomore season came at the Coliseum, where I returned a punt for a touchdown to help beat USC.

Going down to play in the Rose Bowl was a dream come true. James made sure bowl trips were rewards for having a good year. He gave us time to have fun. Yet there was discipline. You didn't hear of anyone getting into trouble. There was no mayhem going on.

The guy I was going to match up with was Anthony Carter, probably the best receiver I faced in college. We met one-on-one before the game during a hula contest. I think he won the most applause.

Michigan fans celebrated 16 unanswered second-half points in their 23–6 victory. I felt I held my own against Carter, even though we lost. Carter had five catches for 68 yards and one touchdown.

Returning to the Rose Bowl my junior year gave us a chance to redeem ourselves. Both our offense and defense dominated. Our 28–0 win over Iowa was the first Rose Bowl shutout in 29 years. A memorable play for me was my first-quarter, 48-yard punt return.

Because I started school early, I graduated with my sociology degree at the end of my junior year. I wanted to enter the NFL draft, but because of some paperwork, I wasn't eligible.

My senior year we were ranked No. 1 in the country for about six weeks, until Stanford's John Elway beat us. I played much of that year with two jammed thumbs. It's not easy to catch punts without thumbs.

Losing to the Cougars was probably the most frustrating game because it knocked us out of the Rose Bowl. I gave up a touchdown in the corner. I don't think I was the goat of the game, but it had an impact on the game, considering we lost 24–20.

All-American cornerback Ray Horton, who owns Rose Bowl and Super Bowl rings, considered giving up his UW scholarship to be a Seattle fireman but decided to stay in the program thanks to encouragement from his high school coach.

We settled for an Aloha Bowl bid, and my last Huskies game was a thrilling 21–20 victory over Maryland. Turns out we kept a pretty good quarterback—Boomer Esiason—to 251 yards and one touchdown.

Mark Stewart and I were selected to play in the all-star Hula Bowl. James was a coach for the all-star team. We had this luncheon, and Don spoke. He got up and told several jokes, and everyone was laughing. Players came up to us and said how they wished they could have played for such a fun-loving guy.

Mark and I looked at each other and said, "Who is this guy?" We never heard him tell a joke before. We'd never had much one-on-one communication with him. He was kind of stoic and standoffish. Still, we respected him and loved playing for him.

The best respect story about James came at Arizona State. It was Senior Night for the Sun Devils. ASU officials wanted us to come out early and stand while ASU conducted its ceremony for the seniors. Don said, "We're not going out early."

An official came in and ordered us to go out onto the field. Don turned to the whole team and said, "Let's get undressed. We're going home."

He wasn't going to let another team parade in front of us. We said to ourselves, "We have the best coach in the country." Guys played for the man because they respected him and he respected us.

I was drafted by the Cincinnati Bengals and stayed there six seasons before finishing my playing career with four seasons as a Dallas Cowboy. I played in two Super Bowls, losing with Cincy to San Francisco and winning one with the Cowboys in my final pro game. What made it even more special was that that year the Super Bowl was played in the Rose Bowl. It was like I had come full circle—from dreaming of playing in the Rose Bowl as a kid, to winning a Rose Bowl as a Husky, and finally the Super Bowl.

I think I was a pretty good athlete. I could run, catch, and cover. There were far better athletes than me at the UW—I think Aaron Williams and Anthony Allen were the best pure athletes I played with at Washington. I was an okay athlete who ended up playing 10 years in the NFL. How could a marginal athlete play a decade in the NFL? Luck? Fate? It's kind of weird.

I've coached in the NFL for 12 years. I get back to Seattle once or twice a year for some charity events, such as Warren Moon and Steve Poole's golf tournament. I cross paths with Huskies every now and then.

My oldest brother is a referee in the NFL, but they don't allow him to referee my games. I am currently the secondary coach for the Pittsburgh Steelers.

So, no, my brother didn't referee the 2006 Super Bowl between the Seattle Seahawks and Pittsburgh. To tell you the truth, I thought the referees only missed one call—the penalty on Matt Hasselbeck for the low tackle. That's in the rule book, but in 10 years as a player and 12 as a coach, I've only seen it called twice, and both of those were in 2006. If those two teams played 10 times, we beat them nine. Neither team played very well that day.

Now that I have Rose Bowl rings as a player, and Super Bowl rings as a player and a coach, there's only one thing left. My ultimate dream now would be to come back and be the head coach at Washington.

Ray Horton was an outstanding one-on-one cover defender. He had 14 pass break-ups and two interceptions his senior year to earn All-America honors. Horton was a first-team All–Pac-10 selection and an honorable mention All-American in 1981. His 15 broken-up passes is a single-season UW record, and his 22 career break-ups ranks fourth. His 10 career interceptions ranks 10th in team history. Horton's 642 career punt-return yards on 68 catches ranks seventh-best in Huskies history. Horton was drafted by the Cincinnati Bengals in the second round of the NFL draft and played six seasons there. He played for the Dallas Cowboys four seasons, with his final pro game a Super Bowl victory in the Rose Bowl. Horton has coached in the NFL 12 seasons. He is currently the secondary coach for the Pittsburgh Steelers.

CHUCK NELSON

KICKER

1978–1982

I HAD MANY MEMORABLE KICKS at Washington. One of the most unusual happened November 14, 1981.

We were at home playing third-ranked USC on a blustery, soggy day with wind gusts that reached 60 miles per hour and closed the 520 floating bridge.

Marcus Allen was a subplot of the game. The Heisman Trophy winner that year, Allen surpassed 2,000 yards for the season. With 2:19 to play, I kicked a 47-yard field goal to give us a 6–3 lead. I'd say that was my best pressure kick.

Many Huskies fans celebrated us taking the lead by releasing their makeshift raincoats (garbage bags) into the swirling wind. The bags whipped around Husky Stadium and caused a five-minute delay in the game.

I kicked off into the horseshoe end of the stadium. The ball bounced sideways in the end zone, and before a Trojan could secure it, UW linebacker Fred Small recovered it for a touchdown that set the final score, 13–3.

I certainly grew up wanting to be a Husky. My father went to Washington. We were big fans from the mid-1960s on. Pete Taggares and Sonny Sixkiller were my big heroes. I went to one or two games a year.

I started sports by playing soccer. I became interested in kicking a football by competing in Punt, Pass, and Kick competitions. I played high school football at Everett High, where I was the kicker and punter. I also was the starting quarterback. I was nowhere near good enough to be recruited as a quarterback. And as for kicking, my only legitimate kicking scholarship offer came from Olympic Community College.

Washington State did call. The Cougars had a coaching change. An assistant called and asked, "Are we recruiting you? We have your name on our list. Did we offer you a scholarship?"

Coach Jim Lambright did recruit me. He invited me to walk on. Given my Huskies roots, it was an easy choice. I redshirted my first year and then kicked off occasionally as the back-up to Mike Lansford, a pretty good kicker. I earned a scholarship for my final three years. There had been good kickers before, but because of Mike's success, he showed the value of kickers.

Because Coach Don James placed so much importance on special teams, I know I always felt we were a big part of the team. Coach James was always willing to help if we wanted a snapper or holder to come out early.

I got off to an awkward start. Mike Lansford had made 73 consecutive extra points going into our 1980 home opener with Air Force. Two minutes into being the Huskies starting kicker, I missed my first extra point attempt! Coach James let another kicker try the next one, and he made it. We scored 50 points that day, so I got other extra-point chances and made those. I also missed my first two field goal attempts against Air Force, from 29 and 24 yards. What struck me was how fast the game was and how little time I was on the field. It took me a couple plays to realize I wasn't out there very long.

Just before the half, we had a 45-yard attempt. But James had not said whom he wanted to kick it. So I just ran out there and made it. I won the job and was All-Conference.

I learned to keep the blood pumping. When our offense was on the field, I'd kick into the net. When third-and-long situations came up within field-goal range, I'd stand by the coaches to let them know I was ready. I prepared myself as if I would have to kick on the next play.

I learned to be so focused, I couldn't hear much going on around me. Linemen would ask me after the game, "Did you hear those guys yelling at you?" I never really heard it.

Some kickers focus on the holder's hands or the tee. I found it was better to look at the center and watch the football into the holder's hands.

Kicking in Husky Stadium was challenging with the wet weather, heavy footballs, and swirling winds. There were times when the wind would be howling from right to left on the field but from left to right up around the goal post. Early in my career I'd try to work the wind. I might pick a spot

264

Chuck Nelson, a consensus All-American kicker, set an NCAA record for consecutive field goals that still stands, and he remains the second-most accurate field-goal kicker in NCAA history.

outside the goal post and have the crosswind push it inside. But once I missed by doing that, so I decided to never pick a spot outside the goal posts.

I enjoyed kicking off as well. I took a few good pops from defenders. You had to make sure you didn't just focus on the returner or you would get your ear holed. Two or three times a year I had to make a tackle.

A memorable kick that season was a game-winning field goal on the last play against Stanford.

It felt good to play in the 1981 Rose Bowl and make two field goals, even though we lost the game to Michigan 23–6.

My junior year I got a chance to run the ball once. I may hold the UW record for average yards per carry—one carry for 33 yards. Against Stanford, we lined up for a 50-yarder. The snap went to me with holder Steve Pelluer my blocker. I made it to the 1-yard line before being brought down by my face mask.

I made my last five field goals as a junior to start the consecutive streak. Besides kickoffs, my only 1982 Rose Bowl contribution in our 28–0 win over Iowa were two extra points. That was fine with me.

The old NCAA record for consecutive field-goal kicks was 16. My longest during that streak was a 49-yarder against Oregon. I broke the record in the third game of my senior year. I felt nervous on the one to tie it and the one to break it. Other than that, I was just out there trying to make kicks.

Coach James never really said much to me. After a kick, I'd go over to the sideline for the kickoff tee, and he'd tell me what kind of kickoff he wanted. When I broke the record, I went to the sideline. James shook my hand and said, "Nice job. Let's kick the ball down the right hash and get it out." That's about all you got.

So the kick everyone remembers was that one in the 1982 Apple Cup in Pullman. It was a crummy, cold day where we were fighting the elements. After making two field goals that day, I pushed a 33-yard field goal attempt to the right to break my consecutive streak of 30 field goals.

The miss came in the fourth quarter with about four minutes to play. A victory would send us back for our third consecutive Rose Bowl. As soon as I kicked it, I knew I missed it. The kick went well above the uprights, so it was a judgment call. I still don't think it was good.

Because there were four minutes to go, I prepared myself for another chance and rooted to get the ball back. It's without a doubt my most disappointing kick. If I could have one back, that would be it.

That kick is far and away the reference point for fans. I get Cougars fans telling me how excited they were when I missed. Huskies fans tell me how disappointed they were, or how it looked good to them.

Perspective is a funny thing. The drama of things that happen when you're young is not as bad as it seems at the time. I decided that what happened to me in sports was never going to be the highlight or the most tragic moment of my life. That helps me.

Besides, our loss to the Cougars was by four points [24–20]. Field goals are worth three points. My kick would have put us ahead at the time, but who knows if we would've stopped them? We all could've made one play to win that game. I must say everyone was very supportive.

I went on to a successful five-year NFL career before starting my second life as a Huskies sports broadcaster. I've been doing television or radio for UW football games since 1990. We've had a great time doing the games. To still be involved in Huskies football has been a great joy. We've seen great games and losses where you scratch your head.

It's great to still have my foot in the Huskies door and still be an insider. Every now and then I might give current UW kickers some pointers.

I just love the college game. At the heart, it is just a game played by college kids. It's athletics as good as anywhere in the world with 19-to-22-year-old brains. You have kids falling down, running into each other, and making spectacular plays. That adds to the excitement of the game.

College football is a great gathering place with great drama.

For me, being a Husky means having a great sense of being something bigger than the one team you play on or the guys you're with. It's the tradition of success and effort and quality players. It's recognizing the responsibility of that tradition—to win games, be a good guy, and represent the university. To still be a part of that means a lot.

The best part of being a Husky is that's where I met my wife, Nanette. She was a Huskies cheerleader in 1979 and 1981. We met because a good friend of hers was dating, and ultimately married, my good friend, quarterback Tom Flick.

Chuck Nelson earned consensus All-America kicking honors and still holds the NCAA record for consecutive fields goals (30), from 1981 to 1982. His career field-goal percentage of .819 ranks second in NCAA history. Nelson is the third-leading scorer in UW history, with 282 career points. Nelson capped his stellar 1982 season by winning the KIRO Player of the Year, the *Seattle Post-Intelligencer* Star of the Year. His UW career-long, 51-yard field goal against Kansas State in 1981 ranks seventh in UW history. He also was an Academic All-American. Nelson played on three teams in the NFL—the Los Angeles Rams (1983), Buffalo Bills (1984), and Minnesota Vikings (1986–1988). Nelson currently lives in the Northwest and is the director of the Boeing Greater Seattle Classic Golf Tournament and a broadcaster for Huskies football.

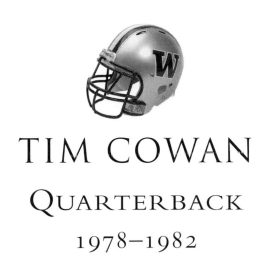

TIM COWAN

QUARTERBACK

1978–1982

TWICE I QUESTIONED my future as a Husky.

The first came about halfway through my first summer practices. I was an all-state and all-league quarterback from Norwalk, California, and I was overwhelmed. I woke up and called my sister, who was my legal guardian at the time, and said, "I'm coming home."

"No, you're not," she said. "Just stay up there and grow up and be a man."

It was the best thing my sister ever told me.

I missed practice and had to tell Coach Don James it was because I was thinking about going home. He went out of his way to set me up with some people to make me feel more at home.

The second time was in the spring going into my senior year. Steve Pelluer had led us to a Rose Bowl victory as a sophomore. My quarterbacks coach, Ray Dorr, told me, "You'll never start another game at Washington again." I went to my apartment after practice and cried for three hours. I had a serious self-evaluation. I couldn't transfer. I could roll over and coast through or continue to work my ass off.

Besides those two moments of doubt, being a Husky was thoroughly the best experience in my life. Being able to play football for a free education allowed me to be able to see things I hadn't seen before. We had great coaching and great character. We went to two Rose Bowls. By the time my class

Quarterback Tim Cowan stuck with the program despite being told he'd never start, and he became one of the feel-good stories in UW history.

268

became fifth-year seniors, we were ranked No. 1 in the country for six weeks.

I grew up the sixth of seven kids. My dad passed away when I was in first grade. My mom passed away my junior year in high school. My sister became guardian of myself and two siblings, and we moved in with her family.

The leap from high school was hard for me. I remember running the scout team. Our first game was against UCLA, so I was running the Bruins' offense. I remember making a fake and running down the line, trying to get around Doug Martin, and thinking, *This guy's a truck*. I finally got around him and turned up, and out of nowhere I got hit in the back of my head, was knocked off my feet, and skidded across the turf.

I thought I needed to get into the weight room to play with these guys. I weighed 175. I realized it wasn't playground stuff anymore. I started from the bottom.

The football experience was just amazing. Some of our games were just mind-blowers.

It was hard waiting my turn, but I knew I wasn't prepared yet. When I backed up Tom Flick, I got to play a little bit when we were winning. I got some confidence my sophomore year. Steve and I battled my junior year for the starting job, and I got the call after fall. So I started the first two games. Then in the second game, I ended up tearing ligaments in my thumb. It was a weird experience. I threw a ball and came back to the huddle, and my thumb was numb. I got the signal, walked to the line, and said, "If I don't get the feeling back, I'm gonna check to a draw." So I ended up doing that, then dropped the ball, but recovered it for no gain.

The next down I knew I had to pass the ball. I got the ball, dropped back, and it just snapped out of my hand, went up in the air, and was broken up. The coach was looking at me, and I said, "Coach, the ball's flat. I swear."

So the referee looked at the ball, and it had all the air in the world. The trainer started looking at my thumb. I looked over, and my thumb was laying on my wrist. We got a quick turnover, and I went back in. We called a quick out, and I went to throw the ball, and it just slid out. I had no feeling in it. So I was sitting there thinking, *Shit*.

I took myself out. Steve Pelluer came in and took us all the way to a Rose Bowl championship. That spring, I told Coach Dorr that I was outplaying Steve. So I asked him, "Am I going to get my job back?"

That's when he said I wouldn't start again. He said, "Look at it from our perspective. You're a senior with eight games as a backup and two starts. Steve is a junior who won the Rose Bowl. Who are you going to start?"

We went into my senior year ranked No. 1 in the country. We were playing well, just not scoring as much. I played in every game through the first four games. Then we played Cal. Steve ran a quarterback sneak in the second quarter. I could see something was wrong. He ran one more play with a concussion. I got to play, and we ended up beating them 50–7. I just had a day. I was 13-for-17 passing. The commitment I made to my team and myself was paying off, and it was gratifying to my teammates because they knew what I had gone through.

A couple weeks later we went to Stanford, and Elway beat us. In that game, they put me in around the fourth quarter, and we ended up scoring twice. So they ended up making me the starter for the rest of the year.

We needed a victory over WSU for a return trip to the Rose Bowl. On the Wednesday practice before the game, something went wrong. I remember hearing a creaking noise from the tower where Coach James watched practices. We knew he was not supposed to be coming down. So he walked onto the middle of the field and said, "Coaches, get your players off the field." Nobody knew what to do.

"Damnit, get off my practice field!" he yelled. "Coaches, get over here!"

We went into the locker room. The coaches came in and said, "See you tomorrow." I said, "Bullshit. This is our biggest practice of the week."

They said, "T.C., go home."

Apparently, James thought we didn't have good focus as players and the coaches were too relaxed.

We came in on Thursday and had a good practice. But our preparation for that game wasn't how we usually did things.

Everyone remembers Chuck Nelson's field-goal miss. But that didn't cost us the WSU game. I threw a corner route for an obvious touchdown catch, and they called him out of bounds. I ran over to the official and expressed my disagreement, and he took me over to Coach James and said, "Coach James, you better tell Mr. Cowan to keep his opinion of the officiating to himself."

Coach James said, "Well, maybe if you make the right call you won't be hearing about it."

The referee actually came and apologized because he knew he'd made the wrong call.

We also could've won on our last possession. I went to the line of scrimmage and realized the Cougars were going to blitz everyone. A missed block let one guy in free who nailed me. All I had to do was get the ball off, and we could've won.

The pilot of our plane home was a Cougar. We got onboard after the game, and there was a 3 x 5 card that said, "Good Job, Cougs!"

The pilot flew us back over the stadium twice with the scoreboard flashing. It was so demoralizing because we could have had the game.

The next thing I knew we were going to Hawaii to play Maryland in the Aloha Bowl. We had about 30 seniors, and we had a great time off the field.

We beat Maryland with six seconds left to play. It came down to our last play from the 11 yard line. We called time out, and I went to the sideline. Receiver Anthony Allen joined my huddle with the coaches and suggested we run our two-point play. I heard Coach Dorr on the headphones say, "I like it."

Allen set up on the left, dragged across the middle, and then cut back to the corner. I got the ball to him for the game-winning touchdown, 21–20. I ended up getting the MVP of the game. The award had been given to Maryland quarterback Boomer Esiason minutes before by the broadcasters, who then changed their minds.

To have gone through the homesickness, my injury, losing the starting job, and then coming back and recapturing success showed that I made the right decision to not give up. I was honored to be awarded the team's Guy Flaherty Award.

I played four seasons in the Canadian Football League with Toronto. After my football career ended, I returned to the Northwest and moved to Kirkland. I was on my way for a job interview and bumped into a UW alum. I told him I was looking for a job. A couple days later, I was in the insurance business. It's a small Huskies world.

Tim Cowan led Washington to a come-from-behind victory over Maryland in the 1982 Aloha Bowl and was named the game's Most Valuable Player. He completed 33 passes that day to set a school record at the time, which now ranks tied for fifth in a UW game. Teammates voted him the Guy Flaherty Award as the team's most inspirational player in 1982. Cowan played four seasons in the CFL with Toronto. He is currently director of business development for an insurance company.

PAUL SKANSI

RECEIVER

1979–1982

IREALLY DIDN'T THINK ABOUT college football until I was in high school. I grew up in the fishing town of Gig Harbor. I loved sports, but I didn't consider playing at the college level until our Peninsula High football team went to the King Bowl twice, losing the first and then winning the second, going 13–0 my senior year.

I was a Huskies fan, but I wasn't a die-hard fan.

I wasn't the prototype wide receiver. I stood 5′10″ and weighed 170. I ran the 40-yard dash in an unimpressive 4.6 seconds in high school. In fact, I turned out for track as a senior to learn how to run. Steve Levenseller was student-teaching at our school and taught me how to run. Steve played football at the University of Puget Sound (UPS).

Not a lot of schools were after me. I got form letters from Big Sky schools, Washington, WSU, and some other Pac-10 schools. My decision came down to two schools—UPS and UW.

Our quarterback from high school went to UPS, and I liked that it was close to home.

During my trip to Washington, I met team chaplin Mike Rohrbach and learned there was a Fellowship of Christian Athletes huddle group at the UW. That was a factor. I also wanted to compete at the highest level. A lot of consideration and prayer went into it. I'm fortunate I made the right choice.

Paul Skansi (7) didn't have great height or speed, but his great hands and 161 receptions placed him on the UW All-Century Team.

I felt I could fit in, but at first I felt the whole thing was over my head. You don't see the details, you just keep going from day to day, spot to spot. Still, I really enjoyed it. I was planning on redshirting my first year, but things progressed quicker than I thought.

Coming into camp, I was last on the depth chart. We went eight deep in receivers on each side. I worked my way up through training camp. I played as a true freshman.

I moved up as a receiver and first got on the field thanks to special teams. I was the punt returner in the season opener.

We played Wyoming. I remember standing on the 10-yard line and thinking about our 10-yard rule—if you have to move backward, you let it go. My focus was to catch the ball no matter what. I caught it on the 8.

The next punt was the same situation. I was at the 10-yard line. I drifted back and caught it on the 5-yard line and returned it five or six yards. I knew I should have let that one go, so I was upset with my decision. The third kick was another 10-yard situation. This time I thought, *I'm not moving backward. I'm going to make the right decision now.* But I followed the ball and drifted back. I caught it at the 2. I thought, *Now I have to do something.* I tried to get to a wall of blockers. I had one guy to beat, but he nicked my leg for a safety.

All the defensive players were muttering, "We have a dumb freshman…there goes our shutout." We won 28–2.

That could have been a negative turning point for me. I could have dwelled on that and gone the other way. I used it as a learning situation. My faith brought me through. One thing I was able to do in my career was block out the surroundings. I could focus on a punt with players running at me. I could focus on the ball and situations on all areas of field.

I returned punts a few more games, then Mark Lee returned from an ankle injury and won his job back.

Halfway through the year, I got to play as a receiver and caught passes for three-and-a-half years.

I was a consistent catcher and route runner. I had soft, quick hands. It was kind of that way throughout my college and pro career. I played a role. I used those talents instead of straight-line blazing speed, which I didn't have.

That first year we beat Texas in the Sun Bowl 14–7. I had the game-winning catch.

I caught 30 passes and five touchdowns that year, way beyond my expectations for my freshman season.

My next three seasons had many highs with back-to-back Rose Bowls—losing the first to Michigan and then shutting out Iowa in the second—and an exciting one-point Aloha Bowl victory over Maryland.

Our match-ups with the Cougars my junior and senior years were special. In 1981 the winner of the Apple Cup went to the Rose Bowl. One of my most memorable catches came just before halftime. Steve Pelluer threw a ball to the corner and underthrew it a little. The defender slipped on the rainy, windy day. I ended up diving over the top of him to make the touchdown catch. That was a big one. It changed the momentum and propelled us into the second half, when we finished it off.

I was honored to be one of four captains on the 1982 team. That year the Cougars knocked us out of the Rose Bowl. Every time we played the Cougars, I knew it was going to be a tough rivalry game, but I always expected we would win. That game was in Pullman, really cold, with snow flurries. I remember sitting down after the game in their locker room, leaning against the wall, and not believing we'd lost. We had a pretty good consolation reward by going to the first Aloha Bowl.

My ride at Washington was great—four bowls and a four-year team record of 39–9.

I went on to play nine seasons in the NFL. After one season in Pittsburgh, I was blessed to be able return home and play eight seasons with the Seattle Seahawks. I was a mortgage banker for two years, then went back and got my degree in sociology and helped coach at the UW. That winter, Chris Tormey asked me to be his receivers coach at Idaho, where I stayed for five years. From there I went to Nevada for seven months before becoming a scout with the San Diego Chargers. I've been married 21 years to my high school sweetheart, and we have two girls, Taylor and Madison.

To me, being a Husky means tradition, privilege, and realizing it's an honor to play there. You don't appreciate it until after you've left. As a kid, you don't appreciate what you've done until you reflect on it.

275

Paul Skansi is a member of UW's All-Century Team. He earned honorable mention All-America honors and was an All-Conference selection as a senior. Skansi is second only to Reggie Williams in UW history with total career receptions of 161. His 1,992 career receiving yards ranks fourth at the UW. Skansi played nine NFL seasons with the Pittsburgh Steelers (1983) and Seattle Seahawks (1984–1991). He is currently a scout for the San Diego Chargers.

ANTHONY ALLEN

RECEIVER/QUARTERBACK/ KICK RETURNER

1979–1982

BEING A HUSKY MEANS MORE to me now than when I was playing. When you're playing, you don't realize how special it is. Now, 20 years later, I can look back and realize that not everyone gets the opportunities and experiences I had.

And I had some great moments to remember, with four straight bowls at Washington.

I still live in Seattle near Garfield High, were I grew up. I see Huskies friends every day. Those connections bring back football memories daily.

I was born in Mississippi and moved to Seattle when I was nine. I grew up playing basketball. In fact, I didn't play organized football until high school. I wasn't a big Huskies fan until my senior year. That year was Warren Moon's senior year, with lots of excitement about the Rose Bowl win. I had many UW connections. My high school coach, Al Roberts, left Garfield to coach at Washington my junior year. Teammate Bruce Harrell went to play for the Huskies.

At Garfield I played free safety three seasons, and on offense I started at receiver two seasons, while being the backup quarterback until becoming the starting QB as a senior.

The UW and Wyoming recruited me as a quarterback. Oregon and Notre Dame wanted me as a wide receiver.

Anthony Allen is regarded as one of Washington's best all-around athletes, as he played quarterback, receiver, and kick returner.

I decided on Washington to stay close to home and because of their Rose Bowl win.

Halfway into my first practice for the Huskies, two quarterbacks went down with knee injuries, and I was moved to backup quarterback.

I entered the program with a lot of confidence in my natural abilities.

As the third-string quarterback, I think I completed one pass and had a few handoffs in games. I learned the offense well. Coach Roberts, the special-teams coach, got me on the field as a returner. I ranked ninth in the nation for kick returners as a freshman. The year was a good learning experience.

I talked with coaches about how I could get on the field more as a sophomore. We decided I should switch to wide receiver. I definitely didn't want to switch to defense and play cornerback.

The next three seasons I played wide receiver. I caught passes from Tom Flick, Steve Pelluer, and Tim Cowan. Flick was the easiest to catch because of his nice soft touch. Playing quarterback was a big advantage. I always knew where everyone was and how to read the defense.

My biggest game came my sophomore year against Arizona. Tom threw me nine passes, which I caught for 140 yards and one touchdown. Tom was knocked out early in that game but came back and got hot. Arizona played man-to-man, and we got into a groove.

Another memorable game was at Pullman my senior year (seven catches, 147 yards, and two TDs). But we lost, and the Cougars knocked us out of the Rose Bowl. I still think Chuck Nelson made that field goal. I still have the tape, and if you watch it, you see the two officials didn't seem to know if it was good or not at first.

That put us in the 1982 Aloha Bowl against Maryland. The game came down to our last-minute, come-from-behind drive. Down by six with 12 seconds left, we were 11 yards from the end zone. We called a timeout. Quarterback Tim Cowan went to the sideline to talk with the coaching staff. In four years of playing at the UW, I had never walked to the sideline during a timeout. This time I did. I had an idea.

So everyone was trying to decide what play to run. We had this two-point play we put in early in the season. So I said, "What about the two-point play?" Everyone kind of looked at each other and finally agreed, "Let's try it."

When we broke the huddle and I saw the defensive coverage, I knew it would work. Cowan found me in the left corner with a great toss for the game-tying touchdown. Chuck Nelson came in for the game-winning extra point and a 21–20 victory. I finished with eight catches for 152 yards and all three touchdowns.

After the game, I was involved with a lot of interviews and lost track of time. Before I knew it, everyone was gone. The team bus left the stadium without me.

I didn't know what to do. So I finally starting walking along the road back to the hotel, still wearing my game uniform! I hitched a ride with a nice family.

I played with great quarterbacks and talented receivers Paul Skansi and Aaron Williams. Skansi ran precise routes and had soft hands. Aaron was a sprinter on the track team. He could fly. I had good hands and could make a move on someone. We all got along well.

In fact, I see Aaron every day. We worked together for Safeway. We hang out a lot. I've also come full circle with Coach Roberts. We are co–head football coaches at Garfield.

What made me a good returner was vision. I had a knack for running because I never wanted to get hit. I never really took a tough hit in a game. I was knocked out during a spring practice. I went up for a ball, was undercut, and hit the back of my head on the turf.

A memorable return was against Sanford my junior year. I took it straight up the gut for a 71-yard touchdown. My longest was a 99-yard touchdown against Pittsburgh in 1979.

Speaking of returns, I fumbled my first return against UCLA. The Bruins recovered the ball at the 10 and scored a few plays later. I got down on myself. Later in the game, I dropped a pass that would have been a touchdown. We lost big.

Coach James called me into his office on Monday. He asked if I knew what waivers were. I shook my head. He said an NFL team would have put me on waivers after my performance. He said I quit the game and lost my focus mentally. I vowed to work harder and never to lose it mentally again.

After eight seasons in pro football, I moved back to Seattle. I live happily with my wife of 19 years, Renee, and daughters, Danielle and Katherine.

Anthony Allen was one of Washington's most versatile athletes, playing quarterback, receiver, and kick returner. He earned All–Pac-10 honors as a returner in 1981. His 118 career receptions ranks sixth all-time at Washington. His career kick-return yards of 1,373 yards on 60 attempts is third most in UW history. Allen's 99-yard return in 1979 against Pittsburgh is the second-longest at the UW. Allen played eight pro football seasons, five in the NFL (the Atlanta Falcons, Washington Redskins, and San Diego Chargers) and three in the USFL. He won a Super Bowl ring while with the Washington Redskins. He is currently a warehouse supervisor for Safeway.

STEVE PELLUER

QUARTERBACK

1980–1983

A HANDFUL OF GUYS FROM MY SCHOOL, Bellevue's Interlake High, had become Huskies and were successful, so I wanted to follow in their footsteps. But all my family went to Washington State, and I considered the Cougars as well. Being able to talk to those guys already at the UW helped me make my decision. So it didn't sit very well with the Cougars side of my family. But my stepdad went to Washington, and my mom was working for the UW, so that helped.

My first year was fellow Interlake grad Tom Flick's senior year. It was great to learn from a future pro as well as a guy I knew and respected. Tom led us to the Rose Bowl. When we lost to Michigan. It was disappointing because we had such a great team. It was such a different feeling, though, when you are actually playing for the team instead of just being on the team. I think I would have felt different if I had been more involved. For me, it was a lot of fun just being in Pasadena. The weather was great in California, and it was fun being with my buddies during Christmas. The loss was disappointing, but I still had a great time.

My sophomore year I got in a game and won the starting job the rest of the year. Our offense wasn't very prolific from what I remember. They'd hardly let me throw the ball. Our defense would dominate, so we didn't have to score too much.

When we played Cal that year, it was a different story. It felt like, before we even stepped on the field, they were up 21–0. We were so used to our defense dominating, it was a shock to be down so early in a game. The coaches decided to let me pass more, and things started opening up. We tied it 21–21 and eventually won 27–26. It was a great comeback. That was the game that turned our team around. Our offense had to produce, and we did. From then on, it seemed like we started to come together

My sophomore season, the USC and Stanford games were ones I remember the most. USC was just a downpour, with windy, horrible weather conditions. That was a good time. Stanford had Elway, and that was a good game, too. The creation of the wave happened during that game. I remember thinking, "What is going on?" It was like a phenomenon created in front of your eyes. They only did it when we were on defense, so we offensive guys on the sideline were loving it because it would distract their offense.

The WSU game was special that year. The winner of the Apple Cup went to the Rose Bowl. Paul Skansi saved my butt with a fantastic catch just before the half. It was a corner route, one of my favorite throws, and I remember it being wet and the ball dying in the middle of the air. I had a lump in my throat when I saw a defender in front of the ball. Skansi jumped over the defender and got the ball, so I was really happy. That really gave us a momentum boost.

281

The second Rose Bowl I was pretty confident. It was so nice playing on grass in nice weather. Throwing a dry football. The two weeks in California just gave me so much confidence. By game time, I was confident in our defense and my skills to win. We were still underdogs. It didn't matter. We crushed Iowa 28–0. Their offense didn't do anything against us.

I was surprised how well Jacque Robinson played. I hadn't seen him make the moves he made that day. He made people look ridiculous. He was a freshman, so he wasn't too bold in the huddle or anything.

The one thing I do remember was Pat Zakskorn lighting up Iowa's mascot in the end zone. On film it was funny because he made it look like he tripped and blew him up, but he did it on purpose.

Winning the Rose Bowl as a sophomore was heavy stuff for me. I wasn't really a cocky guy, and all this success just kind of fell into my lap. My personality is kind of too nice, too light. If there was someone better than me, I felt they should play. I had to know I was the guy, to be the general. I was

282

Steve Pelluer led the Huskies to a Rose Bowl win, lost his starting quarterback position the next season, and then regained it as a senior.

confident and knew I would play with success. There's always the question of what will happen in sports, and at the D-1 level, there's always someone ready to take your place. Going into my junior year I knew we could play with anyone.

We won our first seven games until we played Stanford. I came out for a play or two because I wasn't playing that well, and backup Tim Cowan got a chance. He made the most of it and did well, although we lost the game. Cowan started the next week against UCLA, and I got in only sporadically the rest of the year.

I think if I would have had my head on and been as confident as I should have been, I don't think Tim would've gotten in to start. I kind of lost confidence and started to doubt myself a little bit.

Tim came in and just played great, so it was hard for me to go from the Rose Bowl quarterback to riding the bench. It was probably good for me, though. Adversity makes you stronger and hungry. I think in life, if you take things for granted, you can lose them. To play quarterback, you have to believe in yourself and believe you have what it takes.

I never slacked off or anything. I think I handled it pretty well. I wanted to support Tim. I wanted him and the team to succeed. I had an awareness that I might not deserve the starting job, but it's tough to accept that. Every mistake you make as a quarterback is magnified. We had won some games, but I wasn't playing at the level I wanted to, so I put more pressure on myself and I think that hurt my play. That position is so mental.

The Cougars knocked us out of the Rose Bowl. I remember freezing in that game. I was the holder on field goals for Chuck Nelson. Everyone talks about that missed field goal. I don't know if the hold contributed to the miss. I kind of trapped the low snap on the ground and bounced it once before getting it on the point. I apologized for the hold afterward, but Chuck said it didn't bother him.

My aunt and uncle were huge Cougars fans, so I'm sure they were happy for them.

Both my junior and senior years, the Cougars knocked us out of the Rose Bowl. If not for WSU, my class could've gone to the Rose Bowl four years in a row. Talk about adding fuel to the family rivalry.

In the 1982 Aloha Bowl Tim did well and we won by one point in a thriller over Maryland. I was happy for him and the team. I got to play a couple of series.

My senior year, Paul Sicuro gave me some pressure at the quarterback position. I had high hopes going into my senior year. I think the coaches were questioning how I would do that year. I played great the first two games, so they were on board for supporting me. Our first loss was at LSU, an intimidating place to play. We played pretty well on offense, but our defense couldn't stop them, and we lost 40–14.

A three-point defeat to UCLA was our only conference loss going into my final Apple Cup.

I didn't play very well against WSU. I threw some picks. It was rainy and weather conditions were bad. It wasn't a fun game to remember. The 17–6 loss sent us back to Hawaii for a second straight Aloha Bowl against Penn State.

Unfortunately, we lost that, too, 13–10. It was tough going out with a loss. It seemed that the team was split because some guys were there to win and some to party, so it was disappointing.

What I cherish the most about being a Husky are the relationships I have. I cherished my relationships with friends on the team as well as a great relationship with quarterbacks coach Ray Dorr. I also cherished the journey—the ups and downs, the hard work. It was great.

I was drafted by Dallas and then went to Kansas City. It was a great experience to play in the NFL eight years. I saw tons of Huskies in the pros. I returned to the Seattle area, and I've been in commercial real estate. No doubt, being a Husky has helped in my business.

284

Steve Pelluer earned honorable mention All-America and first-team All–Pac-10 honors in 1983. That season, his 65 percent pass-completion average and 137 passes without an interception set school records that still stand. His 61-yard touchdown run in 1983 against Oregon is the second-longest by a UW quarterback. Pelluer's 4,917 passing yards ranks seventh in UW history. He was a Pac-10 All-Academic selection in 1981. He played eight years in the NFL with the Dallas Cowboys (1984–1988) and Kansas City Chiefs (1989–1991) and two in the World League. He is currently living in the Seattle area and working at Cannon Commercial in commercial real estate.

JIM MORA JR.
DEFENSIVE BACK/LINEBACKER
1980–1984

Whenever I see a Dawg, there's a connection, especially with the guys who played in the Don James era. We all have a bond.

At Washington we kept each other accountable. It was no-nonsense and there was not a lot of showboating. There was trust. We always thought we were pretty darn tough, and we were. Guys in my era, guys who played for D.J., we played for a special guy at a special time. There's a bond between us to this day.

I had a golf tournament recently, and several of my old Huskies teammates came down. I'm still close to Mark Pattison and Hugh Millen.

When I played, the tunnel between the locker room and field was dark and dingy. Water dripped off the ceiling. We had this chant. We'd wait for visitors to get into the tunnel, then we'd walk up behind them and start our "Say Who?" chant.

So during practice, if you needed a lift, someone would just say, "Say Who?"

Some teams tried to wait us out before going out the tunnel. I remember Arizona tried one year. Coach James just parked it. Folded his arms and waited. He was tough. He was beautiful.

The other thing I remember about the tunnel is seeing Momma T. She was an older lady who was a big fan. She'd bake us cookies. On our way out to Thursday practice, she'd be at the end of the tunnel, giving guys cookies.

If you played well the week before, you'd get a cookie. If you didn't play well, no cookie for you.

I was a big Huskies fan, too, during my junior high and high school days. I still remember when Dad got the call from James while we were on vacation. My dad started coaching at the UW when I was in the seventh grade. I wanted to be a Husky, too. In those days, if you were a football player in the Northwest or California, the place to go was the University of Washington.

I had a front-row preview of what to expect. I hung out with the team as much as possible. When you think about it, football has paid for every meal I've ever had. It's paid for every roof over my head and every stitch of clothing. I was a football junkie. I was a ball boy on the sideline at Huskies home games. I'd wear the white-and-red striped shirts. One game, I was on the visitors' sideline and jumped up and cheered when Toussaint Tyler ripped off a long run against Indiana. Coach Bill Mallory kicked me in the butt hard. I shut up in a hurry.

I was thrilled to be the ball boy in the 1978 Rose Bowl. That team captivated me. I especially liked the hard-nosed play of Kyle Heinrich, son of UW legendary quarterback Don Heinrich.

I played high school football on the east side at Interlake High. The Saints had a pipeline to the UW as Coach Rollie Robbins gave them six starters in the late 1970s and early 1980s. John Edwards, Roger Westlund, Chris O'Connor, and Tom Flick went ahead of me, and 1980 Saints classmate Steve Pelluer went to the UW with me.

I had some offers from smaller schools. But Washington is where I wanted to go. I walked on and got a scholarship the spring of my freshmen year. My dad never coached me, though. He took a job with the Seahawks before I got there.

We had a great run while I was there. At one point in every season, we were ranked No. 1 in the country and went to four bowls, including two Rose Bowls.

I knew what to expect before my first practice. No, I wasn't intimidated. I'd been around good players my whole life. I remember Ronnie Lott in my house when he was in high school. I'd grown up exposed to all different races and socioeconomic backgrounds. Physically, it was difficult. I came in 180 pounds with average speed (4.6 seconds in the 40-yard dash). I had to try really hard every day.

Jim Mora Jr. played on special teams and as a back-up defensive back and outside linebacker.

I started playing right away on special teams. I was on the kickoff team my first game as a freshman. It was wild. Something I'd dreamed about.

Returning to the Rose Bowl as a player also fulfilled a dream. I pulled out my Rose Bowl jerseys just last night, as we are doing some remodeling. It was kind of fun to see them again. I remember going out for the kickoff and standing on the Rose image at midfield as a freshman. I got down in my stance and thought about the 80 million people watching. I thought if I could make the tackle, Keith Jackson would say my name. Playing the Rose Bowl was an experience, but losing is never fun.

Guys like Ray Horton, Bill Stapleton, Derek Harvey, and Vince Newsome took me under their wings. I still talk with Newsome and Horton quite a bit, as they both work in the NFL. I roomed with Steve Pelluer.

We were a tight squad at Washington. Sure, there was competition for jobs. But there was a closeness. I think success can bond you. What came first? Is it success that bonds or is it bonding that brings success? I don't know. When you got there, you felt like something special. You pulled for each other and supported each other. We'd fight, but there was a tight brotherhood.

I played back-up defensive back my first two years. My junior and senior years I was a back-up outside linebacker and special-teams player.

Over the years I played here and there, mostly if someone ahead of me was injured. I had nine tackles my senior year against Michigan. Lineman Stefan Humphries had about 70 pounds on me and kept pulling and getting me all day. All my tackles were downfield. We beat them, though. Pattison caught the winning touchdown. It was a good win.

I still have the tape of my worst game. It was against Stanford during John Elway's senior year. We went down there 7–0 and No. 1 in the nation. We lost. I didn't do a very good job on special teams. I had a late hit on the kickoff. Keith Jackson said, "Ah, that's young Jim Mora. That's not very smart." I remember assistant coach John Pease on the sideline yelling at me. I didn't even want to look at him.

I hurt my knee twice. Dinged it my sophomore year and missed four games. Then I tweaked it in the spring. But that was nothing compared to teammate Jim Rodgers. At one point he had a bad broken arm and his jaw was wired shut. He couldn't feed himself. It was real fun rooming with him and dropping McDonald's hamburgers in the blender for him.

My sophomore year I changed my number to 96. I did it in honor of Kyle Heinrich, who wore the number before being involved in a tragic car accident.

Winning the 1982 Rose Bowl was the highlight of my Huskies career. It was huge beating Iowa 28–0 and seeing Jacque Robinson going crazy.

My dad didn't get to see most of my games, but he was there with my family for the Rose Bowl games, which was special.

As a coach, you take bits and pieces from all the people you've been around. My dad has been my biggest influence. Believe it or not, the only thing Dad has coached me on is attitude—being a good team player and never quitting. We still don't talk about strategy or technique. He'll say, "How much is your team hitting? What did you say to your team today?"

Coach James was a coaching role model. I used to babysit Coach James's daughter, Jenny, so I've seen all sides of him. As a coach, he'd get on you as a player. He coached from the tower. You always felt like his eye was on you. The last thing you wanted to hear was his voice out of the tower. Most definitely you didn't want to see him come down from the tower.

When he came down out of the tower, that was not a good thing during practice. The guy had a persona that was all about toughness. We all bought into it.

289

I remember a speech he gave before the UCLA game. We beat them 10–7. He gave one of the greatest speeches on Thursday. It got everyone jacked up. He basically said, "If you don't want to kick UCLA's ass, then get the f*ck out of here." And he didn't swear very much. He gave another great speech during halftime of a WSU game my sophomore year. The Cougars were a Cinderella team. He said, "I'm sick of Cinderella, let's lift up her dress and kick her ass." The way he said it was galvanizing. I remember a lot of his speeches. Not word for word, but the message.

I think playing for D.J. taught me a lot about being a man. He didn't coddle you. He held you accountable. He demanded discipline.

He knew how long, to the second, it took him to get from his office to our meeting podium. When he walked in the back door, the place would go dead silent. Hats off. Feet on the floor. If the meeting started at 4:00, as soon as the second hand hit 4:00 straight up, he'd start talking. He was amazing. He had a great sense of humor, and he cared about his athletes.

James never wanted us to be intimidated. I remember our trip to LSU. It was hotter than crap. Everyone was sweating. Our hotel was a dump. We heard how LSU fans surrounded the visitors' buses and had "Mike the Tiger" in a cage and yelled "Tiger bait!"

James said, "We're not going to be intimidated by these clowns." So before we dressed for the game, we walked around the stadium. The student section was full and they were drunk. They were screaming "Tiger bait! Tiger bait!" and throwing stuff at us. They beat us bad.

My toughest trip was losing at Pullman. We flew over on two or three Horizon planes, an air caravan. On the way back, I sat next to Chuck Nelson, who missed that field goal. Talk about an emotional wreck. He went from, "It's not my fault" to "I've ruined everything for everyone." That was a tough day.

My only regret during my days at Washington was not taking my academics as seriously as I could have. I got into the jock routine. I tell kids when I speak to them I wished I would have picked a course of study that interested me. I did fine, I had about a 3.0 grade-point average and got a degree in communications. But I was never 100 percent committed to my classes.

After my senior year, I helped the UW coaching staff during the spring and enjoyed it. I knew I wasn't going to play professionally. I got a job with the San Diego Chargers right out of school, working with the coaching staff and front office. I was hired as the secondary coach at 24 and spent seven years with the Chargers. I coached for New Orleans and San Francisco before joining the Falcons.

I got a little disillusioned with the UW program for a while. I think we're on the right track now with Tyrone Willingham. I considered coming back when I got a call about the UW opening. If I ever went back to coaching in college, it would be at the UW. The college team I always want to win is Washington.

Jim Mora Jr., who grew up the son of NFL coach Jim Mora Sr., has spent his career in coaching. After seven years with the San Diego Chargers, and stints with the New Orleans Saints and San Francisco 49ers, he was named the head coach of the Atlanta Falcons in 2004. During his three years there, he led the team to an overall 26–22 record and an NFC Championship Game.

MARK PATTISON

RECEIVER

1980–1984

MY DEFINING MOMENT OF HUSKIES FOOTBALL came while I was a freshman. I really had never had to work for my athletic success. My first year at Washington, I really wasn't working the way I should to compete at a high level. It was a day of reckoning. I had to get it together and get dedicated, or it wasn't going to happen.

I lived in a fraternity, and it wasn't the most conducive environment for what I was trying to do (although I did meet my future wife at a fraternity function). I made a decision. I moved home, recommitted myself to the books, and hit the weight room more.

The move wasn't far. From my parents' View Ridge home window I could see Husky Stadium.

My mother and aunt had been Huskies cheerleaders. My grandfather was a prominent Seattle businessman, and he took me to a lot of games in Husky Stadium. I remember the games were a lot of fun because Sonny Sixkiller was throwing the football like crazy and scoring touchdowns.

Like all the kids in my neighborhood, I started playing football with the 89ers—eight- and nine-year-olds. It came naturally to me. I played football at Roosevelt High. We had an all-state quarterback when I was a sophomore and junior. I received a lot of letters from colleges to be a wide receiver. Future Huskies quarterback Hugh Millen was a year behind me, but he was awkward for his age. He was pretty tall, but his coordination hadn't caught

Mark Pattison, who led the Huskies in receiving in 1983, grew up with a view of
Husky Stadium from his house, and his mother had been a Huskies cheerleader.

up with his body. My senior year, Hugh still wasn't ready. He couldn't get the ball to me. So I played quarterback for the Roughriders.

Oregon, Oregon State, and Hawaii, among others, recruited me as a quarterback. But I wanted to be a Husky and be part of what Don James was building. Washington recruited me as a wide receiver, although at 6'2", 195 pounds, I did play quarterback on the scout team as a freshman. A bunch of injuries left our quarterback depth shallow. So I ran the scout team for a while. Ray Dorr asked me if I wanted to switch to quarterback. But Coach James said no. He wanted me to stay at receiver.

In my five years at the UW, we went to five bowls. The first year it was great to just go to the Rose Bowl. The next year even better with a Rose Bowl win. We missed a third straight Rose Bowl trip when the Cougars beat us, sending us to the Aloha Bowl. The same thing happened a year later. Then we had the "Purple Reign" and played in the Orange Bowl, beating Oklahoma.

In my first chance to play at wide receiver, we had Michigan at home. We came back from 14 points down for a thrilling victory with a seven-yard touchdown pass to me in the final 27 seconds. I scored my first touchdown and the crowd went berserk. It was very cool. Then *Sports Illustrated* came out that week with a picture of me leaping over a defender for a catch.

293

My career-high 114 receiving yards came in a loss at LSU. When we lost to Penn State in the Aloha Bowl, I had a couple of breakers and a bunch of yards.

The best regular-season victory had to be beating Michigan on the road. In that game I had a special 73-yard touchdown catch from Hugh Millen in our 20–11 victory.

I was able to make some big plays with three game-winning touchdowns. When the games were on the line, good fortune came my way. I was prepared well. Don James did a great job of reloading. I spent a few years on special teams, so by the time I was put into a starting role, pressure was not new. There was pressure every day in practice. So it wasn't new in a game. You'd get into a zone and go out and do it. People get all tense in the stands because they're not involved. When you're out there, it's different. I was able to tune in during those tense situations.

One catch I wish I could have made came against USC in 1984. We had a critical third-down play at around the 50-yard line. I dropped a pass I should have caught. We ended up missing a field goal. That had an impact on the game, and by losing it knocked us out of the Rose Bowl and into the Orange Bowl.

The Orange Bowl proved a poetic ending to my Huskies career because of my connection with Hugh Millen.

After high school, Hugh went to Santa Rosa Junior College. He called me up my junior year and said he was thinking about walking on at Washington. He did and lived with our family for a year. As you can imagine, we spent a zillion hours together throwing and catching the football.

Even though we were ranked No. 1 in the country at the time, Hugh lost his starting quarterback job midway through the season. My heart ached with his.

So when Hugh came into the Orange Bowl game off the bench in the fourth quarter with us down 17–14, I was proud to see him back in the huddle. Then he led us on a 74-yard drive that ended in a 12-yard touchdown pass to me to give us the lead for good with five minutes to play. Amazing!

One cool thing about playing at Washington was my grandfather got to see me play from the same seats where he took me to games. I actually lived with him my junior year, and we watched film together. My dad, who went to Oregon State on a track scholarship, would come over, and we'd have fun chalk talks about the games. My dad and I are still talking Huskies-Beavers smack.

I went on to play in the NFL—five seasons with the Oakland Raiders and New Orleans Saints. Upon my return home to play for the Seattle Seahawks, I was cut.

It took about a year-and-a-half to deal with the death of my playing days. My grandfather passed away shortly thereafter. In a way, I'm following his footsteps into the Seattle business world. I've started three businesses here in Seattle—The Pattison Group (imports), Front Porch Classics (coffee table games), and 16 Mile Solutions (buyer/supplier visibility software).

Being a Husky has led to a lot of introductions and contacts around town. There is a great network of UW people. It's still fun to be part of something big.

Mark Pattison led the Huskies in receptions in 1983 with 44 catches for 455 yards. He played five seasons in the NFL with the Oakland Raiders and New Orleans Saints.

JACQUE ROBINSON

RUNNING BACK

1981–1984

PEOPLE REMEMBER ME for my start and my finish.
    I was the first freshman to be named the Most Valuable Player of the Rose Bowl, and in my senior year I was named MVP of the Orange Bowl.

It's a good thing to be able to play in the Rose Bowl, especially as a freshman. We beat Iowa 28–0 in the 1982 Rose Bowl, and I finished with 142 yards on 20 carries and two touchdowns. Not bad, considering I didn't even play until the second quarter. Three years later, we beat Oklahoma in the Orange Bowl. I felt the Orange Bowl victory meant more because we were playing for the national championship.

Ironically, I came to Washington thanks to basketball but played football. My son, Nate, went to Washington thanks to football and eventually switched to basketball.

I was recruited by Marv Harshman to play basketball. I told him my sport was football. So he showed the Huskies football coaches my football tapes. The football recruiters came to look at me at San Jose High School. I felt like getting away from California but wanted to be close enough to home. So I thought by staying in the Pac-10 I could still be close enough to home. The Huskies had made it to the Rose Bowl the year before, so it was kind of a no-brainer. I had a great visit to WSU, but they weren't very good. I came to Washington. It was in the middle of the city, and I liked that because it made me feel more at home. It reminded me of San Francisco.

I definitely felt like I was going to start before I got there. But then I saw the speed of the other running backs, and I was like, *Oh, my God!* I was running a 4.5-second 40-yard dash, and they were running 4.3s. I thought, *These guys are track stars.* I didn't think I was going to play much. Once we got pads on, they started slowing down, and some got scared to get hit. So then I thought, *Oh, I can play with these guys.*

No one really took me under their wing. You get to meet 30 or 40 other freshman when you come here, so they're your friends.

Once I put the pads on, it was on. Scrimmages were great because I could run the ball. I weighed 202 pounds and stood 6'. I played special teams my first year on the punt team. I broke my finger that year and had to play on the scout team for a few weeks. Cookie [Ron] Jackson was ahead of me.

We were playing USC, and I was on the scout team. They gave me No. 32, and I was supposed to be Marcus Allen. They told me to run wherever I wanted to go. I was all over the place and running over the number-one defense. Then the running backs coach said I was going to be practicing with the varsity. I said, "Okay, cool." They told me I might get to play on Saturday, so I went from scout to second-string.

I got to play some at running back against USC in the fourth quarter. Marcus had 155 yards, and I had something like 55 yards and a couple crucial third-down carries. The game was real close. It was kind of scary for me, being a freshman and playing during crunch time. I remember being in the huddle in the fourth quarter and a lineman told me to hold onto the ball and run like I always do. I said, "Why are you putting that negative thought in my head?" So that was kind of funny. Kind of like, "Don't drop the ball." I think I fumbled once.

The day was pretty exciting. We won 13–3.

I played the first half against Washington State. I had two fumbles that game. One was kind of a bad handoff exchange—but when you're a freshman, it's always your fault. But I ran pretty well. They could see I could run the ball. The whole thing was: Could I hold onto it?

During the Rose Bowl warm-ups I didn't know if I would get in or not. We were warming up for the game, and Al Roberts, the running backs coach, came up to me and saw this towel with a Rose on it. A couple friends and I had them. He came over and snatched it.

"Take that off," he said. "Wide receivers wear those, not running backs."

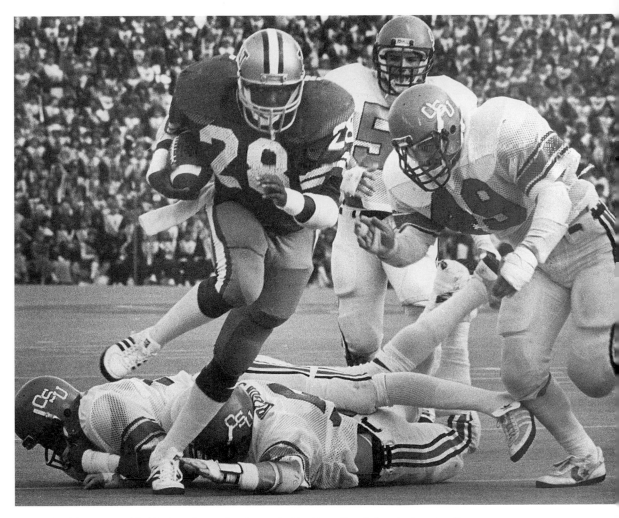

Jacque Robinson got his big break as a freshman in the Rose Bowl thanks to a push from a teammate.

A few drills later, he grabbed my face mask. Roberts screamed, "God damn it, wake up! I see a little freshman in that fat little face. Wake the hell up!"

And I said, "I'm ready to go, Coach. What are you saying?"

I guess he saw me standing there looking around the stadium. It got my butt ready to play.

No, I didn't start the Rose Bowl. Cookie did. A friend of mine on the team, Michael Collins, said I needed to be close to the coach so he'd know I was ready. So I got up close to Coach Roberts. Then Michael kept pushing me from behind so I'd bump into Roberts. The first time I bumped him, Roberts turned around and said, "What?"

"Coach, I'm ready," I said. After a few more pushes from behind and bumps, Coach Robs got pissed off. Finally he said, "Okay, get into the game!"

It was 0–0 when I got in during the second quarter. The first couple carries I got four or five yards. I was feeling comfortable. The holes were there, and it was about getting through them. We drove 65 yards, and I scored on a one-yard dive to put us up 7–0. My best carry of the game was a 34-yard run up the middle and then to the sideline for a touchdown in the fourth quarter. I finished with 142 yards on 20 carries.

After the game was kind of crazy. I got pulled into this press room with 65 reporters from all over the country. They asked all these questions. It was overwhelming. I'd never experienced anything like that, so it was kind of crazy. They told me I was MVP after we were finished in the locker room. I wouldn't say I was shocked cause I thought I had a good chance to get it.

My family was there for the game. Everyone was just so happy and thrilled.

The next year started slow. I wasn't first-string, so I didn't get the opportunity to run the ball as much. I remember the third or fourth game they let me start. Then I started tearing it up. At the end of the season, I led the Pac-10 in rushing. I hurt my foot in the last game. We lost the last game to WSU and had to go to the Aloha Bowl instead of the Rose Bowl.

My junior year I came back out of shape. Coach James was kind of pissed about that. I weighed about 220. The coaches told me to come back under 210. They started running me. During two-a-days, I had to run a mile before each practice to lose weight. First, I had to run the mile in six minutes, 30 seconds, then they wound it up to six minutes. By the time the season started, I was back down to 205. James still didn't start me. Once again, Cookie was ahead of me again that year. A couple injuries hampered me. Against Stanford I had 77 yards in the first drive and scored. I really bruised my foot badly. I thought I'd broken it. I had a good game against Oregon State and rushed for something like 135 yards in the first quarter and scored three touchdowns. Then against 'SC I turned my ankle.

When I was a senior, we made a lot of goals as a team. We said, "Let's go all the way." That was what we were going to do. It was going to be our year.

It was an excellent year. One of the best memories was our great defense. That was it. Our defense kicked everyone's butt. We used to lead the nation in turnovers. Even if our offense sucked, they'd always be giving the ball back to us on offense. It was great.

Our only loss of the year was to USC, 16–7. The coaches had a brain fart. We started passing too much. We were running well. We didn't stick to the game plan, and things fell through. We were running the ball at will, but we got behind and started to panic. It was a bad game.

We got a second chance with our Orange Bowl bid. The Oklahoma game I remember vividly. They ran their mouths so much. We went out on this cruise with them days before the game, and we almost fought on the dance floor. I started and played the whole game. I was on the sideline when the Sooner Schooner went on the field and took away a field goal. We thought it was pretty funny. That was kind of a big swing, though.

I was running effortlessly that day. The best play was probably this trap play. We got 15 yards out of it every time. Fullback Rick Fenney was running well, too. We had a great one-two punch with him and me.

Brian Bosworth played on that team. We talked one time on the sideline. I heard him tell some guys to wrap me up. So I said, "Why don't you wrap me up?"

We talked after the game about how they'd never missed so many tackles before that game. They hadn't allowed more than 100 yards rushing all year, and we went out there and got around 250 or something.

We felt like national champions after winning the Orange Bowl 28–17. We really knew that we were. I wish we'd had the BCS back then so we could have proved it on the field.

Yes, 1984 was a good year. My first child was born. We named him Nate.

Watching Nate play on the same field I did was great, too. He got to go to a bowl game, and it was just awesome to witness that. Ironically, he really wanted to play basketball at USC. The UW coaches were calling me all the time about him. He went to Washington to play football and basketball. He was good at football, so he liked to play it. He had good year in basketball, too, and so the time came where he had to decide to focus on one or the other. Nate really wanted to be a running back. If the coaches had given him a chance to run the ball, he might have stayed with football. I told him, "You've got to choose which one you want to become a professional in. So he decided to play basketball."

After Washington, I didn't play much at all. I played with the Philadelphia Eagles a few games. But that was it. For most of my adult life, I've been a working with kids as a counselor. My focus has been to work with inner-city kids and kids from abused homes. It's been very rewarding.

For me, the games were probably the most memorable thing about being a Husky. When it was the fourth quarter, it was Dawg time. Toughness is what it means to be a Husky. We were the toughest guys on the field. We had heart and confidence. Everyone on the team was tough and fearless. We all had pride.

Jacque Robinson is the only player to be named the MVP of both the Rose Bowl and Orange Bowl. He earned honorable mention All-America honors and was an All-Conference selection in 1982. Robinson's 238 carries in 1982 is the fifth-most for a Huskies ball carrier in a season, and his 2,636 career yards also ranks fifth. His 14 rushing touchdowns in 1984 is third-most in team history, and his 27 career touchdowns ranks sixth. He is currently a social worker in California.

TIM MEAMBER

LINEBACKER

1981–1984

MY DAD CAME HOME HIGHLY INTOXICATED and told me to figure out what I wanted to do. If I wanted to be a lawyer, go to the library. If I wanted to be a ditch digger, start digging. If I wanted to pursue sports, choose one and work at it.

So my goal was to be a college football player. It was my dream. I worked out with Steve DeClerk three years in high school every day. The first day, I was the only guy who couldn't lift the bar off my chest. Three years after that, I had a scholarship. I accomplished my dream. Nobody in sports history had a better experience than I did at the UW. It was a four-year dream.

I came from Yreka, a little town in the hills in California. Earl Nordtvedt, who found Sonny Sixkiller and alerted UW coaches, found me and convinced UW coaches to recruit me. Coach Jim Lambright came down, and he really fit in with my high school coaches.

When I arrived, I wanted to redshirt. I was a little undersized for a linebacker at 6′3″, 198 pounds (I eventually played at 227). After summer practices, I went into Coach Lambright and said I wanted to redshirt. Lambright and I were on the same level—hard work, no shortcuts. That mentality paid off. Lambright decided he couldn't afford to redshirt me. Two games later, I was starting on special teams and earned a letter. I even got to play in our Rose Bowl win over Iowa.

All-American inside linebacker Tim Meamber played with heart and passion, collecting four bowl rings, two of which were buried with his grandfather and father.

302

My sophomore and junior years, everyone was disappointed as we were knocked out of the Rose Bowl by the Cougars and went to back-to-back Aloha Bowls.

I almost didn't play in one of them. I rented a Jeep to go body-surfing with some players. I left the keys in it, and it got stolen. I called Coach James;

he said get the best attorney I could. The day of the game, they were about to throw me in jail. The president of the Aloha Bowl paid the deductible so I could play in the game.

When I was voted team captain my senior year, I remember saying we wanted a national championship. Goal-setting was part of Coach James's philosophy. The coaches bought into it, and in the opening game I had three interceptions. We had to go to Ann Arbor, and we kicked their butts. At that point, we had buy-in from everyone, and it started to become special.

We didn't really have an offense. We would go three-and-out on defense and get standing ovations. We were keeping teams in negative rushing. We set the record for turnovers. We'd stuff teams. We'd go through the whole lineup and it was a solid defense. It was fun because we loved each other. The defense didn't change at all. We ran a basic 3-4 defense. We just reacted because we had tremendous linebackers. We didn't have a weakness. Offenses were intimidated. We could just look into their eyes, and they knew it was over. Lambright taught us enthusiasm. We'd get on a role and no one could do anything.

We rolled off nine straight wins in 1984 before we lost to USC 16–7.

I remember being interviewed after the USC game, and I was crying. I couldn't do it. It was devastating. We struggled against WSU and we went to the Orange Bowl. James worked us so hard for that game. There was no way they were going to beat us. I remember I had a severe strain in my groin muscle in warm-ups. That was the only time that's ever happened. But I played through it. Our 28–17 win over Oklahoma gave us an 11–1 record. We felt we were the best team in the country.

When BYU was crowned national champions, I was in the lobby in Miami. I was so pissed. We would have destroyed BYU. I get upset over that to this day. We were the first national champions at the UW. One of my goals is to make enough money to buy everyone on that team a national championship ring.

I played in the Senior Bowl with a herniated disc. Minnesota drafted me in the third round. Some were going to pick me in the first round, but after my disc problem, some scouts convinced me to run a 40 and I ran a 4.9, when I really was running a 4.6 during the season. That's why I dropped to the third round. I kick myself in the butt to this day. The 40-yard dash cost me a lot of money.

I played for the Vikings for a year-and-a-half and then the Rams for a year. Then injuries just took over. I returned to the UW in 1991 to be a student coach. That's when I realized my greatest honor as a Husky.

When I was a freshman, every Thursday Coach James would talk about someone who overcame tremendous odds against them. I remember thinking to myself I want to be the person he's talking about. When I came back, I had several players tell me Coach James talked about me in those meetings. He said I gave 100 percent every play. That's the proudest moment of my Huskies career—the best accomplishment.

I had two meaningful conversations with Coach James. We won the first two games my senior year, and the coaches were just riding our asses. I went into his office and told him we wanted the wins just as much as he did. I asked him to stop riding us. He said that they just wanted to make sure.

The other time, I was in the locker room and someone told me that Coach James wanted to see me in his office, now! And I was scared. I saw him, and he said, "I'll talk to you after practice" in an all-pissed-off tone. The whole practice I was trying to figure out what I'd done. Turns out, a Huskies player had been down at a Seattle bar talking trash about someone's wife. The player said it was his birthday. It got back to James, and he checked the birth dates of everyone on the roster. He saw that that day was my birthday and assumed it was me (it was really a walk-on). It got straightened out, but it was an ugly two hours of waiting.

When James resigned, I was sick. He would never violate a rule because he had the most integrity I've ever seen. I think he was so hurt that those sanctions were placed on the program, he couldn't come back.

I think a lot of guys in our class got screwed up. We reached such a high and then we didn't immediately pick it up because we were like, "Now what?"

The great thing is our class is still really tight. We reach out to each other. We've had guys fly into cities and find people who were down and out. We've had guys find teammates in bad areas and pull them out. A lot of tears have been shed and everything. Stuff you can't get anywhere else, and it crosses every barrier. When I went through some rough times, guys picked me up. We remind each other we were successful on the field and we can be successful in life. Our class is all on the upswing now. We're all finally grown up.

I've started my own company making half-popped popcorn, what we call "Half Pops." I spent almost 18 years refining the process, and it's marketed under the name Meamber Snacks Inc. In 2007 we project $2 million in sales. And my high school buddy, who worked out with me, he used to live in a shanty. Now he owns several businesses and is doing well. I have one daughter who is truly a blessing and a gift from God, and will be to the day I die.

When my grandfather and father died, I put one of my four bowl rings on each of their fingers when we buried them. There is nothing like Huskies football. It was about the journey

What does it mean to be a Husky to me? Love and passion. Love the game and the university and the players and you will get the passion to never be beaten.

Tim Meamber earned All-America and All–Pac-10 honors in 1984 as an inside linebacker and ended his Huskies career ranked eighth in tackles by a linebacker with 376. He was selected to play in the Senior Bowl. Meamber's three interceptions against Northwestern in 1984 tied him with eight other Huskies for second-most in a game. He played in the NFL with the Minnesota Vikings in 1985. He is currently founder and CEO of Meamber Snacks Inc. in Yreka, California.

HUGH MILLEN

QUARTERBACK
1983–1985

YOU CAN TELL WHERE YOU ARE IN the team's food chain by the equipment you get. The scholarship players got brand new shoes with their names on them. My shoes had six numbers crossed out. Written on athletic tape on the arch of the shoes was the nameless "F41." That was my locker number, too.

I was an invited walk-on in 1983. I arrived on camps via the long route. I played two seasons at California's Santa Rosa Junior College after playing at Roosevelt High, just a few miles north of the UW.

Even though to some I may have looked good on paper—6'3" and led the Metro League in passing—I wasn't highly recruited because, in part, I was only 16 during my senior year in high school. I wasn't a blip on the UW coaches' radar. I was young and a late bloomer. There just wasn't much indication that I could ever play in the Pac-10.

I went to Santa Rosa because my high school coach knew the Santa Rosa head coach. I was recommended to go down there and play two years and then decide if I could keep playing. I didn't know if I was going to play beyond those two years. It was a great decision because it allowed me to play a couple years and increase my ability. I didn't start as a freshman and had to work my way into the lineup. A lot of quarterbacks are well suited to play junior-college ball. If a guy can play at a four-year school and can play as a freshman and sophomore, more power to him. But if a guy isn't going to play until his fourth or fifth year, it'd be better to play for a junior college.

Hugh Millen came off the bench to lead Washington to an Orange Bowl victory and into history as one of the Huskies' most celebrated walk-on stories.

Coming out of Santa Rosa, I was recruited by San Diego State. It seemed like a good place to go. At the end, they signed a guy named Jim Plum, and he was ranked as highly as Chris Chandler. I looked at the situation and realized it was going to be just as hard to beat out Jim as Chris. I thought if I was good enough to beat out a player of their caliber, then I wanted it to be in the Pac-10 as a Husky.

If they hadn't signed Plum, I probably would have gone there. The more I looked at the Huskies, the more I got excited about playing for a big-tradition school. The Pac-10 was like the NFL to me.

I joined in the spring of 1983, and I redshirted that first year. There was no doubt in my mind I was going to redshirt.

When you're a walk-on, you don't even get to dress, shower, or eat with the varsity. I was fortunate because a good friend and Roosevelt teammate, Mark Pattison, was an established player on the team. He took me under his wing, and I was able to get a great head start on being accepted by teammates.

I was the scout team quarterback. It was a great learning opportunity since I got to play against the starters. When I was playing during those scrimmages, there were no red jerseys, meaning quarterbacks would be hit. One of the biggest hits I took in college was from Fred Small in the spring game. I never saw him coming, and the impact sent us both parallel to the ground. The varsity starters broke my nose twice on scout team and knocked me around. I got the most inspirational non-letterman award. It was a good year for my development.

There was a guy who was a back-up cornerback, and when I was on the scout team he would say every week: "The pros are going to love your arm." I was just wondering if I was going to play. Every week somehow this guy gave me a lot of confidence. I was totally unprepared in the spring of 1983 to play against anyone, but by 1984 I was ready to play because of good coaching.

The next year, every time I came up to the center, I wasn't intimidated by other teams because I'd been playing against our best players my redshirt year. So when I was going against Pac-10 teams, I had a lot of confidence because I had Jacque Robinson and other weapons on the offense.

The thing about Coach James, which I will always respect, was that he was established enough that he'd let the competition be fair. He opened the competition up to whoever could compete, scholarship or not. I went into the spring of 1984 as the third-string quarterback, and after that first scrimmage they put me at number one. Most coaches would give in to politics. Not James. If you got the job done, you could earn a spot. If you were an underclassman, you would have to be better than the upperclassmen at your position. He was not hindered or reluctant to play a young player. You always knew where you stood. There was never politics.

I started the first game in 1984, and it felt odd. In practice you always have the coaches and an army of offensive players behind you. I remember the first quarter in that game and being out there in the huddle. I felt like I was alone out there in the middle of Husky Stadium without anyone standing behind me. That was the first time I played in front of 50,000 people. I didn't have that great of a game, but I didn't play really badly, either. It was enough to get through. We beat Northwestern 26–0.

The next game at Michigan was a great thrill. I lived in Ann Arbor before our family moved to Seattle when I was two. So I was a big Michigan fan growing up because my dad was a Michigan alum and football fan. It wasn't until the Rose Bowl and Warren Moon that I started liking the Huskies.

So because of my Michigan connection, I was determined to enjoy this. I had wanted to do something like this all my life. I was going to compete my tail off and have fun. I didn't have any fear of failure. I had a really good mindset to compete. I was very eager to play.

309

That was the first time I'd ever traveled with the team. I threw one pass to Mark Pattison in the third quarter for 70-some yards. It was kind of surreal being part of a crowd-quieting play. I got hit as I threw the ball, so I never really saw what happened.

My dad was stationed in Germany at the time. The game was on the Armed Services TV network, so he got to see it. The summer before, I went to Europe to see Dad. While there, I bought these wildly ugly pants. So when I packed to go to Michigan, I packed some khakis if we lost and had these wild striped pants to wear if we won. I remember standing at the door when I was about to leave. I left the khakis on the couch. I knew we were going to win and didn't want to even make a contingency to lose that game.

I lost the starting job against Arizona, even though we won the game. I got benched at halftime. The morning we played Arizona we were 7–0 and ranked No. 1. We had scored more points than anyone. I was second in quarterback rating for the conference. But I threw three picks in the first half and had two fumbles. So I can't be critical of the decision to bench me.

The only thing I ever said was during stretching in the first practice after that game. I was in the stretching position behind new starter Paul Sicuro. Assistant coach Gary Pinkel asked me, "How're you doing?"

I said, "I'm gonna get that motherf*cker, that's how I'm doing." On that Tuesday I was confident to show my abilities, and there was no way in hell that was going to be my last play.

I just wish they gave me another chance after that week. I played better on the road, and I think I could have won that game at USC, our only loss of the season. The game was out of hand by the time I got in, so I wish I could've started that game.

I didn't start against Washington State, either. The loss to USC put us in the Orange Bowl against Oklahoma.

Coach James had a way of giving the team so much confidence. We did these elaborate option drills down in Florida and ran these drills so much. All the starters were doing option drills. The defense did so many option drills, we had it down. We were always in position defensively because of his coaching, and that gave us so much confidence. We knew he would prepare us for the game we had to win. When you looked him in the eyes, and you saw how he looked at the team, you knew he was confident. He never thought we were underdogs.

310

I remember being on the bus going to the game from the hotel, and I could tell there was a darn good chance I was going to play that night. Coaches kept telling me to be ready, so I had that feeling.

In the fourth quarter, the momentum was slipping away, so they put me in. I was nervous. On my first play, we had a screen called. If the screen is covered, you are supposed to throw it over the receiver's head. So I did that, and our center happened to be there, and he caught it. We got an ineligible receiver call. We went three and out. It was horrible.

I walked down the sideline and told myself to forget about all the pressures. I said a little prayer. I was going to concentrate on the players on the field, and everything else didn't matter. I don't think I ever had that type of transformation in one series. I was calm as could be, and my vision opened up and so did my judgment. I was ready to play then. That was the one thing I'll always remember.

With 5:42 to play, I hit Pattison on a 12-yard pass in the corner to put us up 21–17. I don't know how to put it into words, really. If you watch someone who's played for a couple of years and has got to the point they've been waiting for in life, and they are successful, it's a great feeling.

We had a phenomenal defense that year. On other teams, quarterbacks constantly have to make plays. That year I only had to make one or two good plays a game, and the rest would be fine.

My final season, 1985, was anticlimactic by comparison. We lost our first two games, won four, then allowed Oregon State their first victory in Husky Stadium in many years, 21–20. That was on me. It's a part of playing the position. The quarterback is the most vulnerable position, and I was the guy, and I lost. No excuses, no complaints; I just didn't get the job done. I hurt my shoulder two weeks later at Arizona State in defeat, my final game as a Husky. My injury made way for Chris Chandler's rise and a Freedom Bowl win over Colorado.

The whole Washington experience, for me, was about Don James and the respect I had for him. There's nobody on this earth I respect more than him. Just being able to play for him, and to see the class he exuded, was enough. He was always the Alpha Dawg. He was always in control with the players, the media, and the officials. He had that George Patton look to him. My Washington memories and experiences are tied to what he did for me and Washington football.

311

Hugh Millen is the only UW quarterback to make the top-15 passing yardage list with fewer than 25 games played. Millen was an Academic All-American in 1985 and is permanently honored in the College Football Hall of Fame as a National Football Foundation Scholar Athlete. During an 11-year NFL career, Millen was the MVP of the 1991 New England Patriots and earned a Super Bowl ring with the 1993 Dallas Cowboys. He is currently a TV and radio football analyst.

ANDRE RILEY

RECEIVER/PUNT RETURNER

1986–1989

MY BEST GAME AS A RECEIVER was against Arizona State in 1989. I had seven catches for 223 yards and two touchdowns. I owned my defender mentally thanks to the first play.

I lined up and told the defensive back covering me that I was going deep on the first play.

He must have thought I was kidding. Our first play was a 76-yard touchdown pass to me.

I talked a lot on the field. I used the mental side to take people out of the game. I had that Sun Devils defender all messed up mentally. He didn't know what I was doing.

Whenever I was on the field, I felt I could go all the way. Whenever I went out for a pass, I didn't think about getting hit. The only thing on my mind was scoring a touchdown—just get me the ball, and I'm going the distance.

When I first arrived at the UW I dreamed of 1,000-yard seasons. I achieved that goal, but not the way I originally planned. I came to the UW as a running back, but I ended up being the first Washington receiver to surpass 1,000 yards in a season.

I redshirted my freshman year and gained some weight for my 5′10″ frame, getting up to 186 pounds. My first couple of years I was really homesick. It

Andre Riley had the hands and moves to become Washington's first 1,000-yard receiver and a leading punt returner.

was tough. I called home to California every day, two or three times a day. I talked to my mom and brothers and friends.

I first got onto the field as a kick and punt returner. I think returning the ball is the hardest job on field because everyone has a running start at you. I felt on any given punt we could return it all the way. I scored a few touchdowns and led the country in returns for a while.

Returning punts affected my smile. Against Stanford, I returned a punt and was tackled and took a forearm under my face mask. I had to put braces back on for another year.

My mom made my teammates smile whenever we played games in California. My family went to every game in California. They all piled into a car. Mom always gave me two big bags of food for the flight back. Everyone knew we'd eat well on the way home thanks to my mom. Everyone acknowledged her, and they knew where the food was coming from.

I was moved to wide receiver at the end of my sophomore year to get more playing time, and for the success of the program. I got the MVP of my first game at receiver. In the second game, I tore my ACL in my knee. I worked very hard on my rehab.

In that game, I was returning a punt and had one person to beat, the punter. I planted on my right foot to go to my left and then was shocked that I fell down because nobody touched me. I think everyone in the Husky Stadium heard the pop. It was my ACL, and that ended my junior year.

I never questioned I'd be back for my senior year. I had the determination and desire to be the best. You always hope for the best and hope you don't get injured. So when it happened, I couldn't focus on *Why me?* I had to focus on getting better and putting in the time to get it better. When you have the mentality to stay focused, you'll come back pretty strong.

My senior year I didn't return punts or kickoffs. I went into my last year with the thought of leading by example. We all thought we could go all the way. I don't think I dropped a ball until the sixth game, and I dropped only two or three balls the whole year.

We were so balanced in 1989 with quarterback Cary Conklin and running back Greg Lewis. Cary Conklin had a lot of targets, including great tight ends. I went over the 1,000-yard receiving mark with a catch on a rainy day at Oregon State. It was a huge accomplishment for the UW and myself.

Each game was exciting in our 8–4 season. If we could have beaten 'SC, we would have gone to the Rose Bowl. Still, I was honored to be one of four captains for our Freedom Bowl win over Florida.

I had lofty goals when I started my UW career. My goal was to help the Huskies win any way I could—as a returner, running back, or receiver. Another goal was to win the Heisman Trophy. Well, I didn't get the national award, but I was voted our team's most inspirational player of the season, which meant a lot to me

I played in the Hula Bowl for seniors and was drafted by Cincinnati. I played a few games before being released and then went to the World League, winning the league title with the London Monarchs. I finished up the preseason with Kansas City. I returned to Seattle to use my degree in human resource management. I've enjoyed reconnection with the Huskies program by serving as a Tyee board member.

To me, Huskies football means great players. Don James's teams were about toughness all the way around—offense, defense, and special teams. We had an aura. Teams knew they were going to be beaten up.

315

Andre Riley became the first receiver in UW history to gain more than 1,000 receiving yards in 1989, and his 1,071 yards ranks fifth all-time at Washington. His career average of 18.8 yards per catch ranks third. Riley's 223 yards receiving in 1989 versus ASU is second-most by a UW receiver in a game. His 460 punt-return yards in 1986 is second-most for a season. He was voted the UW's Player of the Year as a senior. He is currently the general sales manager for Seattle's KBSG radio station.

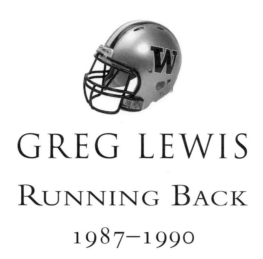

GREG LEWIS

RUNNING BACK

1987–1990

WATCHING HUSKIES FOOTBALL GAMES on TV is what made me a Huskies fan. Family is what made me a Husky. I remember watching Warren Moon throw that touchdown pass to Spider Gaines in the Rose Bowl.

I remember seeing Seattle guys like Anthony Allen and Jacque Robinson being special players. I remember them beating Oklahoma in the Orange Bowl. I drove by Husky Stadium but never had the opportunity to go inside until I was recruited.

During my junior and senior years in high school at Ingraham High, I watched Huskies games from the pressbox. Jim Lambright recruited me, and I liked his toughness. It was the style I thought college football should be all about. His pitch: Washington played hard-nosed football and ran a lot. If I worked hard, I'd get the chance to play. The workman-like attitude, the whole toughness factor, made me want to be a Husky.

It came down to Washington and Stanford. I actually committed to Stanford at first. My mother wanted me to go there. I came out of high school with really good grades and a high SAT score. Brad Muster was graduating, and John Elway's father was the coach. He told me I could possibly come in and take that spot.

My overriding reason to go to Washington came down to the fact that I wanted to stay close to home so my mom could watch me play. Mom had never missed a game since I was eight. During those days, alumni and boosters were allowed to make contact with recruits. They called me and gave me assurances that if I stayed here, and did the right things, then I'd always have opportunities career-wise after football.

"We'll make sure you are part of the family forever," they said. I was able to sway mom's mind and get her blessing to be a Husky. The day before the signing deadline, I told Stanford I changed my mind. They flew up, but I was solid.

The first practice, I realized I'd come to the UW at the right time. Lack of depth gave me early chances to prove myself. I started the day as the number nine tailback and finished the day at number two, behind Vince Weathersby.

Our first game, wouldn't you know it, was against Stanford. I got in a few plays at the end. It was an awesome experience. It was the first game after the northside expansion. The crowd was unbelievable.

My first carry came in the second game, against Purdue, I ran for 35 yards. I could have scored a 70-yard touchdown, but I tripped and fell without anyone touching me. The next day there was a big article in the paper with a picture of me running and a headline: The Future of Husky Football. That was exciting. I was thinking, "I can do this college thing."

Maybe I was a little cocky. Halfway through my freshman year, I started my first game, against UCLA. Led by Troy Aikman and Gaston Green, the Bruins were ranked second or third in the country. The Rose Bowl was filled, and ABC made it their national game. I'll never forget it, but not for good reasons.

I told everyone I wasn't nervous or scared to start. The first play of the game, I fumbled! When I jogged off the field, Coach Don James (D.J., as we called him) came up to me and firmly said, "That's why I don't play freshman."

Next play, UCLA ran for a 35-yard touchdown, and the rout was on. I put my tail between my legs and sat on the bench. I didn't touch the field for two weeks. Nice start.

I had more good days than bad. That year we played in the Independence Bowl against Tulane. I was the leading rusher, so I went into my sophomore season with high expectations.

Overall, the Huskies were 3–0 in bowls while I was a Husky. My sophomore season, however, we didn't attend a bowl for the first time in 12 years. Part of the reason was my fault. At the end of the 1988 season, the winner of the Apple Cup got a ticket to the Aloha Bowl. I was on special teams,

317

GREG LEWIS
Tailback
University of Washington

Greg Lewis, Washington's third all-time leading rusher, rehabbed an injured knee
in time to rush for 128 yards in the 1991 Rose Bowl, despite a torn ACL.

including the punt team. My job was to block the guy farthest outside. On
previous punts, I had helped my teammate next to me because he was a late
replacement. The Cougars noticed it from the pressbox and, in a crucial punt
situation, took advantage. A Cougar grabbed my arm and pulled me inside,

allowing the outside rusher in to block the punt. WSU recovered it at the 2-yard line and scored the winning points.

We finished 6–5. Then things changed. Enter Keith Gilbertson. The offense went from "three yards and a cloud of dust" to opening it up with the spread offense, which really enhanced my career. Being the I–back, rather than being the split back, we went through a transformation trying to figure out who we were. We finished 8–4 and ended on a high note by beating a really good Florida team (9–2) in the Freedom Bowl. Our defense held Emmitt Smith to only 17 yards. Most of my relatives are from Florida. To go into that Gators venue, and having nobody give us a thought, it was a great surprise. But nothing compared to surpassing expectations my senior year.

Our incoming quarterback was sophomore Mark Brunell, so nobody was expecting us to do anything. We didn't have any All-Americans returning. People expected a 7–4 season. Then we came out and set every scoring record the school had ever seen, averaging 50 points a game during one stretch. Players emerged. Mario Bailey suddenly became an All–Pac-10 guy. Donald Jones, who jumped from offense to defense, all of a sudden became an All–Pac-10 guy. Steve Emtman goes from a sophomore to an All-American. And our offensive line had a great season. Nobody believed we'd be that good, other than us.

Going into that season, we made a commitment among ourselves that we weren't going to settle for anything but the Rose Bowl. Our motto was "NBR"—nothing but roses. We believed we'd be that good. So it was great showing everybody what we already knew. Our only losses in 1990 were at Colorado and UCLA at home.

That 25–22 loss to the Bruins changed my life. I hurt my knee that game. I jumped over a guy, and my foot stuck in that old turf, and it tore up my knee. There was no contact on the play. That old turf was not meant for playing football on. So many guys have torn their knees up on non-contact plays. If I didn't go down, maybe we would have been back-to-back national champions. I was never the same player after that, in my mind. It caused me to be drafted lower and ultimately ended my NFL career early. That's the darkest moment of my football career.

I tore my ACL on that play. I had the option of reconstructive surgery, but I would've missed the Rose Bowl and the draft. In those days, guys with torn

ACLs didn't get drafted. I chose to rehab the knee and give it a shot. My rehab was to strengthen quad and hamstring muscles so they would hold the knee together. I rehabbed it good enough to play in the Rose Bowl.

I was supposed to wear a knee brace, but I didn't like it. When nobody was paying attention, I took it off. I had a great Rose Bowl game and ran for 128 yards, even though I didn't play more than three quarters. In fact, that whole year the starters rarely played in the fourth quarter. Whatever records we set, they could've been even more if we weren't beating teams so badly.

Having the opportunity to be a captain and major player, and winning the game by destroying that Iowa team in the Rose Bowl, was awesome. It is still the best experience in football ever, from pro to little league. My closest friends are still guys from that team—Donald Jones, Charles Mincy, and Eugene Harris. I still consider Donald my best friend in the world. The fondest memories are the players. The guys you formed relationships with. The guys you bonded with. The guys you went to war with.

I owe a lot to Jones. He helped me get through practices. I hated practice. I was a great practice player, but I hated it. I worked my butt off and ran as hard as I could. Still, every day before practice, I dreaded it. I was frustrated my sophomore year being behind Weathersby. I wasn't playing as much as I thought I should be playing. I thought about quitting every day. And every day Donald Jones would talk me into going to football practice. He told me to get back out there, to keep working, to keep doing it. "You'll get your opportunity," he said. "This will just make you mentally tougher."

You could tell by the way he conducted business that Coach James was mentally tough. I respected Coach James tremendously, and he taught me a lot. There were times when he and I had the chance to talk. I learned a lot just by observing him and seeing what type of person he was. He was businesslike. He was disciplined and dedicated to his craft. He expected excellence. His system pushed you to work as hard as you could to be the best that you could. I wish everyone, including my kids, could be around somebody like that.

I was called into Coach James's office twice. My wife was having a baby. It was the first day of two-a-days my senior year. I got a call before practice from D.J. He told me I could go to the hospital after practice. He told me to take all the time I needed, stay as long as I needed to, and not to worry about the 11:00 P.M. curfew.

Fortunately, my daughter was born about 11:30 at night. I stayed at the hospital until about 3:00 in the morning. I reluctantly went back to the Crew House and went to sleep. Wake-up was 7:00 A.M., and they had this siren that they played. I was so tired and worn out, I didn't hear it and slept through morning workouts. In the afternoon, I went to the locker room to get dressed and discovered my lock was replaced with a red lock. If you were in trouble, real trouble, you had a red lock on your locker. And Coach James was the only one who could take it off. So I went to my position coach, and he said, "You have to see the coach."

I went to see Coach James, and he started talking to me about responsibility and commitment to the team. He looked at me like, "What's your answer?" I thought for a minute, because I knew this was an important answer, and said, "Well, Coach, there are some things more important than football." He sat back and said, "You're right. Now go to practice."

Being around those coaches and players, and representing the University of Washington is what made the experience special. I graduated in political science. I had some great professors. Ancient political theory was a really fun class. I had a lot of classes that really made me think. I was exposed to things I would have never known. I worked hard at being a student-athlete. Some guys came just to play football. I took it seriously. I had a mom who would not allow me to not take it seriously.

To me, football was not as difficult as other college sports. We traveled on Friday and were back by Saturday night. We didn't miss a whole lot of classes. If you prioritize your time right, you can get it done.

During my time, it was special to have the most 100-yard games, more touchdowns, and more everything than running backs before me. I'm not going to say I was the greatest running back in the school's history—that's Hugh McElhenny, as far as I'm concerned. I set a lot of records, but almost all of them have been broken, between Napoleon Kaufman and Corey Dillon. I may have one or two records left, that's about it. Those records are made to be broken. I appreciate that those guys had a lot of success, too.

Nowadays, people ask if I'm Greg Lewis, and I know they must be at least 35 years old. It does feel good when people remember me. More people recognize me because I worked on TV doing Huskies postgame shows with Bruce King. I was in the finance business for some time after my brief NFL career with Denver. I sold mortgages.

Being a Husky helped me start business conversations with a lot of people. I'd call and say, "This is Greg Lewis." Then they'd say, "*The* Greg Lewis?" And we'd talk football for a while. I think it helped me be successful. I sold a lot of mortgages.

Now, I'm back working for the Huskies as the executive director of the Big W Club, which is for all former UW athletes. You'll see me on the sideline at football games introducing the Husky Legend at the start of the fourth quarter. What the boosters told me is true: once a Husky, always a Husky. To me, one word describes what it means to be a Husky—family.

Greg Lewis holds the Huskies record for most consecutive 100-yard games with 10. His 15 career 100-yard games ranks second. Lewis is also second in most yards in season with 1,407. His career 2,903 rushing yards ranks third among UW runners. Lewis was named the first-ever winner of the Doak Walker Award. The Denver Broncos made him a fifth-round pick in the 1991 NFL draft, and Lewis played in the Mile High City for two seasons before retiring in 1992.

The

NINETIES

DONALD JONES

LINEBACKER

1987–1991

THE FUNNIEST THING THAT I CAN REMEMBER about playing in two Rose Bowls was my experience with Keith Jackson, the national TV announcer.

During my junior year, I had two sacks against Iowa in the 1991 Rose Bowl. On my second, Jackson said, "That's Donald Jones from Gladys, Virginia. I've been to many places in the United States, but I never heard of Gladys, Virginia."

Of course, I heard all about that comment from family and friends after the game.

A year later, I was a captain, so I got to meet Jackson before the game. I told him I was from Gladys, and he remembered me.

My five sacks in two Rose Bowls would have to be my personal highlight of my career next to our team going undefeated. I played my best in our biggest games. I finished with the second-most sacks in Huskies' history with 26. Not bad, considering I began as a fullback my freshman and sophomore years.

The Huskies started recruiting me when I was a junior in high school. They sent me a letter and questionnaire from across the country. They noticed that I had relatives in the Seattle area, so they figured they had a chance at recruiting me. UW coaches just started the process, and I felt that this was a place where God wanted me to be, even though I was 2,000 miles away from Virginia.

I knew all about the Huskies program, and I really loved Seattle. I liked the water. I really felt comfortable with the players there.

I came in as a 6′1½″, 225-pound fullback.

When I started summer practices, I felt ready to play. I had a job to do, and I figured I could compete from day one. I hit the weights really hard. I was ready to play college ball. So I came physically and mentally ready to play my freshman year.

Yeah, it was pretty competitive right from the start, but I knew what to expect. There's a mental aspect to the game that, at times, is overwhelming, I guess, but I would say I handled it well.

While I was prepared to play as a freshman, I didn't get on the field. I came very close. I was one of a few freshmen to make the traveling squad, so I got to practice with the traveling team throughout my freshman year. They were going to play me but just decided not to at the last minute. It didn't upset me because I knew my time was coming.

My redshirt sophomore year, Coach James came to me and asked me what I would think about moving to the strong-side linebacker position. They wanted to give me the chance to play on the field. They changed the offense, and the fullbacks were not going to get the ball like they used to. He was very honest about that. He said I was too good of an athlete not to be on the field. I decided to go for it and try out for the linebacker position.

I got to play in the second half of my sophomore season. We had a lot of good linebackers at the time. Marty Harrison showed me the ropes.

People say our loss to UCLA in 1990 cost us back-to-back national titles. But you know what? We accomplished our goal of getting to the Rose Bowl and winning it. The 1990 team accomplished its goal of getting to the Rose Bowl. The UCLA game was one of those in which everything went bad. And then Greg Lewis went down. That was a nightmare.

Greg was a character. There were those times you had to twist his arm to practice.

That 1991 season was unbelievable, man. That was the greatest time in my experience of sports. We had a lot of fun. We had great camaraderie and pride in what we accomplished at the end. It was just such an honor to be a part of that undefeated team. Everything went according to the script. We were the best team that year, no question.

We really won every game. There were times when we were behind, as we were against Nebraska, but we always felt that we were going to come

Donald Jones was a devastating pass rusher, amassing 26 career sacks.

back and win. That game was close. But we wound up pretty much blowing Nebraska out in the fourth quarter. 'SC was pretty close on the scoreboard, 14–3, but it really wasn't that close. We controlled the game and the line of scrimmage. They couldn't move the ball, so it wasn't like they were a threat.

We were the No. 1–ranked defense the last two years I was there, actually. We didn't really have any weaknesses. They couldn't attack a certain point. We were so quick that we did a great job of confusing the quarterback, which made us even more dangerous.

Steve Emtman was arguably the best defensive player in the country. Believe me, no one could handle Emtman. But we just had so much talent on that team. From that team, there were five No. 1 NFL draft picks, 28 guys who played in the NFL, and another eight who played pro football in Canada, Europe, the XFL, or indoor football.

I received some accolades that year. It made me feel like I had made the right decision to play for the University of Washington. But the best part of it was being with my teammates. To work hard together for a goal and do a really super job was rewarding.

I played three years in the NFL. Then I had a really bad knee injury. I needed three knee operations. I had a lot of problems with limited mobility after that.

I settled in the Los Angeles area, where I'm a major account executive with Sprint. I see fellow Huskies all the time. I volunteer as an assistant coach for head coach Charles Mincy at Inglewood High School. There are several Huskies coaching in the L.A. area, and it's always fun to see them and talk after games. We're giving back to the communities that don't have as much money or the best facilities. We're trying to be good role models for youth sports.

I try to go up to Seattle at least once a year and attend a Huskies game.

Being a Husky means being part of an extended family. You feel like that's your brother. That type of brotherhood and camaraderie is always there. We might not see each other that often, but I still know that they have my back and I have theirs if they ever need me.

327

Donald Jones was a prolific pass rusher with 26 sacks. His 11.5 sacks in 1991 ranks third. He recorded 228.5 career tackles (fourth in UW history). He earned All–Pac-10 honors in 1990 and 1991. Jones played four seasons in the NFL with the New York Jets (2), Indianapolis Colts (1), and Minnesota Vikings (1). He is currently a major account executive for Sprint in L.A. and an assistant coach at Inglewood High School.

ED CUNNINGHAM
CENTER
1987–1991

WITHIN AN HOUR OF OUR 1991 Rose Bowl victory over Iowa, a reporter asked what our team goals would be for the season. Without thinking, I said, "We're coming back, and we're going to play for the whole thing."

A year later, I could feel the prediction would come true during our 45-minute bus ride from Anaheim to Pasadena. I sat with Beno Bryant just behind Coach Don James. There was no doubt what was about to happen. I could see it in the body language from Coach James to scout-team players. We were going to put on a show. Michigan didn't have a chance, and they didn't know it. It was a culmination of talented, dedicated players working for good coaches.

As we pulled into the Rose Bowl, Huskies fans saw us coming and gathered around the bus, clapping, yelling, and slapping the side of the bus. I looked over and saw my mom and dad waving at me. I could see the pride in their faces. It was overwhelming—knowing they were there for me in my biggest moment.

A moment I almost didn't have.

I first visited Seattle in the summer of 1985, between my sophomore and junior years in high school. I competed in the Junior Olympics national track and field championships at Husky Stadium. I threw the javelin. Dad and I looked at the school while there. It was a gorgeous August week. On my flight back home, I told my dad that I'd look into attending Washington. My

Ed Cunningham almost quit the football team, but he decided to stay when Keith Gilbertson was hired, and he went on to be the starting center for two Rose Bowl–winning teams, including the undefeated season.

high school girlfriend was a year older and went to Washington. Dick Baird made sure my girlfriend was included in all the festivities during my recruiting visit. He knew how to recruit. I picked Washington. I knew two people in Seattle—my girlfriend and Donald Jones, a fellow recruit from Virginia. Four months later, my girlfriend and I broke up.

I almost broke it off with the Huskies, too. I was as good as gone. After my redshirt freshman year, I had decided to leave the team. I went home to Alexandria in northern Virginia. I told a friend at the UW I was going to leave. I had Mom look up the phone numbers of those who had recruited me the year before. The Huskies were 6–5 that year, and we had an offensive line coach I didn't like. He treated players poorly.

I called my buddy in Seattle to tell him to box up my stuff and ship it to my home. But his dad picked up the phone. He said, "Hey, James made a change. He's bringing in Keith Gilbertson from Idaho to run the offense." The line coach wasn't coming back. I figured I'd go back to Seattle and give Gilby a chance, at least through spring practices.

One thing Gilby brought was zone blocking. Instead of man-to-man blocking, we worked together to move the line of scrimmage. It made us wonder why we hadn't done this before.

Really, Gilby is one of best men in my life. He pushed me to be a better player and better person. D.J. had never fired an assistant until then. That was a huge moment in his history as a coach.

James was sometimes labeled as unchanging. It couldn't be further from the truth. They started recruiting with a premium on speed. They brought in speed coaches to help us run better. With Keith, they went from an I-back offense to a spread passing offense with a balanced power running attack. Jim Lambright, who had been there forever, invented a defense used now throughout football. The defense was almost impossible to block with everyone up at the line; everything was about penetration. Those changes took us to the next level.

I played guard and tackle in high school. At Washington I started out as a guard and played alongside Bern Brostek. My first year of playing, we didn't go to a bowl and finished 6–5. National publications listed James on the hot seat. But nobody panicked. We new we had talented guys.

My sophomore year, we beat UCLA and earned a trip to the Freedom Bowl. We held Emmitt Smith to 17 yards in a 34–7 victory over Florida. We started to realize we were pretty good. We weren't just good in our conference; we were good nationally.

Years later, I heard from a Florida insider that the coach asked Emmitt if he was going to turn pro during halftime. Emmitt confirmed he was going to the NFL. The coach then said, "Okay, take your pads off. No sense in you getting hurt in this game."

Going into my junior year, I was moved to center, which is more my natural position. A lot of things were better my junior year than my senior year. We couldn't figure out how to be the best, thanks to the UCLA loss. So when we beat Iowa in the 1991 Rose Bowl, we knew those of us coming back had to figure it out.

What we didn't know was that Mark Brunell would get injured in spring practice. And we didn't know how good Billy Joe Hobert was.

We had some guys who didn't want to do the extra stuff when I first got there. My class and the class below us had a bunch of tough, good guys. We got it. No discipline was necessary from the coaching staff. We had strong relationships and disciplined ourselves. Team chemistry is a bunch of guys who care what they are doing and care for each other. We had football coming out of our pores.

331

When a cancer starts in a locker room, it can really hurt a team. If guys thought they were better than they were, we'd shut them up. One addition to team chemistry is when the best players are the leaders. That helps. Steve Emtman, Donald Jones, Mark Brunell, and Dave Hoffmann were the toughest guys. If you didn't live up to what we all expected, your life was miserable. Nobody practiced harder than Steve. How do you not live up to trying your best with that example?

That's when the NCAA passed the 20-hour rule. Teams couldn't ask players to put in more than 20 hours a week in practice, meetings, and games. Our guys did what was necessary. We'd have group film study. As long as a coach wasn't there, it didn't count against the 20 hours.

We were immensely talented. Seven or eight guys that year ended up playing in the NFL. We accumulated amazing statistics. The one I'm most proud of is we only gave up six sacks the whole year. It helped having two mobile quarterbacks, but we dominated people at the line. Our pride came from the fact teams would quit. Opponents would say, "Okay, lighten up, you got it. You've got us beat." We got the other guys to say "uncle."

Besides the Rose Bowl, two games stand out in my memory: Nebraska and Kansas State.

Against Nebraska we were down in the second half and put it into another gear to win 36–21. Our offense rolled for 618 yards! The game marked my most forgettable play and one to remember.

I made my worst snaps ever at the worst time. We were at the 3-yard line and could have cut the Cornhusker lead to three. But the ball slipped out of my hand during the snap and ended up at my ankles. We lost the fumble and momentum, for the time being.

I was up against an all-conference nose guard. In the middle of the third quarter, we were down 21–9 and driving. We needed to convert on a third down. We ran an inside zone play to Beno. I crushed this nose guard, and Beno went 25 yards for a touchdown. My block sprung him. I had to do something to make up for the bad snap.

The next week produced one of the most poignant team moments. We all saw how hard Mark worked during the summer to rehab from his knee injury. I can tell you we seniors were nervous because Billy Joe wasn't a practice player. The older guys were saying, "What the hell are we going to do?" Fortunately, Billy Joe was a great gamer.

But Mark made his return during the Kansas State game, in week three. He came into the game to our surprise. We didn't know when or if he would play. When he ran out onto the field, everyone in the huddle got chills. We all felt he was the guy who would lead us to victory. He was still hobbling a bit. He put aside his personal thing because he had to be on the field. That's what "team" is all about.

So we did make my prediction come true in convincing fashion with our 34–14 trouncing of Michigan. After the game, we hung out at the hotel awaiting the polls. I really didn't care. I knew the voting system wasn't perfect. We were 12–0. We knew. I didn't need the approval from writers and coaches. I was pretty damn content. We were ready to play Miami the next day. Miami didn't have any clue how good we were.

I've been covering college football for 10 years as a broadcaster. I've seen some great teams. Texas had it last year. USC has had it. We had it, too, in 1991. It's not arrogance. It's not cockiness. It's a comfort level. Really good teams don't worry about other teams. They know how good they are.

What it means to be a Husky is summed up in one word—toughness. I think of Seattle as a tough city. There's one way to do things—through hard work. There's no secret to it. We had some flashy players in Mario and Napoleon, but the heart of the program were the big guys. The linemen made Huskies football great.

Playing five years in the NFL never matched my Huskies experience. My NFL highlight was the day I retired, after four seasons with the dysfunctional Arizona Cardinals (I did enjoy my last year with Dennis Erickson and the Seahawks). For linemen, all you have is team achievement. My best year in the pros, our team went 8–8. It's too hard to play for the paycheck. So I moved up to the broadcast booth.

It's been difficult to watch the UW program lose its foundation. Rick Neuheisel didn't get it. He didn't know what it meant to be a Husky. Yeah, he won a Rose Bowl...with Lambright's guys. He did the same thing with Colorado. We lost our sense of toughness. It's not necessarily the wins or losses. It's seeing a purple-and-gold team show up and play soft and undisciplined that hurt the most.

The year before Rick was fired, I was out at the spring game. The Huskies didn't have enough offensive linemen to have a real game. I pulled Gilby aside and said, "What's going on?"

He said, "We didn't recruit enough linemen."

That's what the program was built on—the line—and it was all gone.

Gilby was left to clean up the mess. He had a terrible hand, like sitting in the World Series of Poker with a pair of twos. What's done is done. I'm optimistic about the direction of the program now.

Ed Cunningham earned All–Pac-10 Conference honors in 1991 and was an Academic All-American in 1990 and 1991. He played in the Hula Bowl all-star game and was given an NCAA post-graduate scholarship. Cunningham played five seasons in the NFL with the Arizona Cardinals (4 seasons) and Seattle Seahawks (1). He is currently an ESPN college football analyst.

DANA HALL

CORNERBACK

1987–1992

O UR RUN FOR THE NATIONAL CHAMPIONSHIP—and winning it—was the
most memorable thing about my Huskies career.

The defining moment of that 1991 season was our win against Nebraska
in Lincoln. That game stands out the most because we were on the road
against a very good opponent, and we beat them up for three quarters.

We had an awesome defense. We set so many defensive records. We were
number one in every category that year.

What made us good? It started up front with Steve Emtman, D'Marco Farr,
Tyrone Rodgers, Don Jones, Jaime Fields, and Brett Collins. Then linebackers Chico Fraley, Dave Hoffmann, and Andy Mason…the speed of those guys
up front made our jobs so much easier as defensive backs—Walter Bailey and
me at the corners, and Tommy Smith and Shane Pahukoa in the middle.

Naturally, Steve Emtman was the leader by example. Billy Jo Hobert was
a fierce competitor, and the whole offense took on his personality. Mark
Brunell was a great leader. Mario Bailey was a good one. We didn't have a lot
of vocal guys besides Emtman. We didn't really need to be yelled at because
we knew what we had to do.

There were some guys who were walk-ons who made great contributions
in practices and games, like Curtis Gaspard. He was an integral part of our
receiving corps that year and helped us out a lot with Mario Bailey and
Orlando McKay.

The attack style we played put more pressure on us DBs. Our front guys were so good, it appeared we were blitzing, but we didn't that often. I remember seeing freeze frames, and we had all 11 guys in the close shot, within 10 yards of the line. If the guys up front didn't get home and get the tackle, we were able to hold up under the pressure.

Every team that we faced, we would see the same thing in the pregame press clippings. Every team had the same notion—they were going to come after us, and all they wanted was one or two creases in our defense to break a big play. Our thing was that we were going to go after them, and we were going to hold them up so there were no creases. Our preparation for each game kept us at that level.

The highlight for me of the 1992 Rose Bowl against Michigan was, I think collectively for our secondary, that Desmond Howard, the Heisman Trophy winner, only caught one pass. Unfortunately, that pass was against me. But to collectively hold him down, that was special. We said one person was not going to beat us. Our goal in the secondary was to not get noticed. If you got noticed, something went wrong.

Jim Lambright was good at preparing for a team in one week's time, but give him a month-and-a-half, and they didn't even have a chance.

One play that stands out in my mind was a hit Fields had on their running back in the flat. You had to hear that all the way back in Seattle, that's how hard he hit him.

The best part of having the national championship was winning the coaches' poll. To me, that's the true poll because the coaches are the ones who watch the films and pay close attention to detail. Not to take anything from Miami, but the coaches' poll really is the most important one. The writers don't think we play football on the West Coast and will always vote for the East Coast teams.

I grew up a West Coast guy and went to high school in Pomona, California. A lot of different things led me to Washington. I went to a high school where, traditionally, the head football coach didn't think anyone was worthy of playing college football. He would keep recruiting letters in his drawer from colleges—that's what I heard.

A lot of my recruiting success was due to my high school basketball coach. He wanted us to have an opportunity to play somewhere. He had a friend coaching at San Diego State, who had a friend at Northern Arizona, which became the first school to send me a letter for recruiting. Coaches talked, and

Dana Hall could cover the pass and defend the run from his cornerback position on the record-setting 1991 defense.

others found out I was being recruited, and then I started to get some Pac-10 attention.

I kind of wanted to get away from Southern California, so I started looking at Cal-Berkeley and Washington. When I came to Washington, I really wanted to be here because I wanted to get away from home. I always wanted to play in the Rose Bowl. So Washington was the best choice. Washington seemed to have the best fan support, too.

I never really got homesick. I went home the first summer and decided to come back for summer school. After my first year, I was kind of mad because I thought the politics weren't fair. I think it was good for me, though, because it allowed me to develop my skills. I was 6′3″, 188 pounds when I came, and by the end of the first season I was 208. It allowed me to fill out and sit back and learn. I never thought about quitting. I was frustrated, yes, but I didn't want to quit.

These days I travel a lot, so it's kind of funny when you meet certain people who are big sports fans. As athletes, we are a strange breed. I was in a meeting last week, and a guy sent me an email after asking me if I played for Washington. I told him when I played, and he said, "Oh, you were on the team that split the national championship with Miami." That happens a lot. How people remember that I don't know.

Besides a Rose Bowl ring, I was fortunate to be with the San Francisco 49ers at the right time to win a Super Bowl.

Coming back to Washington, I can say that one of the best feelings was the ovation I got as a Husky Legend—especially when I think that a lot of those fans weren't even born, or were extremely young, when I played. The ovation was an amazing memory.

Being a Husky, for me, during my era, was about having pride and not settling for anything second-best. It was about tradition.

337

Dana Hall earned All–Pac-10 Conference honors in 1991 as cornerback for the record-setting Huskies defense. His 24 broken-up passes ranks second in UW history. Hall played six seasons in the NFL with the San Francisco 49ers (1992–1994), Cleveland Browns (1995), and Jacksonville Jaguars (1996–1997). He is currently vice president of emerging markets for Washington Mutual in Southern California.

MARIO BAILEY

RECEIVER

1988–1991

DURING MY DOZEN YEARS IN PRO FOOTBALL, I tried to come back to the UW and take classes. I'd go and Washington classmates would strike the Heisman pose, just as I did after my last play as a Husky.

I've been recognized around the world for that pose. It's forever in history. If anybody knows anything about Washington football, they know about my pose. I actually got so tired of it, I bought a house in Texas and moved. Everywhere I went that's all anyone wanted to talk about.

But I couldn't stay away from Seattle for long. I returned and got my communications degree in 2006 and have been the football coach at my alma mater, Franklin High, for two seasons.

The pose was how I celebrated my last play—a 38-yard touchdown reception from Mark Brunell in the 1992 Rose Bowl that capped our 34–14 victory over Michigan. All the hype before the game had been about Wolverines receiver Desmond Howard, the Heisman Trophy winner for the 1991 season. He finished with one catch that day. I had six for 126 yards.

My most memorable moment as a Husky came after that final play. I was on the sideline talking to the TV camera. All the players in front of me parted like the Red Sea. Coach Don James walked between them and gave me a big hug and a handshake. I'd never had that happen before, especially during a game. He congratulated and thanked me. That made my career complete right there.

Mario Bailey leaps to pull down an amazing touchdown catch in the 1992 Rose Bowl and moments later strikes a memorable Heisman pose in the end zone.

Coach James wasn't too happy with me when we boarded the flight for the 1992 Rose Bowl.

I almost missed it. I woke up 10 minutes before the plane was scheduled to leave. My brother drove me to Sea-Tac, and I ran straight to the gate. The plane door was closed, so I pounded on it. They let me in.

I walked down the aisle, and as I passed Coach James, he looked up and gave me a little smirk that said, "Yeah, you're lucky."

A few guys did miss the flight, and they had to pay for it with extra running in the mornings.

The funny thing about the Michigan Rose Bowl was that they didn't know how good we were. They knew by the first quarter. I remember the look in their eyes that first quarter, how surprised they were.

The funny thing about that Heisman pose is I've never seen a picture of it. I've seen it on videotape, but I've never seen a picture of it. Enough people saw it on TV.

My only regret at Washington is not having a video camera to record every moment. You don't know how precious every moment is; you're just in the moment. It's unbelievable to me that I got to play against Michigan and scored in the Rose Bowl or even walked on the Rose Bowl field.

The first football game I ever saw on TV was the 1978 Rose Bowl with Warren Moon. My older brother was a big Huskies fan, and he made me watch it. It made a big impression on me.

I loved basketball, but I had a great football season as a junior at Franklin High. I considered UCLA, but I got hurt my senior year. It came down to Washington or Washington State. Dennis Erickson treated me exceptionally well to show I was a top priority. My brother walked on at WSU. Some guys from my high school went to WSU and got into some trouble. My mom wanted me to stay in Seattle, so I'd stay out of trouble. I actually signed both letters of intent to the UW and WSU. My high school coach called Jim Lambright and told him I was thinking of WSU.

I remember seeing Coach Don James at Garfield High to watch our basketball game. It was the craziest place for him to come. It showed he was interested.

My first day of UW practice was with freshman only, and it upset me. I was given No. 80 even though I had been promised No. 5. I was ready to go home after the first day of practice with the veterans. The first thing we did in practice was stretching drills. Captains lined up at the 50-yard line. Then next to them was the first-string offense and defense, behind them the second-string, then third, and so on. I lined up in the back of the end zone, I was so deep on the depth chart. I was still mad about my number. It was just crazy.

I actually called my mom and asked her to call Coach Erickson to see what I needed to do to get the hell out of there as quickly as possible. She called him, and I learned I'd have to go to community college for a year before I could transfer. I couldn't see myself going to a CC. I was miserable, but I decided to try and make it through. My mom did call Coach Lambright and cussed him out (which I wasn't happy about).

The next day there was a No. 5 jersey in my locker. But I took it back. I told the coaches I'd wait until I deserved to wear No. 5.

I barely made it through two-a-day practices. There were a few guys who liked to pick on freshmen. I just kept trying to make the best of my situation. I kept telling myself that I wasn't going to redshirt. I was going to stay and just try to play.

I didn't travel for our first game my freshman year because of a small injury, and it looked like they might redshirt me. During practice a couple weeks into the season, I burned our top cornerback in practice and moved up.

My first game was against Oregon in week seven. Back then, the third receiver only came in on third down. So I got in on some third-down plays. On the film, it looked like I was jogging in a daze. I was nervous as hell. I ended up getting four catches for about 32 yards. But it was a wasted year for me, as we went 6–5.

My sophomore year, I scored the first touchdown of the season in our opener against Texas A&M. I beat an All-American candidate, and it boosted my confidence sky-high. I ended up starting a few games. Keith Gilbertson came in that season and switched us to predominately three-receiver sets. I was the third receiver along with Andre Riley and Orlando McKay. I scored five or six times.

Gilbertson is my favorite guy in world. His offense made Lambright change his defense and made our team change into a new team. Bringing him in changed our entire program. Our glory days were a tribute to him.

My coming out party was the UCLA game in 1989. We were down 21–0 at halftime and came back in the second half to win 28–27. I finished with six catches for 80 yards and a touchdown. From that point on, I was always part of the offensive game plan. Scoring in the Freedom Bowl capped a season of promise.

We struggled in our first two games of 1990. We won, but just barely against San Jose State and Purdue. Then we killed Southern Cal 31–0. 'SC came in and were the monsters of our conference. It was a hot, hot day in Husky Stadium. That was the first time fans saw the new Huskies. It was a glimpse into the future. I remember thinking, *We're a really good team. We could win the national championship.*

The next week we lost to Colorado, which is the worst memory of my UW career. We came from behind in the second half thanks to my eight catches for 147 yards. It was the best half I ever had. We drove down late in the game and were ready to score the go-ahead touchdown. I ran a slant and got open. But a defender tipped the pass, and it went off my fingertips. It would've been a tough catch, but I was used to making tough catches. We lost 20–14.

When coaches handed out the Player of the Week awards, I was overlooked. I felt like they were blaming me for missing that catch.

We rolled from there to a 10–2 season and 46–34 Rose Bowl win over Iowa. Before we left the Rose Bowl for the buses, returning players were already thinking national title in 1991. I never saw so many guys working out in the summer. I was telling my friends at home that we'd win the national championship.

The only doubt on the schedule was the Nebraska game. Then Brunell got hurt in spring practices. That put some doubt into the mix. Billy Joe Hobert looked like a garbage man in practice. In a game, he was a different guy. Some people are game-time players.

The Nebraska game was one of the best college experiences I ever had. There was so much excitement. And it was so loud I couldn't hear Billy Joe calling plays in the huddle. Walking off their field, Cornhuskers fans gave us a classy standing ovation. It was the best feeling.

Everything went according to plan as we went undefeated and shared the national championship with Miami. That 1991 Washington team set a lot of records. For us first-string guys, we were too good. But most of us starters didn't play a lot in the second half. I got to play in the fourth quarter only twice my senior year. So who knows? I might have had 30 touchdowns that season had I played most of the games. The positive side was everybody played. Our team was so close. That's why we won. There were no cliques anymore. We were all in it together.

I had the greatest time of my life being a Husky. I loved everyone. I met some great people. Everything you do you learn from, and everything that happened was supposed to happen.

Mario Bailey earned consensus All-America honors and was the Pac-10 Offensive Player of the Year in 1991. His touchdown receptions for a season (18) and career (30) remain school records. Bailey's career receiving yards of 2,306 ranks second in UW history. Bailey played a dozen seasons in pro football: two seasons with the Houston Oilers, six in NFL Europe, two in the Canadian Football League, and one in the XFL. He also played arena league football. He is currently the football coach at Franklin High School.

343

STEVE EMTMAN
NOSE GUARD
1988–1991

I CAN THANK A WAZZU FOOTBALL BOOSTER for my success at Washington.
I wasn't highly recruited my senior year out of Cheney, Washington.
Four teams showed interest—Oregon, Oregon State, WSU, and Washington.
I took my first trip to Pullman, and Dennis Erickson was the coach at the
time. I was ready to sign with the Cougars that weekend. But then I decided
to at least take a look at the UW.

Then I got a letter from a Cougars booster with some advice. It said I was
WSU's number-one guy, and they really wanted me. It said I would be one
of many at Washington, and that I would never see the field as a Husky.

I went to Seattle to see the Huskies program for myself. The trip went
fine, nothing special happened until I went to the airport with Coach Gary
Pinkel, the quarterbacks coach who was recruiting me. On the way to the
airport, I told him about the letter and asked him, "Hey, do you guys really
want me here, or am I just another guy? I don't want to be lost in the depth
chart. You have so many talented guys here."

Just before I got on the plane, Gary said, "If you are worried about competing, don't come to Washington."

I appreciated that kind of attitude. I decided to be a Husky.

I came into the program at 280 pounds and in good shape. We converted
a shop on our Cheney farm into a weight room, so I had been lifting weights
since sixth grade.

Steve Emtman powers his way though blocks to get into the backfield, earning his reputation as the most dominating and decorated defensive lineman in UW history.

I redshirted my freshman year and spent the season on the scout team. We freshmen went after the upperclass offense pretty good. We had a lot of fun paying our dues. Linebacker Dave Hoffmann and I became good friends. I kept getting him out of fights on the practice field. Since we didn't travel with the team that year, Dave and I made a few road trips back to Cheney and talked many hours about our day coming.

I remember listening to the Oregon game on the radio. We were pissed off because we were losing. That first year in the program, we went 6–5 and didn't go to a bowl. The Cougars made the Aloha Bowl. That Christmas I was home and endured seeing Spokane local TV news showing Cougars players in Hawaii saying, "Ha, ha! Hi, Huskies!" I wondered if I had made a mistake.

I played behind Dennis Brown my redshirt freshman year in 1989. I knew I would not get in much. But Dennis got hurt, and I played a little bit and earned some respect.

Whenever you don't play, it's tough. I bitched about it some to our strength coach. He simply said I had to make it obvious by my work on the field that I deserved a chance. Washington opened the best-equipped weight room in the country the year I came in. I took advantage and worked hard in the weight room, probably overtrained. I felt at home in the weight room. I enjoyed it.

It's a jump from scout team to playing on Saturday. In practice, you think, *Man, I can play against any of these guys. I can do this.*

Then you start thinking, *This isn't the real thing.* You have this doubt in the back of your mind that maybe those first-team guys are taking it easy on you. It didn't set in until I played in front of 75,000 fans. I got in a few plays in the Freedom Bowl, too. I gained confidence that year.

A lowlight of that season actually set the stage for our national championship. We were 2–1 when we played Colorado at home. The Buffaloes ran all over us—420 yards and six rushing touchdowns in a 45–28 loss. That crushing changed our defense and our destiny.

On Monday, defensive coordinator Jim Lambright changed the defensive philosophy to an attack-style. We were going to take the fight to the offense. We didn't perfect it until the next season, but everyone on defense loved the change.

By the time the 1990 season rolled around, I was ready to step in as a starter. Our defense came of age. For a nose guard like myself, when I played a traditional two-gap defense, my job was to tie up offensive lineman and keep them off our linebackers so they could make the tackle. For the new penetrating defense, the bottom line was we were pushing the line of scrimmage backward. People were not running up the middle, they ran wide and we ran to them. The down side was that it put a lot of pressure on the secondary with man-to-man coverage. We had the talent to pull it off. Sometimes our pressure led to bad throws. Sometimes great coverage led to sacks.

People can argue all they want about which were the best defensive teams in Washington history. In my mind, it isn't close. Our statistics speak for themselves, and don't even tell the whole story. In 1990 we led the nation against the run with 1.9 yards per carry. In 1991 we allowed just 67.2 rushing yards and 9.2 points a game. You would see negative rushing yards on the scoreboard with our starters in. But you have to remember, we didn't play a lot in the second half in those years. I remember many games when Hoffmann and I were standing behind Lambright in the second half, screaming to put us back in when a team crossed the 50-yard line. And when you are forcing three-and-outs, the defensive plays are cut down. The Huskies might have 100 defensive plays per game during most seasons. We only had 50 to 60, and the first team had about 35 of those plays.

My favorite stat of our perfect 12–0 season in 1991 is this: only two or three quarterbacks finished a game against us that season—not because we were dirty, but they either got hurt or left in frustration for being ineffective.

What made those defensive teams was the trust we had in each other. You didn't have to worry about the guy behind you or the guy behind him. That was built on and off the field. We watched film together as a defense. Nobody missed a film session. If you did, you had teammates after you. If you heard about it from a peer, you were in big trouble because you'd be out of the family.

347

To me, what it meant to be a Husky in those days was being a family. You didn't want do anything to let your family down. Sports in general, and football in particular, brings guys from all over. People you'd never hang out with otherwise come together and become a family. When you walked on the field, you all respected each other.

One of the traditions handed down to us before each practice and each game was to touch the rose. It was painted on a wall just before the door leading to the tunnel to the field. When you touched that rose and went into the tunnel, that was considered the field. You ran through that nasty, stinky tunnel, never walked. Then we had the "Say Who?" chant before games. Those two traditions were lost—the rose painted over, the tunnel carpeted and lit and made up to look real nice, and the "Say Who?" chant became politically incorrect.

It's hard to explain the energy level of the tunnel back then. It was as close to gladiator days as you could get—like going to the lions. You knew a brawl was coming, and you knew you could count on the guy next to you.

Returning to Washington as a member of the coaching staff, it was frustrating seeing guys walk in the tunnel. We respected all the traditions guys before us passed down when I played. We wanted to walk off the field knowing the guys before us were proud of what we did.

The other difference is we weren't selfish about stats. I didn't care if teams double- and triple-teamed me. As long as our defense did the job, that was fine. Great teams never have selfish individuals.

Our attitude on defense was we didn't care how many points the offense put up—three or 50—we were going to win the game.

The one loss that still hurts today is the 25–22 home loss to UCLA in 1990. We were 22-point favorites! We lost focus, and it may have cost us a national title.

To me, playing Iowa in the 1991 Rose Bowl was just another game. It was a thrill, no doubt. But most of us viewed it as a stepping stone. After our 46–34 win, center Ed Cunningham summarized the underclassmen's feelings about our terrific 10–2 season. He congratulated the seniors on a great year. He said it's back to work on Monday for the returners. The next Monday everybody was in the weight room ready to go.

The Nebraska and California games were the key games of our title year. What I remember about our comeback at Nebraska was thinking after the game, "That's what football is all about, two teams battling in a sea of red fans." Nebraska's fans are classy, not like the idiots at Oregon, who are out of control and throw things at you. After the game, Nebraska fans applauded us. They respected the game. It was like they were saying, "Wow, that was a great football game."

After that Cornhuskers win in the second week, we knew we could run the table.

California had one of its best teams ever. Their line was the best I played against in college. We didn't play to our level that day but still won 24–17 thanks to Beno Bryant's late touchdown.

Each passing week our focus intensified. We weren't going to let another UCLA-type letdown happen this time. Guys would rather study film than go out and chase girls. Football was our priority over everything. Football and classes.

Our scout team did their job, too. The walk-on guys made us a great team. A difference from then and now is teams now have about 100 guys. We had 45 more, and that meant two full scout teams would go against us starters in practice. The two scout teams would trade off every other play. When motivated, rested guys are coming at you, it levels out the talent difference. We were so deep, it felt like we were tested harder during the week than on some Saturdays. Every starter was talented. We had no weak links. If I had to pick the defenders who were the hardest hitters, it would be Hoffmann and Jaime Fields, who tragically was killed by a drunk driver in 1999.

My philosophy as a player was, "I'm going to come at you 100 percent, every play." Sooner or later the guy across me would take a play off, and that's when I'd make a big play.

Going into the 1992 Rose Bowl, I wasn't feeling my best. I had a fever a day or two before the game and even spent the night in the hospital to get my temperature down and replenish liquids with an IV drip. My legs were sluggish for the game, and I didn't feel like I played a good game. I don't know how I got MVP. A lot of guys played better than I did.

Beating Michigan produced such a feeling of accomplishment. There's no better feeling than setting a goal and then reaching that goal a year later.

I didn't have much time to celebrate as speculation quickly turned to whether or not I'd return for my senior season. I really didn't know what I was going to do. To me, it was about the challenge of the NFL. Life isn't about money. I'd give up every dime to play another five years with those UW guys.

349

I decided to move on to the next level and was the No. 1 pick overall by Indianapolis. My six-year NFL career was hampered by serious injuries in each of my first three years, both knees and neck problems.

I returned to the UW campus in 2000 to finish my degree and joined the coaching staff, first as a graduate assistant and then as the strength coach. My contract was not renewed when Coach Willingham was hired, which was hurtful and confusing.

So I'm finally out of football. My energies these days are devoted to my real estate company, Defender Developments, and Dream Turf, of which I'm a co-owner. In business and sports, it's a challenge to find the right people and find that family feeling.

I split my time between Cheney and Seattle. It's sometimes tough being a Husky and living in eastern Washington, especially in the last few years.

Everyone gets busy in life after football. I enjoy the times I can get together with my Huskies teammates. Some things are timeless. Whether it's playing pool or whatever, we go back to the competitive thing and get after each other. I'm sure the wives hate it. That's the way it is with families. Time passes, but Huskies teammates remain family.

Steve Emtman is considered the most dominating lineman ever to wear a Huskies uniform. He is the most decorated UW lineman and was inducted into the College Football Hall of Fame in 2006. In 1991, as a junior, he was a consensus All-American and the only Husky to win the Lombardi Award and the Outland Trophy. He finished fourth in the Heisman Trophy balloting, the highest by a Husky. Emtman's 60 tackles led UW linemen in 1991, including 19.5 tackles for loss. He had 6.5 quarterback sacks. The Indianapolis Colts selected Emtman with the No. 1 overall NFL pick in 1992, the only Husky to be the top NFL draft choice. Emtman played for three NFL teams: the Indianapolis Colts (1992–1994), Miami Dolphins (1995–1996), and Washington Redskins (1997).

MARK BRUNELL

QUARTERBACK

1988–1992

I DIDN'T MIND SITTING OUT MY FIRST YEAR at Washington. I was in no real hurry to get on the field. It was such a big jump for a Southern California kid from a small Catholic school. It was shocking to see big guys with speed.

Growing up in Southern California, all you hear about is USC and UCLA. I didn't really know much about Washington until my junior year at St. Joseph's High. I thought I'd go to a California school until I took my trip to the UW. I wasn't expecting much. I could not have had a better trip—I fell in love with Seattle and the people I met. It all came together.

I played on the scout squad the first two years. I did get to travel my redshirt year, which was a good experience. The second year I was a back-up to Cary Conklin.

My first time on the field, I got in a couple of plays during mop-up time against Oregon State. We were ahead by three or four touchdowns, but I was still pretty nervous. I threw a couple of times and handed off a lot. I did play a little in the Freedom Bowl and scored a touchdown.

Conklin graduated, and I won the job to start the 1990 season. We won our first two games, but our offense didn't have very good games. I was pretty ugly my first two starts. Those were my two worst games as a Husky. UCLA was a tough game to lose that year.

Mark Brunell came back from a knee injury to inspire his teammates and play a supporting role on the national championship team.

Playing in the Rose Bowl made up for all the disappointment. I had never been to the Rose Bowl before, even though I lived about 200 miles from Pasadena. I had lots of friends and family at the game.

It was a great ending to a good season. Our offense and defense both had good days. A lot of people immediately looked ahead to the next season. I've always been a one-game-at-at-time guy, but I was looking forward to the season with everyone else.

The following spring, I blew out my knee during spring practices. Two teammates hit me from either side. Right when I was hit, I knew it was serious because of the pain. I knew it would be a long, hard road to recovery when they told me I needed ACL reconstruction. My doctors were very positive and told me it would take six month to a year to come back. My family was very supportive, too.

Coming back wasn't always smooth. There were a few rough days. The injury itself and rehab were extremely painful. It took a lot of work. I just kept dreaming of getting on the field. It's tough to look beyond that.

Not being able to be a starter was almost as difficult. It was tough. The team goes forward. You never know how long your knee will take to get back. I got on field earlier than people expected. I worked hard to get back on the field in five months.

353

I came in during our home game against Kansas State in the third week. The fans gave me a great welcome home with a lot of cheers. It was a good feeling. That was one of those moments when you soak it all in—one you never forget. Just walking on the field made that one of my highlight games.

There was no quarterback controversy between Billy Joe Hobert and me. I always had a lot of respect for him. It was never awkward between us.

The team had a lot of success without me. Still, I felt part of it. I was able to contribute a little bit to our national championship season.

Winning the Rose Bowl and claiming the national championship—that's a dream come true. My family and a lot of friends were at the Rose Bowl again to share in it. I played two or three series and threw a touchdown to Mario Bailey at the end. There was such a sense of team unity. We realized we accomplished this as a team.

I went into the 1992 season as the backup to Billy Joe. I was able to move around a little more. I started to feel comfortable wearing that big black brace.

I don't think we went into the season trying to live up to ourselves from last year. We lost some key senior players, but I still thought we had enough talent to make another run at the championship.

I became the starter for the Arizona game, the week the Billy Joe loan became public [Hobert's accepting a loan in 1992 led to an NCAA investigation into the UW football program, which resulted in sanctions]. When we lost to the Wildcats, it snapped a 22-game winning streak and knocked the wind out of our repeat title hopes. We lost our last two games of the season, never a good feeling to finish that way. Washington State beat us, and in our third straight trip to the Rose Bowl, Michigan won the rematch.

Being part of four straight bowls was a great accomplish, and I felt fortunate to play with guys who had talent and a lot of character. While we had some disappointments, we all stayed together as a team.

We had some successful years. It was great to be a Husky during that time. Having success in a program that had success for years and years, you were part of something bigger than just yourself.

To me, the word to summarize what it meant for me to be a Husky was "privilege." Not only was there pride and great tradition, but it really was a privilege—not a lot of young men have the opportunity we had.

Mark Brunell was the MVP of the 1991 Rose Bowl and owned five Rose Bowl records. He scored more running touchdowns than any UW quarterback in a season, with 12 in 1990, which ties for sixth with all Huskies runners. His 758 career rushing yards is fourth-most by a UW quarterback. Brunell's 4,008 passing yards ranks 10th at the UW. He leads all UW passers in lowest interception percentage with just 17 picks in 563 career attempts (3.02 percent). He has played on three NFL teams in a 14-year career with the Green Bay Packers (1993–1994), Jacksonville Jaguars (1995–2003), and Washington Redskins (2004–2006). He is currently an NFL quarterback.

LINCOLN KENNEDY

OFFENSIVE TACKLE

1988–1992

THERE'S ONE PLAY I REMEMBER MOST during our Michigan victory in the 1992 Rose Bowl.

We were up by 20 points in the fourth quarter. We were 38 yards away from the end zone. We were having so much fun in that game.

We were in the huddle, and Mark said, "Okay, we're gonna score on this play."

And then I said, "Well, if we score, there's a party in the end zone. Everybody get down there and dance!"

Mark said, "Okay," and called the play. We went up to the line, and you could just feel the air, the air of confidence over all of us. Mark threw it up to Mario Bailey. Touchdown!

And then you saw the whole offense just rip up into the end zone, and we were all dancing in the end zone.

That night everyone stayed up the entire night waiting to see if we got it—the national championship. Everyone's door was open throughout the hotel. Everybody was partying from room to room. People were stepping in and out. Everyone stayed up, glued to ESPN. They had ESPN turned up really loud. And then when they finally came on and said it, you could just hear screams of jubilation.

"All right! We did it!"

Those are some of the fonder moments that I had playing up there.

So after we won the national championship, I had to make one of my biggest decisions. People kept asking me, "Are you going to leave? Are you going to come out early?"

A lot of guys were leaving to turn pro. I had such a great year. I basically just told everyone, "I'm going to stay here."

I wasn't going to leave the UW without a degree. If I lost millions of dollars in the NFL, then so be it. I don't look back and regret it at all because I did graduate with a degree in theater and a minor in communications.

Some guys come to Washington just to play football.

So when the news came out about Billy Jo Hobert's loan [which led to an NCAA investigation and sanctions for the UW], a lot of us, including myself, really didn't understand why it was such a big issue. If the guy wasn't a booster, if the guy wasn't an alumnus, then why was it such a big issue that Billy Joe got paid? So, back then, you didn't necessarily understand all the rules.

I came to Washington because I fell in love with the campus and the vibe.

I didn't grow up in an athletic family in San Diego. I didn't play sports until I turned out for high school football my sophomore year. I had the size. I came out of high school at 6'7", 300 pounds.

My first choice was Michigan. The tradition of college football there and aura of Ann Arbor intrigued me. My high school coach encouraged me to take as many trips as I could.

On my visit to Washington, it was beautiful—sunny and lush. You could see Mount Rainier from Red Square. It was so green. I just fell in love. I committed on that trip.

I made an impression my first day on the Husky Stadium turf. Not a good one. The very first day I showed up, the first day of practice, we had to run 40-yard times. After my first 40, I was coasting to a stop and tripped. I severely sprained my ankle. I watched the first couple days of training camp on crutches. The guys really razzed me. I mean, it was my first time running on the turf, and what did I do? I fell down and sprained my ankle. Guys used to tease me and say that a divot in that end zone near the tunnel came from me.

I redshirted my freshman year and practiced on defense. I remember that I was a little down because I was redshirting and not playing. I wasn't able to travel with the team. But an assistant coach, Myles Corrigan, came up to me and said, "You're as important as anyone else out there. You've got to help keep this crowd into the game."

Lincoln Kennedy came to Washington as a defensive lineman and left as a two-time All-American offensive tackle with a national championship ring.

And so from that point on, I became a cheerleader of sorts. I was in uniform, but I didn't play. At every home game that year, I was on the sideline. I was standing up with the crowd, trying to get the fans into it. That's when I learned to appreciate the love that Seattle fans show for the University of Washington and the traditions behind Husky Stadium.

I learned how seriously the people of Seattle and the students at the University of Washington took it. When you step into a stadium like Husky Stadium and see people way up there, nothing but purple and white except for just a small sliver in the corner end zone of the opposing team's color, it really makes you appreciate everything. I remember taking the bus home from the team hotel and watching all the boats line up on Lake Washington. Seeing all the banners, the purple-and-gold banners flying, and the tailgating. Having to get a police escort just to get on Montlake because it was crawling with cars and trucks with people trying to get to the stadium. It made me appreciate how big it was. It was truly something that was not to be messed with or toyed with. Seattle takes sports seriously, and from that point on, I knew that every Saturday belonged to the Dawgs.

What it means to be a Husky is being a great fan.

I really wanted to play defense the next season. I came in as a defensive lineman and was hoping to take over where Dennis Brown had left off. He was a senior. I told myself I'd learn the ropes and wait my turn.

I learned my redshirt freshman year that I would be switched to the offensive line. I was really nervous. I called my high school coach and told him about the change and asked him if he thought it was a good move. "If you switch to offense," he said, "you'll be All-Pro one day."

Those words kind of stuck with me over the years. That's what I used as my motivation. I went over to the offensive side. I wanted to do everything I could to get on the field, and I didn't care which position. It really turned out better for me.

I'll never forget my first start. We beat USC, blew them out, 31–0. I was at guard, and we threw a bunch of screens and ran the ball well. We totally dominated them. Our two previous games were close, and we were starting to doubt ourselves. So that game and winning the Freedom Bowl built a lot of confidence.

The UCLA loss in 1990, our only defeat that season, is often thought of as a catalyst to our undefeated season. I can tell you after that UCLA loss, there weren't many people thinking about a national championship. Watching the scoreboard cost us back-to-back national titles, in my opinion.

Before the UCLA game, we realized that we were on the brink of something very remarkable. But we fell off when we began to check the scoreboard. We were moving up in the rankings, and we started to watch the scoreboard for teams ahead of us to see where they came up. I didn't take

UCLA all that seriously. I think it was the Virginia game or something like that. So we found ourselves watching the scoreboard, waiting for it to come, and then we realized that we could be in the No. 1 spot. But UCLA had had our number.

Still, 10–2 was a great success. It was something that we had always dreamed of—winning the Rose Bowl. Being in Los Angeles on New Year's Day, playing in Pasadena in front of a sellout crowd of 106,000 people, and then being on national TV in a prime-time game was what we all wanted. You know, we were on top of the world. We were like kids in a candy store.

I remember the very first play from scrimmage in the Iowa Rose Bowl. It was a counter-trap. And it called for me to pull from the right side to the left to clear through for a linebacker. I just remember being amped up. I pulled through the hole, hit the linebacker square, knocked him down, and we had something like an eight-yard gain. I was psyched.

We had a different attitude for our second straight Rose Bowl trip. There was a determination to quiet all the journalists and skeptics. We came in undefeated and had practically obliterated everyone we'd played. I thought we would have gotten more respect than we did. And then came Michigan, who, not taking anything away from what they had done, but all they wanted to talk about was their big-name quarterback who was going to be a first-round draft pick.

I just felt that, as a team, we kind of had a chip on our shoulder, like it was time for us to earn some respect. We were going to go out there and show those people that we deserved to be No. 1. It wasn't a fluke. And we didn't care whom you put us up against. If Michigan was the best they had to offer, so be it. We'd take it and we'd shake it. And we did that.

We jelled. I think just about all of the freshman class that I came in with was playing some significant part on the team. And then the class behind us in 1989 was joining in as well. So we had a few good years of recruiting that all came together at one time. We fed off of one another. We had every weapon offensively. Defensively, we shut down people. Our defense could take over a game. Steve Emtman was a beast back then. He was playing on the other side of the ball just about every snap. And there was Donald Jones. There was a whole host of players on that team. All of us knew our position. All of us knew what our role was. All of us knew what we had to do; and believe me, we went out there and we played above and beyond the level everyone expected us to play.

And we had a one-two punch at quarterback. Billy Joe had a true passing arm, and Mark Brunell was more of a scrambling kind of quarterback. It was kind of the difference between Joe Montana and Steve Young. I was thankful because if one ever got hurt, we always had a competent back-up to come in.

I truly believe the allegations against us in 1992 were about people being jealous. It's like they were saying, "My God, they're too good." Some people began to realize that they couldn't handle us straight up, so they said that we must be cheating.

I look back at all the accolades and stuff that I won over the time there, and I was glad to be appreciated. But I had to start a new chapter in my life shortly after that. And being an All-American doesn't hold weight. It doesn't do anything for you in the NFL.

I was fortunate to play 11 seasons in the NFL. Coming back to Seattle always gave me a boost. Even though I was one of the hated Raiders when I came back and used to play against the Seahawks, I never heard any boos when I was introduced in the Kingdome. I was cheered for when they introduced my name. And that really made me feel good.

Lincoln Kennedy was a consensus All-American, All–Pac-10 first-team selection, two-time Morris Trophy winner (Pac-10 top lineman), finalist for the Lombardi Award, and semifinalist for the Outland Trophy in 1992. He earned All-America and All–Pac-10 honors as a junior. He allowed only two sacks in four years. Kennedy was a first-round pick by the Atlanta Falcons and played 11 seasons in the NFL, eight with the Oakland Raiders.

DAVE HOFFMANN

LINEBACKER

1988–1992

WHEN I THINK ABOUT MY HUSKIES DAYS, I have lots of great memories. I grew up in San Jose, California. I looked at all the Pac-10 schools. The Huskies were a solid team, and Coach Don James and Jim Lambright had great reputations. I was excited to come to Washington.

I redshirted my first year in 1988. The hardest thing for me was missing home. It was rough being 900 miles away in a new city. I knew right away we had a bunch of great guys in our recruiting class who were champing at the bit to get on the field.

During away games, Steve Emtman and I would drive over to his parents' house in Cheney. We'd hang out at his parents' farm and mess around with his high school buddies.

My first year, the team went 6–5 and no bowl. We made a commitment after that season to get better. The work ethic in the weight room, winter conditioning, and spring practice were big reasons we became what we did.

I saw my first action the next season in the opening game against Texas A&M on special teams. I began to start at linebacker about mid-season. We finished the year off with a strong win against Florida in the Freedom Bowl.

Our defense kept improving my sophomore year. Lambright was the captain of our defensive ship. I loved his aggressive style and that of my teammates.

Dave Hoffmann's intensity made him a leader on the 1991 national championship team, and he led the UW in tackles for three seasons.

We finished the regular season 8–2, and barely lost to UCLA. We were in position to win—woulda, coulda, shoulda. We blew it. But we ended the year on a high note by beating a good Iowa team in the Rose Bowl.

The worst thing about the game was that James Clifford wasn't able to play. He injured his knee in the preseason. I wore his cleats in the Rose Bowl. It was great to get back on the field with him the next year.

Senior players like Travis Richardson, John Cook, and Eric Briscoe were the reason we got to Pasadena and got the Huskies defense to become what it was.

We were extremely determined for the 1991 season. Our mission started in January, and everyone was on board.

It was a joy to line up with the guys we had and get after it. We had a crew who were smart and loved to hit. The coaches gave us great game plans and had confidence in us. They let us attack and create havoc for offenses.

No one could match the intensity and excitement of our defensive huddle. We'd challenge each other—who would make the next big play, big hit, who would get the next turnover. We'd celebrate with each other after almost every play.

We loved to have our team chaplain, Mike Rohrbach, with us during the week and on game day. A big group of us would walk into the shower area to pray right before kickoff. I remember the sound of our cleats on the tile floor.

Beating Michigan 34–14 in the Rose Bowl was an exclamation point for our 12–0 season. I would have been shocked if we had not been given at least a share of the national championship. We really only celebrated together in Pasadena. There was not a party or parade for the guys when we showed up in Seattle.

An added joy to the season was having my brother Steve on the team. He redshirted that year, so we looked forward to my senior year when we could be on the field together.

Steve could have gone to any school he wanted. I was pumped up when he decided to be a Husky. He's a true warrior. There was nothing like playing with my brother. Steve was the epitome of the class of player the Huskies were getting in those years. He was a great athlete with a great attitude who could strike and also had the team player mentality.

Steve and I often talk about the great guys we played with. We had all kinds of characters, and every one of them would always cover your back.

We had another great run the next year, and then the wheels came off after some off-the-field issues came up. Although the team went through a rough few weeks, we never had any animosity toward any of the players.

Our loss in the Rose Bowl was a hard one. It was tough knowing it was the last time I'd play for the Huskies and with my brother. That was the hardest time I had at Washington, right there at the end of my last game.

It's part of life, things come to an end. The hardest thing is when that fight is over. Steve and I did not want to leave the field. We were the last two Huskies off the field. We took our time getting back to the locker room.

The Bears drafted me, but I was caught between a coaching change and let go at the end of camp. I went to the Steelers and played special teams. I tore my groin the second year. By my third year, I was with the 49ers, back near my home town. But I started having problems with my neck, and I knew that was the end for me.

What being a Husky means to me is…being blessed to be associated with the players, coaches, and support staff who were at the UW during those years.

Dave Hoffmann's fearsome hitting and intensity were traits that helped him to consecutive first-team All-America selections as a linebacker, the first Husky so honored since linebacker Rick Redmond in 1963–1964. He collected several other honors: a Dick Butkus Award finalist; Pac-10 Defensive Player of the Year award; Pac-10 All-Conference (twice); the Husky Tyee Club Football Athlete of the Year award; the KIRO Pete Gross Player of the Year award; and the Guy Flaherty Award for most inspirational player. Hoffmann led the UW in tackles three straight seasons and ranks fifth all-time in tackles for loss with 46. Drafted by the Chicago Bears and released, he played in the NFL three seasons with the Pittsburgh Steelers (2) and San Francisco 49ers (1) before injuries ended his career. He currently works in personal security.

CHARLES MINCY

DEFENSIVE BACK

1989–1990

I ALWAYS TELL THIS STORY: I always dreamed of scoring a touchdown in the Rose Bowl. My mom used to drag me to church on Sundays. When I was in high school, I'd sit in church and daydream of making an interception and scoring in the Rose Bowl.

And the weird thing is, it happened just like I dreamed it.

In the 1991 Rose Bowl, I did intercept a pass and returned it 37 yards for a touchdown in the first half. It was like déjà vu.

We changed from a zone team to a blitzing team. We disguised our defenses well. The Iowa quarterback came to the line and checked off. I don't think the receiver picked it up. I don't think the receiver stopped where he was supposed to. The quarterback threw it right to me.

Later in game, I caught a tipped pass when we pressured the quarterback on a rollout. I had a forced fumble and four broken-up passes that day. It was a great way to end my Huskies career. Especially considering my road to Washington.

I didn't get any Division 1 offers coming out of Los Angeles's Dorsey High. I really wanted to go to the University of Southern California. I remember the first football game I ever went to was 'SC vs. Washington in the Coliseum. Washington won. Still, I was a big 'SC fan.

So I went to Pasadena Community College for two years. 'SC wasn't interested in junior-college players at the time. I was recruited by Washington almost by accident. The Huskies were scouting Scott Miller, a highly touted wide receiver at Saddleback Junior College. We played them, and I shut him down and had two picks. The UW coach was impressed. Miller went to UCLA (and played with the Miami Dolphins), and I went to Washington. Everything works out for a reason.

It wasn't too much of an adjustment going to Washington from a junior college. We didn't have a lot of depth at corner at the time. Le-Lo Lang was the only senior corner. It was good timing for me. Dana Hall, William Doctor, Ivory Randle, and I all played quite a bit my first season. I started most of my junior year.

I also won the punt-return duties. I took my first punt return for 39 yards, but it was called back. Then against Purdue, on my second return, I scored a touchdown, but it was called back, too. Those were my two longest returns. My senior year, Beno Bryant, my high school teammate, took over returning punts. I couldn't argue with that one.

The Arizona State game my junior year was my worst. I got beat for a touchdown, and if Eugene Burkhalter had not picked off a pass, I would've given up two touchdowns. When you fail, you have to be able to let those things go. You try, but it's tough. That was the worst I felt after a game about my individual performance.

366

Beating the hell out of 'SC in Seattle my senior year was most gratifying. If the Rose Bowl was my best game, this was my second best. We beat them 31–0. I was matched up against Gary Wellman. I was jamming him so much he was complaining to the refs all day.

My senior year we had such a great team. It was such a privilege to play with those dudes up front—Donald Jones, Steve Emtman, and Jaime Fields. They made things so much easier for us DBs. The quarterbacks didn't have a lot of time to throw. If I ran down the field and cut them off, I'd be okay. We didn't have to cover our guys very long.

That UCLA loss was the most disappointing game overall. I woke up the next day, and I really didn't believe it happened. That was unreal.

My two years at Washington were the most memorable days of my life and the most fun. I played nine years in the NFL and I never had a better experience of being on a team, especially my senior year. That 10–2 season was so memorable and the camaraderie so strong. Those teammates are some of my best friends. I have three guys I keep in contact with from the NFL. But I see half the guys from that team at least once a year, starters and walk-ons.

Charles Mincy didn't have a single Division-1 offer out of high school, so he went to a junior college before playing two years at the UW and earning All–Pac-10 honors.

I see a lot of Huskies down here in L.A. because I'm the head football coach at Inglewood High. There are several Huskies involved in high school sports down here. The biggest thing I learned from Coach Don James that is making me a better high school coach is how to delegate responsibility to my assistant coaches. Coach James instructed the coaches on what he wanted done. Now, I'm learning more and more you can't do it all yourself. You have to let other people do their thing, too.

Charles Mincy, a junior-college transfer, made an immediate impact on the program. He was named the Huskies' Most Improved in 1990 and earned All–Pac-10 honors as a senior. He played in the East-West Shrine Game. Mincy played nine seasons in the NFL with the Kansas City Chiefs, Tampa Bay Buccaneers, Minnesota Vikings, and Oakland Raiders. He is currently the head football coach at Inglewood High, California.

BILLY JOE HOBERT

QUARTERBACK

1989–1992

M Y RECRUITING STORY TO THE UW is easy. Our Puyallup High football team won the state championship my junior year with me at quarterback, and I received a letter in the locker room after the game. It said: "You are officially being recruited." It was signed by Don James.

Until then, I had not given college football a second thought. Baseball always had been my passion. That letter clicked on the idea that maybe I could be a college quarterback.

I've always been a Northwest and Puyallup boy. I've always been a UW fan, still am. Once I was recruited by Washington, I immediately decided I wanted to be a Husky. They didn't have to give me a sales job. Everyone knew it.

I went to see UCLA and Troy Aikman play in Husky Stadium the fall of my senior year. It was my first time seeing the Huskies at home in person. I was sitting in the horseshoe end when I heard the roar of the fans as the players came out of the tunnel. Hearing the cheers coming off the aluminum roof floored me.

I was most nervous about the schooling aspect of the UW. Nobody in my family had gone to college. For me, sports was about going out and playing as hard as I could.

The first two guys I met were D'Marco Farr and Jamal Fountaine, both up from California. I don't think I could've gone out of state. I would've been too homesick.

Football was hard all the way around. We had major competition at every position. We wanted to compete with each other in everything. To be around the strongest, fastest level of competition raised everyone's effort.

Learning the UW offense was an easy transition because my high school coach, Mike Huard, father of Damon and Brock, ran the UW's offense at Puyallup. So I had been running the same offense for two years. As a freshman I knew 60–70 percent of the plays. It was a huge advantage for me. The UW offense did evolve to more of an open passing attack as I was there.

Speaking of the Huards, Damon was a tight end while I was quarterback at Puyallup, and Brock was my ball boy. Both, of course, became quarterbacks and went on to record-setting Huskies careers. Every time I see Brock, all I see is my ball boy.

I sat out my first year as a redshirt, and it was the worst experience of my life. I didn't get on the field for a game for a full year. I played primarily on the scout team. I don't recall ever getting beaten up. I think quarterbacks were wearing red shirts so defenders wouldn't hit us. I missed the contact.

I'm a bit of an egomaniac. I have to get involved. I'd do anything I could to be involved with the team or be on the field. There was this quote by Coach James: "Billy Joe thought he could do everything because he tried everything."

Going into the spring practices of my sophomore year, I seriously considered my options of playing a different position to get on the field. I talked to coaches about playing tight end. I continued to work on my punting. I was a good punter and even started against USC as a punter my redshirt freshman year. That's when 'SC said if Billy Joe started as a punter, he wouldn't finish the game. They went after me on my first punt, and eight guys ran me over.

I thought of other positions because quarterback Mark Brunell was the guy. He led us to a Rose Bowl victory the season before. One play, however, changed everything. Mark went down with a terrible knee injury in practice. I didn't know how severe it was. I got to go out and finish the drills, but I didn't anticipate how long he might be out. D.J. is very loyal to his players who go out with injuries. I was sure I'd relinquish the position soon. That is, until we all found out the seriousness of Mark's injury. We were told Mark might miss the whole 1991 season. Then I knew I was the starter. I never thought about being nervous about it. I had a job to do.

Coaches and many teammates weren't so sure. You see, I'm a horrible practice quarterback. I'm very unsettled in practice. I'm not a prototype

Billy Joe Hobert is the only quarterback to lead Washington to an undefeated season and never lose a game as a starter.

quarterback—mentally or physically. I have a natural aggressiveness that's not conductive to being a quarterback. Practices were often a nightmare. Offensive coordinator Keith Gilbertson never uttered so many four-letter words, because I'd have poor practices three times a week.

At least I got the opportunity to show I'm a gamer. I focus extremely well in games. I want to beat every person who steps in front of me. I was cocky enough. I didn't stop being cocky until my third year in the NFL. I felt nobody could beat me. Teammates never expressed it in front of me, but after the season some said to me how worried they were when I became the starter. "Man, we thought you were going to suck this year," they said.

I had the whole summer and summer camp to prepare mentally for our season opener against Stanford, a smashing 42–7 victory.

The second week we played at Nebraska. If I had to pick one game, other than the Rose Bowl, Nebraska is my favorite. What I remember most is the euphoria of being around fans. The Cornhuskers fans were calling me "Betty Sue" and "Bobby Jean." They threw drinks and ice cubes on us. It was pretty cool seeing nothing but a sea of fans in red. When we walked off the field, 36–21 victors, we anticipated being bombed, but they all stood up and gave us a respectful clap. It was insane.

The key play of the game, and the season, was a fourth-and-eight play near their end zone. I remember coming to the sideline, and Coach James expressed how big the play was. I remember going back to the huddle and thinking, "If we get this first down, we're going to win the national championship." We scored!

I've never told anyone that. It was one part wishful thinking and one part bartering with God: "If you get me out of this one, I'll promise I'll never do anything bad."

We had two close games that season, USC and Cal, and I played badly enough for us to lose both. In the Cal game, Walter Bailey broke up a pass at the end to preserve our 24–17 win. At 'SC, nothing was clicking with the offense. I threw a pick and fumbled. I remember flying home from the USC game, and I wasn't able to sleep. Even though we won, I vowed that that would not happen again. It was horrible. We just weren't scoring.

In our final two games, we put up 58 and 56 points to end the regular season 11–0. Going into the Rose Bowl against Michigan, Coach James and Coach Gilbertson had me so focused. I had the entire game plan memorized two weeks before the game. All I remember hearing about was Desmond

Howard and Elvis Grbac. I didn't think they stood a chance in hell competing against us.

Every Husky did his job. After a scoreless first quarter, we scored first in
the second quarter on my two-yard run. Michigan answered with a touchdown, but then two field goals by Travis Hanson put us ahead for good. Our
UW defense dominated. I threw two short touchdown passes in the second
half, and Brunell hit Mario Bailey on a 38-yard touchdown pass in our 34–14
victory.

To win in the fashion we did was the perfect ending to a 12–0 season. It
was such an honor to be part of that. I remember sitting at the hotel waiting
for the polls to come out. When it was announced we were No. 1 in the
coaches' poll and Miami was No. 1 in the writers' poll, I felt such joy and
ache. I felt half-full. I was so mad we couldn't play Miami to settle it.

The glow of winning a national championship didn't last long. After the
first week of 1992, the rest of the year was a tough, tough year.

That summer I was married and broke. I wasn't allowed to do anything
but small summer jobs. I remember being 20 with my wife pregnant and
thinking, "How am I going to go to college and support a family?"

I was working at a golf course and playing golf once a week with a buddy
of mine. We talked about how I was getting nervous trying to figure out how
I was going to make it. He introduced me to his father-in-law, who lived in
Idaho, about a personal loan.

My wife and I separated, and I had about a billion distractions. I turned 21,
and sometimes you don't make a lot of good decisions at that age. My life was
such a freaking joke. Still, when it came to football, I was able to pull it
together on the field. I didn't think we were as good as the 1991 team, but
we got the job done and were ranked No. 1 or No. 2 through the first eight
weeks with an 8–0 record. My first start was against Stanford, and a 41–7
home victory over Stanford in week eight of 1992 was my last game as a
Husky.

The first inkling something was wrong came during an interview with a
Seattle Times reporter. I was trying to get my life in order. My wife and I had
just gotten back together. A guy was mentoring me in Christianity, and I was
eager to try to turn my life around. So the interview turned out to be smoke
and mirrors. The article was supposed to be about my new lifestyle. So at the
end of the interview he asked, "So with all this stuff going on, how do you
deal with the fact you took out an illegal loan?"

I was stunned. "The loan was 100 percent legit," I said. "I have to pay back the money."

The story exploded the week of the Arizona game, and all hell broke loose. I think most people don't understand the loan wasn't from a booster. I wasn't spending it on drinking, drugs, or guns. I've never taken an illegal drug in my life.

One thing I'd like to express is that I never ever desired to put the UW in a situation that would cause such uproar. At that time, I bled purple and gold. I put my life and career on the line for purple and gold. I was requested to stay quiet. And I did. Knowing what I know now, I would've stood up for myself and defended myself to avoid the death threats and public scrutiny, all to protect two or three people. People don't like me because they were told not to like me. Someday, the truth will come out. If I had acted accordingly, a lot worse things would have happened than a two-year bowl ban. In the end, the UW did not receive a single sanction because of my loan. Granted, I take responsibility for the fact that it opened the door for an investigation.

The Huskies fans are phenomenal. I understand why many reacted the way they did because they felt someone was slighting their school. I appreciated playing at Washington. I'm very proud of their tradition. We've had so many great players. It's impossible not to be proud of being a Husky.

I'm proud to be the only undefeated starting quarterback with more than a dozen starts. UW teams were 20–0 when I started at quarterback. I was more interested in a trophy. I never cared about my stats. As far as pride, I'm most proud of being part of that national championship experience than anything else.

I went on to a nine-year NFL career with the Raiders, Bills, Saints, and Colts. My first marriage, sadly, didn't survive, and I've since remarried. I'd like to think the lessons I've learned the hard way make me a better man, better husband, and better father. I cherish my wife and family. We've been raising our family in Southern California. I've worked in real estate and the travel industry. I do long to return to the Northwest.

I've actually had to block out my future regarding the UW. As I said, I'm a Northwest boy through and through. That part is tearing me up inside. I'm not home.

I'd love to be a part of UW again because I have so many experiences— good and bad. I'm not counting on it or even anticipating it. Until people understand how loyalty and a locker room works, they won't understand.

Washington state is my home, and I will be back someday. I'm still a Huskies fan and have attended a lot of away games.

I've been back to Husky Stadium once, when I was with Indianapolis for a preseason game. I'm not going back to Husky Stadium unless I'm invited.

It was so humiliating the way everything happened. And since then I've felt every opportunity was closed to me. Now, 15 years later, I don't know if I would be emotionally able to handle it. My ultimate Huskies dream would be to join the Huskies coaching staff.

Billy Joe Hobert is the only UW quarterback to lead his team to a 12–0 season and a national championship. He was 20–0 as the UW's starting quarterback. Hobert played in 27 UW games (four as a punter only) and never lost. He has the fourth-lowest career interception percentage (3.05 percent—16 interceptions in 464 attempts) in UW history. His 2,463 passing yards in 1991 was second-most in UW history at the time and now ranks sixth. His 3,220 career passing yards ranks 13th. Hobert's 24 touchdowns in 1991 set a school record (now ranks third). Hobert played nine NFL seasons with the Oakland/L.A. Raiders (1993–1996), Buffalo Bills (1997), New Orleans Saints (1997–1999), and Indianapolis Colts (2000–2001). He is currently living in Southern California and working on a "semi-fictitious autobiography."

BENO BRYANT

RUNNING BACK/RETURNER

1989–1993

I GREW UP IN SOUTHERN CALIFORNIA, and that's where I make my life now. These days I go by the name of Wilson Bryant. Huskies fans still remember me as Beno (the nickname handed down from my grandfather to my father, and then to me).

Despite living in L.A., I'm still a die-hard Husky. I live for Huskies football. To me, being a Husky means having character, being a man, and being tough as nails. It's about being a good citizen and representing the university wherever you go as a player. I think in the past few years, they either don't know what it means to be a Husky or those who do didn't care. It hasn't been about the team. It's been about themselves. But being a Husky means you are always optimistic, I think we'll be fine. My time is over, and I really want them to get back to that zenith.

All I have to do is play video football to remember that zenith. Whenever I play football on PlayStation, I always pick the Huskies. If I want to beat someone badly, I grab our 1991 national championship team. I know the offense and defense so well, nobody can beat me. It's fun. It brings back a lot of memories. As an interesting aside, I was hired to do a lot of the motion captures to help the games be more realistic.

My career at Washington was a blessing. I made the best of my opportunities. I got injured, so that cut into my time on the field. But I had fun and learned a lot. I played with the greatest player in college history, Steve Emt-man. I had the greatest coach, Don James. We had great assistant coaches ded-icated to Huskies football. Coach Myles Corrigan, for example, had a heart attack during the Cal game and continued to coach us to victory. I met a lot of great individuals.

For those who look at records, Beno Bryant is still scattered throughout the UW books. Records were not important to me. It was about being accountable. I was more about getting the crowd into it than trying to get records. At that time at Washington, everyone took it upon himself to take his game to a higher level. I just want to be remembered as a good person who gave his best because records come and go. As long as I'm remembered, I'm okay with that.

I played during an exciting time at Washington. I saw it all—my freshman year we were rebuilding from a 6–5 season the previous year. I played on Washington's only undefeated team. And I was there when Coach James resigned.

I decided to go to Washington the day before the official signing day. I was overlooked coming out of Dorsey High in Los Angeles. I think Washington recruited four or five running backs ahead of me. They all went elsewhere. I was set to go to Oregon State before Washington made me a scholarship offer at the last minute.

376

Washington was taking a chance because I was a little guy. There were no Warrick Dunns or Bookers in college football. There weren't any small backs in D-1 football taking a pounding before I got there. My success as a small back opened the doors for others my size in college football, including my successor, Napoleon Kaufman, the fastest tailback in Huskies history. People don't want to give me my props for that. I just laugh because it's the truth. I showed I could run, catch the ball, run back kick returns and punts. And I could block.

Greg Lewis was a great teacher for me. I was arrogant coming in. And I got banged around in two-a-days. I finally asked him, "Why is this happen-ing?"

He sat me down and started teaching me blocking responsibilities and how to read the front line and the linebackers, and then how to understand what the safeties and corners would do. Hugh McElhenny is called "the King" and is recognized as the greatest running back to come out of Washington. I call Greg Lewis "the Prince." He was a great mentor.

Beno Bryant's success as a running back and returner opened the door for other "small" running backs to come.

When I arrived at Washington, I thought we had the talent to run the table. My freshman year, we lost to Colorado in the fourth week. I felt kind of bad because I wasn't used to losing. I looked around at those other players, the expressions on their faces and their mannerisms, I could tell we had something special. It was just a change of mental attitude after that. We started caring about each other on and off the field. We became a family, and it was a special feeling.

The first time I got on the field as a running back was the Freedom Bowl when I was a freshman. There was 39 seconds left, and I went in against Florida to run out the clock. I was lined up in the I formation. It was still exciting for me.

The start of my sophomore year, I earned the punt-return job. Before our season-opening game against San Jose State, I told UW basketball player Laurie Merlino I'd score on a punt. I saw her coming out of the weight room, and she said, "Good luck."

"I'm going to score," I said.

The day before, I told punter Darryl Green, who I'm still close to, "I'm going to score me a touchdown tomorrow on a punt return."

"All right, I believe," he said.

On my first punt return, I got smashed. This dude hit me just after I caught the punt, and the impact bent in my face mask. Each punt I gained confidence. I could feel it coming. We were trailing with about three minutes left, and I busted it. I ran it in from 54 yards for the 20–17 win. I ran back two others for touchdowns that year, 82 yards [vs. ASU] and 70 yards [vs. Arizona]. I got my fourth career punt-return touchdown the next season with a 53-yarder against Kansas State.

My only real embarrassing moment on the field came my sophomore year. I missed a block in the backfield that led to a sack. The coaches called me on it in the film review. I buckled down and learned how to block. I didn't miss another block the rest of my Huskies career. I didn't want my quarterback to get hit.

I can remember all of the games. One of the games that sticks out the most was the Nebraska game in 1991. We were down 21–6 in our second game of the season. I started seeing how offensive coordinator Keith Gilbertson was pressing their defense, and then I saw what defensive coordinator Jim Lambright was doing to disrupt the continuity of their offense. Before that I just played football. I hurt my knee that year during summer practices. Instead of calling plays for me to run laterally, I was going up the middle, running downhill so I didn't have to cut hard. I didn't understand that until later. It worked out. I finished with 139 yards as we scored 27 unanswered points to win 36–21.

I ran for a few yards that year (981) despite my knee. The coaches used to say when a person is sick or hurt, you still have to go to work. The coaches would say, "We didn't ask you to play football. You wanted to play football. So play when you have the opportunity to play, go out and play."

I think Coach Gilbertson was an offensive genius. His philosophy was to take what the defense gave us. If they closed the gaps to stop the run, then we'd beat them with the pass. We had two great quarterbacks in Mark Brunell and Billy Joe Hobert. We had great receivers, and the offensive line was killer. We knew how the move the ball, and Coach Gilbertson knew how to distribute the ball. And we didn't have a drop-off with the second team. I give a lot of credit to the offense for our national championship, but our defense was just amazing. That defense was impenetrable.

That 1991 year, the Southern Cal game was special. We hadn't won in the Coliseum in about a decade. Our defense won that one 14–3.

It all came down to the Rose Bowl, with only Michigan standing in our way of perfection. We knew we had the Wolverines the moment we knew we'd play them. Just the Rose Bowl presence was great. We were mini-celebrities down there. One of the best parts was we got to see coaches in a different light. We'd see them with their families. We'd see the coaches calling their wives, "Honey," and calling their sons, "My boy." We saw them as real people. It was a lovely experience.

379

I found out after the game from a couple Michigan players that their staff had a plan to get me out of the game. They respected me and thought I'd quit running hard by pounding me until I came out of the game. I was taking everything they were dishing out. Then a guy pulled me down on a punt return and twisted my ankle. It knocked me out of the game in the third quarter. I kind of felt like I let the team down by being injured. But Jay Barry came in and ran well.

After our 34–14 victory, I was emotionally drained from the intensity of going undefeated for 12 games. I was just happy to relax.

My senior year, I was extremely comfortable with the offense because I really understood how it worked. It would have been an explosive year for myself, but I got a hamstring injury before the season started during two-a-days. I was running a pass route. I sat out that whole year.

My relationship with Napoleon Kaufman was great. He came in, and I showed him the ropes. We started hanging out and became good friends. The media wanted to make it as if we had problems. I've never had a problem with him. We had a good relationship. Napoleon and I would watch film together, and I would let him know he was going to carry on the Huskies running back tradition. He was an exceptionally blessed player. So who was faster? We raced in a 60-yard dash indoors, and I beat him. I always remind him of that. But he beat me by three steps or so in the 40. He had a great start. He ran a 4.19 and a 4.24 twice. My fastest 40-yard time was 4.31.

Before the start of my second senior season, Coach James stunned us all by retiring. James was great. His way of letting us have fun was getting us prepared to go out and kick people's butt. When he told the team of his decision, it was probably one of the worst moments of my life. He gave me the opportunity to play, and I still had things I wanted to show him that I could do on the field. I wanted him to see me graduate (I earned a degree in ethnic studies). It brought tears to my eyes when he stepped down. For a man with such immense integrity and character to be criticized and tarnished for no reason at all, it's very hard for any young man to swallow. We lost our leader. It was tough. The things that were stated about him were hurtful, not just to him, but to the players and coaches all around.

Napoleon came in and did well while I sat out a year, so I had to wait my turn and play a back-up role. It's not the ending I hoped for, but when you are on a team, you don't have control.

I took everything as a challenge. If we needed two yards, I'd fight for those two yards. I liked the zone plays the most. I could run downhill and hit a crease, and it was over. I didn't feel one guy could tackle me. If I got to the safety, it was over.

I felt I was a threat no matter what. When I ran, I ran in silence. I couldn't hear the crowd, only me talking to myself. If I went through a hole and people were swinging for the ball, I'd whisper, "No, no. You're not going to get it."

If a dude was hanging on me, I'd say in my head, "Let go, get off me!"

If I was running away from someone, it was, "You're not going to catch me!"

After my Huskies career ended, I played for the Rams and Seattle a little bit. I floated around and played in the World League. I learned more football, and it was fun. But it was nothing like Huskies football. It wasn't about how much talent you had in the pros. They weren't going to play a guy making $250,000 over a guy making millions.

I returned to my high school as a teacher and assistant football coach. Going back to my inner-city high school was one of the greatest feelings ever. You see yourself in a lot of those kids. It's great to see ambitious kids out there doing a sport and going to school.

Those are the same reasons I still follow the Huskies.

Beno Bryant paved the way for small backs at Washington. He earned All-Pac-10 honors in 1990. He is the UW's career leader in punt-return yards (1,086), total kick returns (154), total punt returns (112), and punt returns for touchdowns (4). Bryant ranks first in punt-return yards in a season (593), second in punt-return yards per attempt (15.6) for a season, fourth in UW career all-purpose yards (3,981), fifth in career rushing yards per attempt (5.2), 12th in career rushing yards (1,826), and 13th in rushing yards for a season (981). He played briefly for the Los Angeles Rams and Seattle Seahawks, and in the World League. He currently works for a utility company and in real estate in Los Angeles.

NAPOLEON KAUFMAN
RUNNING BACK/RETURNER
1991–1994

M Y DEFORMITY WAS offset by a blessing.
I really couldn't carry the ball with my right hand because of a deformity in my wrist. I can't turn my wrist all the way over, so I couldn't cradle the football in my right hand as well as I could with my left hand. I had some fumbles, but I did pretty well keeping the ball in my left hand as I ran. I managed to catch passes, punts, and kickoffs.

After my four seasons, I had carried the football for more rushing yards, more touchdowns, and more all-purpose yards than anyone else in Huskies history.

They say no UW player has run 40 yards faster than my 4.22 seconds. Yes, I was blessed with speed, but I also had drive and a love for football.

I stand just 5′8½″. I never felt small, however, as I worked hard to build my body. I could bench press 420 pounds. I loved practices because I loved to play football, anytime, anywhere.

When I ran, everything would go quiet. I was so focused, it was like tunnel vision. Then, when I got to my destination, all my peripheral vision and the sound would suddenly rush back and bring me back to reality.

When I'd get the handoff, I could sense electricity in the air and a hush in Husky Stadium. I could see it when I watched tape of the games. You could see people on the edge of their seats, as if they were thinking, "What is this guy going to do?"

Napoleon Kaufman, the UW's all-time rushing yardage leader, is considered the fastest player in Huskies history.

What I tried to do is help Washington win games. We had some great wins during my four seasons. We had some tough times, too.

To me, my time at Washington was a privilege. A privilege to be part of the school during a time when there was a lot of excitement. It was also a privilege to be in college. I came from a small town in Lompoc, California, and not many people in my family had gone to college.

I had my pick of colleges. I was recruited by everyone from Notre Dame to USC. I wanted to get out of California. Mark Brunell lived close to me in Santa Maria, and he was influential. When I took my trip to Washington, the Huskies were doing great at the time. The people were great, too. I felt comfortable. I can't put my finger on one thing. I liked what I saw.

Once there, my first impression with the program was I thought it was very professional. I thought Coach Don James always had his finger on the pulse of the team. I thought the organization was run very clean. I was pretty nervous, in the sense of being at a new school and making new friends. I was still confident in my abilities. I came to play.

There was an adjustment being away from home. The big adjustment was that everyone there was the star on their high school team, and then each of us got to the UW, and they treated us like everyone else. We were each just one of the guys. Beno Bryant and Matt Jones took me under their wings.

I started on a scout team for a little while. Then I was moved up to the second and third teams. I probably got hit harder in our practices than I did in games. I was pushed up the depth charts relatively quickly.

I played in every game my freshman year, on kick returns and runs here and there.

I had a few nice runs as a freshman. I had a memorable kickoff return in the national championship game in the Rose Bowl. That was fun. You don't really appreciate things until you are a little older. I took it for granted. I wish I had enjoyed it more. I was naïve coming out of high school. The hype of it all and the crowd of 100,000 is what I remember most.

I became a starter as a sophomore. Even though we lost a lot of talent, I believed we had a shot at repeating as national champions. Injuries to Beno and Jay Barry made the season my coming-out year. I had 159 yards, including a 70-yard breakaway, against Arizona State, and after that the floodgates opened. I had 1,000-plus yards rushing my last three seasons.

One fumble I do remember, that still bothers me, was the one in the 1993 Rose Bowl against Michigan. It did kind of turn the game around. Since we lost by seven points, all I can say is, yeah, I blew it.

Going into the 1993 season, I heard about Coach James stepping down like everyone else—I heard it on the news. We had a meeting, and that was my saddest day as a Husky. I cried. It was really tough.

I thought we did a great job of bouncing back from adversity. We had some great wins my junior and senior years with back-to-back 7–4 seasons. We were not eligible for bowl games thanks to the Pac-10 sanctions.

I went on to a six-year career in the NFL with the Oakland Raiders. I had the money, the cars, the house, but still didn't feel like I had it all together. My life was heading in the wrong direction. You can look like you have everything going right, but inside you know something is not right. Some people try to fill that void with drugs and sexual relationships. A Raiders teammate ministered to me, and as a result I gave my life to Jesus Christ and felt the call of God. I decided to retire and plant a church in Dublin, just outside of Oakland. It's called The Well Church. So I've been the senior pastor there since.

Being a Husky, number one, helped me to grow up as a young man. I believe it helped me to develop more discipline in my life. The career records mean the most to me now. It's one thing to come in and have one good season. To have the longevity was important to me. I like to be a finisher. More than the records, I hope I brought excitement to Huskies fans who watched our team.

> Napoleon Kaufman, the fastest Husky ever, thrilled fans for four years and broke many records as the only Husky to run for more than 4,000 yards in a career. He earned All-America honors in 1993 and 1994 and All-Conference three times. He owns UW records for career rushing yards (4,106), rushing attempts (735), rushing touchdowns (34), all-purpose yards (5,832), 100-yard rushing games (17), most 200-yard games (4), and most 50-plus yard runs (6). Kaufman played six seasons for the Oakland Raiders, where he owns the single-game team record for rushing yards (227), and his 4,792 career rushing yards ranks fourth in team history. He is currently senior pastor at The Well Church in Dublin, California.

MARK BRUENER

TIGHT END

1991–1994

TWO DAYS BEFORE I PLAYED in my first game as a Huskies freshman, our starting tight end, Aaron Pierce, a senior whom I looked up to, gave me some advice.

"You need to prepare yourself as if you are a starter because you never know when you'll play," he said.

He was so right. You have to be ready for your chance. That's a message that has stuck with me. You never know what play is going to be the game-breaker. I still use the philosophy in football and life. I've been fortunate to play a dozen seasons in the NFL as a tight end. In the NFL, the difference between teams is so slim, there are usually three or four plays that determine a game, so you have to play each one like it's the most important. You can't take anything for granted.

I was fortunate to be recruited by every Pac-10 school and Notre Dame while in high school at Aberdeen. My mom wanted me to attend Stanford so much she wrote "Stanford" on my pillow so I'd sleep on the idea.

Being a Huskies and Seahawks fan growing up, I wanted to stay close to home. When I made the decision to be a Husky, Mom didn't talk to me for two days. She got over it. My parents gave me tremendous support and attended every home and away game while I was at Washington.

Two weeks before the 1991 season started, it was decided that Napoleon Kaufman and I would be the only incoming freshmen who would not sit out

Two-time All-American Mark Bruener elevated UW's tradition of producing standout tight ends with a school-record 95 career catches.

the year. They put me at second-string tight end. They liked my 6′4″, 216-pound size and good hands.

One of the freshmen traditions is to sing in front of the team at the Crew House at mealtime. So Napoleon and I had to get up and sing one day after practice. Napoleon is such a great singer, the team made him sing a couple songs. I, however, didn't want to sing at all, so I made sure mine was horrible so I only had to do it once.

We opened at Stanford and beat them 42–7. After the game, I asked Mom, "Aren't you glad I didn't go to Stanford?" She nodded.

To be part of such a great football team in 1991 was amazing. It was a perfect season.

I realized how good we were after the second week of the season when we beat Nebraska on the road, 36–21. After the game, I remember the feeling in the locker room was we could really run the table.

The amazing thing about our team was how dominate our defense was at every position. They were constantly making big plays, and our defense was scoring a couple touchdowns a game, too.

I played three games before attending my first class. Coaches forced us to go to study hall every day for an hour or two. Defensive line coach Randy Hart, who recruited me, and my position coach, Myles Corrigan, were constantly asking me, "Are you going to class? How are your studies going?"

At the time, I thought, *These guys are so annoying, why can't they leave me alone?* Then you realize afterward how much they cared about athletes and how they impressed on us that we were there to play football and get an education. It's like you appreciate your parents more as you get older. Their monitoring really helped me. Randy and I are still good friends.

I caught my first collegiate pass in the back of the Rose Bowl end zone. It was a broken route against Michigan. We were at the 5-yard line, and I went across the middle. I saw Billy Joe Hobert was under pressure, so I stopped and went back to the corner. My parents have a poster-sized picture of the catch at home, and it's still a cherished memory.

To win a national championship in my first UW season was unbelievable. One thing about that team is how everyone fed off each other. What impressed me was how individuals could play so well as a whole. So many people were not afraid to have their number called in clutch situations. They wanted to make the play. That's what separated us, so many were willing to step up to make big plays at opportune times.

The coaching staff kept us humble that off-season. Coach Don James had a knack for keeping his players working to be the best they could be. That first off-season they were constantly on us to get in our winter workouts.

I got to catch footballs thrown by three great quarterbacks—Billy Joe, Mark Brunell, and Damon Huard. Billy Joe and Mark had different rotations on their ball, since Mark was left-handed. Billy Joe was a heck of an all-around athlete with an extremely strong arm. He never lost a game he started. Brunell had great touch. Both prepared as if they would be the starter. Damon broke most UW passing records at the time, and we are close friends.

We made it back to the Rose Bowl my sophomore season, despite the off-field distractions of 1992, and lost to Michigan to finish 9–3. We were hit hard with news of Billy Joe [his accepting of a loan launched an NCAA investigation into the UW program, which led to sanctions], but I don't blame any of the losses on the situation. I still don't know all the issues that were brought against him. We were all very supportive of Billy as a player. It seemed like they were trying to find ways to bring us down, and one of the ways was to sideline our quarterback.

Near the end of summer training camp going into my junior year, Coach James called a team meeting. I'll never forget that meeting and the anguished look on Coach James's face when he told us he was resigning. We were all shocked. For such a great person, who gave his heart and soul to the university, for him to end his coaching career that way did not seem right, not at all. I felt like I got run over by a tank. I felt like I lost a family member.

We all wanted Jim Lambright to take over, and I thought he did great, given our situation. Huard stepped in at quarterback, and we won some big games. I led the team in receiving, and one of the games where Damon and I really connected was at California. The first half we didn't play well at all. But we had a two-minute drive in which we hooked up about five times before Damon hit me for the game-winning touchdown.

That was the game Corrigan suffered a mild heart attack during pregame warm-ups and coached from the sideline on crutches because he had no feeling in his legs. He did go to the hospital before the game was over and recovered.

We were placed on a two-year bowl ban by the Pac-10, so when we played at Miami my senior year, we treated it like a bowl game. We were not intimidated at all by their home winning streak or when Hurricanes fans wrote "RIP UW" on a tombstone before the game. I didn't have any touchdowns that game, but I had some key catches to keep drives alive.

We finished 7–4, and losing to WSU in my last game was a sad ending to an otherwise rewarding and enjoyable UW football career.

Something I do before every NFL game is get a roster of the team we are facing to see if any players went to Washington. If so, I always try to say hello

389

before or after the game. Obviously, some of the younger guys might not know me, but I always try to acknowledge them and say, "I went to your school," to keep the Huskies tradition alive.

Mark Bruener earned All-America honors twice as a tight end and finished his career as the reception leader for UW tight ends with 95. He led all UW receivers in 1993 with 30 receptions for 414 yards. Bruener has played for two NFL teams during his 12-year career—the Pittsburgh Steelers (1995–2003) and Houston Texans (2004–present). He is currently a player in the NFL.

DAMON HUARD

QUARTERBACK

1991–1995

I'D DESCRIBE MY OVERALL EXPERIENCE of playing quarterback at Washington as up and down. That comes with the position. We had some dramatic highs and a couple bad lows. It prepared me for life—it's not always going to be rosy.

My experiences at the UW helped me be a better pro quarterback for the last 10 years. I played for three different offensive coordinators in five years at the UW, much like my pro career. I've had to learn how to adapt to new coaches in the NFL. I wouldn't trade it for anything. I have many great memories. We won a lot of games, and I made a lot of friends.

I was there during the head coach transition from Coach Don James to Coach Jim Lambright.

It was an awful day when Coach James resigned—a complete shock. It was like, "What are we going to do? We have a game in a couple of weeks."

Here's a guy who had done so much for program. You had a conference seeing him win all these games, winning bowls, recruiting from Southern California, and they decided to take away for two years the thing that kids and coaches play for—bowl games. The Pac-10 is the only conference to have a separate committee to determine rules. I don't blame Coach James for what he did. I understand his reasons. We were confident in Lambright. We were able to win a lot of games.

Damon Huard broke Sonny Sixkiller's all-time UW record for passing yards in his final game in Husky Stadium during a victory over Washington State.

The Miami win was a highlight, as was our comeback against Cal after being down by three touchdowns. Beating Ohio State at home stands out, too.

The thing I remember about that Miami game, known as the "Whammy in Miami," is it being so hot I couldn't breathe. I was so sweaty, I couldn't grip the ball. We went down a couple days early, but you couldn't relate to the heat being from the Northwest. We had guys hooked up to IVs and laying on ice blocks.

Everything went right for us to start the second half as we scored three quick touchdowns. Then we started to lay down the hammer on them. Napoleon Kaufman had a great night running, and Mark Bruener made key catches. One of the great plays was a screen pass to Richard Thomas that went for a 75-yard touchdown, thanks to Napoleon's awesome block to get Thomas into the end zone. Since we were on probation, it was our bowl game.

I'm also part of a famous Oregon play, what they call "The Pick." We were nine yards from a go-ahead touchdown with minutes to play in 1994. I threw an ill-advised pass in the flat, which Kenny Wheaton intercepted and returned 97 yards for a touchdown and a 31–20 Oregon win.

There are always Ducks fans I cross paths with who bring up their one glory moment that put them in the Rose Bowl for the first time in decades. I'm so past it. People still make a big deal out of it. I guess it is still shown on Ducks broadcasts every time the Huskies and Ducks play. As a quarterback, you have to have a short memory. I made a terrible play but moved on and had a great game the next week.

I think most Huskies fans are forgiving. In the Northwest there is so much to do, there are more things to life than sports. I've played in other cities where fans don't forgive you for those kinds of mistakes, like Boston and Kansas City.

My senior year, I was proud of the fact we were co–Pac-10 champions with USC. They got to go to the Rose Bowl by virtue of their non-league schedule. In our game with USC, we were ahead 21–0 at the half and became too conservative as the Trojans came back for a 21–21 tie.

I broke Sonny Sixkiller's all-time UW record for passing yards at our home victory over Washington State in my final game in Husky Stadium. It was a neat way to finish my career with a close game down to the wire. To me, playing football is all about wins and losses. I don't think people remember you for all the yards you pass for. To me, records are made to be broken, and most of mine were surpassed by my brother, Brock.

My senior year was special because Brock was a freshman. I actively recruited him. I remember asking him, "Where are you from? Where do you want to live and raise your family?" So I think I played a part in him being a Husky.

I don't remember much about our Sun Bowl loss to Iowa, my final Huskies game. They got the momentum early. I think we were so excited to be back in a bowl. We spent 12 days in El Paso. It sounded great at first, but after the first few nights, we looked at each other and said, "What are we going to do now?"

There were many fellow Huskies teammates who inspired me. I could go down the list and name a couple dozen guys. Two guys that come immediately to mind are Eric Bjornson and Bruener. Bjornson and I battled for the quarterback spot. Then coaches asked him to move to receiver, and he did for the good of the team. He had a great attitude. The move paid off for him as he became a very good receiver and played in the NFL. Bruener was just a stud, an old-fashioned football player who could've played with a leather helmet.

Being a Husky taught me how to get back up when you're knocked down.

Damon Huard finished his UW career as the Huskies' all-time leader in season (2,609) and career passing yards (5,886), and career passing touchdowns (36). His career passing yards and touchdowns now rank third, and his season yards ranks fifth. His .597 career completion percentage (472-for-790) and career passing efficiency rating of 130.29 remain school records. Huard has been in the NFL since 1997 with three teams—the Miami Dolphins (1997–2000), New England Patriots (2001–2003), and Kansas City Chiefs (2004–present). He earned two Super Bowl rings while playing with the Patriots. He is currently an NFL quarterback.

STEVE HOFFMANN

DEFENSIVE END

1991–1995

THERE'S THE BOND BETWEEN BROTHERS, the bond between teammates, and then there's the bond between competitors.

I played on the defensive line. There were many games when I'd go out and battle offensive linemen all game long. Then, after the game, you give those guys a hard handshake. There's a deep admiration on both sides when you both know you played extremely hard against each other. You appreciate their effort, and they appreciate yours. That's one of the real rewarding things of playing sports.

One of the moments that sticks in my mind happened with Eddie George of Ohio State at midfield before a game. He was such a great player, and even early on, we knew he was a great player. We played the Buckeyes three straight seasons, from 1993 to 1995. The first meeting was in Columbus. It was the second game of the season. I was battling a back injury and played as best I could. But that injury forced me to end my season after that game because I needed back surgery. We didn't win the game, but I had a couple of good hits on George. I didn't remember them that well. You remember the hits better when you win the games.

I have fond memories of our 25–16 home victory over Ohio State the next season. I was thankful to be back playing. I had a solid game. I do remember getting in some great hits on Eddie. Going up against George was great because he really enjoyed the competition.

We were both captains the next season. Before our rubber match, we met at the 50-yard line for the coin flip. When we shook hands, he smiled at me and said, "You're not going to hit me as hard as last time." We kind of just chuckled and laughed. That meant a lot to me for a guy of that caliber to have that much class about him. I admired his humbleness. It meant a lot because he remembered. That tells you that he's going back and looking at the film from last year, really studying the games. That speaks a lot to his thoroughness.

Bowl games are always helpful in developing team bonding. I was fortunate to experience three bowl games. The first one was our 1992 Rose Bowl victory over Michigan for our national title. I had a sideline view as a redshirt. It was amazing just to be part of that and see it happen up close. All the redshirts were able to go down to the game and play in the practices and be a part of that. On game day we suited up and stood on the sideline. We went through all the warm-ups even though we knew we wouldn't step on the field.

My redshirt freshman year, I was honored to make the travel squad to the Nebraska game. During Pac-10 games, teams are limited on how many can travel. When we played Nebraska, Coach James said, "We are going to bring one extra scout guy on defense and one extra on offense. Whoever really performs well that week and gives us their all, I want to take as a reward." He selected me to go. And that meant a whole lot to me. I suited up for that game, went through the warm-ups, and watched us beat those guys that year. That was a pretty cool deal.

There were a lot of fun games. As a freshman I remember playing against Stanford at home. I remember being in on important downs and recovering a fumble that stopped one of their drives to solidify a win. And that was a fun game because the whole defensive line was given the Defensive Player of the Game award. So that was really kind of neat to be given an honor like that with D'Marco Farr and Andy Mason and the other solid guys at the time.

Speaking of D'Marco, I remember laughing in the film room with him as we watched one hit I had my sophomore year. My helmet was coming off as I was coming around to sack a quarterback. I remember I was running and thinking about getting my chinstrap back in order. But I just kind of said, "Screw it." My helmet was half-off as I hit this quarterback really hard. I remember watching it with D'Marco in the film room and laughing our heads off about it. My helmet kind of came back on when I made the hit. It

Steve Hoffmann followed his brother Dave's footsteps to the UW and overcame a back injury to be a standout defensive end.

showed how you do whatever you need to do to make a play. You didn't let a chin strap slow you down.

I remember some of my teammates' hits just as much as my own hits. One of the great hits was Mike Ewaliko's in the Miami game. The Hurricanes had a guy called "the Blitz Buster." Whenever there was a blitz, he was the guy they would throw a screen pass to, and he'd sneak around the defense and get a first down. Well, he got a little screen pass, and it was when we had called a zone blitz. In that situation, our coaches sometimes sent Mike or myself into coverage, and it was where we'd fake a rush, let one of the linebackers get by, then retreat to coverage. It was a scheme Randy Hart and Jim Lambright learned from the Pittsburgh Steelers. Mike was dropping back, and he just cleaned that guy's clock. It was a loud pop. He had to be helped off the field. He was okay, but he didn't come back. We played defense with a team attitude. If you made a great play, you went over and celebrated with your teammates. Unfortunately, I see too many players in this day and age celebrating by themselves in an effort to make sure everyone realizes they made the play. That is a selfish attitude in my humble opinion, and I was glad that our team focused on each other, versus ourselves.

One of the all-time best hits I ever saw was by my brother, Dave, while playing linebacker for the Huskies against Stanford.

When I was a senior at Pioneer High in San Jose, I went to watch the Huskies play in Palo Alto. Dave came across the middle and leveled Ed McCaffrey. Ed had to be carried off the field. Dave was able just to get a great clean shot off, and that was one of those hits heard all around Stanford stadium.

I'm two years younger than Dave. I became a Huskies fan when he went to Seattle. I took four recruiting trips before deciding on the Huskies. At the end of the day, I felt like UW was a great spot for me. I felt like it was a city I could eventually live in. It had a great academic reputation and a great football team, plus my brother was there. All the stars aligned. It wasn't an easy decision, but, when I did make it, I felt very comfortable and confident in it.

Dave wasn't pushy at all. His attitude was probably more hands-off. He was there to answer my questions when I had them. I think one of the things I appreciated was I knew the program inside and out. I knew it wasn't going to be snow white—as many recruiters claim. I got to know a lot of his UW teammates while in high school. A lot of those guys are still my close friends. They played football hard and are also just great guys, and they were humble when it came to school and keeping up.

Playing on the same team with Dave was special. We played high school basketball together one season, but never football. My first year was his junior season.

I came in as a defensive end. I played most of my career at UW as a defensive tackle on the inside, mostly because they needed more support on the inside. Defensive ends for a period of time were a little bit on the shorter/smaller side. One of the things that happened was that Donald Jones came in as a linebacker and played defensive end. He was an absolutely phenomenal athlete. I think the coaches started to think of him and his type of frame as a prototype defensive end—a little bit shorter and a little quicker than your average defensive lineman.

I started six games during my redshirt freshman year. Those 1992 games are some of my fondest memories—first just being on the field with Dave, then starting together and playing together in the Rose Bowl.

We just had fun. We would just look each other in the eye—he could tell I was playing hard, and I could tell he was. Having fun but being aggressive at the same time. He was our main leader on the defense at the time. He was the linebacker calling plays. He was out there in the middle of everything. The most fun was whenever he made a big play, I was there to give him a big high five and laugh about it and have fun. And when I had a big play, he was one of those guys that would be right there pumping me up. That was a lot of fun.

My first game was against Arizona State. That was a game I can vividly remember—going down to Sun Devil Stadium and getting in and making a couple tackles. That was a confidence booster just because I was able to go out there and make plays at the Pac-10 level.

399

That same year we went down to Arizona to play the Wildcats. It was right after a lot of the Billy Joe Hobert stuff [surrounding his loan and the NCAA investigation into the UW football program that followed] started coming out. I thought our defense just played a great game. Even though we lost that game, it was one of those games we walked away from and felt like, *Man, we gave it our all*. I'm not ashamed of the way we played at all.

I'd say the same thing about our 1993 Rose Bowl loss to Michigan. The first half I thought the defense played pretty well. I thought that we played decently in the second half, too. It was one of those games that went back and forth. And after the game, you could go up to each and every one of those players on that O-line on Michigan and say, "Good game." Because they played a good game. And, in a lot of ways, we played a good game, too. There was a lot of admiration.

That was an emotional game for the Hoffmann family, as Dave and I knew it would probably be our last time on the field together.

My junior year, after returning from back surgery, the "Whammy in Miami" was the highlight of that year. We went there and beat those guys on their home field to end their winning streak.

My senior year we went to the Sun Bowl. Unfortunately, we didn't win that game. It was not one of the Huskies' better performances that year. It was actually a decent year where we came pretty close to being Pac-10 champs. It is something I think is often forgotten. That was the first year back after the [NCAA-imposed] probation that we were eligible for a post-season bowl game. I am proud of my teammates through the years that had to stand strong through the probation's impacts. None of the guys on that team had anything to do with the issues, but we were the ones who had to suffer the punishment. However, through those times, the Huskies stayed strong and united.

Not to talk bad of El Paso, but it is not the most glamorous of places. I think one of the highlights was going to the boot factory and seeing what kind of boots were coming off the assembly line. We all made it into Mexico. There wasn't a whole lot to see. Actually, I was married the previous summer, so we spent our first Christmas together in Juarez, Mexico.

I married Heidi Hills, who played basketball at Washington. We met in the training room. She was a freshman my second year. I saw her coming through the training room along with the other freshman basketball players. I finally got the nerve to walk up to her sorority, midway through the year, and introduce myself. I took her out on a couple dates. We kind of started it slow. We became friends, started dating, then got married. I was 22 and she was 21. We now have two great boys, and life is very fun and blessed.

It's funny because I think we started a trend—a UW football player marrying a UW women's basketball player. There were a couple other guys who followed suit. For example, my sister-in-law, Molly Hills, married Brock Huard. We found a good place to look for gals.

What does it mean to be a Husky? It's all about the bonds that unite us and playing with a high degree of excellence.

Steve Hoffmann excelled on the field and in the classroom. Hoffmann was named to the Pac-10 All-Academic team in 1992, 1994, and 1995. He is currently a senior project manager for GLY Construction, Inc. in Bellevue.

INK ALEAGA

LINEBACKER

1992–1996

MY GREATEST ACCOMPLISHMENT at the University of Washington was getting my degree.

I say that because coming out of high school in Hawaii, I didn't have the SAT test scores to attend Washington.

Coach Jim Lambright was one of the few coaches who recruited me. I committed to Washington because of Jim. After I graduated from high school, I spent a whole year in Hawaii improving my SAT scores and sitting out of football. When my scores improved to get into Washington, Lambright kept his promise to me and offered me a scholarship. Spending that year focusing on academics was a good learning experience for me.

Not only did I appreciate the opportunity to play football—that was the easy part—I appreciated the opportunity to attend the University of Washington.

In 1992 I redshirted my first season at Washington. It was hard. I knew all the hype going into the 1993 season. Washington had won the Pac-10 title three consecutive years. We had a number of good players on offense and defense returning for the 1993 season. We were very confident. We knew we'd be in contention for another Pac-10 title. Then Coach Don James stepped down. When he addressed the team and announced he was stepping down, nobody knew what had just happened. That was a big blow to the football program.

I didn't consider leaving. Our seniors and juniors at that time made a commitment to stay to keep the program afloat. When we saw that, we followed that commitment. It was a really tough time for us.

I was recruited as a linebacker, and that's where I played. I was an inside linebacker, where we were expected to learn all three positions—outside, weakside, and strong. Linebackers were expected to know the responsibilities of all defensive positions on the field.

I loved playing the attacking style of defense Coach Lambright used. I think he changed college football when he implemented that defense in 1989. Nobody ever saw that kind of defense or scheme before. It allowed a lot of freedom for linebackers to roam around. We got to do a little bit of everything—blitzing, jumping back to defend passes, disguising our alignment on the line of scrimmage. Jim only gave us the freedom to do that if we knew our responsibilities.

The game that was so memorable for all of us was the "Whammy in Miami" in 1994. The best game I played was the Arizona State game the same season. I got almost every defensive stat that game—15 tackles, an interception return for a touchdown, a fumble recovery, a tackle for loss, a quarterback sack—everything but a caused fumble.

My worst game was against USC in 1993. Tony Boselli, he just kicked my butt the day we played them.

A goal of mine was to win the Rose Bowl. My redshirt freshman year, we went to the Rose Bowl. We never made it to the Rose Bowl when I played, but we went to the Sun Bowl and Holiday Bowl. We were 0–3 during my tenure. It's always crushing to lose in the bowl games.

I went on to play three seasons in the NFL with the New Orleans Saints. It was a dream job, but at the same time, it was a business.

I graduated from the UW with a double major (sociology and American ethnic studies) in the spring of 1996. I'm working on my master's degree in education and will be graduating in the fall of 2007.

I've started my own family. I recently was honored as a Husky Legend at the wonderful UCLA home win in 2006. I went out at the beginning of the fourth quarter with my daughter, Malia, who is seven. It was cool to see her face. When she saw my face on the big screen, she said, "Is that you, Daddy? What did you do here?" I was surprised to learn I was one of only four linebackers in UW football history to be named All-Conference two years in a row.

Linebacker Ink Aleaga sat out a year to improve his grades and then redshirted a year before becoming a leading tackler for three seasons.

I'm now the UW academic coordinator for the Student–Athlete Academic Services in the UW Athletics Department.

What does it mean to be a Husky? It means a lot. It means tradition, pride, a blue-collar mentality, and having a big heart. It means family, being surrounded by a lot of good people, including coaches, administrators, and professors.

Ink Aleaga was among the top two leading tacklers at Washington for three years. He earned All-America honors and was named to the Pac-10 All-Conference team two years in a row. Aleaga played three seasons with the New Orleans Saints (1997–1999). He is currently the academic coordinator for the UW Athletics Department.

BOB SAPP

OFFENSIVE LINEMAN

1992–1996

I WANTED TO BE A DOCTOR. Now I'm a doctor of pain.

I'm in a unique situation. I'm world famous for being a kickboxer and movie star.

I have a house in Kirkland and Las Vegas, but I spend a lot of time in Japan. I've been in six U.S. movies. I've done two movies in Japan and about 70 commercials.

Before all that I was a Husky.

I was recruited out of Mitchell High in Colorado Springs by the UW, USC, Oregon, Colorado, and Ohio State. I chose the UW because I wanted to go pre-med.

My senior year in high school, the Huskies won the national championship. It was a very attractive program at the time. It was awesome going from high school to that type of major university—a dream come true. I didn't even know I was good enough to play in college until these colleges sent me letters. I could've gone anywhere in the country. I was 270 pounds, 6′4″. I had 5 percent body fat. My 40-yard time was 4.9 out of high school and peaked at 4.7. When I left the UW, I was 318. Now I'm about 350 or 360.

I was recruited as a defensive lineman. I redshirted my freshman year. I was moved over to the offensive line my sophomore year. I did find it difficult switching. We always had to move from left and right side of the center, depending on the play. I found it difficult, so I wore a black and white glove to remember which side to switch to. Rashaan Shehee used to tell me go to the black glove. It was great.

I felt like quitting, especially when I had a serious injury to my right foot. My position had been changed, and I was on crutches. I didn't think I was going to come back. To be honest, my parents really didn't want me to go to Washington. My dad changed his home phone after he dropped me off on campus, so I couldn't call home. That was my freshman year. When I was injured, there was no calling anyone.

I enjoyed being around my teammates, and they really enjoyed my personality. I can have a good outlook in bad situations, like during two-a-days. We had a ball; it was crazy. I look back on it and enjoyed every moment. A favorite hangout for us linemen was any restaurant. We went to Tony Roma's for all-you-can-eat rib fest. We took the whole offensive line, and we tried to eat them out of ribs. They still have a picture of us on the wall. We used to just pig out. The Sun Bowl was exciting. Every time we had an opportunity to go out, we'd have dance contests and giant buffets. I love to dance. It was a lot of fun.

I was a little intimating at times. I had a problem of always looking older than I was, so they'd call me a junior-college transfer. I didn't have any facial hair, yet my face looked old. I'm really a gentle giant.

The worst day as a Husky was when Don James brought us in to say that he was resigning and Jim Lambright was taking over. It was crazy. People were upset. I really wasn't aware of what was going on.

My best game was the "Whammy in Miami." I got a touchdown in Miami and didn't even realize it. I picked up the ball in the end zone, and I thought it was a safety. I thought I did something wrong. I walked to the coaches, and they were all excited and everyone else was, too. It was pretty funny. That was the highlight of my career.

That game meant everything to us. The week before, coaches had us wear sweaters underneath our pads to adjust for the heat down there. It was 80 degrees and we still had to wear all that. I don't know if it helped, but I think it helped the morale, if anything. I wouldn't recommend it now. We were picked as 40-point underdogs, and it was incredible. We scored 21 points in a minute-and-a-half.

The most disappointing loss was the Notre Dame game. We almost beat them when I was a junior.

I went to the Sun Bowl, Rose Bowl, and Holiday Bowl. I have all the bowl rings. It was awesome. I will always remember the highlights at the

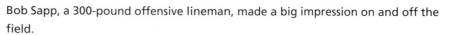

Bob Sapp, a 300-pound offensive lineman, made a big impression on and off the field.

University of Washington, no matter what. Winning the Morris Trophy as the Pac-10 Lineman of the Year showed I really did it. I was able to perform the position change and earn the respect of my peers. Interestingly, the league's offensive players vote on the best defensive lineman, and the defensive players select the top offensive lineman.

The biggest moment at the University of Washington, outside of football, was the time I spent at BF Day Elementary School, where I was a teaching assistant. I taught kids how to read and how to problem-solve without using violence. The kids really took a liking to me. I got a 4.0 in the class. I'd take the city bus to BF Day and would do my thing with the kids. I really enjoyed it.

I did do some odd summer jobs. I worked around the UW and cleaned up the stadium. I'd go from work to football to class to work to football. I got a degree in sociology and a degree in pre-pharmacy but didn't try to go to pharmacy school. I went to school year-round and graduated early. When [my kickboxing career] ends, then I will go back to school. I love animals and I would love to do something with animals.

I played from 1997 to 2000 in the NFL. I didn't play much. I played with the Vikings, Bears, Raiders, and Ravens. I bounced around a little bit. Bob Morton, the Huskies offensive line coach, told me after I was released twice, "Make them cut you, don't cut yourself." I've kept that attitude all the way.

407

I got my big break at WCW [World Championship Wrestling], where I got a job as tough man. I got a knockout in the second round. It opened some doors. I talked to some people from Japan, and they asked if I wanted be a professional fighter.

To be a Husky means to use the body, mind, and spirit to get through anything. That's one thing they always taught me. You can never keep a good Dawg down. I will always stand back up if I get knocked down. Being a Husky has made me a better man. It showed me how a man should act toward his loved ones. It prepared me for the future and real life outside of college. From the weight room to the classroom, it taught me lifelong values.

Bob Sapp was the Pac-10 Offensive Lineman of Year in 1996 and anchored a line that opened holes for Corey Dillon's record-setting season of 1,695 rushing yards. He played in the NFL three years for four teams—the Minnesota Vikings, Chicago Bears, Baltimore Ravens, and Oakland Raiders. He is currently a K-1 fighter and actor with nine movie and TV roles and 70 commercial credits.

JASON CHORAK

DEFENSIVE END

1993–1997

MANY PEOPLE WERE SKEPTICAL that a guy from class-A Vashon High would be able to play for the Huskies. I read that the Huskies had given 40 scholarships to guys from class-A high schools, and only three had successful careers. I made that number four by becoming a two-time All-American defensive end.

I didn't follow football much growing up on Vashon Island. I just loved playing. I was impressed with the atmosphere at Husky Stadium and the integrity of Coach Don James. When he came to my house, he was very humble. During my recruiting process, I met a lot of coaches who weren't afraid to show their confidence. Coach James said Huskies football was a family. That was a big reason I went there. Being from a Croatian family, we had strong family values.

My belief has always been that, if you have the heart and desire and motor, you can do whatever you set your mind to. It helped that I stood 6′4″ and weighed 275 pounds.

There were adjustments. My graduating class numbered 72. My first class at the UW had more than 1,000 students. That took a while to get used to.

Before I could get used to Coach James's style, he resigned before the 1993 season. Suddenly, one of the main reasons I went to the UW was gone. They offered to let anyone from my class transfer, but we all stayed. I believe our

Defensive end Jason Chorak penetrated offensive lines at the corner to set a UW record for most career tackles for loss.

class kept the program going and had the most players drafted [by the NFL], even more than the 1991 national championship team.

Jamal Fountaine, a senior, helped me out tremendously. He showed me the ropes and told me what I needed to do. I redshirted that year and played on the scout team. Every day I was fighting with the offensive linemen because I was dominating them as a true freshman. To play defense at Washington, you had to be aggressive and fight to make the tackle every play.

We didn't play in the Rose Bowl while I was there. After the two years of bowl probation, we went to the Sun, Holiday, and Aloha Bowls.

Coach Jim Lambright was one of the best defensive coordinators in the country. I think the change to head coach was something he wasn't as good at. When you are affiliated with the defense for so long, it's tough to do everything.

I probably learned the most from my position coach, Randy Hart. He's one of the best I've been around. He cares about his players, and I still have a relationship with him. He got everything out of us. If someone wasn't going to give everything, he wouldn't be around long.

One of our highlight games came early in my first year of playing. The "Whammy in Miami" was a great college game—two proud traditions facing off. My big play of the game was causing a fumble that led to one of our touchdowns. To go down there and physically beat them up gave us a lot of confidence.

Our worst game was our 1997 WSU loss in our house that sent the Cougars to the Rose Bowl. That was my last home game and left a bad taste in my mouth.

A game that showed my drive was our season opener at home against Arizona State. Our training camp had been overcast and cool. The temperature topped 85 degrees on game day. I cramped up so badly I couldn't move anything, even my toes. They had to carry me out of the stadium and fill me with two IV bottles in the locker room. I came back out and played well.

One of the things I'm proud about is that I never missed a home practice (I did miss a few bowl practices due to injury). There wasn't a week that went by that I was fully healthy, but I never wore the red jersey.

Being a two-time All-American, I was living the dream. I got to meet the best players of my day at the Playboy Mansion and had my picture on the cover of *Athlon Sports* magazine and in *Sports Illustrated*.

St. Louis drafted me, but I only made their travel squad. I played for Indianapolis, Denver, San Diego, and in the XFL. I didn't have any hard feelings about hanging up my cleats and moving onto the next phase of my life.

I returned to the Pacific Northwest and became a co-owner of mortgage company, Pine Lake Financial. Our company has been successful, and it's been my pleasure that our company has been a sponsor of the Big W Club, a group open to any former UW athlete.

Being a Husky is being proud to have worn the purple and gold. A lot of great athletes have worn the uniform, so there's always a bond when you run into a former player. There's mutual respect because players from any era know what it took to play for the Huskies.

Jason Chorak, a two-time All-American and All–Pac-10 Conference selection, posted one of the most dominating seasons for a defensive lineman in 1996 with 14.5 sacks and 22 tackles for loss, both team records. His 61.5 career tackles for loss is best in school history, and his 25.5 career sacks ranks third. Chorak played in the NFL with the Indianapolis Colts, Denver Broncos, and San Diego Chargers, and played in the XFL. He is currently a co-owner of Pine Lake Financial mortgage company.

TONY PARRISH

DEFENSIVE BACK

1993–1997

WASHINGTON HAD BEEN TO THREE Rose Bowls, won a national championship, and had one of the best defenses in the nation when I was in high school. I was a West Coast guy from Huntington Beach, California, and Washington was dominating. I thought, *Why not go to Washington?*

I was hoping Seattle was big enough. When I took my visit, I saw Seattle was not out in the woods. When I walked into Husky Stadium and saw Lake Washington, I was impressed.

I was a safety in high school, and that's where I wanted to play in college. The defensive coaches wanted me to move to cornerback and play as a freshman. I wanted to redshirt and have a year of development. I went and talked to the coaches and told them that corner was cool, but my heart was at safety. So they moved me back to safety and let me redshirt. When I first got to Washington, I was 171 pounds. By spring ball, I was 202, faster, and grew an inch to 5′11″.

The class of 1993 players were first-year freshmen when Coach Don James stepped down in protest because he felt we were being treated unfairly by the NCAA and Pac-10 Conference.

It was a very emotional time. All incoming freshmen were given the opportunity to transfer without penalty. We had meetings among ourselves to talk about whether we should stay or leave. In the end, everyone stayed. We became the class that held the program together.

Tony Parrish's aggressive, physical style helped him to All–Pac-10 honors as a defensive back.

My sophomore and junior years ended with losses to Iowa and Colorado in the Sun and Holiday Bowls.

It meant a lot to me when teammates voted me a team captain my senior year.

We started 7–1 and then had some injuries, which led to our losing our final three games of the season. That put us in the Aloha Bowl against Michigan State. Coach Lambright finally let us loose. The first play of the game was a forced fumble followed by a touchdown run by Rashaan Shehee. The best part about it was everyone was healthy and having fun in a 51–23 win. I had a couple of interceptions, including a 56-yard interception return for a touchdown. That game was one of my fondest college memories.

We had a lot of talent in 1997. We had 12 guys drafted [by the NFL].

We were some of the strongest teams in Washington history. And we took pride in that. We may have lost some games, but we knew we couldn't be "out-physicaled."

College football was a special time. As much as playing in the NFL is a completion of a dream, I miss playing with the boys. College football is a soft-spot for all players. Some of that purity of playing ball with the guys changes in the NFL as it becomes big business.

Looking back on my Huskies experience, I realize football has contributed to my focus, drive, and resilience.

414

Tony Parrish was an All–Pac-10 Conference defensive back in 1996 and 1997. He was voted a team captain in 1997. His four fumbles recovered in 1996 tied a UW season record. Parrish was the 35th pick in the 1998 NFL draft and has played nine seasons in the NFL with the Chicago Bears (1998–2001), San Francisco 49ers (2002–2006), and Dallas Cowboys (2006–present), and was an All-Pro twice. He is currently a football player in the NFL.

BENJI OLSON

OFFENSIVE GUARD

1994–1997

I HURT MY BACK DURING MY SOPHOMORE YEAR. The trouble started after I matched up against USC's All-American lineman Darryl Russell. I played a really good game against him, and it helped me gain some national recognition.

About a week after that game, however, I felt a strange pain shooting down my leg. I thought it was a hamstring problem, but it got progressively worse. Anytime you hurt your back, any movement is painful. Just getting into my stance as the strong-side offense guard was a challenge.

We played in the Holiday Bowl that year. I was proud of the fact I just played in the game. My back was on fire the whole game. I played through extreme pain. For me, that was a memorable moment — to know I could handle such discomfort and still be productive.

Turns out I had a herniated disc. I had surgery during the off-season. It sucked because it was a scary thing. They found a bone chip in one of my nerves, so it's good they got to that. It's been 10 years since my back surgery, and it's held up pretty good.

Despite my back problem, I have many great memories of my days at Washington. Husky Stadium is one of the greatest places to play, especially for a local guy. I grew up in Port Orchard. My 6′4″, 290-pound frame out of high school gave me opportunities to play at any school in the country. I always enjoyed watching the Huskies, so I wanted to stay home.

Benji Olson (76) overcame back surgery to be the UW's first two-time All-American offensive lineman. *Photo courtesy of Getty Images*

My first start my redshirt freshman year was memorable because it was against Ohio State in front of 100,000 people. It was a crazy first start. I played against an All-American and passed the test. We played at Notre Dame one year, and that was a good experience. I had a great time at the bowl games, especially the Aloha Bowl.

Missing a block happens now and then, but giving up a sack is the worst for an offensive lineman. I don't remember giving up any sacks, except maybe in the Holiday Bowl because of my back. I don't remember many plays when I screwed up too badly. But you have to remember, a good football player will forget about the mistakes and focus on the next play.

Being part of a rushing record is also a source of pride for linemen. It was special to help Corey Dillon set a single-season rushing for the Dawgs in 1996. He was fun to block for.

My size and strength helped me be a quality lineman, but I've always had really good coaching from high school on. I've always been a coachable guy and paid attention. You've got to have a little bit of everything—size, strength, athleticism, good hand-eye coordination, and overall football knowledge to be a good lineman.

I was fortunate to be drafted in the fifth round by Tennessee in 1998, and I'm still in the NFL, riding that train.

To be a Husky meant a commitment to excellence and being involved in great tradition. Growing up here just makes it special to be part of the UW program.

Benji Olson is Washington's first two-time All-American offensive lineman. Olson helped open holes for Corey Dillon, who set a school rushing record of 1,695 yards and 22 touchdowns in 1996. He has played nine seasons in the NFL with the Tennessee Titans. He is currently a lineman in the NFL.

JEROME PATHON

RECEIVER

1994–1997

I WANTED TO BE A HUSKY WHILE I was in high school. I watched from north of the boarder as the Huskies competed for national championships.

But Canadians are not considered must-have recruits. I grew up in North Vancouver, British Columbia. Nobody from the States showed interest in me in high school. So I played a year of Canadian university football. It paid off as I was the rookie of the year.

I gained a little more interest. I had the talent, but could I compete at the college level in the U.S?

A friend of mine got together with Dick Baird at the UW. I made a visit, and they looked at my film. The stars aligned, and I became a Husky.

I redshirted my first year, which was fine. I had never lifted any weights before coming to Washington. Strength-wise I was way behind everyone else. I worked hard. You find a way to catch up pretty quickly.

I hung out with my classmen, but you always try to learn from the older guys. I first roomed with Bob Sapp, who took me under his wing. It was nothing but laughs with Bob. It's so funny to see him on TV as a K-1 fighter. He's this monster figure who will break you in half. Honestly, though, he is one of the most good-natured people I've met.

My first big break occurred when somebody got injured. I was next up. I went out and made a few plays. He was out for a number of weeks. I played at a high level and took advantage of opportunities. My playing time

North Vancouver, British Columbia, native Jerome Pathon needed a friend's introduction to become a Husky, but he quickly became a star receiver and team leader.

escalated my sophomore year. I caught my first touchdown in the 1995 Sun Bowl on a 30-yard pass from Shane Fortney.

My junior year, I started playing a lot more. I had a hand in one of many exciting Apple Cups. In 1996 we had a 24-point lead, but Ryan Leaf led a charge that sent the game into overtime. Brock Huard hit me for a three-yard score for the lead. We watched from the sideline as Leaf's fourth-down pass was caught out of bounds, giving us the win. In the 1996 Holiday Bowl, I returned a kickoff 86 yards for a touchdown, but we lost that bowl, too.

I came into my own as a senior. I was honored to be named a team captain. Early in the season I had a stretch of four games where I really did well with 100-plus yards a game. That put me on the national map. My most memorable game was on a huge national stage, even though we lost. It was an ABC game versus Nebraska. Brock Huard went down, and Marques Tuiasosopo stepped in as a redshirt freshman. He was running for his life. I found a way to make plays, but it wasn't enough. I felt like I never gave up, and I felt Marques never did, either. We were both out there gun-slinging and making something happen. It's always nice to go out a winner. In my third bowl, we beat Michigan State 51–23 in the Aloha Bowl.

For every great game, you probably have more bad games. I remember dropping a few I should've caught. You never know whether that one catch could've led the team to something great. When a ball bounces off your hands, it's embarrassing. It's very difficult. It comes with the territory of being a good athlete. You mourn the drop or mistake that night, then you have to let it go. Whether you did your best or didn't concentrate or ran before you made the catch, you learn from those experiences. It's like a great cornerback. They get beat, but they bounce back.

One of the more interesting plays came against Arizona State. I scored a touchdown, but it was called back. Offensive coordinator Scott Linehan, who's now the head coach for the St. Louis Rams, called another play for me to score on the next play, and I did. To get your number called twice in a row was something special. That shows they have confidence in you.

When I was drafted, we had so much talent come out that year. I was drafted by Indianapolis in the second round. I was in a meeting, and in walks Jason Chorak, whom I had roomed with at Washington. It was so nice to see a familiar face. He stayed at my house, and we roomed together again and experienced the NFL together for the first year-and-a-half, which was cool.

For me, there's no memory of Washington that could be bad enough to detract from my time there. The worst memory was about a friend of mine, Curtis Williams. I was in the NFL when I heard that Curtis was paralyzed in a freak football accident and later died. That had a lot of impact on a lot of people who knew him. It's difficult to accept. I've been hit so hard and flipped upside down and landed on my neck. I don't know why he was taken from his friends and family.

I was released by Atlanta during the season in 2006. If I play again, great. If not, I've had a great career, and I'll go back and finish the quarter I need to get my degree in marketing and communications. I'm not really a records guy. I took a look one time and saw my name at the top of some receiving records among all the Huskies legends. I thought, "That's not too bad." It gives you a sense of accomplishment, but you realize so many greats played this game. We had really good teams my junior and senior years. The guys I played with made it happen. Quarterbacks, lineman, receivers—you need every component to set records.

Being a Husky is about sharing moments. When you have a group of guys that are together four or five years and you come through a program that was first-class, not only do you have the opportunity to get an education and camaraderie, you share those special moments. It's a unique opportunity— to do what you dreamed of doing and love. I think it transcends being a Husky. I think you have a connection with anyone who plays NCAA football. Those are some of the best years of your life. I cherish the relationships I have with people I met at the UW.

421

Jerome Pathon left Washington with the most productive season ever by a Huskies wide receiver, with records for receptions (73) and receiving yards (1,299). (His records slipped to second when Reggie Williams ended his UW career.) Pathon became the first Huskies receiver to earn first-team All-America honors since Mario Bailey in 1991. His yardage total was the second-most for a receiver in a Pac-10 season at the time, trailing only Johnnie Morton's 1,373 yards at USC in 1993. Pathon finished his career second on UW's career receiving yardage list (2,275). He was drafted by the Indianapolis Colts in the second round in 1998. He has played nine seasons in the NFL for Indianapolis (4), the New Orleans Saints (3), Seattle Seahawks (1), and Atlanta Falcons (1).

BROCK HUARD

QUARTERBACK

1995–1998

PLAYING ON THE SAME FOOTBALL TEAM with my brother, Damon, for the first time showed me what it's like to be a parent.

When you are playing, you sit there and see your parents getting stressed out. You think, *What are they worried about?*

Now I know.

When I entered the University of Washington, Damon was the senior starting quarterback for the Huskies.

People don't believe it when I tell them this, but my redshirt freshman year was one of the toughest years I've ever had in football. It very much made me sympathize with parents whose kids play sports. Just being there and not being able to play and control the environment, I had so much emotion wanting Damon to do so well. I'd hear teammates whisper this or that behind my back about Damon. It was just incredibly more difficult than I thought it would be. It was hard to really enjoy a lot of that year. I certainly enjoyed the upsides and some of the wins—we were a field goal away from vying for the Pac-10 championship with USC—but it was a very draining year, very hard.

When I was deciding on where to go, I narrowed it down to UCLA (Terry Donahue was still there) and the University of Washington. And in that year, coming out, I happened to be the number-one guy on the West

Coast, and Cade McNown was number two out of Oregon. And I think he still, to this day, holds a grudge that I kind of got to pick while he played second fiddle, waiting for me to pick one school, and he got the other.

I was really enamored with UCLA and sunshine and Terry Donahue and really liked a lot of its aspects. I enjoyed certain parts of it and came home and even told friends that I was leaning that way, that I thought I'd go to school down there, enjoy the sunshine and get away a little bit. I had some heart-to-heart conversations with my dad, with Damon, and some other folks. And the bottom line, which I would tell any recruit selecting a school, is that if you want to live in the Seattle area, if you want to work here someday, and if you want this to be your community, you better go to school here. If you go to UCLA or USC or Oregon, or some other place, you're going to have a tougher time making inroads back into this community, because this still is, ultimately, number one, a Huskies football town.

It was a great decision for me. I'm talking about the business side of it, the media side of it, the relationship side of it. Just every aspect of community, including great things with schools, within the churches, within the youth groups. I've been fortunate to go to places and know lots of people. Not just simply getting a job, but making inroads into a community. Had I gone off to a UCLA or USC or the University of Miami and left home, I don't know that I would have ever been able to establish that sense of community that I have here.

423

One of my favorite photos from that year was taken after the Army victory. A guy from Port Orchard took a series of photos. Damon threw a big touchdown pass. At the end of the game, I was out on the field, and he jumped into my arms, and probably hurt my vertebrae right there, but that was a special moment to have in pictures.

I came into the program knowing more than the average freshman about the UW program, thanks to Damon, my father, the head coach at Puyallup High, and Billy Joe Hobert, who also went to Puyallup High. I'd been to all their bowl games and been to a lot of practices. I went to every home game through high school. I felt very comfortable, as comfortable as any freshman could coming in. I certainly had a lot to learn and new relationships to build— a dorm to live in, and all those things—but as far as having a leg up on the average freshman coming in, or on my roommate who was coming in from Arizona, I would probably say I did, just because I'd been around it so much.

We went to a bowl game all four years I played. My first year was the first year we were eligible again for a bowl game, and we played down in the Sun Bowl against Iowa. And then we went to the Holiday Bowl, the Aloha Bowl, and the Oahu Bowl.

The first game of my redshirt freshman year, I thought I'd play a few series, depending how the game went. We opened at Arizona State. Eight months before, the Sun Devils lost to Ohio State in the Rose Bowl, their only loss of the season.

I remember getting my first series at the end of the first half. I can close my eyes and still picture that. We were deep down in our own end zone. The first play was a run. We came back to the huddle, and the linemen were yelling at me that they couldn't hear me. It was very loud—kind of a tough environment. And that first series I think was a three-and-out. And then we came back in the fourth quarter. I believe we were down 42–21 when I got put in there. Things just were remarkably in slow motion for me. You hear of first-time players, getting their feet wet, say the speed of the game is so fast. They can't adjust to it. I just remember, pointedly, how the game seemed to slow down, and I was able to put the ball right where I wanted to.

I threw a hook-and-go to Jerome Pathon for a big gain, ran for a touchdown on an option run, and hit Gerald Harris on a deep post for a 70-yard touchdown. All of a sudden we were right back in there.

They fumbled, and Corey Dillon had a 20-yard touchdown run. And before we knew it, it was 42–42, and we had a game going. They drove down and we intercepted, and I was thinking, *This is going to be terrific.* So we got the ball, drove it down, and were going to have an unbelievable win and start out my career the right way. We had a decent drive. I think we got about midfield and had a third-and-five. I dropped back and threw it a little bit too quickly to my pitch route, Jerome, before he was ready for it, and it bounced off of his hands. I said, "Okay, it's fine. We'll pin them down here and go to overtime."

We had a nine-yard punt. And two plays later, they kicked a 45-yard field goal to win it. And that was the first taste of it. Bittersweet. Like I said, it was remarkable for me that I could go in there and the game was slow enough for me, and I felt like I could really play. It was a great start to my career.

That ended up being our only Pac-10 loss that year.

We came home to play BYU, and there was some talk and some grumbling. Some thought I should be the starter. They kept Shane Fortney as the

Brock Huard had the prototypical quarterback size at 6'5", 230 pounds, and he set 20 Huskies passing records.

starter. He played a pretty good game. Near the end of it, he hurt his knee. He ended up tearing, or partially tearing, the patella tendon in the back of his knee. I went in there and mopped it up. He was hurt the next game, and that was officially my first start, against Arizona at home.

I probably couldn't have had a better team to match up with—a team that loves to play man-to-man defense. And we knew pretty much what they were going to play, which is always nice for an inexperienced guy.

I think the first play might have been a little fade route to Jerome over Chris McAlister, which he caught for a big play. We ended up throwing for over 300 yards and three touchdowns in the first half. I just had a ball.

I just remember, vividly, sitting outside the stadium. Damon was home that year. That was the one year he was out of football—working for Paul Allen, actually, and the Seahawks. I remember him and Dad sitting in the car and just going, "Man, you couldn't have asked for a better start."

"You are the man now."

"This is gonna be your team." Yadda, yadda, yadda.

I can vividly remember what a great memory that was.

So I was feeling pretty good about myself. Cary Conklin, a former UW quarterback who had returned as a volunteer coach, called me and said, "Let's watch the game."

We broke down the game. And there's an old adage in football: "The eye in the sky doesn't lie." That is, the video camera never lies.

You never ever play as well as you think or as badly as you think you did. I remember Cary and I broke that game down, and he said, "You threw for 340 yards, but you could've thrown for 450 yards if you just watched this and looked at that."

That brought me back down to reality. We ended up going on having a pretty good year. We beat Stanford the next week. Then we went to Notre Dame and got crushed out there. That was a huge part of our season that year, and a very humbling part for me. As high as that Arizona game was, that was a pretty low time. I got absolutely pounded and beat up. I had a couple bad interceptions. We just got really thrashed on national TV.

It really set the tone for us. We had great senior leadership that year.

If you bide your time and pay your dues, it's going to be your time when you're an upperclassman. And, really, Shane had done that through his career, playing under Damon, and it was going to be his time and his opportunity.

And there were many of the guys of his class, some of the older guys, that weren't very excited about some freshman redshirt coming in and taking over some of the role that they felt should have been Shane's, especially with his being injured. It felt like he wasn't getting a fair shake at it. Fortunately, we rattled off six straight wins after the loss to Notre Dame, which put us at 9–2, and we had a pretty productive year.

Corey Dillon was great for our passing game. We established a pretty neat identity where we could pound the ball with Corey and run it and run it, and then hit that deep play-action pass. I loved it.

Speaking of Corey, I remember he cramped up in our Washington State game that was played in sub-freezing temperatures. A whole bunch of guys went all out to protect themselves from getting cold. Corey looked like he had scuba gear on, gloves and a jacket underneath. He got so hot and dehydrated, he was cramping.

Everyone was asking, "How in the world do you get cramps when it's 15 degrees outside?"

That was the Cougars game we pulled out in overtime.

We went down and played Colorado in the Holiday Bowl, and they were a good team. I think we were both right around top 10, and they were a loaded team. We played them pretty tough. Corey actually got hurt, separated his shoulder in that game, and that took a big chunk of our offense out. We just didn't quite pull that one off.

427

Next year, Shane transferred before our season started. We came in as a top-five team. We had a lot of people back. Corey ended up leaving for the NFL, but Rashaan Shehee came back after missing a lot of that previous year with an injury. We were a talented a team. I think eight guys got drafted from that team. A rash of injuries hampered us. Rashaan got hurt, and I missed a couple games with a high ankle sprain. And that really was unfortunate. Because I think if we would have all been healthy through that year, we would have been 9–2, at minimum.

Our glaring weakness that year, a lack of depth, really showed how probation hurt the program. If we'd had those other 15 or 20 scholarships that were taken away, it could have been a different story. That to me was the first straw.

My junior year was a really tough year, and not just because I separated my shoulder. We lost a large talent pool, and that put a strain on a lot of true freshmen, who were called upon to fill the void.

I wish, in some ways, the script could have been: I endured a few bumps early in my career and went out 9–2; but that's the way it goes.

I would say the hardest pill we had to swallow really had nothing to do with me but with the coaching staff getting fired after that year and, for whatever reason, just feeling responsible for that. I came back and thought we could really do some neat things that season. And still, to this day, I certainly wish things could have worked out and those coaches could have stayed there.

There were a lot of guys who bled purple and gold, guys who absolutely loved Huskies football, and it was a real bummer to see them let go and then ultimately to see the program go through great highs with the new regime before that regime left in shambles.

I heard about Lambright being fired while I was interviewing an agent. I didn't see that coming. It really surprised me because it wasn't too long after Barbara Hedges had come out and voiced her approval and said Lambright would remain at Washington. Then to see that happen was pretty disappointing.

I technically had another year of eligibility, but I was getting married that year and was graduating. I knew, going into my junior year, that that would be my last as a Huskies football player. I played three years and had gone through some real ups and downs and great times. Unfortunately, I injured myself a number of times, but that's the way the game goes.

Dad always understood. And, certainly, by the end of my career we had some great ups and some tough downs. Husky Stadium can be a difficult place for a parent of a player, particularly a quarterback, when things aren't going well because of that community, and the people who care. It was tough on him, I think, at times. But, I think, all in all, Dad and Mom had to look back, much as I do, and see that the good far outweighed the bad and what an incredible experience it was to have had their boys start for five-and-a-half years.

As I look back with perspective, I can still say it was absolutely enjoyable.

I'm an analytical guy. I remember so much of it. I can go back, almost per game, and tell you the ups and downs of it and all the excitement and fun times, and every win and every loss. But more than anything, you just always hear it, and it's so true, that the relationships and the friendships that you build are what matters most.

Being a Husky is really about community. I see people, people recognize me, and I'll go places, and it isn't, "Oh, you're that Seahawks quarterback." I spent four years playing with the Seahawks here. And it's never, ever, "Oh, you're that Seahawks quarterback, aren't you?" It's always, "Oh, you're that Huskies guy." And I say, "Yeah, but that was about eight years ago." But that is what is remembered, and what this community is really about.

Brock Huard surpassed his brother, Damon, as Washington's all-time leading career passer, at the time, with 6,391 yards and 53 touchdowns. Huard held 20 UW records and still holds school records for passing yards per attempt in a season with 8.46 (2,319 yards, 274 attempts), most passes thrown in a game (62), most career passes without an interception (151), highest passing efficiency in a season (156.8), and most touchdown passes by a freshman (13) and sophomore (25), among others. He also excelled in the classroom and was honored as a two-time Academic All-American. Huard played six seasons in the NFL with the Seattle Seahawks (1999–2001, 2004) and Indianapolis Colts (2002–2003). He is currently a TV football analyst and lives in the Puget Sound area.

JOE JARZYNKA
RETURNER/RECEIVER/ KICKER
1996–1999

IREALLY DIDN'T KNOW MUCH ABOUT the Huskies when I was an invited walk-on. At first, it didn't really mean much to be a Husky. In the beginning, it meant an opportunity to showcase my skills at the D-1 level. It took a few years to kick in what it meant.

When you are 5'7¼", you have to prove yourself every day. I worked hard every day and proved I could play with the big boys. After redshirting my freshman year, I played in every game four straight years and played in four bowl games.

My high school career gave me the confidence I needed to walk-on weighing 155 pounds.

I played receiver, defensive back, kick returner, and kicker. I was one of the top kickers in the state and was voted to the all-state team my junior and senior years as both a receiver and defensive back. We played in the state championship my junior year but lost to Prosser by two points.

I really wasn't a huge Huskies fan in high school. I moved from Michigan in the eighth grade, so I had only spent five years in the state.

My first day at Washington practice, I was the smallest guy on the field. I stood out, though. I had hair down to my nipples and a little bit of a swagger.

I remember going against guys I didn't know anything about. I was a little nervous. But after I got out there, I had to do what I had to do. I wasn't overwhelmed. I knew I was as good of an athlete as anyone else, and I knew I could be effective.

I took jersey No. 21. I was No. 1 in high school, and my brother wore No. 2.

I remember one practice, running pass patterns against Lawyer Milloy. He kind of took it easy on us new guys and wouldn't blow us up. I worked him pretty good a few times, and everyone was hollering at him, including coaches and players.

The first game of my redshirt freshman year, I was on the kick-return team as a returner, and the punt-return team as a punt rusher. In the last game against Washington State, an injury to the starting punt returner gave me an opportunity to field my first punt, and I almost broke it for a touchdown. I caught the ball and took it 30 or 40 yards before being snared by a shoestring.

I knew some people thought I was a novelty. So I worked out and gained 15 to 25 pounds. Got up to about 183, then realized I was too heavy. My optimal playing weight was 172.

431

The spring before the next season, I came on strong as a receiver. No one really wanted me to be in that position. An assistant coach told me he didn't want me to be there. He put it, "To be honest, I want someone 6' running a 4.3, but you'll catch the ball if we throw it to you; and we don't have anyone else."

You can imagine what that does to a young kid.

My philosophy is: if you don't have anyone sticking up for you, you've got to do it yourself.

My teammates were great to me. Jerome Pathon, Dave Janoski, Fred Coleman, and other receivers were awesome. They taught me more than I could have asked for. Dave and I were similar size-wise, so we had a connection. Janoski was definitely inspiring as a person. Pathon was a superstar, but still he was really cool with me. We went out off the field and goofed around during practice.

Coach Al Roberts gave me some opportunities as a young player that other coaches wouldn't have given me. He was honest with me and taught me some great lessons. Rick Mallory was another coach who was great and fun to work with.

Joe Jarzynka, a fearless punt returner, played in every game for four straight seasons despite being one of the smallest players on the field.

Most would agree that I made my mark as a returner. I carried myself with a fearless attitude, and I like to think that attitude influenced those I played with. Occasionally I'd let a punt hit the ground, but I'd still pick it up and run.

I returned punts and kickoffs, caught passes, and kicked extra points and field goals.

Standing there waiting for the football to come down while 11 guys are running to knock your head off is a little nerve-wracking. The 300-pounders didn't worry me. I was scared of the 210 guys running 4.5s. I knew if I could catch a ball and make one guy miss, I could get 10-plus yards. When big guys are running down the field as fast as they can, they are typically out of control. I could juke one way or the other, then go up the middle, and it was off to the races.

My most memorable return came against Cal my junior year when I took my only punt return back for a touchdown, and then kicked the extra point afterward. It was pretty unbelievable. There were several other memorable returns that come to mind…against San Diego State, there were three or four guys in front of me, all running down the sideline…that was fun. I broke off Utah State for over 100 yards in punt returns, had another 100 yards against Oregon State as a senior. It didn't take long for people to notice I could make an impact.

There was a time when I was close to quitting. After my second season, I wasn't sure what they were going to do about a scholarship for me. They were kind of stringing me along. After two years, a walk-on is eligible for a scholarship without detracting from the incoming freshman scholarships. The staff hadn't given me the go-ahead yet, and I just wanted to say, "Hey, if I don't get this scholarship, I may have to reconsider my situation." I wanted to be appreciated and be involved. I got the scholarship.

My punt-return lowlight was against Oregon State. I took the worst hit a returner can have in that game. I got a helmet in my chin while looking up for the ball. In the same game, I got a pooch kick and went to pick it up. It took a funny bounce, and while I was trying to pick it up, an OSU player crushed my hand with his helmet, and the other team recovered. After that game, I couldn't eat because my jaw was so swollen. My chin felt like I got punched. My hand was all busted up. I couldn't even hold a fork.

But I played the next week. We taped everything up, put a huge glove on my hand, and I was ready to go.

Opposing fans used to get on me, and that was fun. They called me "Billy Ray Cyrus" and "Goldielocks."

I caught passes from two great quarterbacks who had opposite styles. Brock Huard liked to stand back and deliver in the pocket. Through those years, we had Freddy, Jerome, Chris Juergens, Dane Looker, Gerald Harris…all bigger targets. Marques Tuiasosopo was the other quarterback I played with. I appreciated the way he played the game because he liked to improvise and scramble. I have a similar view of the game.

My senior year, Jim Lambright was replaced by Rick Neuheisel. There were mixed feelings on the team. We had lost six games that year, and everyone was a little disappointed. When the change happened, we were excited for a fresh start. I was grateful to Coach Lambright because he gave me a lot of opportunities that Neuheisel wouldn't have given, and didn't give, me.

I finally understood what it meant to be a Husky and what kind of respect we demand when we play to our potential. I don't remember exactly what game it was, but I remember realizing the meaning. For me, the games that meant the most were when it was close and we pulled it out as a squad. That's what it was all about.

While being a Husky was the first time anyone had told me they didn't want me on the team, that was a wake-up call that nothing is ever handed over to you. It definitely shaped my character. Working that hard day-to-day prepared me to do anything after college. Realizing what it takes to be a team made me want to maintain contact with those guys who formed the great teams we had.

After working for years in the Alaskan bush as a fishing guide, I'm now in commercial real estate back in the Puget Sound. People recognize my name every now and then. Every once in a while, I watch the word spread around an office. That kind of thing cracks me up. It has helped me out.

Now, to me, being a Husky is about grit, about getting dirty, and never giving up. That's the attitude that I felt was a Husky. It was after I was done that those feelings were reiterated. These guys gave everyone a chance to work hard. I took advantage of it and others did, too. They wanted guys who were mean, nasty, and played harder than anyone else on the field.

Joe Jarzynka stood just 5′7¼″ but stood out by being fearless. He earned All-Conference honors in 1998 as an all-purpose player and was voted the team's Most Valuable Player. He caught passes, returned kicks and punts, and even kicked field goals one season, the longest one being 44 yards. He led the 1998 team in scoring with 50 points by converting 20-of-24 extra points, six-of-eight field-goal attempts, and scoring two touchdowns. He holds the school record for combined kick and punt returns in a game (10) and season (65), and is second only to Beno Bryant in career combined returns with 147. His 91-yard punt-return touchdown is the UW's third longest. His 166 punt return yards against California in 1998 is a school record. Jarzynka is third in season (425) and career (860) punt-return yards. He ranks fifth in team history in kickoff-return average, with 18.9 yards per return on 46 returns for 870 yards. He is currently a commercial real estate broker in Puget Sound.

The
NEW
MILLENNIUM

MARQUES TUIASOSOPO

QUARTERBACK

1996–2000

THE BIGGEST HIGHLIGHT OF MY Huskies career also showed me two poignant examples that sports are still just a game.

The team captains took a separate flight to the 2001 Rose Bowl. We stopped in San Jose to see teammate Curtis Williams, who had been paralyzed by a head-on tackle during our Stanford game about two months before.

What happened to C.W. was a complete shock to everyone. To see a guy you played with for three years, spent a lot of time with, who one day was fine and the next day struck by tragedy, definitely brought another perspective to the team. You never know what's going to happen. I think everyone understands that football is dangerous. But, yes, it was scary to see what happened to Curtis.

When we first saw Curtis in San Jose, he couldn't talk. We could tell he was happy to see us. And he knew it was uplifting for us to see him. Curtis did come to the Rose Bowl game and was with us in the locker room before and after the game.

Winning the 2001 Rose Bowl against Purdue was the perfect way to end my UW football career. We got the program back on the national scene as we finished 11–1 and No. 3 in the national rankings. I'm very proud of that. I'm proud of the guys I played with and have a lot of love for all of them. I miss playing with those guys.

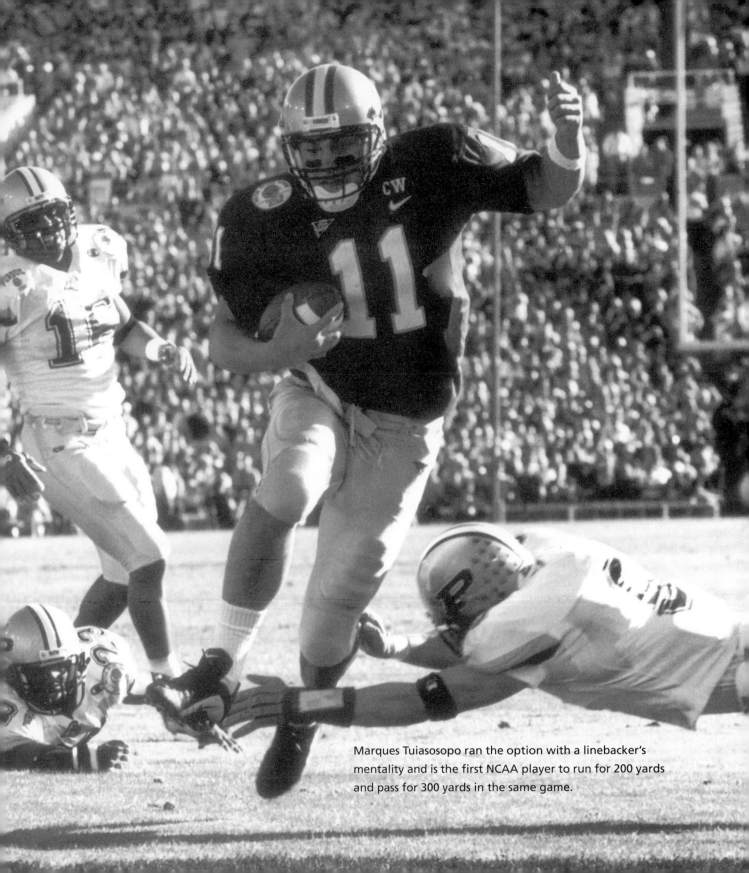

Marques Tuiasosopo ran the option with a linebacker's mentality and is the first NCAA player to run for 200 yards and pass for 300 yards in the same game.

I had a good game. Everyone had a good game in our 34–24 victory over the Boilermakers and Drew Brees. What made it sweeter was that my brother, Zach, was on the team. He redshirted his freshman year. We didn't get to be on the field together, but not too many brothers play on the same team. We got to practice together. To go through that year with him was special.

As I was getting back from postgame media interviews and celebrating in the locker room, my dad was waiting for me outside. He'd never done that. I was surprised to see him. He said, "We have to go."

I didn't know what was going on. After Zach and I dressed, we went to be with our grieving family. My dad's cousin, Amia Amituanai, who we called "Auntie" and who made us cookies and candy, came down next to the field after the game to congratulate Zach and me. She had a big smile on her face. She then walked out of the stadium tunnel and collapsed—her heart gave out. No matter how important the Rose Bowl seemed, it didn't compare to the significance of a life lost. I felt so badly for my cousins who didn't have a mom anymore.

There were a lot of mixed emotions that day.

Our only stumble that season came in the fourth week against pesky Oregon, a 23–16 loss.

Beating Miami 34–29 at home in the second week put us on the fast track. That was the loudest game I've ever played in at any level. Huskies fans like to stomp their feet to make extra noise. A couple of times in the game it was like an earthquake. It was amazing.

Then beating Colorado the next week on the road made us 3–0 going into Oregon.

My junior season, the game that stands out was the Stanford game at home. It was a big game to beat Stanford 35–30 and push us up in the standings. I knew we had to play well. They were leading the Pac-10. I think they were leading the league in sacks, too.

Guys made big catches, and we just kept answering them. Winning always supercedes individual accomplishments. If we lost, any record would not matter. That's how we did things there. Everyone comes together. Guys will have big days because other things are going well.

That was a great game, but a hip injury in the first quarter almost sidelined me. I had a deep hip bruise and a minor hip pointer. I was rolling out to the left and landed hard on the turf. I took some anti-inflammatory medication and kept moving. I didn't sit down the whole game. I knew if I did, my hip would stiffen up. I walked up and down the sideline when our defense was on the field.

Despite that painful injury, I had a record-setting game. I became the first player in NCAA history to pass for 300 yards (302) and run for 200 (207).

People said I had a linebacker mentality while running the option. I'd rather pass if I had a choice—it's a lot easier on your body. But I didn't mind running. It helped us be harder to defend. We put a lot of pressure on defenses to prepare for us. It gave us one more weapon to use.

I wasn't going be stupid and take chances to get hurt. But if there was a guy in front of me to get a first down, I wasn't shy.

I played my heart out every time, trying to win the game. If I wasn't going to be tough, how could I expect a teammate to be tough? I led by example, but if we weren't practicing at a certain level, I wasn't afraid to bring it up. We held each other accountable.

I had fun playing quarterback. Most other colleges wanted me to play defense. Only Washington and UCLA saw my quarterback potential.

My father played at UCLA, and I'd been a Bruins fan growing up. I crossed over to being a Huskies fan in 1991 when they beat Nebraska. One of my reasons to be a Husky was to play for national championship. When I was a senior in high school, UCLA was 5–6. Washington was ranked No. 1 in the preseason. I really liked what Coach Jim Lambright was doing. I think UCLA went on to a 20–2 record, but I didn't have regrets.

439

Speaking of Coach Lambright, it was sad for me to see him go after the 1998 season. I thought he would be there my whole career. That's part of the football business. At the time, we were coming off a 6–6 season, and I had been waiting my turn behind Brock Huard. All I knew was we wanted to turn it around and get going. We knew we had to bring our hard hats. Coach Rick Neuheisel came in, and within a few years, we accomplished our goals.

I got along great with Coach Neuheisel. He let me be me. I had a wealth of resources and information about the quarterback position with Neuheisel being a former quarterback, Keith Gilbertson on staff, and quarterbacks coaches Steve Axman and Karl Dorrell.

Still, we opened the 1999 season with two losses in my first two starts. We fell at BYU in a heartbreaker and lost by 10 at home to Air Force. That was a very humbling experience. That's not the way it was supposed to be. It wasn't pretty. Everyone was looking around and wondering, *Can this guy and team do it?*

The next week we faced Colorado, the team Coach Neuheisel left to come to Washington. We answered the questions with a 31–24 victory. I'd say, next to the Rose Bowl, that was the second-biggest game of my career.

Our second-to-last regular-season game was a tough overtime loss to UCLA. I felt responsible for that. For the second year in a row, we fell one win short of a Rose Bowl trip. We had our chances.

I loved throwing to all my receivers. To me, they were all equal. Gerald Harris, Chris Juergens, and Jerramy Stevens were all hard workers. Jerramy was a big target with a long wingspan. I always loved finding a big target.

It's hard to believe I've been in the NFL for six seasons. I've learned a lot. I'm still waiting for a chance to play consistently and show what I can do.

What being a Husky means to me is pride and toughness. We had pride in the way we played. And we were going to be tough people. We weren't going to back down. We believed we were the best and could beat anyone. If we went up by a lot of points, we would put our foot down. If we were down, we'd fight back. We were going to be physical and put a hurt on you. When teams got done playing us, they were going to feel it. We were going to grind you.

Marques Tuiasosopo was voted the Pac-10 Player of the Year in 2000 and the 2001 Rose Bowl Most Valuable Player. He was eighth in Heisman Trophy voting. He was the most prolific multidimensional quarterback, becoming the first in NCAA history to pass for 300 yards and rush for 200 yards in a game. His 1,495 career rushing yards is the most by a UW quarterback. He set a career mark at the time for career total offense with 2,989 yards. Tuiasosopo also excelled in the classroom and was awarded an NCAA post-graduate scholarship. He has been with the Oakland Raiders six seasons. He is currently an NFL quarterback.

LARRY TRIPPLETT
DEFENSIVE LINEMAN
1998–2001

I BECAME INTERESTED IN WASHINGTON because Westchester High School [Los Angeles] teammate Chris Waddell became a Husky after my junior year. He came back and told me about the program that had Corey Dillon and Lawyer Milloy, and finished ninth in the college rankings.

Growing up, I always wanted to play in the Rose Bowl. I figured going with the Huskies gave me the best chance of accomplishing my dreams.

The summer practices were tough, I'll be honest. The toughest experience I've ever gone through. Line coach Randy Hart was such a nice guy when he recruited me. He was a completely different guy as a coach. That's fine, they had to do what they had to do.

To me, I learned what it means to be a Husky my freshman year. I just remember the toughness. As a freshman, we had to sing in front of the team. We also had to answer a question. You'd stand in front of the team, and they'd ask you, "Are you going to quit?" "I ain't never going to quit!" I yelled.

No matter how bad the situation, I never was going to quit. That's what it meant to be a Husky.

There were times I wanted to quit. Being from L.A., I hated the rain. I remembered it rained for about 100 days in a row. I remember being at practice, and it would be so cold with freezing rain and the cold breeze coming in off the lake. I was redshirting and on the scout team. There were times when we were on the sideline with nothing to do.

Two-time All-American Larry Tripplett anchored the defensive line with a career-high 14 tackles for loss during the 2000 season.

A bunch of us freshman would huddle up together in a tight circle to stay warm. Guys would break out and sing some rap. We were freezing.

The first year was bleak, 6–6. The younger guys talked about when we got our opportunity we'd take advantage of it and how it as going to be special. All in all, we won our share of games. We were 26–10 in the three seasons I was a starter on the defensive line.

We had so many special games—the Miami game my junior year and, of course, playing in and winning the 2001 Rose Bowl.

During that 2000 season, my personal highlight game was the Oregon State game. I was cramping up and in a lot of pain. The Beavers were driving the ball in the last two minutes. All they needed was a field goal to win. I needed a break on the sideline, so I came out for a few plays. Strength coach Steve Emtman came over and yelled, "Get yourself in the game!"

I went back in and, on a crucial third-down play, broke through the line and got the tackle for a loss. OSU was out of timeouts, so they had to rush on the field for the field goal. They missed, and we won.

I had a pretty good game against Colorado that year and was honored to be named National Defensive Player of the Week.

Winning the 2001 Rose Bowl over Purdue was unbelievable. In L.A., what you do on New Year's Day is watch the Rose Bowl parade and the Rose Bowl game. To play and win…it was truly a dream come true for me. Our MVP, Marques Tuiasosopo, is such a great leader. Whenever we needed something special, he was able to do it. He gave it his all. I just hope an NFL team gives Marques a chance to play.

The worst game of my career was that terrible Stanford game when Curtis Williams took a hit that paralyzed him. Patrick Reddick, Odell George, Chris Waddell, and I visited him in Fresno. Curtis was a special guy. Everyone on the team loved him. I think about him even to this day. I think about the opportunities he could have had.

The danger of football runs through your mind. But it's football, one thing I've been doing all my life. I have to trust and believe God will take care of me. I put it all in God's hands when I play.

I know Coach Rick Neuheisel has taken a lot of criticism. He was good from what I saw. He was always fair to me. All the conflict and turmoil while he was there is unfortunate. I had two years with Coach Jim Lambright. I was real young then and didn't expect the coaching change. It definitely surprised me. You have to say Neuheisel did bring excitement to Huskies football, and we were able to win games.

I've run across a number of Huskies being in the NFL. Playing against [the Chicago Bears'] Olin Kreutz brought back feelings of being on a scout team. It was funny. He left school early, as a junior, when I was a freshman. He's a Pro Bowl–caliber center, and I always want to prove myself against him.

The rebuilding year of 2001 was disappointing. But I played as tough as I could, with a career-best 14 tackles for loss. I'm proud I was able to start 36 consecutive games from 1999 to 2001.

443

Larry Tripplett earned All-America and All–Pac-10 honors two seasons. He anchored the 2001 Rose Bowl team with a career-best 14 tackles for loss. He was one of 12 finalists for the 2001 Lombardi Award. He was the 1999 team's Academic Player of the Year. He was selected by the Indianapolis Colts in the second round of the 2002 NFL draft. He is currently a defensive tackle with the Buffalo Bills.

PAUL ARNOLD

RECEIVER/RUNNING BACK

1999–2002

GROWING UP, I WAS ALWAYS PLAYING SPORTS, but I never watched sports on TV. I remember the first time ever seeing a football game. My cousin and I were watching the 1990 Huskies, with Greg Lewis and Beno Bryant and all those guys. And he was saying, "Wow, look at that Beno!" He was pointing out all the guys to me. It was kind of ironic to have that be my first experience. I was 10.

I started playing youth football in the sixth grade. It was the first time I played football, and I played ever since then. I was actually a lineman. I was big and stayed the same size. I liked being a lineman. I was just happy to be part of the team and play sports. I was happy about doing it.

By the time I was a senior at Kennedy High School, I was one of the most highly recruited running backs in state history. I had over 50 scholarship offers. I was recruited by just about everybody in the country. I took five trips: Colorado, Notre Dame, Washington, UCLA, and Michigan. I was recruited by Coach Rick Neuheisel while he was at Colorado and when he became the Huskies coach.

In Colorado he said, "You have to come here, it's a great place to play."

Once he switched, he'd say, "You gotta play at Washington—it's a better place to play. You can't leave. You'll be successful."

I joked with him a little, "Hey, do I still have my scholarship at Colorado?"

Marques Tuiasosopo was my host during my Huskies trip. I felt like I was meeting a legend. His advice: "Stay here because Huskies run the city. Everybody follows the Huskies. There's not a better place to be."

So I stayed. During summer camp, there were times when I wanted to leave. There were times it was hard. Doubts came into my mind, and I wondered if this was really what I wanted to do. The first words of encouragement I remember came from teammate Curtis Williams. He didn't say much, and we were just hanging around. He had a little brother named Paul. He said, "You remind me of my little brother." I remember that it probably didn't mean anything to him. But to me, I had been through all this exhausting work, and it was the first word of encouragement that I really received.

All coaches love speed, and I had it. I ran 40 yards in 4.33 seconds. I played as a true freshman and lettered. I played special teams and running back, and carried the ball in every game.

I remember running out into that stadium. I remember walking down that tunnel doing our chants. There were kids looking over the tunnel. And we started to hear kids say, "Here they come, here they come!" We noticed it really filled up. It's a big deal. People started rushing the tunnel, watching the guys come out and trying to get high-fives and everything. I remember when we all took off, we could hear the band start playing, and the crowd would erupt. It looked like everybody was on their feet. It's a super adrenaline rush you can't match. People can talk about it and describe it, but it's one of those things that you have to experience, because talking about it does not do it justice.

I caused some excitement in our Air Force game when I returned a kickoff 100 yards, the longest in Huskies history.

I had a few fumbles that year, but my biggest freshman mistake was dragging my feet in celebration after I scored a touchdown at Arizona. The penalty led to a missed extra point. I apologized to the team before the half, and some of the guys on defense said, "We don't care, do it again!"

A big win was beating Colorado for Neuheisel's first win, and the UW's 600th victory. It was a big deal.

I started the season as a nervous rookie and became a part of the family. I wore No. 20, the number Greg Lewis wore. Greg really mentored me. He was always there to talk. He helped me realize it was special to play as a true freshman.

445

A stress fracture in my back hampered my sophomore year. I missed the last four games but was able to suit up for the Rose Bowl. A highlight for all of us happened before the game. Curtis Williams, paralyzed in the Stanford game, came into the locker room. We were all excited to see him. He was in there and wasn't able to move much, but he was in good spirits. He was leaning back. We couldn't see much expression, but we could tell he was excited.

Paul Arnold, a highly recruited local running back from Kennedy High, made the switch to receiver at Washington.

We knew he was happy to be there. A couple guys teared up. We all got really excited. We started hooping and hollering. We were all saying, "We are going to go out and get this." It was definitely a big deal for us to see Curtis.

Even though I wasn't a factor in the game, I felt I contributed during the first six games to help the team produce an outstanding 11–1 season.

Watching Marques up close was amazing. It was like in the movies. We'd be behind, and Marques would come into the huddle and say, "Okay, okay, enough of this. We're going to score and win this game." When Marques said something, everyone believed him. We had so many come-from-behind victories.

While I was waiting for clearance to play, I wasn't able to do anything physical. So that's when the thought came up of my being a receiver. When I was bored, I'd line up with the receivers and run deep routes.

My junior season, we had a new running backs coach and a new receivers coach. We talked about my going out for receiver, but we never made it official. Everything I did was still with running backs. I remember the first day of spring practice, I went out with the running backs. The running backs coach said, "Are you with me or not?"

I wanted to say farewell. I remember Coach Neuheisel pulled me aside after practice and said, "I've been telling everyone that you are going to be a receiver. What's going on?"

I said, I knew I was going to be a receiver, but I wanted to go out for the last day.

We still had four running backs at that time and only five receivers returning. The more and more we thought about it, it made sense. My dad would tell me through high school, "You aren't a running back, you are a receiver." It was his idea. I called him and said, "Pops, I'm going to be a receiver." He said, "I told you. I told you."

Coach Neuheisel was a different kind of coach. A lot of people say a lot of different things about him. I can only speak from my own experience. The things I remember is that he made sure we got everything we deserved. If we needed extra gear, he made sure we got it. When we had bowl trips, we always felt like we had the best bowl experience.

I was excited for my junior season to try a new position. I was a starter at my new receiver spot right away. We had a great season, even though we ended the year with a Holiday Bowl loss to Texas, led by Major Applewhite's comeback heroics. I only caught one pass that game and had a drop. You always want to win the last game. It's always a big deal to the seniors. They talk about the seniors paying their dues and ending right, and you feel really disappointed, like you let down the seniors. You have to deal with that. So you use that motivation to work hard in the off-season.

That season, I saw the most courageous act. Cody Pickett played the whole season with a third-degree separated shoulder. When he was tackled, you could just tell he was hurting. Most guys would have this "come get me" look. But he'd pop up and get back in the huddle. Cody set Pac-10 passing records that year. He always mentioned that his dad, a hall-of-fame rodeo cowboy, put that toughness in him.

I came into my senior year confident. I knew the receiver position well. I worked out as hard as I had ever worked out that summer. I was really excited. We had Cody coming back. We had Reggie Williams, Todd Elstrom, Patrick Reddick, Wilbur Hooks, Charles Frederick, and me. That was our receiving core. We had everybody coming back.

I had some dreadlocks, too. They called me E.T. I had to chop them off so they'd stop calling me that. I always wore braids.

448

We finished 7–6 that year. We were in the middle of the pack. We went to the Sun Bowl and played Purdue again, a rematch from the Rose Bowl. We lost that game. We said, hey, we beat you guys when it counted; we won the Rose Bowl. But it was a tough one.

A memorable game was UCLA. That's because Rich Alexis, a good friend, and I both had big games. I caught four or five passes for 150 yards and he had two touchdowns.

Rich and I we were running backs at the same time. We were really close. I consider him my little brother, even to this day. I remember that was a big deal because we both had good games that day.

That triple-overtime win in Pullman [vs. Washington State] was one of the craziest games I ever played. To make that comeback was unforgettable. I scored a touchdown in my first Apple Cup, an 80-yard touchdown run, and one in my last one. I remember John Anderson having to make all those field goals. You never lose hope about winning the game. It was real iffy. But we just went out there and continued to play hard. We felt like we were a better team. We had to win that game. We had to keep it up and continue to play hard even though it didn't look very good.

My most cherished memories are everything. I spent so much time with these guys that they became like family. I think about the times we had a hard practice and I was sitting with my buddies, asking, "Is it going to be a long one today?" Or going in after the game with the music playing in the locker room and celebrating with all my teammates. The biggest thing for me was everything that went along with football—the relationships. Just spending time. I have teammates who are like brothers to me.

After my senior year, I signed as a free agent with Indianapolis, but I was released. I felt like I got a fair shot in the NFL.

So I came home. I knew that Dawgs take care of Dawgs. The reason I stayed here for college was because I knew one day I wasn't going to play football. The one thing everybody talks about is that Huskies will take care of their own. I found that to be true. Actually, my current boss is a die-hard Huskies fan and season-ticket holder. That helped me become a real estate agent. It's helped me get some appointments. I do open houses and say my name and show my ring. It's a good conversation-starter that's helped me in my business. At the same time, the ring is a reminder of my past. Going through school, managing my time, my social life, and playing football all prepared me for life at the end of the day.

Paul Arnold set the school record for longest kick return (100 yards) as a freshman. He was voted the team's Most Improved Player in 2001 and won the Coaches Award in 2002. His 97 career receptions rank 13th at the UW. He is currently a real estate agent in the Puget Sound area.

JOHN ANDERSON

KICKER

1999–2002

IN MY FINAL APPLE CUP, I missed my first three kicks. Two of them were from beyond 50 yards, but those were makeable for me. Since it was my last regular-season game, I was bummed.

That was the wild 2002 game in Pullman that went to three overtimes.

We were down 20–10 with under four minutes left. Then I made one to force overtime, and suddenly it became easy. In overtime, I tried to have more fun with those pressure kicks. I've made kicks from those distances a million times before. I tried not to think about it too much. I'd laugh and have fun with it. I made field goals in the first and second overtimes. In the third overtime, I hit a 49-yarder to win it 29–26.

I was really lucky in my career. I never missed any big kicks. My first clutch kick was at the end of my freshman year at UCLA in the Rose Bowl, when I kicked a 56-yard field goal to send it into overtime. We ended up losing, but that was probably one of the biggest kicks of my career. I also had two walk-off, game-winning kicks my junior year, against USC and Arizona.

I almost wasn't a kicker. I earned high school all-America honors in punting (averaging 47 yards a kick) and place-kicking at Boynton Beach, Florida. I originally committed to Georgia Tech. I was going to punt there, but I really wanted to place-kick. I took a couple of trips to Big Ten schools and then visited the UW in December, right before they were about to go to the Aloha Bowl. I really wanted to kick right away, and they needed a kicker for

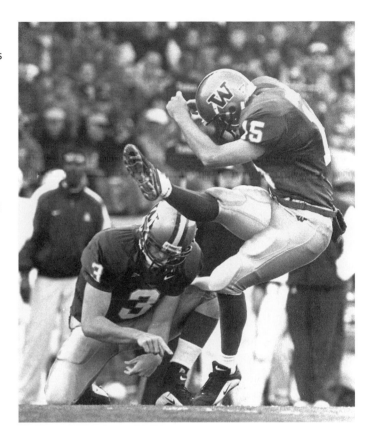

John Anderson kicked field goals four seasons for the Huskies and never missed a clutch kick, including his legendary three overtime field goals in the 2002 Apple Cup.

the next season. I went to Washington because I knew I would have a chance to play as a freshman.

I won the job on one of the last days of summer camp and was the starting kicker for four years. It was really exciting to play at the D-1 level. Two years before I arrived, they lost a few games because of kicking, so a lot of the older guys were really encouraging, and I was very lucky because overall I was encouraged and believed in.

I had two holders. Ryan Miletich was the holder for my freshman year, and then Cody Pickett my last three years. Ryan was very dedicated to Huskies football, and he was very tolerant of the freshmen. Every time I was out there, he looked at me as though he had confidence I could do the job.

Playing in the 2001 Rose Bowl was a big deal. It was a special game. I kicked two field goals in the third quarter, a 42-yarder and one from 47. A lot of schools had grass, so it wasn't that big of a deal. I tried to treat it as just another game. I just concentrated on what was happening on the field. When

I was at Washington, everyone had a job, and that was mine. I didn't feel I had more pressure than anyone else.

For everyone on that team, the memories of the Rose Bowl also include Curtis Williams, our teammate paralyzed in a game that season.

I was in the first bus going to the Rose Bowl on game day. Coach Neuheisel and Coach Gilbertson were on the bus. About 10 minutes before we got to Pasadena, Coach Neuheisel got a call that Curtis wanted to visit the locker room. I remember Neuheisel and Gilby argued about it. Gilby said it wasn't a good idea. Neuheisel finally said, "We'll do whatever Curtis wants!"

Everyone went to Curtis and hugged and kissed him. Everyone was crying. We weren't going to lose that game. That emotion carried us to a 34–24 win over Purdue.

Two seasons later, my final game was a loss to Purdue by the same score in the Sun Bowl.

I played in a senior all-star game and was drafted by the Chicago Bears. The strangest thing happened in that all-star game. I was kicking my normal, right-foot, soccer-style kick, and I felt a snap in my hip. It was like a rubberband snap on my hip. It was a freak injury. But that injury ended my career. I couldn't kick anymore without pain. It still hurts to this day. I was bummed, but I knew I wasn't going to play football forever. I got my degree is business management.

I was really lucky to be at Washington, though. There's nothing better than that. I'm still close to some of the players. I'm in touch with about a half dozen people. I work for my family business, a contracting management company. One of my hobbies is tournament fishing. We've spent way more than we've made. It's something my dad and my cousins enjoy doing.

To be a Husky is an honor. Washington has a lot of history, and it's something that I'll always be proud of.

John Anderson's 56-yard field goal against UCLA in 1999 is tied as the longest in Huskies history. His five field goals in the 2002 Apple Cup tied a UW record for most in a game. His 159 career extra points is the most in Huskies history, and his 42 in 2002 is the most in a season. His 68 career field goals ranks second. His 68 percent conversion rate for field goals (68 of 100) is fifth-best. He is currently the manager for his family business in Florida.

CODY PICKETT

QUARTERBACK

1999–2003

ONE THING I'M PROUD TO SAY about my career at Washington is I never lost to Washington State.

My junior year it took three overtimes to keep that streak alive. That was a great game. The Cougars were ranked high, and we beat them twice. I threw a touchdown in overtime that was called back.

That game was one of the coldest I've ever played in. As I drew the ball back, it slipped out of my hand, and rolled off my shoulder pad and onto the back of our lineman. I quickly recovered it and threw a touchdown pass to tight end Kevin Ware. The refs took it away—they said I threw two forward passes. But it was okay because we got out with a field goal.

One of the key plays of the game was a 48-yard pass to Reggie Williams. It was third and long with 4:41 to play. We weren't moving the ball much. In the huddle, I said to Reggie, "I'm throwing to you no matter what, even if you're covered by three guys."

"I'm ready," he said.

I threw it up with a lot of air, and Reggie made a spectacular catch over two guys now in the NFL—Marcus Trufant and Jason David. We scored a few plays later to pull within a field goal.

Reggie was a great target. He had height (6′4″), speed, competitiveness, and confidence. He's a very confident guy—a guy who wants the ball. I did

454

Cody Pickett, Washington's all-time passing leader, set a school record for most passing yards in a game—while nursing a separated shoulder.

everything I could to get him the ball as much as possible. Reggie and I are still tight.

Playing in Pullman was the closest I got to home—Caldwell, Idaho—where I was an all-state football player and the state's high school basketball player of the year.

When the WSU game is the last of your Huskies career, that's not a good thing, because it means no bowl game. Even though we underachieved my senior year with a 6–6 record, it was a good feeling to beat WSU at home on a touchdown pass to Corey Williams.

A lot was made of the "Northwest Championship"—beating Oregon, Oregon State, and Washington State—many remember the T-shirt Braxton Cleman made my junior year. But I have to say that beating the Northwest schools was always our goal and always a big deal for us.

Setting Huskies passing records was the last thing on my mind while I was playing. It wasn't even a thought. I was just trying to prepare for each game. The ultimate was to win. I wish we could've won more games. Still, it is a good feeling to know I hold some UW records.

I think my 10,220 career yards passing almost doubled the record. I almost broke the career mark in one season when I threw for 4,458 in my junior year. We threw the ball a lot.

That's no surprise, considering I played for a Rick Neuheisel, a former quarterback, and offensive guru Keith Gilbertson.

I was recruited by Jim Lambright's staff, but by the time I arrived for summer practices, Neuheisel was the head coach.

It's unfortunate how things turned out with Coach Neuheisel, because I thought he was a great coach. We got along great and won some big games. Neuheisel came in, and he was a very energetic, positive guy. It was the same when he left at the end. Coach Gilbertson came in, and we had high expectations. All and all, my experience was great. I had great coaching staffs.

I also had quality teammates. We were a very close bunch of guys. I was really close to Reggie and Khalif Barnes. We hung out on and off the field. We had a tight bond. We were inspired by tradition and what we had to do.

I was able learn about leadership by watching Marques Tuiasosopo. I learned how to win while he was around Washington. You kind of look to your elders and try to do things the way he did. Marques was a winner. He practiced hard and played very well. I tried to follow his way.

I actually played five seasons at Washington. My true freshman year, I played about 20 minutes before a back injury sidelined me for the season. I just wasn't used to lifting weights, and my back had problems.

My first memorable game was our 2001 Rose Bowl win over Purdue. I was the guy who hadn't played at all and came in and completed a couple passes to keep our drive alive when Marques got hurt. That was a good feeling.

That game was dedicated to Curtis Williams. Seeing his paralyzing injury absolutely affected me. It was a terrible tragedy—being paralyzed and then passing away. I've seen two football tragedies firsthand. While playing in a preseason game with the 49ers, we were driving for a score at the end of the game. Everyone was tired. In the huddle I was saying, "Come on, we've got to push through this." We scored, and everyone felt good about it. The game ended, and we went to the locker room. Suddenly, Thomas Herrion suffered a massive heart attack in front of us and died. It makes you appreciate what you have.

My first start, a home victory over Michigan, was special. But a game I'm proud of is a victory over Arizona in 2001. The week before, I blew out my shoulder. I was fine when I threw the ball. But when I took a hit, it didn't feel too great. My 455 passing yards set a school record in a game, all with a separated shoulder.

456

I had my share of injuries here and there. I tore my pectoral muscle in my throwing side versus Indiana. I swelled up like I had implants. I played through it. I had a concussion against Oregon and played the next week. Injuries are part of the game.

I felt like I played no matter what—separated shoulder, concussion. I was going to do whatever I could to be successful. That was my team. When I had a concussion, the staff had to hide my helmet from me. The last thing I wanted to do was stand on the sideline. No matter what, I wanted to be with my teammates.

The Holiday Bowl loss to Texas was very disappointing. It was one of the all-time greatest Holiday Bowl games. We were way ahead, and they came back, led by Major Applewhite, and got us in the end, 47–43. That's a game we should've won.

Another disappointing game came my junior year when we played at Michigan on national TV. We had those guys beaten, but they made a 47-yard field goal with no time on the clock.

Losing tight end Jerramy Stevens was a big loss my junior year. And then we lost some key linemen my senior year. That's not an excuse. I just wish I could have won more games, especially my senior year.

Being a Husky was an honor. All the tradition made it a great honor to put on the uniform. I played for my teammates and all the players who had played before. You walk down the tunnel and all you see is tradition. Going out and playing in front of 70,000 every weekend and having everyone count on you to get the wins—I loved that feeling. I played in a lot of big games in a big-time atmosphere.

> Cody Pickett's 4,458 passing yards in 2003 made him the first 4,000-yard passer in Pac-10 history. His career total of 10,220 passing yards set a school record and ranks fourth-highest in Pac-10 history. Pickett has seven of the UW's top-10 single-game passing yardage records. He holds 21 UW passing records. He is currently seeking a spot in pro football after two NFL seasons with the San Francisco 49ers.

RICH ALEXIS

RUNNING BACK

2000–2003

M Y PARENTS DIDN'T ALLOW ME to play football for fear I would break bones.

I mainly played basketball in Florida at Pope John Paul II High. I dreamed of playing basketball in college. My basketball coach left after my junior year in high school, and I was getting pretty nervous about my basketball career.

I played one football game as a freshman and two as a junior. I hid my participation from my dad. Our high school had spring football practices, so I had a great game the spring before my senior year and finally showed my dad the videotape and asked if I could play my senior year.

Dad surprised me by saying that if I wanted to play, I should "go for it."

I immediately loved playing running back. I picked up the sport quickly. I had natural running instinct. I didn't have any technique, just raw talent. My coaches just gave me the ball and told me to run. I had some good games. I had size—6′ and 200 pounds—and speed.

I ended up at Washington because my high school teammate, John Anderson, a UW kicker, sent my tapes to the UW coaches.

Miami and Indiana showed interest but wanted to switch me to defensive back. I really didn't want to learn another position.

Coach Rick Neuheisel made me feel comfortable. Even though it was far from home, I decided to be a Husky.

In his second game as a Husky, Rich Alexis scored a 50-yard rushing touchdown against Miami, a team that advised him to be a cornerback.

Our summer training camp was at Evergreen State College. I went from sunny Florida to gray skies and hippies running around playing banjos. I was freaking out. I locked myself in a room and wanted to go home. I thought, *I can't do this anymore.* Neuheisel came and calmed me down.

Before our second game, against No. 4 Miami, Neuheisel said he wasn't sure if he'd put me in the game or not. He said there might be a chance for my parents to see me.

When I got in, quarterback Marques Tuiasosopo changed the play at the line of scrimmage to an option. I forgot everything. So I just trailed him. I got the pitch and raced down the sideline for a 50-yard touchdown. It was exciting, especially against a team that said I shouldn't play running back.

During the season, defensive back Curtis Williams gave me encouragement. Curtis seemed very quiet and low-key. I didn't know how good of a player he was. On the field, I saw an animal come out of him. He was a very explosive player. One day I was feeling down. He came and talked to me and told me to keep my head up and things would work out.

When a tackle paralyzed Curtis against Stanford, I couldn't believe it. I was like, "Curtis, get up!" When they moved him off the field, I went to another place. I couldn't believe what had just happened. To be raised fearing something might happen if I played football, and then to see that nightmare come true right before your eyes…it affected me. It affected everyone. You know that can happen anytime you play football. We said our prayers and took it in stride, but we never forgot about Curtis. That gave us extra motivation, knowing we could finish what he started.

That season, I set a record for most rushing yards by a freshman with 816. My average of 6.4 yards per carry is the most in a season at Washington.

I was able to contribute in our Rose Bowl victory over Purdue with a 50-yard pitch down the sideline. To be on a D-1 team and win the Rose Bowl in my first year, I couldn't write a better script.

I loved playing for Coach Neuheisel. I think he was the best coach to this day. I can't understand people who say he was soft. That was false. He knew how to relate to players. He didn't have to motivate players every day. To some, if you don't yell, you're soft. You're not soft when you can win a Rose Bowl.

Marques eased me into my role. I saw the way he played, and it inspired me. I couldn't be a freshman around him. I had to know what I was doing.

I wasn't a star, but he gave me a break. He'd ask, "What's up?" to check how I was doing. He said if I forgot a play, I could just ask him, and he would let me know what to do. He kept me motivated and my spirits up.

We couldn't help but get up just walking through the tunnel to the field. I would get real hyped up seeing posters of the bowl games on the walls. The tunnel was our sanctuary on game day. We had a couple chants, too. We'd shout, "Whose house?" and then answer, "Dawgs' house!" We also had the "Say Who?" chant. I thought, *Dang, I didn't know they did all this to get ready* In the tunnel was when we got together.

The first year, I was just happy to put on the college uniform. The second year I got to know the tradition and understand all the great players before who bled for Huskies football. Each year I understood what it meant to be a Husky…to lay it on the line and not let anyone disrespect your home. Each year you know more and more.

I struggled with some injuries while at Washington. Most players do. I had two shoulder surgeries and blew out my quad. I had a shoulder problem my first year and played the whole season with it. My sophomore year, I got a shoulder injury again in the Holiday Bowl versus Texas. I hurt both shoulders from two different hits. On one, I took a hit and felt my shoulder dislocate and then pop back in when I hit the ground.

461

My sophomore season was my hell season as my yardage was cut in half. I was hurting so much, I didn't even want to go out there and suit up. I could have blamed a lot of things—the injury, the weight I gained, the new offensive line, and a new running backs coach—but I didn't.

Our heartbreak game that year was a loss to Oregon State. We could've gone back to the Rose Bowl. Instead we went to the Holiday Bowl.

I had a few fumbles. In college I was a north-and-south runner. I tried to run you over. I ran hard all the time toward the end zone. I heard critics who said I should make more moves. People thought I should be a slasher. You can try to please people, but in the end you have to do what makes you successful—hit the hole when it opens. The holes in college don't stay open very long.

Because of finances, my parents were only able to fly out to Washington for one game during my time in Seattle—and that game I was injured and didn't even play. They were able to experience a game at Husky Stadium, though, so I was happy about that.

In the end, everything worked out. Playing for the Huskies and being out there on field made me stronger. I learned I could deal with any adversity. I've experienced highs and lows. One day people love you, the next day they are not so sure—that's sports. I was happy to go out and play for Huskies.

Rich Alexis burst into the Huskies football records with the best season by a freshman running back. His 816 yards is the most by a freshman, and his 6.4 yards per carry in 2000 is the most by anyone in a season at Washington. His three runs for more than 50 yards (including an 86-yarder) as a freshman are tied for most 50-plus-yard runs in a season with Napoleon Kaufman and Hugh McElhenny. His 28 career rushing touchdowns placed him tied for fourth with McElhenny. Alexis's 596 rushing attempts ranks fourth in UW history, and his 2,455 yards rushing is seventh-best. Alexis signed as a free agent with the Jacksonville Jaguars and was with the team for three seasons before signing with the St. Louis Rams. He is currently a player in the NFL.

ZACH TUIASOSOPO

FULLBACK

2000–2004

WHEN THE COACHING STAFF ASKED ME to redshirt my first year at Washington, I was bummed. It was really hard to sit out.

One reason I went to the UW was because of my older brother, Marques. We had always missed playing together on the same team by one year. With my first year being Marques's senior year, I thought we would finally play in the same game.

From the sideline, I watched as my brother quarterbacked the Huskies to the 2001 Rose Bowl victory. I was so proud when Marques was named Most Valuable Player of the game.

It was exciting for me to watch that game and the whole season. I always looked up to him as a leader. When I watched him play, I envisioned myself playing with the same passion and drive.

The Rose Bowl had a mixture of intense emotions. My mom and dad were from Southern California, so we had a lot of relatives at the game. After the game, our Auntie, Aima Amituanai, came down to the edge of the field to congratulate us. She said, "We're going to party at our tailgate; we'll see you out there!" A few minutes later, Dad came into the locker room and said, "We have to go; Auntie has collapsed." She collapsed and died of heart failure just steps outside the stadium. It certainly put the importance of sports in perspective.

Linebacker-turned-fullback Zach Tuiasosopo, a co-captain going into 2004, lost most of his senior season to an untimely injury.

When I got my chance to get on the field the next season, I played linebacker. I started five games and played in every game. My memorable play of the season was my first sack. It came at home against Arizona. I was on top of the world. I finished with 41 tackles, and I wanted more. People forget we were one win away from going back to the Rose Bowl that year. We played in a thrilling 2001 Holiday Bowl—although Major Applewhite did us in, 47–43.

That spring, the fullback position was thin. Coaches asked if I'd move to offense. At first it was a hard decision because I loved linebacker, still do. At that point, however, it was about how I could help the team. The move was not about me. I learned to understand that.

I think I fumbled my first carry as a fullback against San Jose State. I guess that established me as a blocker. The season ended with another bowl appearance and another bowl loss—to Purdue in the 2002 Sun Bowl. Still, a bowl is a bowl.

I learned a valuable life lesson that spring, the hard way.

I was arrested for malicious mischief (damaging four cars). Being a Huskies football player, combined with my famous last name (my dad played at UCLA and for the Seattle Seahawks), made my arrest newsworthy.

It's not something I hide from. It's not a highlight of my college career or life. It happened, and I hope everything is resolved and forgiven. I've expressed my sincere apology. It was one incident. I'm not that kind of person. It was embarrassing for my family and the UW football team and coaching staff. I moved home because I needed to work out things in my life. I needed to get away. It helped. My family was unbelievable. They stood by me and have always been there for me. The thing I expressed to younger teammates was that the things you do don't just affect you.

My junior year also brought change in the coaching staff, as participation in an NCAA basketball tournament betting pool eventually led to the dismissal of Coach Rick Neuheisel, who was replaced by Keith Gilbertson.

It was really surprising to us players when Neuheisel was fired. But we had to say, "Hey, let's kept the ball rolling. Let's keep Huskies football alive. We can't worry about the distraction." Coach Gilbertson was excited about the opportunity. I don't think we gave him reasons to be excited by our performance on the field.

I did score two touchdowns during my Huskies career, both during my junior year. I didn't expect to score as the fullback, so when it happened, it was fun. One was a 12-yard option up the middle that I broke to the left. The second was a one-yard dive against Cal. But for the first time in 10 seasons, the Huskies didn't go to a bowl game.

The real heartbreak came my senior season, in 2004.

We lost our home opener to Fresno State. That hurt, but it wasn't the heartbreak. That was my most productive day as a fullback. I popped a 50-yard run before being tackled at the 1-yard line. I kept saying to myself as I was running, *Don't get caught!* I finished the game with 98 yards rushing on two carries, and five receptions.

In the third game, in a 38–3 loss to Notre Dame, I fractured my fibula [calf bone], and that knocked me out the rest of the season.

I went from being a co-captain, receiving national attention as a top player, to not getting a chance to help my team. That humbled me a lot. At first I felt sorry for myself and thought how unfair my fate was. In your last hurrah, if you go down in the eighth or ninth game, okay. But in the third game? It was a big blow. My grandma says everything happens for a reason.

I never thought I was done. I kept pushing with my rehab. I kept thinking I'd play in the last game. But I didn't make it. I did stay involved with the team, though. I dedicated myself to be there as a cheerleader for my teammates. I decided I'd go to every game and did. I made my own arrangements to fly out to every road game. I'd fly in the morning of the game or the night before and stay at the team hotel.

The ball didn't roll our way the whole season. I believe four of our five captains didn't finish the season. Our 1–10 season was the worst since 1969.

In the five years I was in the program, UW football went from one loss to one win: 11–1, 8–4, 7–6, 6–6, and 1–10. It didn't take away from my football experience. You have to turn the page. You can't change what happened yesterday. You can change tomorrow.

I'm fortunate to experience how it goes both ways—three bowls and then two frustrating seasons. The last two years gave me another type of learning experience—just because you accomplish something one year, you can't expect people to roll over. I think we lost sight of that.

You can't deny there was a different atmosphere, a different attitude from when I arrived at Washington to when I left. I don't believe it's on Coach Neuheisel. Some say it's the coaching change that brought us down. Coach Gilbertson wasn't the one with the pads on. It comes back to the players. If you don't have toughness, it's on the players. I know something was lost somewhere in the mix. Not that the players didn't have it…just the thinking you can show up and play because you wear the gold helmet and purple jersey.

People can say what they want about our record, but I never lost my pride of being a Husky. There's nothing like being there for each other. It's easy to be there through the good times. It's hard in the bad times. Are you going to be there arm-in-arm no matter what? I think we did stick together.

Being a Husky means it's great to be part of such an established organization and family. You're not just a Husky four or five years—it's a lifetime, like a brotherhood or fraternity. When I see players from other times, there's a common bond. When you see guys you played with, it's like you never missed a beat.

I did try to convince my younger brother, Matt, to be a Husky. I thought that would've been fun. His freshman year would've been my senior year. Matt decided to sign with the Seattle Mariners. I think he made the best decision for himself, and I can't argue with that.

I did realize my dream of playing at the same time with Marques. We both played for the Oakland Raiders for a short time in 2006 until I was traded to the Philadelphia Eagles.

Zach Tuiasosopo, younger brother of Huskies quarterback, Marques, began his Huskies career as a linebacker before switching to fullback in 2002. Though primarily a blocker, he scored two touchdowns from the fullback position and was elected team co-captain before suffering a season-ending calf injury in his senior year. Though undrafted, he signed with the Philadelphia Eagles in 2006. He is currently a player in the NFL.

REGGIE WILLIAMS
RECEIVER
2001–2003

W HEN I ANNOUNCED THAT I'D DECIDED to be a Husky, I did it on Fox Sports TV. I said I wanted to be a Husky and then play in the NFL.

My predictions came true, but I never dreamed of breaking UW receiving records or of finishing my career as the second-leading receiver in Pac-10 history.

To be the Huskies' all-time career receiver in both yards and catches is an honor. There's been a lot of great quarterbacks and great receivers, like Mario Bailey and Jerome Pathon. Those are great accomplishments to look back on. I never set out to break records. My only concern was to help the team win.

I almost was a Michigan Wolverine instead of a Husky. I really didn't like Washington while in high school at Lakewood, near Tacoma.

I didn't think it fit me. Coach Rick Neuheisel changed my mind. I started talking with him after he took the UW job.

I was torn between Michigan and Washington when it came time to make a decision. A week before signing day, I talked to the Michigan coach, and in 30 minutes I was convinced I'd go to Michigan. The next night I talked with Neuheisel, and then I decided to go to Washington.

I was anxiously excited when practices started. I was ready to get out there and see what this college thing was all about.

The receiving corps received me with open arms. We became a tight group, with guys like Ty Ellingston, Wilbur Hooks, and Paul Arnold. We were deep at the position.

I guess I was able to show my talent early on, and being 6′4″, 218 pounds, with speed and hands didn't hurt. I started every game of my true freshman season. Our opener in 2001 was a nice 70-degree day in Husky Stadium. The experience was more than I expected. Until you actually go out and do it in a real game, and walk down the tunnel for the first time with everyone screaming, you don't know how you will react.

As fate would have it, my first Huskies game was against the team I turned down—Michigan.

The second series I caught my first pass. It was a fade down the sideline. I made a good play on the ball and ran 74 yards. I was pulled down by my foot, and it knocked my shoe off. I had four catches for 134 yards in my debut. That first game was a big boost for my confidence.

I was fortunate to be teamed with quarterback Cody Pickett, the Huskies all-time leading passer. Cody's a great quarterback and made my job a whole lot easier. He's such a competitor. He takes it to the next level every play.

469

All the Apple Cup games stick out for me. Those were always exciting games to play in. There was one catch at Pullman that was special. I leaped over a couple defenders to keep a drive alive. I don't even know how I caught that one. That was a one-hander. We were down, and we needed a little momentum. That play really changed the game.

The couple of catches I remember most were long touchdowns against Arizona and San Jose State. Against the Wildcats, we were losing by four and backed up on our 20. Cody checked to my side. I ran a slant, broke a tackle, and went 80 yards. My longest catch, the longest in UW history, came against San Jose State. It was a curl route I ran across the middle for an 89-yard touchdown.

While I was at Washington, we played in the Sun Bowl and Holiday Bowl. I had some pretty good catches in Texas. My junior year we didn't go to a bowl but we won the Northwest Championship!

College was one of greatest times of my life. Being around teammates was the best part. The guys took me in and made me feel part of family. I just liked hanging out with the guys, whether it was going to a mall or just walking around.

Reggie Williams's 6'4" stature, his speed, and his soft hands—combined with the UW's pass-happy offense in the early 2000s—led to broken receiving records.

470

Being a Husky meant playing for a great team and being part of a great family and tradition. I just wanted to be accepted. Being a Husky is about having the heart of a champion. A football team is such a diverse group—black, white, so much culture bound into one.

Being a Husky taught me tough times never last, tough people do.

It was a sad situation, what happened with Coach Neuheisel. I love Neuheisel. He's a great coach and motivator. I was sad to see him go. He moved on, and we moved on. I thought Coach Gilbertson was a great coach, too. Seeing the team win just one game after I left was tough to watch. I'm still in touch with some of the players.

I remind them of the promise all freshman made when I was at Washington. They had all the freshman stand up in front of the team and answer a question. They ask you, "Are you going to quit?" And you yell back, "I'm never going to quit!"

I took that promise to heart...and never did quit.

Reggie Williams shattered UW receiving records on his way to being an All-American in 2002. Williams posted 1,000-yard receiving seasons in each of his three seasons as he set career UW records for receptions (243) and receiving yards (3,598). His 94 catches and 1,454 yards in 2002 was just two yards shy of the Pac-10 single-season record and left him the second-most-prolific receiver in Pac-10 history. His 89-yard touchdown catch from Cody Pickett is the longest scoring reception in UW history. His reception yards per game are UW records for a season (111.8) and career (97.2). He averaged 6.57 receptions per game (also a UW record). He is currently a receiver playing in the NFL for the Jacksonville Jaguars, who drafted him ninth overall in 2004.

ISAIAH STANBACK

QUARTERBACK

2002–2006

FOR ME, BEING A HUSKY HAS BEEN about perseverance and dedication. If you start something, you finish it.

When I was a junior at Garfield High, the Huskies won the Rose Bowl. My senior year they went to the Holiday Bowl. In my five years at Washington, the football program didn't have the success we envisioned as we had three head coaches and just one winning season: 7–6, 6–6, 1–10, 2–9, and 5–7.

For those who criticized our commitment the past three seasons, I wish they could have walked in our shoes for a week. There were a lot of positives not in the public view. For us to go through all this downturn makes us stronger people. It didn't go the way I wanted, but I think my experiences at Washington will be beneficial to me. It's been a good environment, a family environment.

That family feeling is one reason I decided to be a Husky. I had a lot of options. I narrowed them down to USC, Arizona State, and Washington.

Coach Rick Neuheisel was probably the biggest influence on my going to the UW. He's very people-oriented. He tried to make it a family environment on the team, and that made it much more comfortable. It didn't hurt that Neuheisel was a quarterback.

I think I fit in well. I had watched practices before I joined the program, so I wasn't amazed or in awe. I caught up to the game speed pretty quickly.

Isaiah Stanback endured as the starting quarterback through one of Washington's lowest points, a one-win season.

I mainly played quarterback on the scout team. One week, however, I played receiver to prepare for the WSU game because they had some tall receivers.

A memorable moment that year came when a teammate was late for a couple meetings. The whole team had to pay for it. We had to show up at the stadium at 6:00 AM to run as punishment.

Unfortunately, Coach Neuheisel left before I got in my first game. Coach Keith Gilbertson took over. Where I would play caused much discussion. I was behind Cody Pickett, Washington's all-time leading passer. It was a problem my first couple years. I came to Washington to play quarterback, and I wasn't going to be derailed. I wanted to prove people wrong—those who doubted my quarterback abilities.

I saw my first quarterback action in a big win over Indiana my redshirt freshman season. I came in, and we had a couple runs and a few passes. It was cool. It was exciting because of the crowd.

I played some at the flanker position as well. I wanted to be on the field. I told Coach, if I had the opportunity to play quarterback next year, I had no problem trying to help the team as a receiver.

My best receiving game was against Arizona. I had three or four catches and almost scored.

I learned a lot from Cody. I learned a lot from everyone. I try to pick up whatever I can from anybody, as far as passing. Learning how to become a D-1 quarterback was difficult. I didn't have any stability with coaches to help. I had three different offensive coordinators and three different position coaches.

It's hard to believe we won only one game my sophomore year. It wasn't easy. I truly believe God doesn't give us more than we can handle. I got through thanks to God and the support of family and friends. You hear criticism all around. You can't pay attention to it. I chose to use it as motivation.

When I got stressed out, I'd go home or call Mom or my brother or the people I'm closest to. I tried to deal with most of those things by myself and just went to my place and chilled out.

My first touchdown came in our 2004 home opener against Fresno State, a short-yardage rushing touchdown. I wish I could've kept that football. They don't let you keep footballs in college. Next year, when I get my first NFL touchdown, I'll keep that one. There's not a lot to say about that one-win season. Our only victory was against San Jose State.

A special pass came just before the first half of my junior year. The play was: trips left, formation protection, Hail Mary. We were 69 yards from the goal line when we lined up for last play of the half. Arizona had a good defensive end, so I dropped back and then stepped up into the pocket and launched that ball about 75 yards in the air. Craig Chambers came down with it in the end zone for a touchdown. That's the farthest I've thrown a ball in a game, but I've thrown some farther in practice. Everyone was pretty excited. Almost our whole team rushed onto the field. The play propelled us into the second half with momentum, and we won our second game of the season.

My senior year we started to turn things around.

A key game was a come-from-behind home win over UCLA. I remember sitting on the bench, and we were behind. Hall of Fame quarterback Warren Moon came over and whispered encouragement into my ear. He told me to relax. He said to start hitting the easy throws and everything would fall in line. Warren has been a big influence. He offered his friendship and advice. It's something I've very much appreciated.

The game went as Warren predicted, and we won 29–19 to start the 2006 season 4–1.

Then fate threw us a couple bad breaks.

We went straight up with USC and were moving toward a game-winning touchdown. We drove 65 yards in 10 plays in 94 seconds. With just a few seconds left, we were at the 'SC 15, and then everything went crazy. I don't know why referees stopped the game to talk or why they let the clock run out on us. The whole game, the ref told us we had to wait on him and not snap the ball until we heard his whistle. So we were set up for the snap, awaiting his whistle, and the clock ran out on a 26–20 loss. It hurt to be that close and not get that last play. If we had the chance and didn't score, then that's on us. But we didn't get the chance.

The most painful play was my last. Against Oregon State at home, we were down by 10 points early in the fourth quarter. We were backed up at our own 4-yard line with a third-and-26. I broke free on a scramble and was close to the first down. I tried to make a move, put too much pressure on the outside of my foot, and went down two yards short of the first down. It ended my season and UW career with five games to play. Doctors told me I had torn ligaments in the Lisfranc joint in the middle of my right foot. I had never heard of that injury before.

On crutches, I watched as we lost four straight before ending the season with an encouraging 35–32 win over the Cougars.

Everyone has to take some blame for the program's fall. The coaching changes played a huge part. You can see how much progress we made in 2006 by having the same staff the last two seasons. Imagine if we had four or five years with a stable staff. People don't understand how hard it is to get used to another staff and system.

Going through such a low point in a program tests everyone. Heart and dedication…that's what you really learn. You question yourself when things are going badly and wonder if you should stay. That's where the dedication comes in. You just try to do your best and prove everyone wrong. I never seriously thought about leaving.

Huskies fans never mistreated me. I received nothing but love from fans one on one. We had a lot of support, even though the attendance at games slipped. Once they start winning, fans will come back. I'm proud of how far we've come and of our growth and improvement. We set a foundation in 2006 to build on.

Isaiah Stanback endured an up-and-down career at Washington, with losing seasons, two coaching changes, and being switched from quarterback to wide receiver and back again. He emerged as an outstanding passing and running quarterback in his senior year (2006) under Coach Tyrone Willingham, but suffered a season-ending foot injury in week seven, against Oregon State. Despite his injury, he was selected in the fourth round of the 2007 NFL draft by the Dallas Cowboys as the 104th overall pick.

M. "JIMMIE" CAIN · BY HAINES · BUD ERICKSEN · WALTER HARR
OUSTON · STEVE ROAKE · LUTHER CARR · CHUCK ALLEN · BOB SC
HELL · ROD SCHEYER · NORM DICKS · JIM LAMBRIGHT · DAVE KC
BLEDSOE · CALVIN JONES JR. · SONNY SIXKILLER · BILL CAHILL ·
BUSH · WARREN MOON · MICHAEL JACKSON · NESBY GLASGC
AND · BRUCE HARRELL · DOUG MARTIN · JOE STEELE · TOM FLIC
OWAN · PAUL SKANSI · ANTHONY ALLEN · STEVE PELLUER · JIM M
N · ANDRE RILEY · GREG LEWIS · DONALD JONES · ED CUNNINGH
KENNEDY · DAVE HOFFMANN · CHARLES MINCY · BILLY JOE HO
O · STEVE HOFFMANN · INK ALEAGA · BOB SAPP · JASON CHORAK
NKA · MARQUES TUIASOSOPO · LARRY TRIPPLETT · PAUL ARNOLD
E WILLIAMS · ISAIAH STANBACK · JAMES M. "JIMMIE" CAIN · BY HA
BOHART · WENDELL NILES · JIM HOUSTON · STEVE ROAKE · LUT
TA · BEN DAVIDSON · CHARLIE MITCHELL · ROD SCHEYER · NOR
BRAMWELL · DAVE WILLIAMS · MAC BLEDSOE · CALVIN JONES J
ALDASSIN · MIKE ROHRBACH · BLAIR BUSH · WARREN MOON ·
S · TOM TURNURE · RONNIE ROWLAND · BRUCE HARRELL · DOU
ORTON · CHUCK NELSON · TIM COWAN · PAUL SKANSI · ANTH
SON · TIM MEAMBER · HUGH MILLEN · ANDRE RILEY · GREG LEV